In *A World Theology*, a Christian theologian and an atheistic Buddhist philosopher examine five major world religions – Hinduism, Buddhism, Judaism, Christianity, and Islam – to demonstrate that each is a particular expression of a central spiritual reality shared by all humankind. They argue that the differing concepts of ultimate reality in these religions can be understood as symbolic expressions of a common spiritual reality that transcends the bounds of any one religious tradition.

The book begins by identifying and validating three essential characteristics of ultimate reality that are affirmed by each of the religions considered – undeniability, desirability, and elusiveness. Employing a novel concept of "symbolism," the authors develop a paradigm within which to examine sympathetically and concrescently the varying expressions of ultimate reality encountered in the world's religions. After a discussion of the successes and limitations of atheistic critiques of religion, they systematically pursue this paradigm by examining the most important intellectual, moral, mythological, and spiritual symbols encountered in five major religions.

The authors explain both the differences and the essential commonalities of these religions, and argue that the religions are mutually complementary rather than contradictory. Without undermining the identity or integrity of individual religions, this book points the way toward integrating the respective messages of the world's religions in a comprehensive and systematic manner that constitutes world theology – religious thought that is informed by the faiths of all humankind but dominated by no one of them.

A World Theology

We dedicate this book to our mothers
GENEVIVE H. REAT and RUBY GRIFFIN PERRY

Contents

Preface

For over ten years N. Ross Reat and I have worked together on *A World Theology.* Dr. Reat began his academic career in my "Religion in Human Experience" class at Northwestern, and I take pride in that fact; on this project, however, we have worked, from the outset, as colleagues and peers. Dr. Reat initially composed the bulk of our manuscript – the introductory first chapter and the chapters on Atheism, Hinduism, Buddhism, and Islam, while I wrote the chapters on Judaism and Christianity. Although he was living in Brisbane, Australia, and I in Evanston, Illinois, we maintained close contact and a constant exchange of mutual, constructive criticism throughout the project, at considerable expense in airfares and telephone bills. Because of our close collaboration, we share responsibility for the entirety of the book.

The first inspiration for this book came in 1979 in a telephone call from a Methodist bishop, Charles Wesley Brashares, then retired, now deceased. In that call, at 2:30 A.M., Bishop Brashares proposed that I write a book that would take full account of the best that people in all religions have said about their experience of "the phenomenon called God," the bishop's expression for ultimate reality. Quite some time later Dr. Reat and I discussed with Bishop Brashares our concept of a global theology and received his encouragement. We record here our gratitude for his vision of a theological statement informed by the religious affirmations of humans universally.

Among our numerous academic colleagues, we single out the Venerable Professor Emeritus Walpola Rahula of Sri Lanka for special acknowledgment. In the confidence and informality of his friendship with my family since 1964, I have learned most of what I know about Buddhism and a great deal about the phenomenon some of us call God. As an undergraduate student, Ross Reat began his Buddhist studies in Dr. Rahula's classes during Dr. Rahula's tenure as the Bishop Charles Wesley Brashares Professor of Religion at Northwestern University. Since that time, Ross too has maintained a close personal and professional relation with "Rahulji."

We requested and received technical information on various points of scholarship from Professors Vincent Cornell, John Hunwick, Richard Kieckhefer, and Manfred Vogel. Thanking them sincerely, we hasten to add the obvious: We alone are accountable for what appears in our text. We have ineffable gratitude to Elizabeth Stegner and Erik Webb: The speed and high quality of their typing and word processing took a lot of anxiety out of our labor and gave our finished manuscript a professional appearance.

We thank the Cambridge University Press editorial staff who have worked patiently and supportively with us over the five years our manuscript has been under contract. Finally, in advance, we thank our readers, especially those who will give us the benefit of their critical comments, whether published or in private communication.

Edmund F. Perry

Abbreviations

A	Aṅguttara Nikāya
B.U.	Bṛhadāraṇyaka Upanishad
C.U.	Chāndogya Upanishad
D	Dīgha Nikāya
Kena	Kena Upanishad
Khp.	Kuddaka Pāṭha
Lk	Laṅkāvatāra Sūtra
M	Majjhima Nikāya
Mk	Madhyamika Kārikā
Mu.U.	Muṇḍaka Upanishad
Q	Qur'ān
Ṛg	Ṛg Veda
S	Saṁyutta Nikāya
Sn	Sutta Nipāta
Sp	Saddharma Puṇḍarīka Sūtra
T.U.	Taittirīya Upanishad
V	Vinaya Piṭaka

CHAPTER ONE

The Central Spiritual Reality of Humankind

Openly or secretly, all people believe their lives have meaning and purpose. Even the most cynical, in unguarded moments, betray a tacit conviction that their lives have significance exceeding biological survival and the pursuit of pleasure. This conviction is the essential message of all religions, from the most primitive to the most sophisticated. To this extent at least, all religions are in agreement.

Moreover, all religions attempt to express this conviction by viewing human life against the backdrop of a nonmaterial realm. All of the major world religions, and many of the so-called primitive religions, assert that it is in this nonmaterial realm that an ultimate reality is to be found. The present book argues that this conclusion – that ultimate reality is a nonmaterial reality – is unavoidable for any thinking human being with sufficient opportunity to ponder human existence.

In pursuing this argument, we examine five world religions – Hinduism, Buddhism, Judaism, Christianity, and Islam – and show that they are *different expressions of the same valid ultimate reality*. In doing so we construct a "world theology" along the lines proposed by Wilfred Cantwell Smith in *Towards a World Theology*.[1] In essence, Smith proposes that henceforth normative religious thought must be informed by the faiths of all humankind and dominated by no one of them. The days are past when religious thought could adequately serve humanity by championing the religion of a single civilization.

In the present age of instant global communications, rapid global trans-

---

1 Wilfred Cantwell Smith, *Towards a World Theology* (Philadelphia: Westminster Press, 1981). Although indebted to Smith's work, we do not adopt his suggestion that religions should not be personified. We do accept his observation that religions do not exist; only religious people exist. Strictly speaking, one should not say "Buddhism asserts," but rater, "Buddhists assert." We have chosen to follow conventional usage and employ both types of statement.

portation, a massive global economy, entwined global politics, and potential global annihilation, the desirability of worldwide religious understanding is self-evident. Therefore those who read this book will not be wasting their time. Its reading may, however, require concentrated effort because, in the first place, much of the material will be unfamiliar to most readers, and in spite of our efforts to achieve simple and straightforward communication, the concepts involved remain somewhat demanding. Second and more important, our determination that this book be globally informed requires that our readers temporarily suspend some of their most cherished convictional judgments, whether the bias of these judgments is for or against religion.

The results of our research require that we acknowledge at the outset that the ultimate reality to which five world religions commonly point *does not exist* in any conventional sense of the term. It is neither empirically verifiable nor logically demonstrable. It is, however, a universal and necessary *reality* of the human condition. Anyone who honestly and consistently observes one's own *behavior* has to admit to being influenced by a nonmaterial ultimate reality, which each of these religions affirms. To admit this, as one must, and yet to deny the reality itself would be such a radical self-alienation as to be untenable.

This is not to say that one must affirm or should embrace any of the traditional modes of response to this nonmaterial ultimate reality. The various organized religions may well have enough negative qualities that one would be well advised to steer clear of them. The five religions we have examined, however, have at least one positive quality in common: Each addresses in a coherent and systematic way a fundamental reality of the human condition. All people, not only religious people, grant at least implicit assent to the same nonmaterial ultimate reality commonly expressed by Hinduism, Buddhism, Judaism, Christianity, and Islam. The unavoidability of this assent makes this reality as influential as any existing thing, logically demonstrable truth, or empirically verifiable fact.

The Phenomenon Some Call God

The argument in this chapter concerns human necessity, not logical or empirical demonstrability. It exposes and analyzes the human necessity of a nonmaterial ultimate reality. This ultimate reality is *a phenomenon some call God.* Others have different names for it: Allāh, Brahman, Nirvana. The five religions we have examined elaborate extensively and distinctively upon it, yet none of them claims to capture it in its entirety. None of these religions will regard our argument as a validation of its entire concept of ultimate reality, but neither can any of them deny that the phenomenon we describe is central to its own concept of ultimate reality.

When we use the term "valid" we do not intend "verifiable." We use the word, as most dictionaries define it, to signify "well founded, reasonable, and defensible." By using the term "phenomenon" we do not imply the objective existence of God or indeed of ultimate reality by any name. The original Greek roots of the term "phenomenon" justify our using it to mean *anything that causes human experience.* We use the term "reality" as a synonym of phenomenon. Obviously, one cannot observe other people's experience to verify its content. We can observe their behavior. Therefore, our working definition of the synonyms phenomenon and reality is *that which influences human behavior,* whether existing or not. Many things may influence human behavior – may be real – and yet not exist. In the present sense of the term, for example, ghosts assuredly are *real,* because some humans experience them, and the behavior of these people is influenced thereby. These ghosts are phenomena even though they may not exist.

The uncritical materialism currently in vogue tends to dismiss as invalid and trivial anything that does not exist as a material reality.[1] Uncritical materialists may assert that in examining ultimate reality as nonexistent we are dealing with a "mere concept," a "figment of the imagination." Some materialists, of course, are not uncritical, and recognize that there may be dimensions of reality that materialism does not address. They may doubt this but nonetheless remain open to perspectives other than materialism. We see no compelling reason why critical, open-minded materialists should reject the position we set forth in the following pages.

We acknowledge that ghosts may indeed be figments of the imagination. Some nonmaterial, nonexisting realities of human experience, however, are not at all imaginary. On the contrary, they are fundamental and obvious realities of human consciousness. The number three, for example, is nonmaterial and does not exist. One can never point to something and say "There is three itself." One can only indicate examples that point to the reality of the number three: three coconuts, three rocks, three fingers. Nonetheless, three is not *merely* a concept. Even the most brutish human, having gathered three coconuts and gone to sleep, would be perturbed to wake and find only two. Three is a universal reality of the human condition, a phenomenon some call three; others have different names for it.

We will show that the phenomenon some call God is exactly analogous to the phenomenon some call three in the following ways: (1) Neither the phenomenon some call God nor the phenomenon some call three is material; nonetheless both phenomena are universal realities of human experience. (2) Although one cannot locate either phenomenon itself, one can specify examples that point to these phenomena. (3) Although neither phenomenon exists, neither is trivial; neither is a "mere concept" or a "figment of the imagination." In fact it is impossible to imagine human consciousness or to explain human behavior without recourse to the phenomenon some call three and the phenomenon some call God. Such universal *phenomena* definitively shape human experience.

Conceptual phenomena, such as the number three, are not the only nonmaterial realities that are universal in human experience. Most emotions fall in this category. Consider for example fear. It may indeed be the case, as some scientists claim, that fear and all other emotions are caused by hormones and electrical impulses in the nervous system. If so, this means that fear has a material cause. Nonetheless, fear itself, as experienced, remains a nonmaterial reality. It may be possible some day to control a person's emotions in a laboratory, but it will never be possible to put fear itself in a test tube. Upon reflection, it is clear that the whole of human consciousness as such comprises nonmaterial phenomena. Scientists may be able to map out in the human nervous system the causes of many of these phenomena, but the phenomena of consciousness as experienced will remain forever in the nonmaterial realm. Along with the physical similarities that allow us to identify *Homo sapiens,* the universal similarity of our experience of nonmaterial realities allows us to identify our common humanity. The implicitly recognized commonality of our experience of nonmaterial realities is definitive of what it is to be human, every bit as definitive as physical characteristics and genetic makeup. One of the most fundamental of these realities is a phenomenon some call God.

The universality in human experience of the phenomenon some call God allows us to formulate a valid concept of ultimate reality. We show that the five religions we have examined implicitly express the phenomenon to which this concept refers. This is to say that the *ultimate referent* of each of these religions points toward, but does not encompass, an *ultimate reality* that they all affirm in common. Our findings may apply to other religions as well, but we will show that at least these five religions share a valid central reality, which each discloses inadvertently in its symbolization of its own *ultimate referent* – Allāh, Brahman, Dharma/Nirvana, or God. All religions are not the same; however, a common, fundamental reality informs and inspires each of the major world religions we examine. The differing doctrines and practices of these religions may be regarded as divergent expressions of the same central reality. This suggests that philosophical critiques of religion are effective only when directed against the terms in which a religion expresses its divergent elaboration upon this central reality. These terms of expression, the doctrines and practices of an individual religion, we regard as *symbolic expressions* of the central reality that these five religions share.

Symbolic Expression and the Ultimate Referent

Our use of the phrase "symbolic expression" requires explanation. The meaning we intend for it has a strong bearing on our understanding of the religious data we investigate. This specific meaning is based upon a widely accepted distinction between signs and symbols. Symbols, like signs, point to something beyond themselves. Unlike signs, symbols participate in the reality to which they point. For example, the ringing bell, red light, and dropped barrier at a railroad crossing are *signs* that point to a coming train. Of course, these signs may activate accidentally and give an erroneous signal. If, however, one looks down the track, one may see the light on the front of the train's locomotive, or without looking one may hear the locomotive's whistle. Like the signs of the crossing, the locomotive's headlight and blowing whistle point beyond themselves and indicate the approach of the locomotive. The locomotive's light and whistle, however, are more convincing indicators than the paraphernalia at the railroad crossing. The light and whistle are part of the locomotive to which they point. They illustrate what we mean by *symbols* first of all because they participate in the reality to which their functioning points. Furthermore, when one sees the light and hears the distinctive sound of the train's whistle, one knows two things. One knows that at least a locomotive is near, and that one should make whatever personal decisions are appropriate when a train is coming down the track.

In our use, then, *a symbol points beyond itself to a larger reality in which it participates and whose larger dimensions it makes present and known.* We regard the doctrines and practices of the religions we have researched to be symbolic expressions of spiritual realities to which they point, in which they participate, and whose presence they make known for personal response or reaction. Analogous to the whistle or light on the locomotive, the cross on a church altar points to Jesus' crucifixion, which in turn, in certain circumstances, points to, participates in, and makes present for personal decision the reality of God's redeeming love. The cross on the altar is, in the terminology of our analysis, a symbolic expression of the spiritual reality that Christians identify as God's redeeming love. The redeeming love of God points, of course, to the larger reality of God, the fullness of which constitutes Christianity's *ultimate referent.* Each of the religions has its analogous symbolic expressions for its *ultimate referent* and, like the cross and redeeming love, all of these symbolic expressions are effective within their respective provenances.

In explaining each religion, we treat four types of symbolic expression:

intellectual, moral, mythological, and spiritual. We find these four symbolic expressions in each religion's teachings, doctrines, and practices. Each type of expression has its own distinctive aim and means. Intellectual symbolism appeals to the intellect by argument, evidence, or proof. It intends to convince the mind of the reality, character, and decisive significance of the religion's ultimate referent. Moral symbolism appeals to the conscience and intends to induce the will to behave in accord with the character of the religion's ultimate referent. It makes its appeal by illustrating the negative consequences of behavior that differs from the religion's character and the positive results of behavior that reflects its character. Mythological symbolism appeals to the imagination with images of power, grandeur, and sublimity. It intends to evoke awe toward the religion's ultimate referent. Spiritual symbolism engages the whole person by presenting the religion's ultimate referent as decisive for the person's present existence and eventual destiny. It intends to secure personal commitment to the ultimate referent of the religion in question.

We have found that the symbolic expressions with which various religions represent their *ultimate referents* intimate other, more universal dimensions of their ultimate referents. These intimated dimensions indicate the possibility, if not the necessity, of reconceptualizing the ultimate referent of each religion so that its universal validity is no longer obscured. In exposing the larger dimensions of a religion's ultimate referent and its symbolic expressions, we do not intend to discredit either its ultimate referent or its symbols in their respective contexts. In an open forum of debate, however, where unbelievers and adversaries are given a fair hearing, the beliefs and practices of individual religions often lose credibility. The central, shared reality to which the beliefs and practices of each religion point can maintain credibility in such a forum. Although widely varying and often conflicting in relation to each other, these systems of belief and practice disclose themselves under investigation to be symbolic expressions of the same *central spiritual reality.* Recognition of this, we believe, will facilitate understanding among the religions and will validate rather than discredit their respective claims to express ultimate reality.

The Central Spiritual Reality of Humankind

We identify the phenomenon some call God as the *central spiritual reality of humankind,* aspects of which are disclosed by the ultimate referents of the five religions dealt with in this book.

Definition

Central: This phenomenon is "central" in two senses. It inheres in the center of each of the individual religions we have examined, and it is the common, albeit unrecognized, center from which these religions diverge. The religions we have examined may be viewed as divergent symbolic expressions of this central reality. These divergent expressions are meaningful and evocative in their given cultures, but not universally valid. The central reality to which they all point is universally valid.

Spiritual: Our use of the word "spiritual" is not a special pleading for exemption from the critical standards of intellectual discourse. "Spiritual" indicates that which pertains to human aspirations and needs beyond material sufficiency. The term "spiritual," as we see it, refers specifically to aspirations and needs that relate to the meaning and purpose of one's life as a whole and entails the freedom and responsibility to pursue this meaning and purpose. Circumstances from birth and accidents of various kinds deprive some human beings of the freedom and responsibility necessary to pursue the meaning and purpose of their lives in the present world. The behavior of these deprived people does not contribute data applicable to our study. The nature of their spirituality does not belong to our inquiry. We note that every religion we know makes an effort to provide some meaningful interpretation of these special humans and their relation to the phenomenon some call God. Our investigation inquires into the behavior of humans who are spiritual in the sense that they have sufficient opportunity to ponder human existence and sufficient freedom to participate responsibly as independent agents in their own existence. For humans who have the opportunity to behave with responsible freedom, the phenomenon some call God exercises influence on their pursuit of meaning and purpose.

Reality: The term "reality" indicates, to repeat, *that which influences human behavior*, whether existing or not, whether material or non-material. Use of the terms "reality" and "phenomenon" does not imply that the central spiritual reality of the major religions is an objectively existing thing. Rather, the central spiritual phenomenon is a reality in the sense that it influences human lives. As we have already acknowledged, in this sense ghosts are also real. Whether or not they exist, they influence those who experience them. Similarly, only some people are influenced by God. All people, however, are influenced by a central spiritual reality. This phenomenon is *a universal reality of the human condition.*

Essential Characteristics

Our examination of five religions has disclosed that although they vary greatly in doctrine and practice, they all affirm and express three essential characteristics of a central spiritual reality. These essential characteristics are *undeniability, desirability,* and *elusiveness.*

These characteristics constitute the substance of the *world theology* that we construct. This construction is in essence the formulation of a concept of ultimate reality that fulfills two necessary requirements of any world theology worthy of the name: (1) Admissible concepts must be common to many, if not all world religions. (2) Admissible concepts must be valid in the specific sense that they are *well founded, reasonable,* and, in a universal forum of critical discourse, *defensible.*

We list these requirements in this order because in practice world theology proceeds from research on the religions to formulation of concepts. For the sake of clarity in our presentation we deal with the second requirement before the first by demonstrating three things in this chapter and the next: (1) A nonmaterial, ultimate reality that is undeniable, desirable, and elusive is *well founded* in human experience universally. (2) It is *reasonable* that human beings respond to such a phenomenon. (3) The three characteristics – undeniability, desirability, and elusiveness – define a concept of ultimate reality that is defensible in a universal forum of critical discourse. We satisfy the first requirement of world theology by demonstrating in Chapters Three through Seven that the phenomenon these characteristics identify is affirmed by five major religions.

Because we have researched and formulated our concept of ultimate reality in accordance with these two requirements, it is a *mediating, valid,* and *validating* concept. It *mediates* among widely varying symbolic expressions of ultimate reality by allowing us to demonstrate that each of them *points to* the same phenomenon, the same reality of human experience. It is *valid* because we can demonstrate that all people, not only consciously religious people, are influenced by a spiritual reality that is central in their lives, whether they recognize it or not. Being itself valid, this concept *validates* many of the symbols of the five religions by enabling us to establish that the reality to which they point is universal in human experience. The significance of undeniability, desirability, and elusiveness will become clearer as our argument and then our comparative study proceed. By way of preliminary definition, however, we offer the following.

Undeniability: Each of the five religions we have examined holds that its ultimate referent cannot effectively be denied. Nonbelievers may, of course, deny the ultimate referent affirmed by any religion and may offer valid arguments to refute that religion's concepts of ultimate reality. As a result, concepts of ultimate reality may change. For believers, however, denials of ultimate reality itself lack any real force. For religious people, other realities *derive their meanings* from the ultimate referent of their religions, not vice versa. Therefore the ultimate referent that a religion affirms cannot effectively be denied, for its adherents, by appealing to other realities. It is the ultimate norm of verification for the people who affirm it. For example, the Christian doctrine of creation by God has been altered by scientific explanations of reality, but Christian certainty of God has not been diminished.

Christian certainty and the similar certainty found in all religious persons is not unreasonable. It reflects the fact that it is impossible to live our a human life without at least implicitly affirming an ultimate spiritual reality. As we explain more fully below, the *undeniability* of a central spiritual reality is in essence an expression of the human necessity of affirming meaning and purpose in one's life as a whole. The behavior of all people, not only religious people, bears witness to the universality of this affirmation.

To be sure, each religion characteristically denies the concepts of ultimate reality found in other religions. These religions agree that the central reality of true religion is undeniable, but they disagree sharply as to what it is that is undeniable. Regardless of how irreconcilable such disagreements may seem, there remains an overall agreement among major religions that the central reality of true religion is an *undeniable* reality. This means that undeniability is universally affirmed to be a characteristic of ultimate reality.

Two considerations, then, attest *undeniability* to be a characteristic of ultimate reality: The behavior of people in general bears witness to this *undeniability*, and five major religions affirm it.

Desirability: Each of the religions we have examined holds that the ultimate referent it affirms is ultimately desirable. For religious people, other realities, in addition to deriving their meaning from an ultimate referent, also *derive their value* from such a referent. Therefore the ultimate referent that each religion affirms cannot effectively be devalued by appealing to other realities. It is the ultimate valuational norm for the people who affirm it.

Again, this is not unreasonable on the part of religious people. Humans by nature evaluate in absolute terms much of what they experience. No human confines this evaluation to judgments such as "*A* is different from *B*" or even "I prefer *A* to *B* at this particular moment." Instead, all humans sometimes conclude, whether they express it or not, "*A* is better than *B*." This conclusion, that *A* is better than *B* – for example, that democracy is better than communism or vice versa – implies some ultimate standard of desirability that *A* approaches more nearly than *B*. Proponents of democracy or communism may or may not appeal overtly to such a standard in arguing their cases. They may argue instead on the grounds of freedom of choice or the greatest good for the greatest number. Such arguments, however, also presuppose an ultimate standard that freedom approaches more nearly than regimentation or which the greatest good for the greatest number approaches more nearly than the greatest good for a privileged few. Regardless of the outcome of such arguments, their very existence implies universal, though often preconscious, assent to an ultimate standard of desirability. The behavior of all people, not only religious people, attests the universality of such an ultimate standard.

Each of the religions we have examined holds that its ultimate referent serves as an ultimate standard of desirability. As in the case of undeniability, the religions disagree among themselves as to what precisely is ultimately desirable, and they tend to deny the desirability of ultimate reality as expressed by other religions. Nonetheless, these religions agree that the central reality of true religion is an ultimately desirable reality. *Desirability* as a characteristic of ultimate reality is commonly affirmed by the religions we have examined, and is validated in human experience in general.

Elusiveness: Each of the religions we have examined recognizes that its ultimate referent eludes human grasp, that it exceeds human comprehension and control. Each religion admits that its doctrines do not fully comprehend its ultimate referent. Moreover, each of these religions admits to a "missing link" in its scheme of salvation. There is a universally recognized gap, unbridgeable by human effort alone, between the world and the ultimately real. Each religion we have examined admits that its ultimate referent eludes both its doctrines and its practices. Recognition of the elusiveness of any reality conceived to be ultimate is self-evidently reasonable.

We have noted that each religion characteristically denies that the ultimate referents of other religions are undeniable or desirable. It is perhaps ironic that they tend to highlight and ridicule expressions of elusiveness in other religions. For example, in Christianity the necessity of grace and faith exemplify the elusiveness of God; some critics from other religions ridicule grace as indicating lack of nerve, and faith as indicating gullibility. Still, each religion asserts that true religion must recognize the elusiveness of ultimate reality. This recognition is self-evidently valid if one grants in any sense the possibility of an ultimate reality.

Having briefly defined the central spiritual reality that five world religions affirm and from which they diverge, we proceed now to illustrate the inescapable influence in human life of this undeniable, desirable, and elusive reality. This inescapable influence, we argue, constitutes the universal validity of this central spiritual reality. This validity is the topic of the rest of this chapter. The chapters that follow present five world religions as complex symbolic expressions of this universal reality of human experience. As such, they may be sympathetically understood and appreciated by any inquiring human mind.

The Validity of a Central Spiritual Reality

The universally recognized gap between the material world and the ultimately real makes the terms "existence" and "being" inappropriate with reference to the central spiritual reality of humankind. Some religions employ these terms in their symbolic expressions of their ultimate referents, but others do not. The being or existence of the ultimately real is therefore debatable even among the religions themselves. We argue only that a phenomenon central and common to five religions is *real*, that it influences human behavior. As stated before, we readily acknowledge that in this sense ghosts are also real. Whether or not they exist, they influence the behavior of those who experience them. Whereas, however, only some people experience ghosts, all people experience the central spiritual reality that each of the religions we examine expresses in its own characteristic way. This reality is a necessary "given" of human experience. It influences the behavior of all people, including skeptics.

A phenomenon central to human spirituality is valid as a human necessity rather than a logical necessity, and as real rather than existing. A variation upon Anselm's ontological argument for the existence of God illustrates this validity. According to Anselm, once one understands the definition of God, one must agree that God exists. God, according to Anselm's definition, is "that than which nothing greater can be conceived." Anselm argues that having understood this definition, one must agree that God is more than a mere concept, for it is better to exist objectively than to exist only in the mind. One can readily conceive of something greater than anything that exists only in the mind, namely, a corresponding thing that also exists objectively. Thus, if one adheres to the definition of God as "that than which nothing greater can be conceived," one must agree that God exists objectively as well as a concept in the mind.

To exist objectively as the greatest conceivable thing is certainly great; but Anselm argued that one can conceive of something still greater. One can conceive of a being that exists in such a way that it is impossible to conceive of its not existing. Thus, if one adheres to Anselm's definition of

God, one must agree that God cannot be conceived not to exist. Usually modern interpreters of Anselm regard this notion as equivalent to the notion of logically necessary existence. While this interpretation may be true to Anselm's original intent, we propose that the ontological argument is more persuasive if interpreted behaviorally: that it is impossible to *behave* in such a manner as not to affirm the existence of God. Clearly, it is possible *to say* or *to think* that God does not exist. It is also clearly possible to say or think that God does not exist necessarily. We suggest, then, that the ontological argument can be taken more seriously if it is understood as urging that it is impossible for a human being to *behave* in a way that does not indicate at least preconscious affirmation of the existence of God.

We would prefer "reality" over "existence" in this reformulation of Anselm's argument. We recognize that the ontological argument itself set out to prove the "existence" of God, and that it may not work if "reality" is substituted for "existence" throughout the argument. We recognize too the anachronism of interpreting Anselm behaviorally. Nevertheless, interpreted as urging that preconscious assent to the reality of God is universally apparent in human behavior, Anselm's argument illustrates that aspect of the central spiritual reality we call "undeniability." The definition "that than which nothing greater can be conceived" is one that the religions dealt with in this book would readily accept as applying to their respective notions of ultimate reality. Other than Christianity, no religion has applied Anselm's reasoning to demonstrate the undeniability of its ultimate referent. But each religion would readily agree that it is impossible effectively to deny the reality of its essential core.

Thus, each of these religions claims undeniability as a characteristic of its ultimate referent. We argue that this common claim is valid if by "undeniable" we understand "commanding necessary behavioral assent." It is clearly possible to *speak* or *think* a denial even of the *reality* of a religious ultimate. We argue, though, that it is impossible for human beings to *behave* in such a manner as to deny the *reality* of something "than which nothing greater can be conceived." Our argument has two parts.

First, we show that all human beings behave in ways that are inexplicable without reference to a nonmaterial reality. Second, we seek to show that this nonmaterial referent, if consistently conceptualized, must be conceived in terms of ultimate good. These two parts of the argument correspond to the *undeniability* and ultimate *desirability* of the central spiritual reality of humankind. Humans necessarily behave as if in response to nonmaterial motivations. In this sense a central spiritual reality is undeniable. When one reflects upon such nonmaterial motivation, it becomes clear that in order to be reasonable such motivation eventually requires conceptualization in terms of ultimate moral good. In this sense a central spiritual reality is desirable. We recognize that a large part of the human response to the nonmaterial realm has been characterized by fear, superstition, and occasionally outright evil. We will argue, however, that such response is inherently self-contradictory and that the only consistent and reasonable response to the central spiritual reality of humankind is to regard it as ultimately desirable in terms of moral good. This ultimately desirable phenomenon may not have any objective status whatsoever. At the very least, however, it inheres in the fundamental structure of human consciousness. Human minds and human behavior cannot be fully understood without reference to this undeniable, ultimately desirable, and elusive phenomenon.

The Undeniability of Nonmaterial Motivation

In order to illustrate the undeniability of nonmaterial motivation in human life, let us consider the behavior of three jet pilots, each finding the plane on the verge of crashing into a crowded school building. Each must make a split-second decision. The first pilot self-sacrificingly guides the plane to a crash landing in an adjacent field and dies. The second pilot bails out and, watching the plane crash into the school building, feels remorse. The third bails out laughing.

In the first case, behavioral assent to a nonmaterial reality takes the form of willingness to sacrifice oneself for others without any hope of a material reward. Such behavior is irrational from a materialistic point of view, wherein death represents an utter final blank, the avoidance of which would outweigh all other pragmatic concerns. In the second case, behavioral assent takes the form of remorse. It is irrational from a materialist point of view to feel remorse upon having saved one's own life, at whatever cost to others. What materialist could possibly blame the second pilot?

The first and second pilots typify the vast majority of human beings, but the third case is too common to be ignored, and it brings us to the heart of the issue of universal assent to a nonmaterial reality. The third pilot would have to be something like a political terrorist or a capriciously malicious lunatic. In the case of a terrorist, willingness to risk one's life, and invite the possibility of punishment, in service of a cause of some sort indicates assent to a reality other than material pragmatism. No matter what political gains one may hope to enjoy as a consequence of a terrorist action, they are decisively outweighed, materialistically speaking, by the immediate risks involved in committing such an act. Again, from a materialistic point of view, the behavior of the terrorist is irrational.

The case of a lunatic is similar. Even a lunatic's behavior implies assent to a nonmaterial reality. Perhaps the lunatic simply enjoys seeing others suffer and die. This wish itself, however, is irrational from a materialistic point of view, for one receives no material benefit from gratifying such a desire. The random suffering and death of others does not conduce to one's own survival or material well-being. Moreover, the risks the lunatic undertakes are as considerable as in the case of the terrorist.

Let us suppose, however, that our "lunatic," rather than being merely capriciously malicious on the basis of perverse, irrational hedonism, is actually trying to make an existential statement. Perhaps this person is trying to act out existentially Sartre's famous paraphrase of Dostoyevski, "Everything is indeed permitted if God does not exist."[2] Let us suppose that, as an act of rebellion against the supposedly restrictive and "inauthentic" norms of society, the apparent lunatic is actually attempting to commit himself or herself totally to the performance of evil. Let us suppose, in other words, that this person is attempting to be the antithesis of the saint, who attempts to be committed totally to good. We should note again that this would-be totally evil pilot behaves in an irrational manner for a materialist, in that again, he or she can reasonably expect no material reward for this action. If one hopes to communicate to the human race at large some "truth" about the nature of life and social standards, one is again motivated by nonmaterial concerns and, from a materialistic point of view, is behaving irrationally.

It is conceivable, some might argue, that there is yet a fourth type of pilot to be considered in this example: one who would bail out feeling a sense of relief at having saved his or her own life, but would feel absolutely no remorse, guilt, satisfaction, or glee at seeing hundreds of children perish as a result of this action. There could be, in other words, a person who, even in the most extreme situations, is motivated exclusively by entirely materialistic concerns. This would also have to be a person who, in less extreme circumstances, would have no interest in music or art, would not prefer polite treatment to indifference, would not prefer freely and enthusiastically given sex to the well-performed sex of a prostitute, would not in fact prefer an attractive sexual partner, would have no hobbies, no favorite color, would never travel for recreation, socialize for fun, or feel lonely. Although such a person is conceivable, we defy anyone to bring forth an actual example from the ranks of *Homo sapiens*. This person, by the way, would not be embarrassed by such attention.

So long as such a person is not forthcoming, we maintain that all human beings sometimes behave as if in response to nonmaterial realities – for example, beauty, love, or variety. This response, at its most basic level,

2 Jean-Paul Sartre, *Existentialism and Humanism*, trans. P. Mairet (London: Methuen, 1948), pp. 33–4.

takes the form of nonmaterially motivated preference of one thing or situation over another. The undeniability of *some* nonmaterially motivated behavior in *all* people is the basis of our argument that undeniability is a *valid* characteristic of a central spiritual reality of humankind. No one behaves as if only the material world were real. Instead, all people are sometimes motivated by nonmaterial realities. In regarding their own *ultimate referents* as undeniable, religions express this inescapable reality of the human situation.

Desirability and Ultimate Good

Since nonmaterial realities motivate behavior it is clear that they have value. To be sure, some people are very materialistic and some even claim to be materialists, but no one actually *behaves* as if only material realities had value. Various forms of sociology and psychology have attempted to give materialistic explanations for the reality in human life of various nonmaterial desirables, and it is possible that one or a combination of these explanations is correct. This would not, however, alter the fact that all people are motivated by nonmaterial desirables in addition to material desirables.

When one reflects, it becomes clear that nonmaterial desirables constantly impinge upon the lives and influence the behavior of all people, including those sociologists and psychologists who try to explain away these realities. Consider purity as a desirable. For high-caste Indians all meat is impure, and they will not eat it. Purity in this case is a nonmaterial desirable. It has nothing to do with the material or nutritional qualities of meat, and this seems to us in the West an odd way to think. Most Americans, however, will recoil in disgust at the prospect of eating dog meat. Dog meat is impure for Americans, even sociologists, psychologists, and skeptics. Neither this American instance nor this Indian instance of purity as a nonmaterial value has any validity in the material world, as is demonstrated by the fact that many Chinese relish and thrive on dog meat.

Like purity, many similar nonmaterial values constantly impinge upon the lives of all humans. That these values differ from society to society indicates that they have little or no grounding in the material world. Such values may indeed be nothing more than social conventions. This possibility, however, does not lessen an American's revulsion at the thought of eating dog meat. Nonmaterial social values – like purity, beauty, femininity, masculinity, style, and etiquette – impinge upon all people's lives as experiences of nonmaterial realities. Even rebellion against such values, as is now common, bears witness to their reality in human life. Many women will now consciously seek out an effeminate man. Seeking to avoid

masculine men confirms masculinity as a nonmaterial value, albeit a negative value.

Moral values, though still nonmaterial, are more widely consistent than
"social values," although they still may vary from person to person and
society to society. Moral values may indeed be nothing more than universally recognized "social values," conventions that facilitate the formation
and maintenance of human societies. Nonetheless, this is not how they
are experienced.

Consider the statement "I would like to sleep with you, and I could get
away with it, but it would not be fair to my spouse." Some people would
make such a statement out of fear of domestic strife and loss of property,
and these people would be materially motivated. Many people, however,
would be motivated genuinely by the nonmaterial criterion of fairness,
without any expectation of material gain. Many, of course, commit adul-
tery with abandon, but surprisingly few of these think it is fair for their
spouses to do the same. Even people who are not themselves fair expect
fairness from others, and regardless of the fact that they may not deserve
fair treatment, they genuinely feel wronged when they perceive that it is
not forthcoming from others.

The same is true of honesty. "That dirty, rotten, filthy, stinking used-
car dealer sold me a lemon!" Such statements are common and are not
justified with reference to the material world alone. If material criteria
alone are considered, it is reasonable to lie in order to sell a bad auto-
mobile, and in most situations it would not be reasonable to do otherwise. Nevertheless, many people try to avoid lying under any circumstances. Many people, of course, lie easily and frequently, but they
usually feel moral outrage when they are themselves the victims of dishonesty. Neither group can validly claim to assess reality on the basis of
material values alone.

Eventually, even the most materialistic, calculating, callous, and immoral person will be caught affirming nonmaterial values. For most
people, the compulsion to act on the basis of nonmaterial values such as
fairness, honesty, and compassion is frequent; for some it is less frequent.
Such compulsion is never completely absent in any human life, and even if
it were, these same values would be affirmed by appealing to them in
others and feeling wronged when others do not act on the basis of such
values. When one feels that one has been wronged, vengefulness affirms
the nonmaterial value of justice just as much as fairness. Much revenge,
like much fairness, does not result in any material reward and in fact is
often disadvantageous with reference to the material world alone.

We argue that all people are compelled, because they affirm nonmaterial
values, to behave in ways that are not intelligible or reasonable with
reference to the material world alone, ways that result in no material

reward and even in material disadvantage. It is true, of course, that we have not had an opportunity to observe the behavior of all human beings. Technically, our argument would be falsified by finding even one utterly materialistic person. Since many people who once lived are now dead, our argument must forever remain technically inconclusive. Nonetheless, we state our points in universal terms such as "all human beings" because the issue at stake is so fundamental to humanity.

Response to nonmaterial realities is *an* essence, if not *the* essence of humanity. It is so essential as to be definitive of fully human status – every bit as definitive as phylogenic or taxonomic considerations. To say that human beings invariably respond to nonmaterial realities is not to say that response to nonmaterial realities is incontrovertibly reasonable. To evaluate its reasonableness, however, would require a perspective of omniscience, or at least a qualitatively superhuman perspective. Because no human operates from such a perspective, it is highly unlikely that the issue will ever be determined. Being ourselves human, we can never evaluate objectively whether it is reasonable to be as humans are.

We argue only that to exist and behave as a human being and yet to deny being influenced by nonmaterial realities is such a radical self-alienation as to be untenable. It is pointless to speculate about whether all members of the species *Homo sapiens*, without exception, have responded to nonmaterial realities. This is not the substance of our argument. We are confident that all of our readers – after having recalled with suspicion an obnoxious neighbor and a few hated rivals – will concede that the compulsion to respond to nonmaterial realities is a defining characteristic of the human race as we know it.

Because human behavior is motivated by nonmaterial values, and this is simply the way human beings are, we can only ask if such behavior is conceivably reasonable. Such behavior is clearly not reasonable with reference to the material world alone. It may yet be reasonable with reference to a nonmaterial dimension of human life. We have cited examples of various forms of assent to such a nonmaterial dimension of life. These examples indicate that it is not possible, and may never be possible, to reach universal agreement concerning the nature or priorities of the values that this dimension of humanity comprehends. Therefore, the only way in which behavior motivated by this essential dimensions of human life can be regarded as even conceivably reasonable is on the basis of its consistency in any individual. Nonmaterial values must be constant and must be consistently pursued in order to be regarded as reasonable.

It is reasonable to respond randomly to material desirables and to pursue them independently of one another. Most people desire both food and sex, and when these two desirables come into conflict, they may simply choose one or the other. The physical existence of the food or the sexual partner justifies the choice and renders reasonable the resulting behavior. Nonmaterial values, by contrast, must be constant and must be consistently pursued in order to be regarded as reasonable. It is not reasonable, for example, to pursue truthfulness, compassion, and justice independently of one another. There is no tangible basis for choosing between truthfulness and compassion in a situation where "the truth hurts." Unlike food or sexual partners, these desirables do not exist in the material world. Like sexual partners and food, they do occasionally come into conflict.

In many instances one may behave truthfully or compassionately in expectation of a material reward, or one may seek justice because there is a material advantage to be gained. In such cases conflicts between these values are not problematic. But often, people respond to conflicting non-material values with considerable disregard for the material consequences. In these instances one's behavior is not even conceivably reasonable unless one is able to resolve conflicts between these nonmaterial desirables. The only way to resolve such conflicts and yet maintain the requisite constancy of nonmaterial desirables is to seek to integrate the conflicting values into a higher value. Eventually such higher, integrating values must themselves be integrated in yet higher values. This integration of values creates a hierarchy of value that converges implicitly upon an ultimate, non-material good.

Consider the case of a young man who has committed a serious crime and the one witness to that crime. It is conceivable that the witness might reason as follows, through a series of conflicts between nonmaterial values. "From the standpoint of truthfulness I should testify that the young man has committed a crime. From the standpoint of compassion I would like to see him spared punishment. This conflict can be resolved from the standpoint of justice, and I concede that he should be punished. But this young man is my son and I love him. Faced with a conflict between justice and love, in order to be true to myself I should follow the dictates of love, but in order to be true to humankind I should follow the dictates of justice." This final conflict between nonmaterial values – being true to oneself and being true to humankind – can be resolved only by appealing to some ultimate, universal standard.

Behavior motivated by nonmaterial, moral criteria such as truthfulness and compassion can be regarded as consistently approaching an ultimate criterion of desirability, a greatest good, which renders such motivation reasonable. There may in fact be no greatest good, but moral behavior that presumes such an ultimate criterion of desirability can be consistent and thereby reasonable. It is, moreover, possible to conceive of the perfection of behavior so motivated. Although one may never attain this perfection, it is reasonable to attempt in all situations to behave in ways conducive to the greatest good for all beings. Because such behavior is conceivably perfectible, one can conceive of it actually being in the best interests of all beings including oneself. There is, then, no inherent contradiction in regarding nonmaterial, moral motivations as being universally valid.

Nonmaterially motivated immoral behavior, by contrast, cannot be consistent or reasonable. Let us consider deceitfulness and cruelty – in contrast to truthfulness and compassion – as nonmaterial values. Most deceitfulness and cruelty, like much truthfulness and compassion, is motivated by material desirables and therefore need not be consistent in order to be reasonable. If one lies to keep one's job, it is reasonable behavior with reference to the material world. If one is cruel to one's rivals, this too is materialistically reasonable. Similarly, being truthful in expectation of a reward or compassionate in expectation of gratitude is immediately understandable behavior on materialistic grounds. As nonmaterial values, however, deceitfulness and cruelty cannot be reasonably pursued, because they cannot be consistently pursued. This is so because nonmaterially motivated deceitfulness and cruelty cannot be viewed as being integrated in an overarching criterion of desirability, in this case, a "greater evil." As nonmaterial values, cruelty and deceitfulness are divergent, whereas truthfulness and compassion are convergent. Divergent randomness is, in fact, essential to deceitfulness and cruelty, whereas convergent consistency is essential to truthfulness and compassion.

To illustrate this contention, let us reconsider our hypothetical jet pilot who is devoted to the performance of evil. Practically speaking, the task set is impossible even to attempt. Whereas it is possible at least to attempt always to perform good actions that have universally good effects, it is impossible even to attempt evil in all situations. One who is committed to evil must perform good in some situations in order to be effectively evil in others. For example, our hypothetical devotee of evil must occasionally tell the truth in order for lies to create the desired evil effects. Every time he or she lies, the ability to tell effectively evil lies in the future is undermined. The truthful person, on the other hand, enhances the power of his or her truthfulness each time he or she refuses to lie. While truthfulness may occasionally produce undesirable results – such as anger at the harsh truth that one drinks too much – when the motivation behind such truthfulness is known, it will encourage universally desirable results and a similar moral motivation in others. When the true motivation behind evil behavior becomes known, however, it foils the plot and in many cases even produces morally desirable reactions in others. Many, for example, feel compassion for intentionally malicious people once they are caught and brought to justice. The perfection of evil, then, is inconceivable as well as impossible because: (1) Evil must be inconsistent; (2)

it tends to undermine itself; and (3) when understood, it often produces good.

Practically speaking, the perfection of good may also be impossible, but it is at least *conceivable*, and therefore it is reasonable to attempt it. Few people, of course, attempt to be perfectly good, but far fewer if any fail to perceive in their lives a dimension beyond mere material self-aggrandizement. When they respond to this dimension by behaving morally, out of *spontaneous regard for the welfare of others*, they participate in and thereby affirm a venture that is at the very least reasonable. Nonmoral responses to the nonmaterial dimension of human life, while they may occur, are not even conceivably reasonable, because they cannot be integrated into convergent hierarchies of value.

The hierarchies resulting from integration of nonmaterial moral values may differ from person to person, and may be changeable for any one person. When truthfulness and compassion come into conflict, a person may appeal to justice as a higher value. Another person, or the same person at a different time, might appeal to compassion as an integrating, higher value in order to resolve a conflict between truth and justice. Such variation is of little consequence in the present discussion. The essential point is that any attempt to integrate one set of nonmaterial values in a higher value establishes a pattern of convergence tantamount to at least implicit affirmation of an ultimate nonmaterial good that orients one's spiritual life. The reader will remember that we use the term "spiritual" to indicate "aspirations and needs beyond material sufficiency that relate to the meaning and purpose of one's life as a whole."

To be sure, the ultimate referent of meaning and purpose in one's own life, whether explicit or implicit, may not correspond to the ultimate referent of anyone else, but most if not all people think otherwise. Human beings do not confine their judgments to statements like "I personally prefer A to B," whether such statements evaluate material or nonmaterial realities. Instead, all people often say or think "A is better than B." Such statements or sentiments imply affirmations of an ultimate, universal standard of goodness, which A approaches more nearly than B. Many of the most common human sentiments are unintelligible without reference to such a standard: simple aesthetic judgments like "Navy blue is a better color for trousers than red"; heartfelt political judgments like "Democracy is better than Communism"; moral sentiments like "It is better to be honest than to be rich"; or the hedonistic reverse "It is better to be rich than honest." Each of these statements, even the last, implies assent to an ultimate, universal, and nonmaterial standard of value. This is so because none of the preceding statements, not even the last, are intelligible or verifiable with reference to the material world alone. To say that it is better to be rich than honest or vice versa requires reference to nonmaterial value in addition to material value, and in order to refer reasonably to the nonmaterial value of honesty, it is necessary that one regard honesty as occurring in an integrated hierarchy of nonmaterial desirables. Moreover, every such statement of "better," in order to be reasonable, requires assent to the notion of a universal "best." Otherwise one could reasonably say only "I personally prefer A to B."

Obviously, one may not be able to articulate the nature of that implicit "best," and it may remain forever impossible for human beings to agree on what it is. We may never agree on even the early stages of a hierarchy of values that approaches it. The world's religions, however, attempt to give structure and evocative power to the universal notion of that which is ultimately desirable for all humankind. They do this by proposing ultimate referents that can serve to integrate and render reasonable non-material human values. In doing so they affirm and guide the universal human urge to affirm meaning and purpose in one's life.

It may indeed be the case, as some sociologists and psychologists hold, that human morality functions as a survival strategy facilitating the formation of societies, and that beyond this it has no objective validity. Be that as it may, upon reflection it becomes clear that the basic principles of morality – truthfulness, compassion, generosity, and justice – inhere in human consciousness in a way that makes them fundamental realities of human experience, with or without objective verification.

Our argument can be summarized in nine steps: (1) All people are motivated by nonmaterial desirables. (2) Behavior motivated randomly by nonmaterial desirables is certainly unreasonable. (3) If nonmaterial motivation is consistent and the nonmaterial values regarded as constant, one's behavior may still be unreasonable, but such behavior is at least conceivably reasonable. (4) When nonmaterial values come into conflict, the only way to regard them as constant and to remain consistent is to integrate them somehow in a higher value. (5) Such higher, integrating values themselves eventually require integration in yet higher values. (6) The resulting hierarchy of values sets a pattern of convergence tantamount at least to implicit affirmation of an ultimate good to which all of one's nonmaterially motivated preferences point. (7) No one confines one's judgments to personal preferences. Instead all people make judgments that have universal implications, as in the judgment "A is better than B." Such judgments, unless they can be materially validated, imply that one affirms a universal hierarchy of nonmaterial values and thereby a universal ultimate good. (8) There may be no such ultimate good, whether individual or universal, but the behavior of people who implicitly or explicitly affirm either is at least conceivably reasonable. (9) The only reasonable alternative available to humankind is to formulate hierarchies of nonmaterial value. Religions do this by conceptualizing ultimate spiritual referents that serve to integrate nonmaterial values and thus make them reasonable.

Elusiveness and the Variety of Religions

We have already observed that no one, religious or otherwise, can reasonably claim that any human or group of humans comprehends ultimate reality in its entirety. All of the religions we have examined explicitly disclaim total comprehension of ultimate reality. Yet each of these religions maintains that its symbolic expressions of its ultimate referent conclusively present ultimate reality to human apprehension. Each claims that its doctrines pertaining to its ultimate referent definitively explain ultimate reality to human understanding and that its prescribed ritual and moral behavior decisively relate responsive humans to its ultimate referent. For each religion, its own ultimate referent is identical with ultimate reality. Each religion thus embraces in its very heart a paradox. On the one hand, each disclaims that it totally comprehends ultimate reality. On the other hand, each claims to have supreme access, understanding, and relation to ultimate reality. This paradox signifies more than any religion has discerned, or has admitted responsibly. No religion has accepted fully the implications and consequences of the twofold assertion that each of them makes. The dimension of elusiveness in each religion's account of its ultimate referent signifies that the ultimate referent of each religion is itself a symbol of a yet more ultimate reality. The ultimate referent of each religion points beyond itself to a more ultimate reality, participates in that more ultimate reality, and discloses some but not all dimensions of that more ultimate reality.

For example, normative Christian thought has held continuously that God revealed in Christ (*deus revelatus*, in the Latin, technical vocabulary) suffices for all needs whatsoever that humans have for the meaning, purpose, salvation, and sanctification of their lives. Yet all along, this same Christian thought has held simultaneously that there are hidden, concealed, unfathomable dimensions of God (*deus absconditus*) and that the revealed God and the concealed God are one and the same ultimate reality. Christians commonly assert that the redeeming love of God revealed in Christ is itself an unfathomable mystery, especially to Christians themselves. They find it incomprehensible that they who are sinners are recipients of fellowship with free, saving divine love. The love given is inscrutable, the fact of its being given is impenetrable. To the detriment of the religion, Christian thinkers have characteristically neglected to draw out the implication and consequence that God-revealed-in-Christ is relative to God-concealed. That implication and consequence are that Christians have no wherewithal to set any limits on the scope of God's revelation.

When adherents of a religion concede that their religion's ultimate referent is relative to a more ultimate reality, they become more honest and their religion becomes more universally credible. At the same time, when a religion admits that its ultimate referent symbolizes an even more ultimate reality, it effectively negates its exclusive and proprietary claims on ultimacy. This admission renders plausible the possibility that the ultimate referents in other religions authentically symbolize distinctive dimensions of ultimate reality. When a religion surrenders exclusive and proprietary claims on ultimate reality – by granting that the ultimate referent of the religion is a symbol – it validates itself by making credible, in a forum of universal discourse, the claim that its ultimate referent presents an authentic dimension of ultimate reality.

We submit that the elusiveness of ultimate reality, as commonly attested by five major religions, accounts for and justifies the existence of different religions based on their respective symbolic systems. Furthermore, the elusiveness common to each religion's referent suggests strongly that the several religions may be mutually complementary rather than mutually exclusive of each other. Viewed as complementary, the world's religions present a solid front against criticisms from the antireligious and against apathy from the irreligious.

Symbolic Expressions of the Central Spiritual Reality

We now turn to illustrate briefly how the central spiritual reality is differently expressed in five major religions. We show that the three characteristics of what we refer to as "the central spiritual reality of humankind" can be accepted by each of the major religions as appropriately descriptive of its ultimate referent. We will illustrate how each religion conceptualizes and evokes response to a reality that all affirm as being *undeniable, ultimately desirable,* and *elusive.*

As mentioned previously, we refer to the conceptual and evocative methods – the myths, doctrines, and practices of the several religions – as symbolic expressions. For a given religion's believers, they point to, participate in, and make present a reality beyond themselves. In the religious context we are accustomed to looking beyond mythological symbols such as an image of the Buddha or the Garden of Eden to a deeper reality that these symbols serve to represent and evoke. We suggest that one should also look beyond even the doctrines and practices of the respective religions to discover their meaning for all humankind. These doctrines and practices, though often thought to conceptualize and manifest universal truth in themselves, are actually religion-specific, symbolic expressions. They are supremely meaningful and evocative in a given culture, but they cannot successfully claim universal validity. Within a specific culture, however, they may validly claim to express and guide a fundamental and universal human urge, the religious urge to respond to *the central spiritual reality of humankind.*

To illustrate this contention, we give an exposition of four types of symbolism that the five major religions use to express the *undeniability, desirability,* and *elusiveness* of their respective *ultimate referents.* These are the four symbolisms – intellectual, mythological, spiritual, and moral – that we characterized early in this chapter. Our intent should become clearer as our examination of the several religions proceeds, but by way of preliminary orientation we may indicate briefly the general function of these symbolisms in expressing the three fundamental characteristics of the central spiritual reality of humankind.

1. *Undeniability: Intellectual symbolism* of undeniability attempts to establish that an ultimate spiritual referent is real and is the reality upon which all other realities depend and from which they derive their ultimate meaning. *Mythological symbolism,* employing images of power, expresses undeniability as irresistibility. *Spiritual symbolism* appeals for personal consent to the inevitability of living with reference to an ultimate spiritual reality. *Moral symbolism* seeks to disclose this inevitability by exposing self-contradictory behavior.

2. *Desirability: Intellectual symbolism* identifies a spiritual reality as the ultimate valuational norm and seeks thereby to make other expressions of desirability reasonable. *Mythological symbolism* of desirability depicts ideals evocatively in the forms of paradise, heroes, a golden age, and so on. *Spiritual symbolism* emphasizes the personal benefits of response to an ultimate spiritual reality. *Moral symbolism* defines desirable human conduct with reference to the ultimate desirability of this reality. In so doing, it transforms self-interested morality into spontaneous regard for the welfare of others. Authentic morality is not based upon fear of punishment or expectation of reward, but upon a free decision to serve, submit to, emulate, or realize an ultimate spiritual reality. Religions employ moral symbolism of desirability to integrate their ethical precepts into their larger, overall expressions of the meaning and purpose of human life, thus minimizing selfish motivation for good behavior.

3. *Elusiveness: Intellectual symbolism* attempts to make the elusiveness of ultimate reality reasonable. *Mythological symbolism* provides illustrations of its elusiveness. *Spiritual symbolism* encourages sustained discipline despite this elusiveness. Although morality defines

itself with reference to an ultimate spiritual reality, *moral symbolism,* in each of the major religions, emphasizes that good behavior in itself is insufficient for personal perfection. In the interrelated spiritual and moral components of each of the schemes of salvation there is a "missing link," the expression of which is spiritual and moral symbolism of the elusiveness of the central spiritual reality of humankind.

By examining these four types of symbolism under the headings undeniability, desirability, and elusiveness, we can give a balanced and accurate account of the essential affirmations of each religion. This demonstrates that undeniability, ultimate desirability, and elusiveness – the characteristics that define a universally valid reality of human experience – are not merely peripherally affirmed by five world religions. Instead, affirmation of these characteristics, and the central spiritual reality that they identify, are integral to the fundamental self-understandings of these religions. Before examining these five religions in detail, it is first necessary to consider further the *validity* of a *central spiritual reality of humankind* by examining atheistic critiques of religion.

CHAPTER TWO

Atheism and the Central Spiritual Reality of Humankind

Some readers may find the three characteristics we assign to the central spiritual reality of humankind – undeniability, desirability, and elusiveness – unsatisfyingly vague and abstract. This abstract characterization of the phenomenon some call God is essential to the twofold purpose of this book: first to show that this phenomenon is universally valid, and second to show that such a reality does indeed operate at the core of the five major religions we have examined. Consideration of modern atheistic critiques of religion will serve to illustrate the necessity of the abstract characterization with which we operate. Because these critiques are *atheistic*, because they attack specifically concepts of God, in this chapter we are justified in using the word "God" to refer to the central spiritual reality of humankind.

Modern atheism successfully attacks several attributes widely regarded in the West as essentially characterizing the core of religion. In the wake of these critiques, it seems impossible to claim responsibly that God created the universe, governs the universe, is a personal deity, or indeed that God exists in any conventional sense of the term. These successes of atheism may seem at first glance thoroughly to refute religion in general. When one looks beyond Western theism to the Eastern religions, however, one finds that these refuted characteristics are not regarded universally as essential attributes of the core of religion. When one adopts a universal view of religion, these refuted attributes appear to be what we have termed symbolic expressions. That is to say, they are supremely meaningful and evocative in some religions – namely Judaism, Christianity, and Islam – but not in others, for example Hinduism and Buddhism.

This finding does not establish the falsity of the doctrines in question or the truth of any other religious doctrines. It does show that in attacking several supposed attributes of God, atheism does not attack the entirety of religion. From a universal perspective, atheistic critiques have not even damaged Judaism and Christianity, the religions that the critiques attack. From such a perspective, atheism attacks theistic symbols rather than theism as such. Such an attack is analogous to a critical appraisal of a symphony that judges, without having considered the work as a whole, that its several instrumental parts are not beautiful by themselves. One does not appreciate a symphony by listening first to the violins, then to the horns, and so on. Similarly one does not appreciate theism by dismembering the organic expression into its component parts and evaluating each part separately.

The dismembering of theism, it must be remembered, was not initiated by atheists, but rather by theists who insisted upon the literal truth of each of several propositional tenets of their respective theisms. In Europe, for example, Christian doctrines concerning the nature of God were promulgated for centuries as a set of independently demonstrable truths. The ontological argument confirmed the existence and perfection of God. The cosmological arguments confirmed God's creatorship, and the teleological argument confirmed God's governance of the universe. Philosophical theists severed these arguments from the organic whole of Christianity and considered them independent demonstrations of the existence and nature of God. These arguments assumed for many the role of pillars of the faith. The philosophical reasoning that set up these apparently freestanding pillars, however, can also undermine and topple them. Recognition of this ambiguous role of reason in religion has created a widespread crisis of belief in modern Christianity.

Maintained as literal and exclusive truths, the doctrines of all religions are vulnerable to the same sort of antireligious criticism that has borne against Christianity. Most of the atheistic criticisms of Christianity apply to Judaism and Islam, and with slight modification to Hindu theism as well. Thus far, Buddhism and nontheistic forms of Hinduism have not met with much modern philosophical criticism, but there is scope for such criticism if their doctrines are regarded as literal truth claims. We will illustrate the vulnerability of religious doctrines maintained as literal truth claims by considering in this chapter the most important intellectual criticisms of religious doctrines of God.

In each case we note that these criticisms do not apply across the board to all religions. The modern Western world which spawned these criticisms was theistic in outlook, and therefore the criticisms are atheistic. As such, they do not apply to Buddhism and nontheistic forms of Hinduism. This belies their validity as critiques of religion as such. We do not suggest that this situation indicates that the doctrines of Buddhism and Hinduism are more true than those of the theistic religions. On the contrary, it indicates that when the doctrines of any religion are promulgated as literal truth, that religion loses credibility in the modern world.

Only when a religion regards its doctrines as literal truths does it declare other religions to be false. Ironically, by maintaining the literal truth of its doctrines a religion also opens itself to being proved false by philosophical criticism. In one stroke, the concrescent treatment of religions that we offer facilitates understanding among religions and undergirds the validity of all religions. Without some such understanding and undergirding, no valid argument is possible for any religion in the modern world. If the atheistic thought now to be considered serves as it should – to urge the world's religions toward harmony, mutual understanding, and a cooperative mission – it may be regarded as a contribution of the highest order to religious thought.

The sections that follow demonstrate the inadmissibility of regarding several theistic concepts as essential characteristics of ultimate reality. In the chapters on Judaism, Christianity, and Islam, we show that these same concepts are valid symbolic expressions of the wider spiritual reality they intimate but do not affirm directly.

God as Creator of the Universe

Thomas Aquinas, in the first three of his "five ways" to prove the existence of God, set forth the classical theistic argument that God is a necessary postulate to explain the existence of the universe. His first way begins by noting that there is motion, or more precisely change, in the world around us. He noted too that nothing moves or changes unless something else moves or changes it. In order to cause motion or change, the source of change must be in motion, so that it too must have been set in motion by a prior source of change. Thus, unless one is prepared to accept an infinite regress of sources of change, one must agree that there must be an ultimate source of change or motion that itself is not changed or moved by anything else, an "unmoved mover." This, said Aquinas, is what "everyone understands to be God."

Aquinas's second way to demonstrate the existence of God proceeds by considering the nature of causation. Everything we see, he noted, has a cause or causes, without which it would not exist. These causes also have causes and so on. So, again, unless one is prepared to accept an infinite chain of causes, one must agree that at some point there is an ultimate cause that is not caused by anything else, a "first cause." This again, according to Aquinas, is what everyone understands to be God.

The third way, the argument based on contingency, is a philosophical abstraction of the first two ways. In this argument, Aquinas observed that nothing we find in nature exists necessarily. Everything we encounter in nature did not exist at some point in the past and will not exist at some point in the future. With all things continually coming into and going out of existence, it is possible for all things to cease to exist at the same time. This possibility is remote, but Aquinas reasoned that if the universe was not created at some point in time, there has been an infinite amount of time in which this possibility could have become an actuality. In an infinite amount of time, all possibilities would at some point necessarily be actualized. But if at some point in time it came about that nothing existed, nothing would exist now, since there would have been nothing to cause the existence of anything else. Viewed another way, the contingency argument holds that the existence of everything we encounter in nature is explained by the existence of something else, which is itself explained by something else, and so on. Another infinite regress commences unless one agrees that ultimately there must be something that exists necessarily, not contingent upon or explained by any prior condition or thing. This again, said Aquinas, is what is meant by the word God.

Modern interpreters of Aquinas generally think that Aquinas's first three arguments, the so-called cosmological arguments, are strengthened by construing the priorities of mover to moved, cause to effect, and explanation to existence as logical priorities rather than temporal priorities. For example, consider a train moving along a track. Each car is moved by the car in front of it, which thus causes or explains its motion. But this second car's motion also requires a mover, a cause, and an explanation. Ultimately, one understands the motion of the cars only when one discovers the locomotive, which moves itself and all the cars at the same time. The locomotive's motion is not temporally prior to that of the cars, for the whole train moves simultaneously. The locomotive's motion is instead logically prior, for it *explains* but does not precede the motion of the cars. Similarly, modern Thomists argue that Aquinas's cosmological arguments should be understood as demanding an explanation of the universe rather than an origin of the universe. The existing universe – with its motion, its causes, and its contingencies – is intelligible only with reference to a self-explaining being, namely God.

The most devastating refutations of these cosmological arguments are usually credited to the eighteenth-century philosophers Hume and Kant, but as these refutations go somewhat beyond strictly cosmological arguments, we will ignore them for the moment and note some of the more obvious shortcomings in these arguments for the existence of God. In the first place, each of the cosmological arguments relies on the impossibility of there being an infinite regress. There is, however, no valid reason to suppose that there may not be such a regress, either logical or temporal, of movers, causes, and conditions. On the other hand, perhaps all of the world's movers, causes, and conditions are thoroughly interdependent, like the stones in an arch. Perhaps the lines of causation move in large circles. Within the universe, one cannot construct a perpetual-motion machine, an apparatus that continues to function without additional energy from an external source, but this is not to say that the universe itself cannot continue in self-contained perpetual motion.

In the West, because of our historical orientation, we tend to pose the exasperated question, "Yes, but where did this dynamic universe of matter and energy come from in the first place?" If, however, one is prepared to accept the existence of God without an explanation of God's existence, why not accept the existence of the universe without further explanation? When challenged to explain the existence of the universe without recourse to God, the famous atheist Bertrand Russell remarked revealingly, "I should say that the Universe is just there, and that's all."[1] Thus, while one might want an explanation for the origin of the universe, and while God is a possible explanation for its origin, no such explanation is necessary.

Some religions, most notably Buddhism, do not assert that the core of religion created the universe or explains its existence. Most forms of Buddhism, in fact, specifically deny that the universe has any such origin or explanation. If, as we hold, there is a central spiritual reality affirmed by all of the major world religions, neither the cosmological arguments nor their refutations reach it.

God as Governor of the Universe

In addition to conceptualizing God as creator of the universe, the theistic religions depict God as the ultimate source of natural and moral order in the universe. Like divine creation, when divine governance of the universe is asserted as a literal truth, it becomes vulnerable to philosophical refutation. In the West, symbolic representation of God as universal governor effectively becomes a philosophical truth claim with the advent of Aquinas's design argument, the fifth of his five ways to prove the existence of God.

The design argument is in a sense an extension of the cosmological arguments and is often included in the cosmological category, because it urges that the postulation of an uncreated universe that is "just there" does not account for the orderliness and regularity of the observable universe. "How is it," ask proponents of the design argument, "that there are regular, invariable natural laws that allow intelligent beings like ourselves to comprehend the world around us? The world could be – and, indeed, unless it is designed by an intelligent being, should be – utterly

1 Originally broadcast in 1949 by the BBC in a debate between Russell and F. C. Copleston. Reprinted in *The Existence of God*, ed. John Hick (London: Macmillan, 1964), p. 175.

random, undifferentiated, and incomprehensible: a seething, senseless chaos. But instead we see myriad discrete entities – stars, planets, oceans, continents, mountains, potholes, and pebbles – all enshrouded in a vast yet delicate regularity, and serving admirably to sustain life and accommodate that wondrous, radiant miracle: consciousness. How could such a marvelous universe evolve through random fluctuations of brute matter and undirected energy, even if one allows, for the sake of argument, that matter and energy have existed, uncreated, throughout eternity? In conjunction with the cosmological arguments, which ponder the miracle that anything at all exists, does not contemplation of the variety, orderliness, and beauty of what does exist render inescapable the conclusion that an intelligent being designed the universe and governs its workings?"

Again, such musings can be profoundly moving to the theistically committed, but they carry little weight for a nonbeliever. An atheist too may find the variety, orderliness, and beauty in the universe a source of endless fascination, but will see no necessary recourse to an intelligent universal designer to explain it. Astronomy, geology, and biology offer cogent theories to explain the evolution of galaxies, stars, planets, life, and consciousness without recourse to divine intervention. Moreover, if there are gaps and inconsistencies in the scientific account of the development of the universe, these may be overcome and corrected by additional research. By contrast, religious cosmologists often deplore and defy amendment, as evidenced by the reaction of some sectors of Christianity to the discoveries of scientists such as Galileo and Darwin.

Not all religious people, of course, mistrust scientific knowledge. In fact, in the seventeenth and eighteenth centuries, scientific discoveries generated a flurry of religious speculation regarding the design of the universe. Developments in astronomy and biology provided hundreds of examples of specific natural mechanisms that seemed to confirm the existence of an intelligent universal designer. The anatomical and botanical sciences in particular began to uncover a previously unimagined functional adaptation to the environment by plants and animals. The teeth of cows, for example, are admirably suited for grinding the grass that their digestive systems can assimilate, whereas wolves' teeth are admirably suited to their carnivorous digestive systems. What is more, all of the plants and animals found in nature appear to be constructed through variations on a few central themes. For example, the bird's wing, the horse's leg, and the human's arm are all structurally analogous, and yet each, by a subtle modification of the underlying structure, is admirably suited to its particular purpose. The broad leaves of the moist, tropical jungles reappear as thorns, a more protective and frugal structural variant, in the harsh and arid deserts. Thus, not only are plants and animals well adapted to function in the widely varying environments in which they find themselves, but it also appears that the tremendous variety found in nature is actually a result of subtle modifications upon a few basic ideas. Surely, it was thought, such discoveries constitute conclusive evidence in support of the existence of an intelligent designer of the universe.

With the publication in 1859 of Darwin's *The Origin of Species*, however, the marvelous adaptability of biological mechanisms to their environment appeared to be adequately explained, without recourse to a designing deity, as a mere hit-or-miss process governed by no more sublime a principle than survival of the fittest. Nevertheless, some see in the process of evolution yet more evidence for the existence of an intelligent universal designer. Some theists find the process of evolution, as described by Darwin and his intellectual heirs, incredible without postulation of an intelligent agent standing behind the process and guiding it to completion. It seemed preposterous, for example, that the complex human eye evolved by pure chance from some crude reaction to light on the cell wall of a primeval amoeba. Similarly, the theologian F. R. Tennant argued that the theory of survival of the fittest does not adequately explain "the arrival of the fit."[2] The French theologian Teilhard de Chardin based much of his writing on the idea that astronomical, geological, and biological discoveries reveal a sweeping evolutionary plan that can be recognized as converging upon a divine purpose, which he calls "the Omega point," the penultimate approach to which is evident in the evolution of human beings and societies.[3] Such arguments, which discern a specific purpose or end (*telos*) in the supposed design of the universe, are known as teleological arguments for the existence of God.

Arguments that point to purpose in the structure and workings of the universe all suffer from a fault that David Hume called "anthropomorphism," "in-the-form-of-man-ism." In teleological arguments, the mind alleged to be responsible for the purpose or design of the universe is invariably conceived of as being like a human mind. In other words, the purposes we see in nature are projections of our own human purposes in seeking to manipulate the world around us. When we propose, for example, that the purpose of grass is to feed cows and the purpose of cows is to feed us, we elevate our own purposeful reaction to nature to the position of being the guiding force behind nature. We tend to forget that many of the species that appear to have been purposefully produced through the process of evolution will become extinct when their environment changes and they are not longer adapted for survival. When a life form thus becomes extinct, the matter within it takes on a different arrangement, which, from a different perspective, might also appear to serve a purpose.

2   F. R. Tennant, *Philosophical Theology*, vol. 2 (Cambridge: Cambridge University Press, 1930), p. 85.
3   See, for example, *The Phenomenon of Man* or *Man's Place in Nature*.

Dead dinosaurs became petroleum. Any arrangement of matter may appear to serve a purpose if surveyed by a purposeful being such as a human being.

Most humans, however, would be loath to accept the proposition that our purpose is to provide food for wolves, or to provide petroleum for a future age. Instead, we see the universe as being purposefully designed for our human purposes. We dovetail the theory of evolution with the religious concept of the human being as the "crown of creation." We suppose, like Tennant or Teilhard, that evolution proceeds in a positive direction and has culminated in the most perfect of all beings, the human being.

It is undeniable that evolution as we know it on earth thus far has tended toward greater complexity in organisms. The instance of life on earth, however, is the only instance of evolution we have been able to observe. We observe it, moreover, in midcourse. It is possible, and it may prove true, that human beings are here to stay. But it is also possible that the human species, like countless other species, will become extinct. It is also possible, as some science-fiction writers imagine, that human beings will evolve into yet more complex, more intelligent beings. Our nuclear weapons, however, are a vivid and persistent reminder that evolution may have reached a high point of complexity, at least on planet earth.

Aside from our own military and environmental irresponsibility, numerous eventualities could result in the extinction of the human species and other complex life forms on earth. From a human point of view, such extinction seems unthinkably disastrous. From the point of view of the theory of evolution, however, such extinction would be merely another of many instances of species dying out due to changed environmental conditions. For all we know, human or higher-level consciousness and intelligence may have evolved and died out millions of times on other planets since the "big bang," the cosmic explosion that theoretically marks the beginning of this universe. This big bang, moreover, may have been one among many or one in a series of big bangs. There may be at present or may have been in the past countless universes where life, consciousness, and intelligence evolve and die out with tedious repetitiveness.

On the one hand, human-level intelligence may be doomed precisely because it is unique to this planet. On the other hand, it may be so commonplace throughout the universe as to need no explanation. Such possibilities render inconclusive those arguments that claim to establish the guidance of God in the process of evolution.

In addition to the philosophical inconclusiveness of the issue of divine governance or design of the universe, neither Buddhism nor many forms of Hinduism ascribe the apparent order in the universe to the activity or will of a divine being. Instead, these religions account for the nature of the universe in one of two ways. In some cases, the universe is said to evolve mechanistically through unimaginably immense cycles of time. Its nature at any given time, whether orderly or chaotic, is regarded as a function of the stage of the world cycle at that time. In other cases, the so-called nature of the universe is said to be determined by the various illusions under which the world's sentient beings labor. Whether we see an orderly, disorderly, pleasant, unpleasant, sublime, or absurd universe, it is because we see wrongly, not because the universe really is one or another of these.

Again, the theistic concept of divine governance of the universe is inadmissible as an essential characteristic of a central spiritual reality. Its essential characteristics must be both philosophically valid and universally affirmed by major world religions. The concept of God as universal governor fails on both counts.

God as a Person

Obviously, the concepts of God as creator and governor both relate to the more fundamental concept of God as a person. That which creates and governs would have to be similar to a person. As we have seen, however, Western atheists have shown that these attributes cannot rationally be assigned to God. They have shown, in fact, that one cannot even demonstrate that the universe is created or governed at all. In so doing, they have invalidated most of the evidence that might lead one to a rational conclusion that God is a person. Hume's critique of the anthropomorphism in the classical proofs for the existence of God, moreover, suggests that the personhood of God is not a conclusion at all. It is instead an unwarranted presupposition, which leads to the erroneous conclusion that the universe is similar to a human contrivance. This critique opened the way for what is probably the most powerful antireligious force in the world today, namely psychological atheism.

The psychological atheists argue that the nature of the human mind is such that it naturally posits and adheres to a concept of a personal God. They suggest that the reasons behind belief in God as well as the nature of the God believed in are not to be found in any objectively existing reality, but in the nature of the human mind itself. In other words, whether or not God exists, humans would believe that a god exists; and whatever God might be like, humans would have conceived of God as a personal being.

The best known of the psychological atheists is Sigmund Freud. Freud theorized that belief in God is a psychological crutch, whereby one seeks to avoid the ultimate responsibility for one's life that comes with adulthood. When we leave the protection of our biological parents, Freud said, we seek to replace the lost sense of security with an imaginary father, God, who governs the wider universe we live in as adults just as our biological fathers governed the small worlds we lived in as children.

The feminist revolution has effectively called into question the gender of Freud's surrogate parent, and modern psychology as a whole has departed from Freudian principles to a large extent. Nevertheless, Freud's basic contention, that religion is a psychological crutch, has survived so well that it is now practically axiomatic in most psychological considerations of religion. Most modern psychologists would not stress the parental aspect of religious belief in God, and many do not regard belief in God as a mental disease. Modern psychology often regards belief in God as an expedient buffer against the vagaries of day-to-day life. For considerations of validity, however, it makes little difference whether belief in God is a mental disease or a psychological boon. The general theory, first formulated by Freud, that belief in God originates and subsists in human psychological inadequacies provides the primary positive complement to the negative atheistic criticisms of belief in the existence of God.

Atheist philosophers have demonstrated that belief in God as a person is not philosophically defensible, and atheist psychologists have contributed an explanation as to why so many people believe it anyway. So pervasive is the psychological explanation of religion that even religious believers themselves are now often willing to admit that they believe in God primarily because they *need* to believe. This theory of religion provides a plausible, naturalistic explanation as to why so many people believe in God even though there is no conclusive evidence that such a being actually exists.

Not all psychological theories of belief in God are as pessimistic regarding human nature as those deriving from Freud's theories. Feuerbach, for example, held that the human mind naturally tends toward superlatives, while the human condition limits these aspirations with the bonds of practicality. Frustrated by the limitations of practicality, human beings, according to Feuerbach, project their most precious traits beyond themselves into a perfected form, and call the resultant image "God." Whatever creativity we actually encounter is human creativity, whatever generosity, mercy, love, benevolence, justice, or forgiveness we encounter, are always human traits. These traits are precious in that they are precisely the traits that differentiate us from brute animals. Projecting these traits into a perfected form could be a positive exercise in self-affirmation, but, according to Feuerbach, in making the projection we obscure the human origins of the attributes we ascribe to God, and thereby the projection of God becomes an exercise in self-negation. God is strong; we are weak. God is good; we are wicked. God creates; we are creatures. Moreover, we construe such self-disparagement as piety, and religious humility becomes an insidious and enervating psychological and social vampire, robbing us of the ambition and dynamism that, if restored, would allow us to realize our own ideals here on earth. "Man created God in his own image," said Feuerbach, suggesting that if we were to become consciously aware of this situation, religion could become a positive psychological and social force by providing us with a ready-made model, in the concept of God, of what we ourselves should strive to become.

Feuerbach's explanation of belief in a personal God, though naturalistic, is less scientific than the truly psychological explanations of Freud and his heirs. Freud, for example, was able to point out striking similarities between the dynamics of neuroses and psychoses and the dynamics of religious belief. There is no such evidence to support Feuerbach's theory. Still, Feuerbach has been tremendously influential through his intellectual heir, Karl Marx.

Marx's primary contribution to atheism was to show that the elite of society has a vested interest in encouraging the masses to deprive themselves of their best qualities by projecting them into an imaginary God. This process, he argued, is the cornerstone of an elitist program designed to deprive the lower economic classes of the ambition and dynamism that would, if unleashed, induce them to rebel against their oppressors. Less controversial figures than Marx, notably Emile Durkheim, have also demonstrated the important sociological role of religion as a buttress of the status quo. The vested interest of societies in indoctrinating their constituents with religious beliefs has become a basic axiom of modern sociology. Thus, modern atheism has not only succeeded in calling into radical doubt the traditional attributes of God, it has also developed viable psychological and sociological theories to account for the origin and tenacious survival of belief in an undemonstrable God.

Many theists, of course, would be quick to agree that the personhood of God is not a reasoned conclusion based on empirical observation and logical deduction. Instead, they would maintain that belief in the personhood of God is based on the experience of a personal encounter with God. If anything, the other attributes of God are deductions based on this transformative encounter. Atheists may be correct in saying that belief in a personal God is a premise upon which the other attributes of God and the universe are based. Such belief, however, is not an unwarranted presumption, but firm knowledge based upon incontrovertible personal experience of God as a living person. Given such an experience of the living God, the theist might argue, the plausible psychological and sociological theories of atheism are of no more consequence than a magician's slight of hand, credible, perhaps entertaining, but ultimately unpersuasive.

Atheists typically answer the argument based on a personal encounter with God by making the observation that many people see ghosts or live under the illusion that dead loved ones or imaginary companions accompany them in their day-to-day lives. All people have dreams and even while waking make perceptual mistakes of one kind or another. People who allow their lives to be guided by such unverifiable experiences are normally considered insane. No one doubts that the experiences themselves are real, and often shockingly vivid, but sane people normally come to ignore experiences for which there is no verifiable object. According to atheism, a personal encounter with God, which is also not objectively verifiable, is not different from an encounter with a ghost or the imaginary companionship of a dead relative. Many theists, of course, claim to have encountered the same God, but this is no more surprising than that the Irish typically encounter leprechauns. We encounter the kinds of ghosts we have been conditioned to encounter.

In the latter part of the nineteenth-century, the pioneering anthropologist E. B. Tylor defined all religions, primitive and modern, as "belief in spiritual beings,"[4] thereby initiating an enduring tradition in anthropology and sociology that regards God as basically a superghost. This theme and variations upon it form the basis of the modern sociological and anthropological approaches to religion as some sort of aberration in the human mind or in human society or both.

Regardless of the drawbacks of the somewhat skeptical approaches to religions that psychologists, sociologists, and anthropologists customarily adopt, it must be admitted that thus far they have done more to give parity status to the various religions of the world than have religious thinkers, most of whom have been content either to ignore other religions or to argue against them. The success of the modern social sciences in equalizing and accommodating the various religions, albeit in an unfavorable light, is one of the strongest cards in the atheists' hand. Psychology, sociology, and anthropology, using varying methods, have been able to demonstrate with remarkable success how the whole range of religions can be regarded as similar human responses in similar situations.

This success, in and of itself, strengthens immeasurably the position of atheists vis-à-vis ordinary theists, who are typically unwilling or unable to extend their defenses of religion beyond the boundaries of their own respective traditions. Religious thinkers cannot hope to be taken seriously in the emerging global community if they cannot generate understandings of religion that function, like the secular theories already mentioned, to accommodate the variety of religious beliefs and practices encountered in the world. As it is, the various religions, oblivious of or hostile toward

4 E. B. Tylor, *Primitive Culture* (London: John Murray, 1873), chap. 11.

each other, are remarkably like several Napoleons in the same asylum or, more to the point, like several passengers trying to waterproof their respective cabins in a sinking ship.

When one does take a wider view of religion, a view that looks beyond the Western theistic traditions, the atheistic theories and arguments discussed in this section once again lose much of their force. As mentioned previously, Buddhism and some forms of Hinduism do not maintain that the focus of religious life is a person. The Buddhist Nirvāṇa or the Hindu Brahman could not possibly be construed as surrogate parents or anthropomorphic projections. Although some Buddhists and some Hindus believe in spiritual beings, Tylor's definition of religion as "belief in spiritual beings" does not encompass Buddhism or most forms of Hinduism.

Once again, modern atheistic arguments and theories refuting the personal nature of God do not apply to religion as a whole. Maintained as a literal truth, the concept of the personhood of God has failed to withstand philosophical criticism. It also fails to find assent in some of the major religions. For these two reasons, we do not regard personhood as an essential characteristic of the central spiritual reality of humankind, though again we acknowledge its evocative power as a symbolic expression of this phenomenon in some religions.

God as Existing

The critiques considered in the previous section refute several attributes of God. Immanuel Kant, though himself a theist, initiated a critique of the very notion of God as existing. Kant claimed to prove with finality that it is impossible rationally to prove the existence of God. His critique hinges on the concept of necessary existence, and all that it entails, as proposed in the ontological argument for the existence of God.

According to Kant, all of the classical arguments stand or fall with Anselm's ontological argument. We have noted that the cosmological arguments and the teleological argument fail to establish the existence of a prime mover, first cause, noncontingent being, universal designer, or universal governor. Kant noted that even if one were to accept these doubtful arguments as valid, they would not establish the existence of the right kind of God. A prime mover, for example, is not necessarily good, just, or merciful. Many would argue that the designer of *this* universe is obviously not good, just, or merciful. And even the most philosophically rigorous devotee would not consider praying as follows: "Our noncontingent being who art in heaven . . ." The theological proofs considered thus far fail on two counts. They fail to establish a God of any kind, and they fail even to argue for a theologically appropriate being that meaningfully could be called God. This double failure, said Kant, renders them dependent upon the ontological argument for vindication.

Kant noted that the ontological argument claims to establish both the existence and the perfection of God, so that if it works, the other arguments are superfluous, and if it fails, the other arguments fail with it. Needless to say, the argument from personal experience, even if it be granted that experiences of God are not illusory, also depends on the ontological argument, for one cannot be certain that the supernatural being one has encountered is in fact *the supreme* being. The superior being of one's religious experience might well be one among many such beings, might not even be the best among them, and certainly might not be the perfect being whom God is supposed to be.

It will be remembered that the ontological argument, which would overcome these problems, begins with what Anselm claims is the proper definition of God: "that than which nothing greater can be conceived." The phrase is considerably less clumsy in the original Latin, but at any rate, in order for the argument to proceed, the definition of God must be stated in just this way. Given this definition, says Anselm, it is clear that the concept of such a being exists in one's mind. But surely it is greater to exist objectively than merely to exist in one's mind, and therefore, if one is true to the definition, one must admit that God exists objectively as well as in the mind. Otherwise one could conceive of something greater than God, namely, a greatest conceivable being which also exists objectively, and the definition would be violated. As normally interpreted, Anselm's argument goes on to say that it is one thing to exist objectively, independent of one's mind, but it is surely a greater thing to exist necessarily. Many things great and mediocre exist contingently – that is, they might not have existed – but the greatest conceivable thing would have to exist with no possibility of ever not existing. In other words, it would have to be necessary and eternal. Clearly the greatest conceivable being would also have to be perfectly good, loving, merciful, just, conscious, and so on, including all of the attributes usually ascribed to God. Thus, in one stroke, the ontological argument claims to establish all that the cosmological, teleological, and experiential arguments claim to establish as well as moving beyond them to establish a being that encompasses the sum of all perfections.

As the keystone of the theological arguments, the ontological argument provides a point that, if successfully attacked, results in the irreparable collapse of all purely rational proofs for the existence of God. The argument from experience, not being rational, cannot be refuted by reason. Nonetheless the failure of the ontological argument weakens the argument from experience. Philosophers and theologians alike agree that Kant accomplished just such an attack, and that there is not, and never will be, an acceptable and purely rational proof for the existence of God. Paraphrased, Kant's argument states that *if* God exists, *if* a greatest conceivable being exists, then it certainly must be supremely good, just, merciful, and so on. *If* God exists, moreover, God must exist necessarily. This much the ontological argument establishes, but no more. *If*, on the other hand, God does not exist, God simply does not exist, and all of the supposed perfections vanish along with the nonexistent being. In other words, one can prove that if one conceives of a supremely perfect being, one must conceive of it as existing, but that does not prove that there is indeed such a being. In Kant's terms, the ontological argument fails because it erroneously conceives of existence as an attribute, whereas, actually, existence is the state of being capable of having attributes. Unsurpassable greatness and perfection are indeed possible attributes of a thing, but to be meaningful as such, they depend on the existence of that thing, not vice versa.

The ontological argument thus fails, and it becomes clear that for our present purposes we cannot regard even existence as a valid characteristic of the central spiritual reality of humankind. This situation, however, is no more surprising than that someone ever wanted to establish the *existence* of God in the first place. Amoebae exist. Kangaroos, as improbable as it may seem, exist. Why would any theist want to put God in a category with such things?

Recently, as the concept of existence has been more clearly formulated in the West, Jewish and Christian theologians have become less enthusiastic about establishing or even speaking in terms of the "existence" of God. Strictly defined, "to exist" means to occur in nature or to be instantiated. As Bertrand Russell has said in mathematical terms, to exist is to belong to the set of all x such that there is one. Thus, if kangaroos exist, the statement, "x is a kangaroo" is sometimes true. If unicorns do not exist, the statement, "x is a unicorn" is never true. It is doubtful that anyone wants to point to something, x, and call it God. Even idol worshipers understand that whatever the focus of their worship, be it a stone or a tree or a mountain, the reality that they hope to approach is not exhausted by something they can point to and call "God."

Given this situation, many modern theologians, most notably Paul Tillich, have come to the conclusion that to argue for the existence of God as one among other existents is not only self-contradictory but even idolatrous. Tillich, like many other modern theologians, preferred to speak of God in terms of "being." According to Tillich, God is, but does not exist. This may be a clarifying theological statement for Christianity, but it contributes nothing toward establishing the ontological actuality of an ultimate spiritual reality.

Atheistic critiques that proceed from clarifications of the term "existence" are not overcome, as some suppose, merely by replacing "existence" with "being" in theological statements. In retrospect, it is obvious that Anselm was not altogether clear about what he was trying to establish when he set out to prove the existence of God. But one does not get any farther with his argument – beginning with the definition "that than which nothing greater can be conceived" – by substituting "being" for "existence" and saying, "It is greater to be than not to be." Instead, it would be better simply to recognize that ontological statements about God, whether framed in terms of existence or being, are not to be taken literally any more than statements such as "God walked in the garden."

To say that God exists, or that God is, is actually to assert an ontological continuity between God and the universe. Such statements are encountered in religions that maintain that the universe has a divine creator or source. Such religions assert that the universe, which "is" or "exists," derives or obtains this quality from an ultimate spiritual reality, which therefore must also "be" or "exist." Some forms of Hinduism make this assertion and would therefore be affected by refutations of the ontological argument. Most forms of Buddhism, however, deny such a continuity between ultimate reality and the world. Thus, again, Western atheism, in refuting existence as a meaningful attribute of God, does not refute or even attack religion in general. Such refutations apply only to expressions of the central spiritual reality encountered in some but not all religions.

A Religious Appraisal of Judaic and Christian Atheism

No one of the atheistic critiques, or all of them combined, refute or even touch all of the religions examined in the remaining chapters of this book. They attack Judaic and Christian concepts of God, but they apply only partially if at all to other religions. Interestingly, none of the atheistic critiques apply to most forms of Buddhism. This does not suggest that Buddhism is better than other religions, but merely that Buddhism is perhaps farthest removed, conceptually speaking, from Christianity. Nor does it suggest that Christianity, the religion most directly affected by atheism, is less true than other religions. That these atheistic arguments apply most directly to Christianity merely reflects the historical fact that they originated and developed in the modern Christian West. Atheism was formulated in response to Judaic and Christian expressions of God and is only marginally applicable beyond this specific context. We are therefore justified in referring to "Judaic and Christian atheism."

In considering the foregoing atheistic arguments we do not intend to detract from Judaism and Christianity. Our point is rather that the most coherent and vigorous antireligious tradition in history does not bear upon religion in general. Nor, we maintain, is it devastating to the religions it does effectively criticize. A rejection of jazz is not necessarily a rejection of music in general, and a study of the goals and techniques of other forms of music and of music in general is likely to lead to an appreciation of jazz. Similarly, consideration of other religions and of the fundamentals of religion in general may be the most effective way to put atheism in its proper perspective and illustrate how the theistic religions can be appreciated as legitimate symbolic expressions of a spiritual reality central for all humankind, even in the face of hostile atheistic critiques.

Aside from not applying to religion in general, atheism has met with only limited success – certainly no more than religions – in formulating a consistent and comprehensive world view palatable for human consumption. By its own standards, atheism fails to demonstrate the unreality of God. Hume himself, one of the most effective spokesmen of atheism, characterized atheism as being merely "negative theism," which affirms the converse of a fundamentally moot question. Moreover, the various brands of atheism fare no better than religions when faced with ultimate and urgent questions concerning the meaning and purpose of human life. True, there may indeed be no meaning or purpose in human life, but thus far no atheistic system of thought has been formulated without affirming some direction and goal in life.

Some of these atheistic proposals of meaning and purpose are straightforward. Marxism and related forms of social atheism urge their followers to work toward a utopian society of one sort or another based on equality, justice, selfless work, and sharing. There is little indication in the material world or in human experience that people are capable or even truly desirous of such a society. On the contrary, there is ample indication that human beings as a whole are not willing to work toward such a society. Why should they? They have no hope of participating in the prophesied Utopia and thereby enjoying the fruits of the sacrifices required of them in their present lives. Social atheism's plea for faith, self-sacrifice, and altruism finds no legitimate motivational basis in the entirely secular world views it espouses. In essence social atheism has replaced the religious "pie in the sky" with a pie in the distant future. Neither fills the stomach.

Why should I be so virtuous if all I have to look forward to is struggle throughout my lifetime and a blank death thereafter? I may join the socialist cause in order to alleviate the current wretched conditions of my life, but as soon as I am adequately fed, clothed, and housed, my mind – and most others' minds as well – will turn to consolidating and protecting my enjoyment of adequacy and parlaying it into a position of superfluity relative to my fellow beings. Moreover, in the wake of a full stomach come nagging questions of the purpose of this finite life I find myself acting out. Such considerations are at least partly responsible for the poor production records of Communist countries. People, it seems, are simply not willing to produce according to their abilities and consume only according to their needs.

In practice, social atheism attempts to deal with human quirks such as greed, competitiveness, individualism, doubt, and rebellion by resorting to indoctrination, the same method these atheists object to in religions. Communist societies put the muscle of coercion behind their indoctrinations of society just as religion has been criticized for doing in the societies it has guided. The ascendancy of Communism in several countries provides evidence that atheistic world views, when entrusted with the helm of society, use the same methods and fare no better than religious world views.

This observation is devastating to social atheism, for its claim to validity and its critique of religion rest upon the claim that its secular world view serves better as the basis of a society than religious world views. Without success in the social sphere, social atheism becomes a blind and pointless Juggernaut, crushing the individualistic and spiritual aspirations of its subjects without even relieving their hunger.

Other forms of atheism are somewhat less straightforward than social atheism in proposing a meaning and purpose in life. Faced with the material world's univocal evidence that life is ultimately meaningless, yet unwilling to accept it, some atheists equivocate. Psychological atheists speak of various forms of "mental health" as an ideal without being able to define it or offer convincing arguments as to why one should desire it. What if my "insanity," religious or otherwise, makes me happy? Why should I give it up for something as bland and nebulous as "mental health"? Nor is mental health proposed as a means to anything beyond itself, other than perhaps jaded, middle-class orthodoxy. Psychological atheism has been convincingly critical of certain aspects of religious belief, but it has not been able to replace religious values with anything more tangible. It has declared religious belief to be a mental disease but has been unable effectively to envisage a healthy state corresponding to removal of the disease. As a result, many if not most psychologists now recognize and recommend religion as an important element in mental well-being.

The existentialists, more than other Western atheists, have been courageous enough to admit that the ultimate implication of secularism is an absurd world, where all values and norms are arbitrary and meaningless. Even so, existentialists generally equivocate by proposing "authenticity" as a unique value that is not meaningless, but ultimate. For existentialism, authenticity means, in essence, to reject "escapist idols" – such as gods, creeds, and nations – and to embrace courageously the meaninglessness of life. There is a paradox here as profound as any encountered in traditional religious doctrines. Why, in a truly meaningless world, does embracing meaninglessness have any more meaning or value than attempting to escape meaninglessness by whatever means, however cowardly or perverse?

Conclusions

Confronted with the realities of human experience, the problems and procedures of atheism are exactly analogous to those of religions. Human beings want to know what to do with their lives, but material reality offers no clues. We want to know what to believe, how to think, and again, the material world is silent. Faced with this situation, the various forms of atheism, like religions, attempt to sway human minds by proposing meanings and purposes in life. They encourage acceptance of various questionable ideals and values by means of indoctrination, the very means they criticize in religions. Atheism, like the theism it criticizes, fails to formulate a comprehensive, normative, and fully rational assessment of the human situation.

In the present age, few would deny that there are intellectual contradictions in religions, both theistic and nontheistic. The intellectual contradiction in atheism, distilled from the foregoing brief considerations, is that it would have us live without an ultimate norm. The human mind simply cannot act in every instance upon the basis of absolute relativity. There is an implicit "best" in every "better," no matter how misguided or perverse one's preferences. Atheists have been less than philosophically rigorous in this regard. Without exception, they hold that A is better than B – for example, that to embrace meaninglessness is better than to seek to escape meaninglessness, that not to believe in God is better than to believe in God. They fail to recognize, however, that to propose a "better" sets in motion an inexorable conceptual chain reaction that necessarily culminates in a "best." Otherwise, one is reduced to relativistic tautologies such as "A is different from B."

In the present age, few would deny that there are existential contradictions in religions, both theistic and nontheistic. The existential contradiction in atheism is that it would alienate us from a fundamental dimension of humanness, the spiritual dimension. We call ourselves *Homo sapiens*, the thinking ape, in order to distinguish ourselves from other primates. In view of the ecological role we have assumed, however, "thinking" is hardly an accurate defining characteristic of the human race. Some have suggested convincingly that it would be more appropriate to call ourselves "Homo religiosus," the religious ape. Even concerning our biological history, we want to know of supposed ancestors of the human race not only "Did they walk upright?" but also "Did they bury their dead?" Though not decisive, the fact that certain extinct creatures buried their dead will be adduced as evidence that they were indeed our evolutionary ancestors. If creatures perceived their world as utterly materialistic, they would not bother with burials. If we took atheism at face value, we ourselves would not bother with burials and other behavior that distinguishes us from brute animals. By denying any nonmaterial reality, atheism, even while claiming to alleviate human alienation, in fact encourages alienation from a fundamental dimension of humanness.

Though flawed itself, Western atheism has exposed many flaws in the provincial, culture-bound Western concept of God. It leaves untouched, however, the commonly affirmed reality central to the religions we examine in the following chapters. Inasmuch as atheism proposes meaning and purpose in human life, moreover, it may itself be regarded as a response to this central spiritual reality of humankind.

The chapters that follow examine *symbolic expressions* of ultimate reality as conceived in five major world religions. Many of the same concepts that in this chapter we have reckoned as invalid will be reconsidered in the following chapters as valid *symbolic expressions* of the undeniability, desirability, and elusiveness of the central spiritual reality of humankind.

CHAPTER THREE

Hinduism and the Central Spiritual
Reality of Humankind

Of all the living religions, Hinduism is arguably the most ancient. Some of its current beliefs and practices can be traced with fair certainty to approximately 2000 B.C.E. No other religion in history has shown such a capacity for diversification without schism, or such a capacity for withstanding, accommodating, and ultimately absorbing alien modes of thought. As a result of this remarkable capacity for assimilating both internal schism and external challenge, modern Hinduism is, in some ways, better described as a mutually tolerant confederation of several religions rather than as a single faith. Many contemporary Hindus, following the lead of several nineteenth-century Hindu modernization movements, are not reluctant to expand this confederation by adding to its ranks the other religions of the world, construing them as being essentially sects of Hinduism. Interestingly, Hinduism's ability and readiness to accept the validity of all religions is perhaps the primary basis of the Hindu claim to be the most valid of the otherwise equally valid religions of the world. Thus far, this unilateral declaration of the equality of all religions has not proved to be an acceptable solution, beyond Hindu circles, to the problem posed by the plurality of religions. Nonetheless, the accommodating posture of Hinduism, even if not always acceptable to those accommodated, makes Hinduism a good starting point for this inquiry into the validity and common center of five major religions.

Hinduism achieves its remarkable capacity for tolerance and assimilation of varying beliefs primarily through a conceptual device that Ninian Smart aptly labels "transpolytheism."[1] According to this Hindu concept, a multitude of symbolic deities are expressions of a single reality beyond literal expression or comprehension. The single reality standing behind these symbolic deities, which need not necessarily be Hindu deities, may

1 Ninian Smart, *Doctrine and Argument in Indian Philosophy* (New York: Allen and Unwin, 1964), p. 215.

46

be theistic or nontheistic, depending upon which form of Hinduism one espouses. In the context of Hinduism, the internal debate between the theistic and nontheistic concepts of ultimate reality is not so much a matter of which is right and which is wrong; it is more a matter of which is more *nearly* correct. To be sure, this debate and its many subdebates have been and still often are heated. Nevertheless, both the theistic and nontheistic alternatives are accepted as equally orthodox forms of Hinduism. It is not uncommon, in fact, to encounter a Hindu who functions comfortably and sincerely in both frameworks without anxiety over the apparent conflict.

Such flexibility arises in part from Hinduism's emphasis upon mythological and spiritual symbolism, rather than intellectual or moral symbolism, in its approach to ultimate reality. Hinduism tends to regard philosophical doctrines as mere abstractions of the concrete truths enshrined in its mythology and in the spiritual experiences and testimony of its saints and sages. No matter how widely they vary, differing religious beliefs can be tolerated and even embraced, so long as they can be seen as approaching in any way the mythological and spiritual truths of Hinduism. If such differing beliefs fall very wide and far short of the mark, it is of no great consequence in Hinduism. Most Hindus accept the theory of rebirth, and in the unlimited course of transmigration that this theory depicts, there will be ample time for even the most misguided soul to follow its own winding path to the eternal truths of Hinduism.

Like one's philosophical beliefs, the details of one's moral code are of no great consequence in Hinduism, so long as the overall moral code can be construed as orienting one in the general direction of eventual spiritual enlightenment. The nature and content of this enlightenment, as well as the final stages of the path to it, are enshrined in the mythology of revealed scripture and in the spiritual tradition handed down by the enlightened Hindu sages of the past. Thus, mythological and spiritual symbolism, the two primary ways in which Hinduism expresses its *ultimate referent*, correspond roughly to the twofold division of Hindu scriptures into *sruti*, "that which is heard" (i.e., revelation), and *smrti*, "that which is remembered" (i.e., tradition).

These two predominant symbolisms also correspond roughly to the dual origins of Hinduism in a Vedic tradition and a yogic tradition. The Vedic tradition, represented in literature by the four Vedas and the several Brāhmanas, is mythological in orientation. The yogic tradition, which first surfaces in the Upanishadic literature, emphasizes spiritual symbolism expressive of mystical release (moksha). The ancient Vedas, composed and compiled in the course of the millennium between 2000 and 1000 B.C.E., are sacrificial in orientation, comprising hymns of praise recounting the deeds and qualities of a populous pantheon. Hindus regard

these hymns as the wellspring of their religion. Next to the Vedas in
authority are the Upanishads, composed between 800 and 300 B.C.E. In
contrast to the Vedas, the Upanishads are contemplative in orientation,
construing Vedic myth and ritual as symbolic expressions of inward,
mystical truths and experiences. Some of the Upanishadic material is
theistic, but taken as a whole, the principal Upanishads lean decisively
toward monism.

Not until approximately the time of Christ and the composition of the
Bhagavad Gītā did devotional theism gain a strong foothold in Hindu
sacred literature. What popular Hindu religious practices may have been
like prior to this time is a matter of speculation only. Suffice it to say that
from very early times to the present, Hinduism in practice has been a
thorough mixture of sacrificial, meditational, and devotional elements.
Different schools of Hinduism emphasize one or another of these elements, and debates between these schools may be intense. Nonetheless,
in the interest of simplification, it is probably not unfair to say that insofar
as Hinduism can be regarded as an integrated whole, its key integrating
concept is the monism of the Upanishads as interpreted by the great
exegete Saṅkara. Hence, Upanishadic monism, as systematized by
Saṅkara in his Adviata or "Nondualist" school, will serve as the focus of
the following exposition of the Hindu expression of the central spiritual
reality of humankind. We will attempt to give appropriate attention to
sacrificial and devotional Hindu theism as well.

Undeniability

Mythological Symbolism of Undeniability

Mythologically and *spiritually,* Hinduism expresses the undeniability of
its ultimate referent primarily in terms of cosmogonic monism, the theory
that in the beginning all was one. This notion differs markedly from the
Western theistic notion of creation ex nihilo (out of nothing), although the
difference is not always obvious in individual passages in the ancient
Hindu texts themselves. Even Hindu theism is concerned mainly with the
source rather than the creator of the universe. Hindu theism, in other
words, is primarily panentheistic, affirming that the universe inheres in
God or in God's activity. For example, in the case of the dancing Śiva, the
cosmos is created not out of nothing, but out of Śiva, through the activity
of dancing. The universe is identified with the dance of Śiva. Because of
the nature of its cosmology, Hinduism, more than any other religion,
conflates the source of the universe and the religious ultimate it affirms. In
Western theism, the doctrine of creation functions only to strengthen a

more essential theistic affirmation. In Hinduism, however, the source of the universe *is by definition* the ultimate referent of the religion. Hindu cosmology, then, describes the ultimate referent of Hinduism rather than indirectly supporting affirmation of this referent. Cosmology is the core of Hinduism's *mythological symbolism* of the undeniability of this refer- ent. In Hinduism, *images of power expressing the irresistibility of this ref- erent* depict the central spiritual reality of humankind as the source of the universe. They are a Hindu expression of the central spiritual reality af- firmed in all human experience and behavior.

The earliest traces of classical Hindu cosmology appear in the Ṛg Veda, where cosmology is expressed in terms of mythological symbolism. The hymns of the Ṛg Veda heap extravagant praises upon a multitude of deities and seek from them assistance in earthly affairs and in the afterlife. Without apparent hesitation, these hymns address several of these gods as the supreme deity. Several different gods are, in fact, given credit for the single-handed creation of the universe.

Wonderful Mitra propped the heaven and earth apart, and covered and concealed the darkness with his light. He made the two bowls part asunder like two skins. Vaiśvānara put forth all his creative power.

(Ṛg 6.8.3)[2]

Lord of all wealth, the Asura propped the heavens, and measured out the broad earth's wide expanses. He, King supreme, approached all living creatures. All these are Varuṇa's holy operations.

(Ṛg 8.42.1)

Thou, Indra, art the Conqueror: thou gavest splendour to the Sun. Maker of all things, thou art Mighty and All-God.

(Ṛg 8.98.2)[3]

Great are the deeds of thee, the Great O Agni: thou by thy power hast spread out earth and heaven.

(Ṛg 3.6.5)

A few hymns in the comparatively late (c. 1000 B.C.E.) first and tenth books of the Ṛg Veda indicate that such passages are not to be taken literally, but are to be construed as addressing several aspects of a single supreme reality.

2 We follow Ralph T. H. Griffith, *The Hymns of the Rgveda*, rev. ed. (Delhi: Motilal Banarsidass, 1973), for translations of Ṛg Vedic passages. Square brackets enclose our clarifi- cations.
3 Ṛg 8.87.2 in some editions.

They call him Indra, Mitra, Varuṇa, Agni, and he is heavenly nobly-winged Garutmān. To what is one, sages give many a title: they call it Agni, Yama, Mātariśvan.

(Ṛg 1.164.46)

Later Hindu mythological expressions of the undeniability of its ultimate referent – such as the famous theophany in the Bhagavad Gītā, chapter eleven – characteristically incorporate, at least implicitly, these interrelated Vedic notions of genesis and all-inclusiveness. Some, of course, do not, but to consider them here would be a digression that would add little to our treatment of Hinduism's mythological symbolism of undeniability. In most cases, one may recognize readily Hinduism's use of *images of power, expressing as irresistibility the undeniability of central spiritual reality of humankind.*

Some forms of Hinduism depict ultimate reality theistically, but the Vedas conclude that the supreme reality is not to be construed as a supreme deity. Like Aquinas, the Vedic sages apparently felt that the universe demands explanation. Unlike Aquinas, they came to the conclusion that any creator god or gods, though possibly instrumental in the development of the universe, must also be subject to the same unitary cause that explains the universe. "The gods," states one famous passage, "are later than this world's production" (Ṛg 10.129.6). The Vedic sages ultimately bypassed the literal terms of their own polytheism and reached the conclusion, still stated mythologically, that the ultimate focus of religion is beyond being conceived in terms of animation, sentience, or even existence.

1. Then was not non-existent nor existent; there was no realm of air, no sky beyond it. What covered in, and where? And what gave shelter? Was water there, unfathomed depth of water?
2. Death was not then, nor was there aught immortal: no sign was there, the day's and night's divider. That one thing, breathless, breathed by its own nature: apart from it was nothing whatsoever.

(Ṛg 10.129.1–2)

Eventually, the cosmogonic monism expressed incipiently here was to have considerable influence on the development of Hindu philosophy. More than a thousand years passed, however, before the philosophical implications and justifications of such a concept were systematically worked out. Chronologically, the next development in Hinduism's expression of the undeniability of its ultimate referent occurred in the Upanishads, which employed primarily *spiritual symbolism* to affirm this cosmogonic absolute and to illustrate its role as the focus of religious life.

Spiritual Symbolism of Undeniability

Vedic monism as an expression of "that than which nothing greater can be conceived" appears to evolve naturally through the dynamics of Vedic mythology, the predominant mode of expressing ultimate reality in the Vedas. The Upanishads contain much mythology as well, but it is not the dynamic mythology of the Vedas. Instead, mythology in the Upanishads is used as a didactic tool subservient to the introspective, spiritual insights of the Upanishadic sages. Thus, though one still encounters creation myths in the Upanishads, the focus of Upanishadic cosmogony shifts, following Upanishadic thought in general, from the external world to the internal world. The Vedas are concerned with capping a potentially infinite temporal regress and arriving at a first cause. Upanishadic cosmogony, on the other hand, is psychological and contemplative in orientation and concerned with the ultimate explanation of our *experience* of the universe. In the Vedas, the monistic origin of the universe lies hidden deep in the past, at the beginning of time. Generally, in the Upanishads, the monistic absolute lies hidden deep within the fabric of the present moment. It is the continuing source of both the material universe and the consciousness that perceives that universe. It is, moreover, eternally unitary, so that our usual perception of multiplicity in the universe is regarded as illusory.

In this framework, the origin of the universe is not an event that occurred in the past but rather a fundamental mistake, that mistake being the bifurcation of the eternally unitary absolute into subject and object. That mistake feeds upon itself and multiplies, resulting finally in the appearance of the manifold objective universe and the multiplicity of conscious subjects. The ultimate goal of religion is to rectify this fundamental mistake by discovering through meditation the nondual source of the universe within one's own mind, at the source of one's own being. The following passage uses psychological terms in a mythological format to express the ultimate identity of the individual, the universe, and the absolute. Regardless of its literal truth, it is clearly an expression of *the inevitability of living with reference to an ultimate spiritual reality;* for it claims that each person is essentially identical with the ultimate referent of Hinduism.

1. In the beginning this (world) was only the self [Ātman], in the shape of a person. Looking around he saw nothing else than the self. He first said, "I am." . . .
2. He was afraid. Therefore one who is alone is afraid. . . .
3. He, verily, had no delight. Therefore one who is alone has no delight. He desired a second. He became as large as a woman and a man in close embrace.

He caused that self to fall into two parts. From that arose husband and
wife. . . .

7. At that time [i.e., before the cosmogonic "I am"] this (universe) was undifferentiated. It became differentiated by name and form (so that it is said) he
has such a name, such a shape. Therefore even today this (universe) is differentiated by name and shape (so that it is said) he [or it] has such a name, such a
shape. He [the self] entered in here even to the tips of the nails, as a razor is
(hidden) in the razor case, or as fire in the fire-source. Him they see not for (as
seen) he is incomplete, when breathing he is called the vital force, when
speaking the voice, when seeing the eye, when hearing the ear, when thinking
the mind. . . . The self is to be meditated upon for in it [the self] all these
become one. This self is the foot-trace of all this, for by it one knows all this,
just as one can find again by foot-prints (what was lost).

10. Brahman, indeed, was this in the beginning. It knew itself only as "I am
Brahman." Therefore it became all. . . . It is the same in the case of seers,
same in the case of men. . . . This is so even now. Whoever knows thus, "I am
Brahman," becomes this all.

(B.U. 1.4.1–10)[4]

The cosmogonic "I am" in the preceding passage in effect sets up a
duality within the unitary absolute. It creates a subject, and thereby an
implicit object. This primordial subject's first emotions, fear and desire,
prefigure the basic emotions of all conscious beings that evolve from it in
the subsequent diversification of the universe. This diversification occurs
through the agency of name and form. In the quoted passage, form represents individual objects, and name represents the subjective concepts corresponding to these objects. According to Upanishadic monism, there
can be no subjective consciousness without an object of consciousness,
and no object without a subject that cognizes it. Thus, the search for
objects – motivated in the primordial subject, as in all subsequent beings,
by fear and desire – actually produces these objects, which then exist in
mutual interdependence with their cognizing subjects. This diversity is,
however, illusory, and the original unitary self remains still unitary, hidden omnipresently within diversity as both subject and object of all experience. Because of the continuing presence of the original cosmogonic self
in all beings, it is possible to conquer the fear and desire that bind one to
the mundane world of objects and to return, introspectively, to the unitary source of all being.

In Upanishadic terms, this psychological cosmogony is expressed as
the identity of Brahman, the ultimate source of the external universe, and
Atman, the innermost soul of each sentient being. When, through

4 We follow S. Radhakrishnan, *The Principal Upaniṣads* (New York: Allen and Unwin,
1953), for translations of Upanishadic passages. Square brackets enclose our clarifications.

wisdom and meditation, one discovers one's innermost self, one discovers also the ontological source of the universe. By discovering this innermost self, moreover, one merges into it and thereby becomes one with the whole universe. By discovering within oneself the identity of Ātman and Brahman, in a sense, one reverses the process of creation, regaining the primordial unity that existed in the beginning. The sage who has accomplished this feat can then meaningfully declare, "I am Brahman," in effect, "I am God."

This unity of the individual with the universe at their common source is not, of course, created by the wisdom and meditation of the sage. It is merely realized through this wisdom and meditation. According to the Upanishads the fact that all is one is eternally and all-inclusively operative. Failure to realize this unity, in which we necessarily participate at all times, is mere illusion, created by our fear of another, our desire for another, ultimately our ignorance. Thus, the sage Uddālaka Āruṇi could identify even his unenlightened son Śvetaketu with the unitary essence of the universe.

That which is the subtle essence this whole world has for its self. That is the true. That is the self. That art thou, Śvetaketu.

(C.U. 6.8.7., etc)

Uddālaka's statement is not based on philosophical acumen or upon extensive knowledge of sacred lore. His instruction to his son consists not of reasoned arguments or reference to the scriptural traditions of Hindu mythology and priestcraft. The authority behind his teaching derives directly from his own spiritual experience, from his personal actualization of the reality addressed in Hinduism's various expressions of Brahman. He attempts to jolt Śvetaketu from his complacency into a similar personal realization of *the inevitability of living with reference to Brahman.* His statement is thus an instance of *spiritual symbolism of the undeniability of the central spiritual reality of humankind.*

Such a personal realization remains to the present day central in Hinduism. Many Hindus seek and find a spiritual teacher (guru) who purportedly has reached such realization. The teachings of one's guru are typically regarded as equal or superior in authority to the approved written texts of Hinduism. Many Hindus, moreover, particularly in old age, seek such personal realization themselves. Some become hermits or wandering ascetics, seeking only enough sustenance to fuel their meditation. For Hindus, the lives of such people themselves become spiritual symbols of the undeniability of the ultimately real. For Hindu monism, then, the undeniability of its ultimate referent is doubly verified, first in scriptural revelation, and then again in the mystical experience of the successful practitioner.

Intellectual Symbolism of Undeniability

The continuing spiritual tradition of verification in personal experience of the ancient truths enshrined in mythology provides for the Hindu such a strong affirmation of the undeniable reality of Hinduism's ultimate referent that philosophical argumentation as such has little to add. As a result, Hinduism's *intellectual symbolism* of undeniability, unlike Western intellectual symbolism, is scarcely concerned with proving the existence of a religious ultimate to skeptics. Instead, most of the philosophical activity surrounding ultimate reality as conceived in Hinduism is debate between believers concerning the finer points of the nature of this reality.

For this reason apparent similarities between some of the foregoing Hindu material and the classical Western arguments for the existence of God may be misleading. Except in the Ṛg Veda, cyclical theories of cosmology dominate in Hinduism. Like modern scientific theories of a cyclical universe, Hindu cosmology envisions a beginningless and endless cycle of evolution and devolution from chaos to cosmos to chaos to cosmos over immense periods of time. Thus, post-Vedic Hinduism posits no first cause as such. The primacy of the absolute is wholly ontological, not temporal in any sense. The absolute is the fountainhead of being but, strictly speaking, not the cause of the universe. The universe as perceived is illusion (*māya*), the great mistake of the cosmogonic "I am." The only reality, subjective or objective, is the monistic absolute. The universe is ultimately only the illusory appearance of this absolute to illusory manifestations of itself in discrete consciousness. This double illusion, engendered by the bifurcation of the absolute into subject and object, has no effect whatsoever upon its real unity. Strictly speaking, then, though the absolute stands behind the universe as its ontological ground, this absolute is not the cause of anything, because in reality there is no universe, only the illusion of a universe. As the ontological ground of the universe, albeit an illusory universe, Brahman is conceived as *the reality upon which all other realities depend and from which they derive their ultimate meaning*. In monistic Hinduism, the ultimate meaning of realities other than Brahman is their illusoriness vis-à-vis this ultimate referent.

Because all things that "exist" are considered illusory, no proof of the "existence" of this absolute is sought. In fact, even in the ancient Vedic passage quoted earlier, the notion of the existence of ultimate reality is viewed with considerable suspicion, if not flatly denied. That Vedic passage stated that in the beginning there was neither existence nor nonexistence. In the Upanishads one finds the point of view that in the beginning there was nonexistence (T.U. 2.7.1), as well as the assertion that in the beginning there was existence (C.U. 6.2.1). From the standpoint of Hindu monism, each of these assertions can be viewed as equally true given the limitations of human language and conceptualization. This mistrust of language and conceptualization, a pervasive characteristic of Hinduism, amounts to rejection of the Aristotelian "laws of thought."[5]

From the point of view of classical Western logic, the Hindu position, expressed in apparently contradictory statements concerning the absolute, appears to be at least agnostic and at worst nihilistic or simply inane. It is, of course, none of these. Far from being agnostic, it claims certain knowledge of the truth, albeit an inexpressible truth. Far from nihilism, it anchors both the universe and the meaning and purpose of human life in this truth. Rather than being agnostic or nihilistic, Hinduism is epistemologically fastidious concerning statements about ultimate reality, any of which, no matter how carefully worded, it regards as potentially misleading. The following passage renders comprehensible the foregoing contradictory statements concerning the existence of Brahman, though of course it does not resolve the paradox to which they point.

There is the teaching, "Not this! Not that!" for there is nothing higher than this. It is called the "Real of the real."

(B.U. 2.3.6)

Here, "Not this! Not that!" translates the famous Upanishadic phrase "*neti neti.*" It means that no matter how one describes or conceives of Brahman, one is mistaken; it is not this or that. Many other Upanishadic passages make the same point.

3. There the eye goes not, speech goes not, nor the mind; we know not, we understand not how one can teach this.
4. Other, indeed, is it than the known, and also it is above the unknown. Thus have we heard from the ancients who have explained it to us.
5. That which is not expressed through speech but that by which speech is expressed; that, verily know thou, is Brahman, not what (people) here adore.
6. That which is not thought by the mind but by which, they say, the mind is thought (thinks); that, verily, know thou, is Brahman and not what (people) here adore.
7. That which is not seen by the eye, but by which the eyes are seen (see); that, verily, know thou, is Brahman and not what (people) here adore.

(Kena 1.3–7)

5 *The law of contradiction:* Nothing can be both P and not-P. *The law of excluded middle:* Anything must be either P or not-P. *The law of identity:* If anything is P, then it is P. To most Westerners, such bipolar thinking appears to be the cornerstone of common sense, let alone logical thought. Thus Westerners typically frame their philosophical inquiries along the following lines: "Either God exists or God does not exist. The universe either has a first cause or it does not." While there may be little likelihood of ever solving such problems, Westerners are characteristically certain that one of the alternatives in such propositions is true, regardless of our ability to determine which one.

In the foregoing passages and many more like them there is a clear basis for a Hindu version of the ontological argument, although no such versions ever emerged. Nor is it any lack of ingenuity among Hindus that prevented such an argument arising in the context of Hinduism. Instead, even though Hindus clearly regard Brahman as being "that than which nothing greater can be conceived," the epistemological fastidiousness of Hinduism prevented either conceptualization or verbalization of this unsurpassable reality. The Upanishad confidently states, "There is nothing higher than this," but in the Hindu framework, the *existence* of such a "real of the real" does not follow from its definition as the unsurpassable reality.

In the Western context, it is better to exist than not to exist, and therefore in that context, "that than which nothing greater can be conceived" must exist; for if it did not exist, a greater could be conceived. In the framework of Hindu monism, to exist is to be either a subject or an object of experience. In this context, it is always possible to conceive of something greater than anything that exists. Greater than anything that "exists" as a subject or an object of experience is that which includes both the subject and object of experience. But that which includes both subject and object of experience is inconceivable, for such a reality includes, absorbs, and thereby negates the conceiving subject.

Therefore, in the context of Hindu monism, "that than which nothing greater can be conceived" is, by definition, beyond existence or nonexistence. Moreover, it is beyond being conceived in any terms whatsoever, for to conceive of it makes it into an object and thereby excludes the conceptualizing subject. Anything conceivable becomes greater by inclusion or the conceiving subject, and therefore "that than which nothing greater can be conceived" is necessarily inconceivable. This situation renders the ontological argument unimpressive in the context of Hinduism, for nothing can be established thereby other than inconceivability.

The ontological argument itself is irrelevant in Hinduism simply because in that framework it is not better to exist than not to exist. If the argument itself loses relevance, however, the basic intuition behind the argument retains its power in Hindu intellectual symbolism of undeniability. This intellectual symbolism is primarily epistemological in nature. It is not concerned with establishing the existence of Brahman. Instead, it expresses undeniability by demonstrating the inadequacy of philosophical thought either to affirm or deny Brahman. In showing that Brahman is beyond expression or conceptualization, it shows that it is beyond denial or refutation. In showing that Brahman cannot be said ultimately to exist, it also shows that it cannot be said not to exist. The undeniability of Brahman is a corollary of its inexpressibility. Paradoxically, intellectual symbolism in Hinduism affirms the undeniability of the central spiritual reality of humankind by demonstrating that philosophical thought is inadequate to that very task.

The foregoing treatment of Hindu intellectual symbolism of the undeniability of a spiritual absolute does not exhaustively represent the great diversity of Hinduism's concepts of its ultimate referent. A brief consideration of Hindu theism, which refers to the religious ultimate as "Īśvara" (the Lord), will serve to balance this account somewhat. The Nyāya-Vaiśeshika school, and some forms of Śaivism, with recourse to arguments resembling the first cause and teleological arguments of Aquinas, hold that the existence of Īśvara is logically demonstrable. Moreover, for these schools, as well as for several others, the concept of existence as a quality or attribute of Īśvara is not as inappropriate as in monistic Hinduism. On the whole, though, Hinduism has remained suspicious of and disinterested in theological proofs. The very notion of the existence of ultimate reality is suspect in Hinduism, which tends instead to declare that the ultimately real is inconceivable and unapproachable by the human intellect unaided by revelation and mystical experience.

One school, the Mīmāṃsā, went so far in this regard as to become formally atheistic. Theirs is not, however, an antireligious atheism. It stems instead from single-minded determination to defend the self-contained authority of revealed scripture. The Mīmāṃsā school is so intensely scripture-based that they deny the existence of God on the basis that divine authorship of the scriptures would entail admission of an authority above that of the scriptures themselves. This would render them at least theoretically fallible and, more immediately important, open the way to appeals for religious authority independent of scriptural sanction. In the course of its crusade for unimpeachable scriptural authority, the Mīmāṃsā school has vigorously attacked those rational proofs of the existence of God advanced within the context of Hinduism.

Likewise, Rāmānuja – the founder of the Qualified Nondualist school, after Śankara the most influential Hindu theologian – attacked all of the theistic proofs of this time, asserting that the existence and nature of God could be known only through recourse to scriptural testimony. The third great Hindu theologian was Madhva, founder of the Dualist school. Unlike Rāmānuja, he did not regard theistic proofs as a positive evil, but held that they are convincing only if revelation is previously accepted. Such views have created within Hinduism a general tendency to rely on scripture and to mistrust rational argumentation concerning ultimate reality, whether theistically or nontheistically conceived. This is in some ways similar to the attitude that prevails in Islam. There, as we shall see, the valid role of human reason is strictly limited to inference based directly on revelation.

Such restrictions upon the role of reason in Hinduism deemphasize intellectual symbolism of undeniability. In Hinduism the preeminence of scriptural authority tends to channel intellectual vigor into debates over which interpretation of scripture is truest to the texts. In themselves, these debates do not concern us here, but their preponderance serves to illustrate Hinduism's emphasis on mythological and spiritual expressions of undeniability. These latter two forms of symbolism dominate Hinduism's scriptural expression of undeniability, and Hindu philosophers by and large have been content to comment upon them.

Moral Symbolism of Undeniability

Like the intellect, morality is regarded in Hinduism as insufficient for realization of the ultimate referent of the religion. Unlike the intellect, morality is deemed necessary for such realization. With regard to the undeniability of the ultimately real, moreover, Hinduism maintains that intellectual symbolism can provide only a weak affirmation. By comparison, *moral symbolism*, based on the theory of karma and rebirth, is thought to provide a strong affirmation of the undeniability of the ultimate referent of religion as variously conceived in Hinduism. Most readers will have heard of the theory of karma and rebirth, but it is so widely misunderstood as to require brief restatement here.

The term "karma" means simply action. Bad or good karma is simply bad or good action, nothing more. Karma is not something that hovers around one like a blessing or curse, although Westerners often speak of it in this way. One does not, then, *have* karma. One simply performs karma, in exactly the same sense that one performs an action. In the sphere of morality, karma implies a *volitional* action, because only volitional actions are thought to have moral consequences. Thus, a driver who unintentionally runs down a pedestrian is legally liable but not karmically liable. If intoxicated or driving recklessly, this driver would be karmically responsible for drunken or reckless driving, but this bad karma would be regarded as only marginally worse, if at all, for having resulted in the accidental death of a pedestrian. This situation, it should be stressed, indicates the karmic gravity of drunken or reckless driving rather than the irrelevance of causing death thereby.

According to the theory, one's good or bad karma bears fruit in this life or in the next or even many lives hence. Popular versions of the theory depict the law of karma as almost a moral equivalent of Newton's law of the equal and opposite reaction, except that, of course, the result of karma is similar, not opposite, to the action itself. Folk versions of the theory sometimes picture the fruition of karma as a fulfillment of poetic justice. If you murder an enemy in this life, he will murder you in a similar fashion in some future lifetime. This interpretation makes for good story-telling and is usually encountered in such a context. The more seriously held popular interpretation asserts merely that in future lifetimes one will suffer from undetermined sources in ways similar to the sufferings one has caused in this lifetime.

More sophisticated, generally scriptural versions of the theory indicate that it is not so much individual actions that are rewarded or punished but rather one's general mental quality that is more influential in determining one's future weal or woe. In other words, it is not so much the act of murder itself that causes the murderer's future suffering. Instead, the killer's violent, hate-filled mind actualizes its own retribution. If one behaves like an animal, one becomes an animal, not as a punishment, but because rebirth as an animal is the natural outcome of animalistic behavior.

In each of these understandings of the theory of karma, the results of good or bad volitional actions come about naturally and relentlessly. There is no divine judge who decides what is right and wrong and what the reward or punishment will be. There is no court of appeal for leniency. Instead, the universe itself automatically actualizes the moral results of volitional actions. Thus, the theory of karma and rebirth, more directly than any of the other moral theories encountered in this book, *seeks to disclose the inevitability of living with reference to a central spiritual reality by exposing self-contradictory behavior.* One normally behaves immorally in hopes of increasing one's own well-being. The theory of karma, however, indicates that such behavior is not only futile but also counterproductive. To resort to an image popularized by Lyndon Johnson, immoral behavior for selfish ends is "like pissing against the wind." It is so obviously foolish that no one in his right mind, whether religious or not, would attempt it.

Just as most of the undesirable results of urinating against the wind are immediately apparent, the more sophisticated versions of the theory of karma and rebirth assert that the results of immoral behavior become apparent in this lifetime. Many of these bad results are, in fact, held to be apparent immediately upon performance or even contemplation of the action in question, if one were but observant enough to notice them. For example, if one steals, one usually experiences immediately the unpleasant emotions of fear and guilt. The habitual thief, who may eventually conquer these immediate emotions, becomes habitually stealthy. He trusts no one and lives knowing that he can be trusted by no one. He is alone in a society of potential enemies who would be eager to harm him, at least in his perception, if they but knew the real nature of his mind and activities. He can share his mind and life with only a very few people, and these will usually be other thieves, as untrustworthy as himself. More important, though, the thief is trapped and oppressed by his own mind.

This oppression may show in observable personality traits such as servile, ingratiating behavior intended to win the confidence and allay the suspicions of potential victims.

Whether observable or not, however, the oppression of mind attendant upon habitual or even occasional immoral actions and intentions is held to be a brute fact, as real as a cancer. Long-time sufferers of cancer may forget what it is like to feel entirely well. They may yet experience days during which they "feel good." Similarly, the thief may have forgotten the joy of an innocent mind. He may cease to notice his own suffering. This, however, does not make that suffering any less real. The theory of karma asserts this with illustrations drawn from the animal kingdom.

Few people would like to be dogs, even though dogs are not necessarily oppressed by any obviously excessive sufferings, and appear to be quite content as dogs. We recognize instinctively, though, that it would be undesirable to be trapped within a mind as limited as that of a dog. This instinctive recognition provides an avenue of illustration for the theory of karma. The thief is like a dog, fearful and ingratiating, or perhaps blustering, seeking only an opportunity to abscond with its sustenance. Traditional illustrations of karma and rebirth, then, suggest that the thief may be reborn as a dog. Actually, though, the thief is already like a dog; he merely has a human body. Rebirth in a dog's body, if it actually occurs, is only the denouement to a plot already complete in its essentials. Thus it is said in the Bṛhadāraṇyaka Upanishad:

According as one acts, according as one behaves, so does one become. The doer of good becomes good, the doer of evil becomes evil. One becomes virtuous by virtuous action, bad by bad action. Others, however, say that a person consists of desires. As is his desire so is his will; as is his will, so is the deed he does, whatever deed he does, that he attains.

(B.U. 4.4.5)

That it is better to be human than canine is, of course, a human judgment. In an utterly material and thereby ultimately valueless universe, such a judgment would carry no real weight. And perhaps it does not. Nonetheless such judgments are for all intents and purposes universal among human beings. This situation, in the light of the theory of *karma* and rebirth, provides an admirable illustration of *the inevitability of living with reference to a central spiritual reality* whether it exists or not. It is here too that the Western mind, which is often incapable of sympathetic resonance with the notion of karma and rebirth, can at least appreciate the genius of the theory as an expression of the undeniability of a central spiritual reality in human life. According to the theory, by thievery one becomes like a dog. Being doglike is tantamount to being a dog, whether this occurs literally via rebirth or figuratively in this very life. Being a dog, or being like a dog, is undesirable, and therefore thievery is undesirable.

But is this human notion that it is better to be human than a dog merely an instance of gratuitous species chauvinism? We suggest that it is not, but rather the result of a preconscious inference based on the perfectibility of good and the nonperfectibility of evil which we noted in Chapter One. Our argument there is graphically illustrated by the theory of karma and rebirth, which with slight variations is common to Hinduism and Buddhism. According to the general theory one who attempts to perfect evil, thievery for example, merely becomes animallike – in this illustration, like a dog. Thievery in dogs, however, is not regarded as evil. It is appropriate behavior for a dog. Similarly, a thief's behavior is not despicable as much as it is pitiable, for it indicates a doglike mind. Like thievery, all evil behavior degrades one's mind to the pitiable status of an animal, wherein one is not evil as much as merely in need of domestication.

An animal cannot contemplate its own behavior and choose to behave in one way or another. So it is also with confirmed evildoers. According to the theory of karma and rebirth, they first become like animals by failing to evaluate the consequences of their own behavior. When reborn they actually become animals, without even the capacity to consider behavior and its results. Once one has reached the state of animal consciousness, according to the theory, rebirth becomes an entirely random, hit or miss process. The likelihood of regaining a human-level mind, with which one can assume control of one's own destiny, is then highly remote. As a vivid Buddhist simile has it, it is about as likely as a blind sea turtle, which surfaces only once every century, putting its head through a wooden ring floating on the ocean (M 3:169).

One who devotes oneself to good, on the other hand, can look forward to open-ended progress toward more and more autonomy in mapping out one's karmic path. One who chooses not to steal may learn not to covet and eventually not even to desire. One who chooses not to kill may learn not to hate and eventually to love. One who chooses not to lie may seek the truth and may eventually find it. To be sure, one who chooses good in these ways may be deluded, but at least there is the rational possibility of perfecting such behavior and volition, whereas the alternative of evil leads inevitably to dissipation. The theory of karma and rebirth, then, depicts the moral alternative as a path converging upon a pinnacle, becoming simpler, wider, and straighter at every turn. The immoral alternative, on the other hand, is a descending path, branching at every turn into an entangled labyrinth of random wandering, illustrated as the impotent foraging of animals.

Desirability

This discussion of karma and rebirth in Hinduism leads directly into consideration of the Hindu expression of the desirability of the central spiritual reality of humankind. The truth or falsity of the theory of karma and rebirth, of course, is not an issue here. We have been concerned instead with its role as *moral symbolism* expressing the undeniability of the ultimately real. The following discussion of desirability must also look beyond the literal terms of the theory itself to its integral function in Hinduism's overall expression of its ultimate referent. Viewed in this way, the theory of karma and rebirth renders reasonable the human aspiration for the ultimate perfection of good. In the course of a single lifetime, the perfection of desirable human qualities may seem unrealistic, but according to the theory of karma and rebirth one has innumerable lifetimes within which to accomplish this task. In its evocative vision of the human being realizing identity with Brahman, the *intellectual symbolism* of Upanishadic-style monism provides a means of conceptualizing this ultimate perfection. In this way, Hinduism's intellectual and moral symbolism of ultimate desirability are mutually supportive.

Intellectual and Moral Symbolism of Desirability

The Upanishads, as we have shown, propose that the absolute encompasses both being and consciousness. The inclusion of consciousness in this definition opens the way for a reasonable human aspiration to full participation in ultimate reality. It renders reasonable the possibility of a thorough sounding of the depths of one's own consciousness resulting in realization of its unity with the totality of being. It suggests, moreover, that anything short of this realization is necessarily less than fulfillment. In this way, intellectual symbolism seeks to establish that the truth is to be found within one's own mind, as well as to conceptualize a successful conclusion of the introspective search for truth. In so doing it inspires the search, by *identifying the ultimately desirable*. It does not, however, indicate the direction in which the search is to proceed other than to indicate generally that it is interior. At this point, Hinduism's moral symbolism becomes vital to full expression of ultimate desirability by contemplating what is good, what is desirable within the existential human mind, for it is within this very mind that the absolute lies concealed. At the same time, moral symbolism takes its cues from intellectual symbolism, *defining desirable human conduct with reference to ultimate desirability*.

Thus, the intellectual concept of the ultimate identity of self and other informs and guides Hinduism's moral expression of its ultimate referent. Given this identity, it is clear that one should not harm others, for in so doing one is in reality harming oneself. Given the convergence of all minds upon the absolute, one should not deceive others, for in so doing, one is only deceiving oneself. These two principles, it will be noted, are a sufficient basis upon which to construct the entire edifice of Hindu morality. These principles of morality are based upon the concept of the ultimate unity of all consciousness. Beyond this, however, Hindu monistic intellectual symbolism asserts the ultimate identity of consciousness and its objects, and this assertion also has moral implications. In the fullness of truth, if it were but realized, the whole of reality is to be found within one's own mind. One lacks nothing, and therefore nothing need be gained by violence or deceit. What one owns legally, one continues to have in reality, whether one keeps it or gives it away. In giving it away, in reality one only gives it to oneself, and in so doing loses nothing. By giving, moreover, one's limited, illusory, existential self grows in the image of the boundless, real, absolute self. Through generosity, one in effect pretends already to have realized the identity of self and other and the all-inclusiveness of one's essential self. Kant suggests the same sort of pretending when he formulates his categorical imperative to "act *as if* the maxim of thy action were to become by thy will a universal law of nature."[6]

In this way, through a confluence of moral and intellectual symbolism of the desirability of its ultimate referent, Hinduism *seeks to transform self-interested morality into spontaneous regard for the welfare of others. It makes true morality possible by integrating morality into its larger, overall expression of the meaning and purpose of human life.* Hinduism holds that the behavior one desires in others is desirable behavior for oneself, and that such behavior discloses the nature and desirability of ultimate reality. So self-evident and so universal are the basic moral injunctions that Hindus say they may be heard in the percussive voice of thunder.

This very thing the heavenly voice of thunder repeats *da, da, da,* that is, control yourselves, give, be compassionate. [Each imperative verb begins with the syllable *da* in Sanskrit.] One should practice this same triad, self-control, giving and compassion.

(B.U. 5.2.3)

Spiritual Symbolism of Desirability

This unrelenting disclosure of moral necessity by the universe itself, through the workings of karma and its results, relates only to the initial stages on the path to personal perfection. Moral symbolism shades into

6 Immanuel Kant, *Fundamental Principles of the Metaphysics of Ethics*, trans. T. K. Abbott (New York: Longmans, Green and Co., 1925), p. 46.

spiritual symbolism, wherein negative and positive moral injunctions become spiritual realizations. The moral control that prevents violence becomes spiritual restraint of senses and the mind. This permits effective meditation and allows the ever-present divinity within oneself to break through one's habitual sensual clamor. The giving and compassion that are initially a pretense of divinity grow into actual divinity as the spiritual qualities of nonattachment and love. The desirable karmic effects of moral behavior translate into spiritual bliss (*ānanda*). The guiding philosophical proposition of the unity of consciousness and its objects becomes a reality, expressed by Śaṅkara in his threefold definition of the absolute as *sat-cit-ānanda,* being-consciousness-bliss. In essence Hindu morality is based on a *free decision to attempt to realize Hinduism's ultimate referent* as spiritual bliss.

The term "bliss" *emphasizes the personal benefits of response to the ultimate referent* as variously conceived in Hinduism. It is central to spiritual symbolism of desirability in every major school of Hindu theology. In no case is bliss conceived as being merely a pleasurable experience. Instead, it symbolizes realization of the ultimate referent of religion as variously conceived in the various schools of Hinduism. In the Advaita tradition that has dominated this discussion thus far, bliss expresses the realization of the unity of being and consciousness, of object and subject. Some readers may feel that the highly abstract, rather colorless goal of this system of theology, as intellectually expressed, is not desirable at all, even if it is true. The Upanishads themselves recognize the apparent blandness of the absolute they describe and do not shrink from it. In fact, they press the point, frequently suggesting that deep, dreamless sleep is the one universally accessible experience most similar to realization of the absolute. Nor is the Indian mind inherently inclined toward a moribund state, as some have suggested. On the contrary, the Upanishads record ancient Indians reacting adversely to the notion that realization of the supreme self entails negation of the individual self. The following passage relates such an exchange between student and master.

"Venerable Sir, in truth this one [who has realized the supreme self] does not know himself that I am he, nor indeed the things here. He has become one who has gone to annihilation. I see no good in this. . . ."

"O Maghavan, mortal, verily, is this body. It is held by death. But it is the support of that deathless, bodiless self. Verily, the incarnate self is held by pleasure and pain. Verily, there is no freedom from pleasure and pain for one who is incarnate. Verily, pleasure and pain do not touch one who is bodiless. . . . Even so that serene one when he rises up from his body and reaches the highest light appears in his own form. Such a person is the Supreme Person. There such a one moves about, laughing, playing, rejoicing with women, chariots or relations, not remembering the appendage of this body. . . . Verily, these gods who are in the Brahma-world meditate on that self. Therefore all worlds and all desires are held by them. He obtains all worlds and all desires who finds the self and understands it."

(C.U. 8.11.2–8.12.6)

This passage shows the same kind of complementarity between the intellectual and spiritual expressions of desirability that has been noted between intellectual and moral symbolism. Without the intellectual expression defining bliss in terms of the unity of consciousness and its objects, the spiritual symbolism of desirability in the previous passage would be at best mumbo jumbo and at worst mere hedonistic fantasy. In the context of the intellectual symbolism that prompts the initial reticence in the pupil, however, reference to serene ascent to the highest light, far from being mere mumbo jumbo, lifts the mind from its conceptual quandary into a new concept of desirability beyond what is accessible to the unaided intellect. In the context of the intellectual expression of desirability as aloofness from pleasure and pain, the symbolism of carefree Elysian revelry transmutes infantile fantasy into a spiritual appeal to an area of the human psyche inaccessible to reason alone. If, as the passage suggests, the lot of the gods depicted in mythology is ideal, it is because they have access to the bliss that ultimately characterizes the absolute. This situation, explicitly stated in Hinduism, provides a clear illustration of the role of hedonistic depictions of paradise in other religions as well.

In the Hindu context, the highest light, Elysian revelry and the enviable gods all express symbolically the desirability of the ultimate referent of Hinduism. All of these expressions rely for their proper interpretation on the intellectual understanding of bliss as the unity of being and consciousness. The intellectual expression, in turn, relies on the spiritual expression to convey desirability to the flesh-and-blood human being.

Intellectual and spiritual expressions of Hinduism's ultimate referent become indistinguishable when bliss is depicted as the cosmogonic absolute.

Non-existent, verily, was this (world) in the beginning. Therefrom, verily, was existence produced. That made itself a soul. Therefore is it called the well-made. Verily, what that well-made, is – that, verily is the essence of existence. For, truly, on getting the essence, one becomes blissful. For who, indeed, could live, breathe, if there were not this bliss in space? This, verily, is it that bestows bliss.

(T.U. 2.7.1)

He knew that Brahman is bliss. For truly, beings here are born from bliss, when born, they live by bliss and into bliss, when departing, they enter.

(T.U. 3.6.1)

Here, Brahman is depicted as both the source and the fulfillment of the inherent and insatiable human quest for the desirable. "Who, indeed, could live, who breathe, if there were not this bliss?" This Upanishadic question expressed in world theological terms might read: "How can one conceive of authentic human existence without reference to the hope for an ultimate fulfillment of desires?" In the universal forum of critical discourse, the real issue is not whether such fulfillment actually exists, but whether one can abandon hope for it without becoming alienated from a fundamental aspect of humanness. Who could live, as a human, who breathe, as a human, without reference to an ultimately desirable?

We have been concentrating thus far upon monistic Hinduism. The spiritual symbolisms of desirability in the various other schools of Hinduism may be delineated conveniently with reference to the monistic concept. All of them make frequent reference to the spiritual symbolism of bliss. In each of them the term "bliss" denotes a concept utterly beyond the pleasurable experiences normally indicated by the term. In a word, in each case the term bliss denotes the ultimate realization of human potential. Naturally this realization is variously conceptualized according to the nature of the intellectual symbolism employed in the different schools.

The Qualified Nondualism (Viśishṭa-advaita) of Rāmānuja, as the name implies, attempts to soften the austere absolutism of Advaita monism in order to accommodate the devotional literature and practices of Hinduism. Rāmānuja thus recognizes as distinct (viśishṭa) three ultimates: matter, individual souls, and the Lord (Īśvara). In order to accommodate the monistic scriptural tradition in Hinduism, however, Rāmānuja also holds that matter and individual souls are utterly dependent upon Īśvara. He illustrates how this is so with reference to the analogy of a person composed of body and soul. Īśvara is the whole person, while matter and individual souls correspond to the body only. Thus for Rāmānuja, the Upanishads are correct in saying that the individual soul is God, but Śaṅkara is wrong in thinking this means that the individual soul is ultimately universal. Instead, according to Rāmānuja, insofar as the individual soul is, it is God, but only part of God. Thus, for Rāmānuja, God may still be characterized as being-consciousness-bliss. Moreover, the meditational practices and pursuit of wisdom enjoined in the Upanishads as a means of realizing unity with this being-consciousness-bliss are still recommended. The unity envisioned, however, is the harmonious unity of the part with the whole.

These intellectual differences between Śaṅkara and Rāmānuja make little difference in their spiritual conceptualizations of the ultimately desirable human state. For Rāmānuja, as for Śaṅkara, the state of release is a state of omniscience, the only difference being that for Rāmānuja, one of the things one omnisciently knows is one's eternal deficiency vis-à-vis God. This deficiency in no way diminishes one's bliss, which is held to be identical with that of the Lord.

This deficiency does have the important effect of altering Śaṅkara's hierarchy of the three types of spiritual practice recognized in Hinduism. These are the three yogas or spiritual disciplines outlined in the *Bhagavad Gītā:* wisdom (*jñāna*), action (*karma*), and devotion (*bhakti*). For Śaṅkara, the yoga of action – implying specifically ritual action and caste duties – and the yoga of devotion to a personal deity serve only as beneficial preliminary practices. Ultimately they must be abandoned for the supreme yoga of wisdom through introspective contemplation, whereby final liberation may be realized. For Rāmānuja, on the other hand, observation of ritual and caste duties are never to be abandoned, for these are not merely expedients. They are existential recognitions of one's actual subservience to the Lord. Meditational yoga is a useful preliminary practice for realizing the nature of the self as distinct from matter, but ultimately, according to Rāmānuja, one knows oneself only by knowing the Lord, and this can be accomplished only through the yoga of loving devotion to the Lord. In effect, the Advaita propounds salvation for the elite and tolerates the religious practices of the masses, whereas Rāmānuja's school opens salvation to the masses and tolerates the elite.

The third great Hindu theologian, Madhva, takes a step further Rāmānuja's emphasis on popular forms of religion. He affirms a total separation – unblurred by any hint of convergence – distinguishing God, individual souls, and matter. In effect, Madhva repudiates the meditational practices of the elite in order further to glorify the devotional religion of the masses. Although Madhva's own work is highly recondite and hardly accessible to the common person, in many ways he might be described as the champion of Hindu common sense. Basically he holds that through the agency of the senses, valid knowledge about the material world as it really is arises in individual souls. And what is just as much a matter of common sense in the Hindu context, Madhva affirms the literal, separate existence of the many deities, all presided over by the supreme Lord, Vishnu. The implications of his system are clear: Each individual soul should worship and contemplate Vishnu as traditionally depicted in Hindu mythology, for this is the only sufficient path to final salvation.

This salvation, as variously described in evocative language by several important Dvaita (dualist) theologians, is often difficult to distinguish from that described in the other forms of Vedānta. Many Dvaitins, in fact, admit that the Advaitin's subjective feeling of unity with the cosmos is a valid form of religious experience, though not the ultimate form. The Dvaitins typically insist that the bliss of ultimate salvation is experienced only by the individual soul, as an individual soul, through the normal sensory channels, primarily the mind, which is widely recognized as a sixth sense in Indian psychology. This is another example of Madhva's commonsense approach to ultimate reality: Everyone wants to experience bliss; few want to be bliss. The bliss of salvation, moreover, is commonly conceptualized by Dvaita thinkers as a quantitative – not a qualitative – improvement in the devotee's present relationship with God. The bliss of liberation is, in other words, ultimate *bhakti*. *Bhakti*, loving devotion to God, is both the means and the end of religious practice. True *bhakti* aims at no goal beyond itself, for the salvation at which it aims is itself *bhakti*. This ultimate, unobstructed devotion is the greatest bliss, equal, according to some, to God's own bliss.

This notion, that in embarking upon the path of loving devotion to God one begins already to experience the bliss of salvation, no doubt played a large part in the development of the intensely emotional, often ecstatic forms of *bhakti* that appear first in history with Caitanya in the latter part of the fifteenth century. The present day "Hare-Kṛṣṇas" are a somewhat Westernized example of this ecstatic approach to *bhakti*. In order to intensify the immediate joy of loving devotion, Caitanya and his followers encouraged devotees to experience their devotion to God in ways analogous to the joy of human relationships of loving devotion. Sexual love is the preferred model, but the devotion of servant to master, child to parent, and even parent to child are also cited as exemplary of the human-to-God relationship. The concretization of the central spiritual reality that such approaches involve may be repugnant to the intellectually inclined, whether Eastern or Western. However, these approaches have the obvious social virtue of reaching out to the masses with a realistically acceptable invitation to expand their realizations of an essential dimension of human life.

In presenting itself to the West, Hinduism has relied primarily upon Śaṅkara's monism, with its emphasis on intellectual expression of the ultimate referent of Hinduism. The theistic views of Rāmānuja and Madhva, however, probably reflect lived Hinduism more than Śaṅkara's system, despite its universal appeal to both the intellect and the spirit. If this is so, it is because Rāmānuja and Madhva concentrate on expressing *the personal benefits made possible by response to the ultimate referent of Hinduism*. By concentrating on spiritual symbolism of desirability, these systems make this ultimate referent readily accessible to the masses. In these systems, symbolism of desirability takes precedence over symbolism of undeniability, and intellectual expression of ultimate reality is deemphasized generally. This may render devotional Hinduism less universal in appeal than meditative Hinduism. For the practitioners of devotionalism, though, the undeniability of this religion's ultimate referent becomes a matter established by immediately accessible experience. Few would doubt intellectually the reality of that to which they have developed loving devotion.

Mythological Symbolism of Desirability

In depicting the ultimately desirable in a popularly accessible way, devotional Hinduism also emphasizes *mythological symbolism* of desirability, often incorporating a literal interpretation of Hindu mythology. Contrary to the Advaita, the Dvaita asserts that ultimate reality in its essential nature has qualities (is *saguṇa*) rather than being qualityless (*nirguṇa*). Most Dvaitins concede that the Advaitin's absorption in *nirguṇa* Brahman is a valid experience of God, but they insist that the experience of God with all his qualities represents the only complete experience of God, the only final liberation. The more extreme forms of devotionalism extend this theological assertion to an affirmation of the literal accuracy of the descriptive and narrative details of Hindu mythology: that Kṛṣṇa really is blue and really plays a flute, that he really was Arjuna's charioteer, and so on. Such literalistic interpretations of mythology may appear untenable to the critically minded, but their value as techniques of expressing the desirability of ultimate reality in a popularly accessible way is obvious.

The more philosophically minded schools of Hindu theology incorporate *nonliteral mythological symbolism* in their expressions of desirability. These nonliteral treatments of mythology express a widespread intuition, common also in devotional forms of Hinduism, that ultimate reality itself is inaccessible to human means of expression or conceptualization. Hinduism's nonliteral use of mythological symbolism expressing the desirability of its ultimate referent unfolds in two interdependent but distinct streams of the tradition: the sacrificial and the devotional. The sacrificial stream, deriving from the Vedas and prominent in the Upanishads, has the most ancient historical credentials.

The Vedas are a collection of liturgical hymns bearing some resemblance to the Psalms of the Old Testament. They lavish praises upon a number of deities, some of whom represent forces of nature and others of whom appear to have originated in forgotten lore. By roughly the time of Jesus, these deities, as portrayed in the Vedas, had lost much of their importance in Hinduism. They were replaced by new deities, some of whom bore Vedic names, but who were expressions of the emerging devotional tradition that has maintained preeminence until the present. The ancient Vedic deities themselves, then, need not concern us here, except to mention in passing that the extravagant praises heaped upon them are an obvious example of literal mythological symbolism of desirability.

A superficial scanning of the Vedic hymns reveals other obvious examples of literal mythological symbolism of desirability. Many of the hymns beseech the gods for mundane favors such as victory over foes, material prosperity, many offspring, and a long life. Others are intended to secure for the performer an afterlife in heaven, pictured as a bounteous paradise where one will enjoy every conceivable convenience and pleasure in the company of the ancestors.

These literal mythological expressions of the desirability of the Hinduism's ultimate referent overlay the more essential concern of the Vedic sacrificial ritual, maintenance of the cosmic order (*ṛta*). This concern remains relevant to an understanding of Hinduism, even though the more obvious concerns of the Vedas have been superseded in Hinduism. Concern with maintenance of the cosmic order is the key to sacrificial Hinduism's nonliteral mythological expression of the desirability of its ultimate referent.

According to Vedic ideas, sacrifice functions to maintain the cosmic order on two levels: the divine and the mundane. By means of power gained through sacrifice, the gods are said to have vanquished the forces of chaos, antideities called asuras. The gods also maintain through sacrifice their cosmic rule, holding chaos at bay. The regular performance and orderly progress of the sacrifice thus symbolize the regularity and order of the cosmos itself.

Human performance of sacrifice on the one hand mirrors divine activity and represents participation in the cosmic order. It is the most perfect human activity because it is most similar to divine activity. This participation, on the other hand, is not merely passive imitation, for the gods are thought to be sustained and empowered by human rituals. They cannot keep up the struggle against the forces of chaos on their own. In the symbolic terms of the Vedas, the gods are fed and invigorated by means of the rituals enjoined upon humans by the Vedas. Human participation in the cosmic order by means of sacrifice is essential to the maintenance of universal order in the face of ever-threatening chaos.

In Vedic thought, sacrificial ritual mediates between heavenly and earthly order in the overall scheme of cosmic order. For Vedic thinkers, the sacrifice served simultaneously to reveal heavenly order on earth and to support the forces of heavenly order in their struggle to maintain overall cosmic order. Modern critics might argue that the sacrifice served rather to project a perceived earthly order upon an imaginary nonmaterial realm. For our present purposes, it matters little which, if either, is correct.

We have suggested that the desirability aspect of the central spiritual reality of humankind reflects, if nothing else, the human necessity to find meaning and purpose in life. We have noted that grounds for an affirmation of meaning and purpose are not immediately forthcoming upon observation of the material universe we live in. Expression and justification of this directedness in human life must then be achieved through a creative leap of imagination that moves coherently and evocatively beyond the confines of the observable, material world. The Vedic concept of sacrifice is an example of just such a creative leap of imagination.

For its practitioners, Vedic sacrifice succeeded in anchoring the inescapable human urge for directedness in a coherent and evocative symbolic construct. This construct effected a smooth transition between the regularity and order of day-to-day life, into the regularity and order of the sacrifice, and finally into a validation, necessarily in a nonmaterial realm, of this very order and regularity. In so doing, it expressed and justified an otherwise inexpressible and unjustifiable, though innate aspect of humanness: the urge to establish a direction in human life that culminates in the ultimately desirable. In the case of the Vedas, maintenance of cosmic order is the ultimately desirable, for if this order fails, earth, heaven, and the gods fail with it.

The success of the Vedic theory of sacrifice in expressing the fundamental human urge for directedness probably accounts in large measure for the continued performance of many of the Vedic rituals among present day Hindus. Even though the Vedic deities themselves have largely disappeared from Hinduism, the performance of Vedic ritual continues to be a conspicuous part of Hinduism as a whole. This somewhat surprising situation is explained by the attitude of Vedic ritual taken in the Upanishads. As we have seen, the Upanishads construe Vedic sacrifice as a symbolic expression of spiritual concerns. In so doing, they indicate a willingness to retain the letter, if not the spirit, of Vedic mythology. Similarly, though abandoning the spirit of Vedic ritualism, Hinduism as a whole has retained the performance of Vedic sacrifice as a mythological expression of the desirability of its ultimate referent.

It is difficult to overstate the pervasiveness of ritual, much of it Vedic in origin, in Hindu society. The sound of it is everywhere, the smell of it, the impressive sight of it. Members of the Brahmin or priestly caste empowered to perform it still enjoy a status and mystique that derives from their role as embodiments of a tradition seemingly older than time itself. The Hindu is born into this omnipresent ritual and grows up in the midst of it. It becomes an expression of tradition, of identity, of life itself, and as such, a tangible representation of all that is desirable. Immediately it represents hope, hope for a better lot in life, a better lot in the afterlife. More subtly, it is security, a comforting clamor that subliminally soothes and reassures. Ultimately it represents cosmic order, and thereby becomes a ubiquitous reminder of the necessity of orienting human life beyond the immediate concerns of material sufficiency. Much of the genius of the Upanishads and those who have expounded them lies in the successful exploitation of this culturally given mythological expression of the desirability of the Hindu concept of ultimate reality.

The Mīmāṁsā or "exegetic" school of Hinduism retains the original concerns of Vedic ritualism more faithfully than those schools that derive from the Upanishads. Mīmāṁsā's mythological expression of the desirability of Hinduism's ultimate referent appears to have developed out of purely Vedic concerns, albeit in a surprising way, without Upanishadic influence. Among the forebears of Mīmāṁsā, the key role of sacrifice itself in maintaining the cosmic order resulted early on in a tendency to devalue the deities addressed in the rituals. When rituals were correctly performed, their results were thought to be automatic, as the cooperation of the deities was assured. This led to a tendency in the Brāhmaṇas, a priestly corpus of literature representing the roots of Mīmāṁsā, to place more importance on the rituals, the priests who performed them, and the texts that enshrined them, than upon the gods they addressed. Finally, when the Mīmāṁsā evolved as a separate school, it actually denied the existence of the deities addressed in the Vedas, and in fact became explicitly atheistic.

The reason for this surprising development was that acknowledgment of any God of gods who authored or stood above the scriptures would weaken the authority of the scriptures themselves. Such acknowledgment would render possible an appeal beyond scripture to a higher authority. For the Mīmāṁsā, Vedic statements are imperatives, not propositions. They command the performance of sacrifice. The Vedic sacrifice does not point beyond itself to a higher reality. Instead it is itself the ultimate reality, which humans realize by actualizing it in ritual performance. The mind-set underlying the Mīmāṁsā position may be likened to that of a nation at war. In such a situation, one does not question. One merely obeys orders, for success outweighs all other considerations of right and wrong, true and false. According to Mīmāṁsā the strategy for success is Vedic ritual. This ritual, in its full-blown reality, is the very order we desire and the order that renders reasonable our other preferences.

In addition to this sacrificial tradition, devotionalism is the second major stream of Hinduism in which mythological expression of desirability is prominent. The evocative depictions of the several major deities current in Hindu devotionalism are sufficiently straightforward examples of such expression as not to require elucidation. As we noted at the outset of this discussion of mythological expression of desirability, however, some forms of Hinduism utilize the popular deities in a nonliteral way that may require some discussion. Again, as in the sacrificial stream, the forces at play in Hindu devotionalism's nonliteral, mythological expression of desirability have their roots in the ancient *Vedas*. Two factors, however, create a wider separation from Vedic concerns than is evident in the sacrificial stream. In the first place, the deities involved are different. Their names and characteristics are different. More important, however, their ontological status is different, this due to the previously discussed phenomenon of transpolytheism, whereas all the forms of extant Hindu theism are monotheistic, or in the case of Advaita, monistic. The several polytheistic gods, then, suffer a decrease in their ontological status. This is not to say, however, that they become any less important in Hinduism's expression of its ultimate referent.

We have noted already a peculiar tendency in the Vedas to address several of the gods, each at different times, as the supreme deity, a tendency that Max Müller called henotheism. We find a similar conceptual mechanism in classical Hinduism. It employs multiple deities as non-literal, mythological expressions of the desirability of its ultimate referent. A complex transition in the history of ideas intervened between the Vedas and the classical, Vedāntic theologians, but in essence, Vedāntic treatments of polytheism may be seen as providing philosophical underpinnings for the ancient Vedic conceptual mechanisms. In each case, this underpinning involves the proposition that the several polytheistic deities emanate in various ways from a supreme being. For Rāmānuja and Madhva, this supreme being is monotheistic. For Śaṅkara, it is monistic.

Madhva, as noted previously, affirmed the literal, separate existence of the several popular deities. Still, even in his system, the preeminence of the supreme Lord Īśvara overshadows these several deities to the extent that it would be misleading to call his system truly polytheistic. His doctrine of *sārṣṭi mokṣa,* for example, depicts the deities as enjoying a special kind of liberation (mokṣa) wherein they dwell in Īśvara's body and enjoy there Īśvara's own bliss and power, though they may at will issue forth independently from Īśvara. In effect, Madhva's graphic doctrine illustrates the subtler doctrines of Rāmānuja and Śaṅkara, both of whom picture the various deities as emanations from the Godhead. Rāmānuja accords to these deities, as to everything else that emanates from the metaphysical absolute, more ontological reality than does Śaṅkara, but aside from this, their positions differ little insofar as our present purposes are concerned.

In each case, the various deities converge in a unitary supreme that is the ultimate object of religion. Put crudely, each of these deities is the supreme deity in the same way that the tip of an iceberg is the iceberg, though it is not the whole iceberg. When one worships or contemplates one of the deities, one worships or contemplates the supreme in a distant way. Each of these deities may provide for their devotees a path to the supreme, just as one may enter the same room by several different doors. This creates an expandable pantheon that can accommodate not only many different gods, but even many gods conceived to be supreme. It also creates a flexible pantheon that can accommodate the varying temperaments of individual devotees. This flexibility is accomplished by means of the concept of *ishṭa-devatā* or "favored deity." The studious devotee may be drawn to Ganesha, the passionate to Kṛshṇa, the conservative to Rāma, the ascetic to Śiva, and so on. This situation in Hinduism is a particular illustration of a general characteristic of all expressions of the desirability of the central spiritual reality of humankind. Through the *ishṭa-devatā* concept, Hinduism's ultimate referent, though recognized as unitary, may be expressed in whatever terms the individual human being addressed finds attractive. Even morbid and aggressive temperaments are accommodated by an *ishṭa-devatā* chosen from the more grotesque deities such as Kālī. Moreover, according to the neo-Vedānta movement of the nineteenth and twentieth centuries, Christians may devote themselves to Christ and Muslims to Allāh and still be accommodated in the fold of Hinduism.

This accommodating attitude in modern Hinduism is probably not a solution to conflicting truth claims in various religions. It is, however, without a doubt the most striking example of a traditional recognition that the desirability of a central spiritual reality validates human preference. It can be viewed, and probably should be viewed, not as an attempt to co-opt other religions, but rather as a recognition of the situation that regardless of the objective existence of an ultimately desirable, the innate human predilection for preference presupposes assent to such an ultimate. Modern Hinduism is able to start with the existential phenomenon of preference as it occurs in an individual human being and to express its ultimate referent in terms of that existential preference. Again, Hinduism's emphasis on transition is apparent. In this case, the transition is a smooth movement from the immediate inclinations and preferences of the individual, through a mythological representation appropriate to those immediate concerns, to the reality standing behind the representation.

Neo-Vedānta thinkers have noted a similar transition in the other world religions. In terms of the present paradigm, when the neo-Vedānta declares that all religions are branches of Hinduism, it is calling attention to the similar way in which mythological symbolism of desirability is used in all religions. Each religion leads its adherents from immediate preferences and desires as existential humans, through that religion's evocative mythological focusing of these existential preferences, to an unspeakable yet undeniable reality at once transcending and validating the terms of the mythological expression of desirability.

Elusiveness

Mythological Symbolism of Elusiveness

The same conceptual mechanism that allows for the eloquent mythological expression of the desirability of the ultimate referent of Hinduism simultaneously expresses the elusiveness of this referent. Recognition that ultimate reality may be expressed and conceptualized in several different forms involves recognition that the expressive forms themselves are not the essential phenomenon. Hindus at all socioeconomic levels recognize implicitly or explicitly a "god above god" similar to that described by Paul Tillich. Hindu theologians disagree among themselves as to the nature of this ultimate reality but agree that it eludes human conceptual terms. It is this agreement, formalized in the great theological treatises of classical Hinduism, which allows Hinduism's wide-ranging affirmation of the desirability of its ultimate referent through its own and others' deities. This agreement is also the basis of Hinduism's mythological symbolism of the elusiveness of the central spiritual reality of humankind. The multiplicity of deities thus accepted *illustrates the elusiveness of this central spiritual reality.*

Rāmānuja and Madhva agree in conceiving of the transcendent reality beyond the multiple mythological expressions as a personal god, Īśvara. One's present devotional relationship, pursued via a pantheon of symbolic deities, will eventually blossom into a direct relationship of devotion to Īśvara himself. Since Rāmānuja, Madhva, and their followers are Vaishnavas, "believers in Vishnu," they tend to conceive of Īśvara in terms of the mythological depiction of Vishnu. Many Hindu theists, however, particularly in southern India, are Śaivas, "believers in Śiva," and prefer to conceptualize the transpolytheistic god above the gods as Śiva. Each set tacitly recognizes the validity of the other's conceptualization of ultimate reality, and simultaneously reaffirms the elusiveness of the central spiritual reality of humankind through frequent declarations that the ultimate nature of Īśvara is *acintya*, "unthinkable."

This *acintya* doctrine, while no doubt heartfelt, was in many ways philosophically necessary to combat persistent Advaitin criticisms of the notion of a personal deity. In essence, the Advaitins argued that assigning specific qualities such as personhood to the ultimate reality renders it vulnerable to the same sorts of analytical and inferential evaluations we make upon mundane entities. If, for example, Īśvara is a person, the Advaitin insist that like every other person, he would have to pass away. Such considerations, buttressed by the mystical intuitions of the Upanishads, led Śaṅkara to conclude that the ultimate reality is without qualities, is *nirguṇa*. The Advaitins do not, however, deny that there is a *saguṇa* reality, a personal Īśvara with the qualities of a supreme deity. They hold instead that this *saguṇa* Īśvara, in which the polytheistic deities converge, itself converges in the hither reality of *nirguṇa* Brahman, the qualityless state of utter tranquillity that underlies the Universe and that successful mystics realize at the core of their own being, in the depths of their own minds. *Nirguṇa* Brahman, needless to say, is also *acintya*, unthinkable.

The Advaitins grant limited validity to the theists' claim of receiving salvation from Īśvara. According to the Advaita, devotionalism may indeed result in such salvation, but it is not final salvation. Final salvation can only be realized through wisdom and meditation à la Advaita. Similarly, Hindu theism typically grants limited validity to the Advaitin mystic's experience of union with the absolute. It is valid as a distant, featureless perception of the divine and as an emotional experience of the blissful dissolution of the selfish, willful ego. Beyond such mystical experiences, however, Hindu theists assert that the individual self may have direct experiences of Īśvara with all its diverse and sublime qualities. Thus in Hinduism do monistic mysticism and theistic devotionalism converge in mutual tolerance. This tolerance itself expresses the elusiveness of ultimate reality.

The mystical and devotional orientations comprise Hinduism's two primary categories of religious types. Within each category there is a branching array of more specific orientations and religious preferences. In the wake of the neo-Vedāntin thinkers, many Hindus see this branching array as extending beyond the bounds of Hinduism to include adherents of other faiths as well. From the Hindu point of view, the variety of deities worshiped within this array is necessary for broadly appealing expression of the desirability of its ultimate referent. Tolerance of the various expressions, moreover, is not merely a matter of social expedience, but rather is integral to Hinduism's mythological expression of the elusiveness of its ultimate referent.

Intellectual Symbolism of Elusiveness

Hinduism's intellectual expression of elusiveness, like its intellectual expression of undeniability, grows out of its mythological and spiritual tradition. This intellectual expression of elusiveness is cast primarily in terms of the epistemological limitations that derive naturally from the *acintya* or unthinkable nature of Brahman and Īśvara. The doctrine of unthinkability is for all intents and purposes universal in Hinduism, though it takes several different forms of depending, somewhat paradoxically, upon the different doctrines concerning the nature of what is held to be unthinkable. The doctrine of unthinkability is not, however, special pleading. Instead, it arose as a natural development in the course of attempting to express intellectually the ancient mythological and spiritual insights of the Hindu tradition. We have already shown in our discussion of undeniability in Hinduism that inexpressibility is integral to Hinduism's expression of its ultimate referent.

Even the ancient *Vedas* are concerned with the unknowability and inexpressibility of the ultimately real. Typically, Vedic epistemology centers upon questions of cosmogony. The following well-known verses from a hymn to creation express mythologically the unknowability of ultimate reality.

6. Who verily knows and who can here declare it, whence was born and whence comes this creation? The Gods are later than this world's production. Who knows then whence it first came into being?
7. He, the first origin of this creation, whether he formed it all or did not form it, whose eye controls this world in highest heaven, he verily knows it, or perhaps he knows it not.

(Ṛg 10.129.6–7)

Several verses of the famous Dīrghatamas hymn emphasize the inexpressibility of ultimate reality. Two verses suffice to illustrate.

6. I ask, unknowing, those who know, the sages, as one all ignorant for sake of knowledge. What was that One who in the unborn's image hath established and fixed firm these worlds' six regions?
46. They call him Indra, Mitra, Varuṇa, Agni, and he is heavenly nobly-winged Garutmān. To what is One, sages give many a title: they call it Agni, Yama, Matāriśvan.

(Ṛg 1.164.6, 46)

We have already discussed briefly how first the Upanishadic thinkers and finally Śaṅkara shaped such early mythological intuitions into a coherent metaphysics that offers a philosophical explanation of the inexpressibility of the ultimate referent of Hinduism. We have discussed too how Śaṅkara's rivals, while rejecting his metaphysics, employed the venerable tradition of the unthinkability of the ultimate to defend their own conceptualizations philosophically. Rāmānuja even attempted, while being a theist, to refute the theistic arguments current in his time in order to establish that the nature of the divine could be learned only from scriptural revelation. The result of all this is a tradition in Hinduism of what might almost be called negative philosophy. The elusiveness of ultimate reality is so integral to Hinduism's total expression of its ultimate referent that in many ways Hindu intellectual symbolism is a direct at-tempt to *make reasonable the elusiveness of central spiritual reality of humankind* by explaining why rational thought can never reach ultimate reality.

Moral Symbolism of Elusiveness

Such mistrust of rational thought in Hinduism, however, is not a prelude to uncritical pietism. Hinduism asserts the elusiveness of the ultimate reality in its *moral* and *spiritual symbolism* of its ultimate referent as well as in its intellectual expression. Most obvious in this regard is the univer-sal agreement in Hinduism that morality is not a sufficient path to salva-tion. Good action, good karma, may lead to rebirth in a better situation from which to attain liberation, but, strictly speaking, no rebirth in itself is any closer to liberation than any other rebirth. Many Hindus, like most Westerners, may conceive of karma and rebirth as a sort of ladder to the summum bonum, but sophisticated Hinduism makes it clear that morali-ty by itself is inadequate for final liberation.

In all forms of Hinduism, as in Buddhism, liberation is regarded as the cessation of rebirth. Because of the variety of metaphysical theories en-compassed in orthodox Hinduism, the nature of this cessation, the nature of that which follows one's final rebirth, is variously conceived in the different schools. Nonetheless, all schools of Hinduism regard rebirth as being confined wholly to the realm of *samsāra,* the mundane sphere. Rebirth in *samsāra* necessarily entails death. If one is born, one will die. Liberation is universally regarded as a permanent, everlasting state of bliss, and therefore it cannot be entered via rebirth. One metaphorically "enters" – or more properly "realizes" – the state of liberation via an inexplicable and inconceivable event unparalleled in mundane experience. This event marks a radical break from *samsāra,* the realm of rebirth and death.

Rebirth in *samsāra* is like changing horses on a merry-go-round. One may prefer one horse to another, but none of them will take one to any destination. Similarly, one may prefer one rebirth to another, but no rebirth will convey one to liberation. In large merry-go-rounds, some horses are closer to the edge than others, and so from the point of view of getting somewhere, one might say that one approaches one's destination by moving to an outside horse. Still, although the potential for getting somewhere is greater on an outside horse than on an inside horse, one will never go anywhere unless one gets off the merry-go-round. Similarly, one rebirth may be more conducive to liberation than another, but liberation itself is abandonment, not completion, of the process of rebirth. Thus, all forms of Hinduism agree that morality only leads to "better" rebirths; it does not get one any closer to the realization of ultimate reality. This *missing link* in the moral component of Hinduism's path to liberation *emphasizes that good behavior in itself is insufficient for personal perfection.*

Spiritual Symbolism of Elusiveness

The spiritual practices enjoined by the various forms of Hinduism are also regarded as being unable to bring about realization of the summum bonum. To illustrate this *spiritual symbolism* of elusiveness in Hinduism, we will consider the three broadly representative streams of the tradition: sacrificial, devotional, and meditational.

Already in the Ṛg Veda, the epistemological reflection accompanying incipient monism had begun to express doubts about ritual and the deities to whom it was addressed.

1. In the beginning rose Hiraṇyagarbha, born Only Lord of created beings. He fixed and holdeth up this earth and heaven. What God shall we adore with our oblation?
2. Giver of vital breath, of power and vigour, he whose commandments all the Gods acknowledge: the Lord of death, whose shade is life immortal. What God shall we adore with our oblation?
3. Who by his grandeur hath become Sole Ruler of all the moving world that breathes and slumbers; he who is Lord of men and Lord of cattle. What God shall we adore with our oblation?

(Ṛg 10.121.1–3)

By the time of the Upanishads, such doubts had grown into explicit rejections of ritual as irrelevant or even positively harmful in the quest for salvation.

Whoever knows thus, "I am Brahman," becomes this all. Even the gods cannot prevent his becoming this, for he becomes their self. So whoever worships [using ritual] another divinity (than the self) thinking that he is one and (Brahman) another, he knows not. He is like an animal to the gods. As many animals serve a man so does each man [ritually] serve the gods. Even if one animal is taken away, it causes displeasure, what should one say of many (animals)? Therefore it is not pleasing to those (gods) that men should know this [that "I am Brahman"].

(B.U. 1.4.10)

After its undermining in the Upanishads, ritual never regained the status it had enjoyed in the Vedas as a self-sufficient means of salvation, except perhaps in the Mīmāṁsā school. In Brāhmaṇical circles, ritual was often referred to as karma, because it was held to be the most perfect form of action. After the Upanishadic period, its status had been reduced in effect to that of karma as mere action. It was thereafter generally considered perhaps instrumental in gaining a better rebirth, but ultimately powerless with respect to salvation.

Part of the reason for the decline of ritual as a means to salvation was doubtless the rise of devotionalism, which emphasizes one's personal relationship to Īśvara rather than the formalized rituals that embody the procedures of this relationship. Nevertheless, Rāmānuja and Madhva, the primary theologians of Hindu devotionalism, both asserted in different ways that even the personal relationship of devotion to the Lord is ultimately an inadequate path to salvation. Rāmānuja, as a result of his qualified nondualism – which stressed the interplay among individual souls, the world, and the Lord – expressed the inadequacy of devotion in terms of the necessity of divine favor for salvation.

Let us return to the soul–body analogy referred to earlier. According to Rāmānuja, Īśvara controls the world and souls much as one controls one's body, hence the synonym "inner controller" for Īśvara. No one attains release unless Īśvara wills it and extends his favor and guidance (anugraha). In general, Īśvara may be relied upon to extend guidance to his devotees and withhold it from those who ignore him, but receipt of guidance cannot be assured by human action, even the most fervent devotion. The necessity for guidance from Īśvara constitutes the *missing link* in Rāmānuja's scheme of salvation.

Madhva, more than Rāmānuja, was concerned strictly to distinguish individual souls, the world, and Īśvara. In the Indian context, where creation tends to be viewed in terms of emanation, Madhva's concern resulted in his maintaining that souls, the world, and Īśvara are coeternal and eternally separate. For Madhva, then, salvation results from the fruition of tendencies inherent in each individual soul. This point of view bears resemblance to Western predeterminism, except that for Madhva no one, including Īśvara, does the determining. Instead, individual souls have their destinies eternally imprinted upon them. The result of this doctrine is that again for Hindu theism in the tradition of Madhva, there is a *missing link* in the scheme of salvation.

In the cases of Rāmānuja and Madhva, the elusiveness of Īśvara is expressed as the impossibility of human action securing realization of the summum bonum. In Śaṅkara's Advaita school, the problem is not the action, but the actor. For Śaṅkara the human being in essence is identical to Brahman, and release is merely the realization of this fact. Release results entirely from human effort, without any possibility of admitting divine guidance or predetermination. Anything other than all-encompassing unity is mere illusion. The only thing separating one from release is failure to realize this eternal fact. Human effort in the form of meditation and wisdom can bring about this realization, but the realization entails negation of the identity of the individual involved. The Muṇḍaka Upanishad expressed Śaṅkara's point of view.

> Just as the flowing rivers disappear in the ocean casting off name and shape, even so the knower, freed from name and shape, attains to the divine person, higher than the high.

(Mu.U. 3.2.8)

For Śaṅkara, as for Rāmānuja and Madhva, an unbridgeable gulf separates the human aspirant from the goal of spiritual practice. For Śaṅkara, however, the gulf is one's own individuality and one's own aspiration to gain that which one already is. Each of these representative streams of Hinduism – the sacrificial, the devotional, and the meditational – offers a spiritual discipline leading to realization of its conceptualization of the ultimately desirable state. Each vigorously propounds its own path and goal and criticizes the others, and yet each tacitly admits its own inadequacy for the task it sets for itself. Each, in its own way, *recognizes a missing link in its scheme of salvation,* and yet each *encourages sustained discipline despite the elusiveness of the central spiritual reality of humankind.*

CHAPTER FOUR

Buddhism and the Central Spiritual Reality of Humankind

Widely differing beliefs and practices go under the name "Buddhism," so that it is difficult to specify anything that is true of Buddhism as a whole. The reader will have noted a similar situation with regard to Hinduism, but with Buddhism the problem is compounded by wide geographical expansion involving several different cultural, racial, and linguistic groups. Hinduism has been largely confined to the Indian subcontinent, the land of its birth. Buddhism, on the other hand, disappeared from its mother-land by approximately 1000 C.E. Since then it has developed in several divergent directions without the restraining influence that a continued Indian parent tradition might otherwise have exercised upon the derivative forms of Buddhism that have flourished throughout the Eastern world. As it is, it is impossible to attempt in a single chapter even perfunctory treatment of all the various forms of Buddhism still practiced today. Instead, we will concentrate upon the basic tenets of Buddhism as a whole as expressed in the two primary branches of extant Buddhism: Theravāda and Mahāyāna.

Aside from belief in rebirth and some sort of spiritual release therefrom, one of the few things upon which all forms of Buddhism agree is denial of a creator or ruler of the universe. Buddhism is, then, correctly characterized as an atheistic religion. Nor is it merely nontheistic, for its denial of a God who created or governs the universe is explicit. To be sure, some forms of Buddhism come very close to a theistic concept of ultimate reality, but all stop short of affirming a creator or ruler of the universe, an affirmation that would constitute a Buddhist equivalent of heresy. Nonetheless, not only some forms but all forms of Buddhism do have a devotional component. As in Hinduism, Buddhist devotion is extended toward a number of deities, some of them Hindu in origin, some specifically Buddhist, and some representing syncretisms joining the Buddhist and Hindu deities of India with the deities of alien races and cultures. Again as in Hinduism, Buddhism asserts that ultimate reality lies beyond these various mythological representations, which are viewed as expedients to the realization of a higher, transcendent truth. This situation has led Ninian Smart to characterize Buddhism as "trans-poly-theistic atheism" in order to distinguish it from similar Hindu notions that he labels "trans-polytheistic absolutism" or "trans-polytheistic theism."[1]

Even though it is explicitly atheistic – perhaps because it is atheistic – Buddhism provides some unique insights into the central spiritual reality of humankind. While Buddhism denies much of what other religions traditionally associate with their respective ultimate referents, it nevertheless affirms a *central spiritual reality in human life*. Perhaps Buddhism's greatest lesson to other religions is its demonstration of how little need be said about this nonmaterial reality in order to inspire and guide effectively the human religious emotion.

Buddhism survives today in two main branches, Theravāda and Mahāyāna. Because of this, it will be necessary to discuss two concepts representing ultimate reality in Buddhism. These are Nirvāṇa and Dharma. In general, Nirvāṇa represents the ultimate referent of Theravāda, and Dharma represents the ultimate referent of Mahāyāna. There is some ambiguity in both the Theravāda and the Mahāyāna expressions of ultimate reality, however, in that each combines Nirvāṇa and Dharma in its expression of its ultimate referent.

Undeniability

Intellectual Symbolism of Undeniability

Intellectual symbolism of undeniability arguably plays a more important role in Buddhism than in any other major religion. Modern Buddhists, when presenting their religion to outsiders, typically call attention first to the rational nature of the basic Buddhist doctrines. In so doing, they echo the approach the Buddha himself is said to have taken, over twenty-five hundred years ago, when he delivered his first sermon in Sarnath, near Benares. He recognized that much of what he realized when he attained enlightenment under the Bodhi tree "went against the stream" – it would not appeal to the natural inclinations of human beings. He introduced his teachings to the world, however, by proposing four "noble truths" that Buddhists hold to be undeniable. The first of these is that all life is unsatisfactory (*dukkha*); to live is to be dissatisfied. This is undeniable, the Buddha suggested, because search as one may, one can never discover

1 N. Smart, *Doctrine and Argument in Indian Philosophy* (New York: Allen and Unwin, 1964), p. 215.

anything permanent in the world. All is in a state of constant flux, changing from moment to moment, and finally passing out of existence, and this includes our selves as well. Personal impermanence he termed "soullessness," absence of any unchanging basis of identity that survives death or, for that matter, survives unchanged from one moment to the next. In such a world, pleasure is possible for limited periods of time, but eventually the source of this pleasure will pass away, and the greater the pleasure, the greater will be the suffering when one is deprived of it. Suffering is obviously unsatisfactory. Pleasure, though immediately gratifying, is ultimately unsatisfactory as well because of its inexorable impermanence.

The second noble truth is that desire is the cause of this universal unsatisfactoriness. Impermanence in and of itself is not unsatisfactory. When, however, we desire permanence where there is only impermanence, we create an unsatisfactory situation. We cause our own suffering by desiring reality to be other than what it is. According to the Buddhist notion of causality, removal of the cause of something results in removal of the thing itself, and thus the third noble truth follows from the first and second truths. There is the cessation of unsatisfactoriness, says the third noble truth; for if one's desires were eradicated, there would be no cause for unsatisfactoriness. The fourth and final noble truth is that there is a path to the cessation of desire and thereby to the cessation of unsatisfactoriness. This path is the "noble eightfold path" that enshrines Buddhist practice. These four noble truths form the essence of Buddhism, all of which may be viewed as elaboration upon them. The essence of Buddhism, then, is confined to four rational propositions that appeal directly to the intellect. This emphasis upon rationality has led some to regard Buddhism as a philosophy rather than a religion. We regard Buddhist rationality as a notable instance of intellectual expression of the undeniability of the central spiritual reality of humankind.

It will be noted that none of these noble truths makes reference to a god, a source of the universe, an eschatology, or indeed any metaphysical doctrine whatsoever. Nonetheless, in early Buddhism, represented today by the Theravāda, the third noble truth, the cessation of unsatisfactoriness, affirms an ultimate spiritual reality. It refers to a phenomenon known as Nirvāṇa. According to Theravāda Buddhism, this phenomenon did not create the world, nor in fact does it have any connection with the world. It is not held to be the source, metaphysical basis, or eschatological resolution of the universe. It is not conscious or personal. It does not will, judge, punish, or forgive. In fact, it exerts no influence whatsoever upon the universe. Nonetheless, it may be recognized as the undeniable, ultimately desirable, and elusive phenomenon that inspires each of the major world religions. Beyond these three characteristics, little more can be said about Nirvāṇa. It is arguably the purest expression of the central spiritual reality of humankind encountered in the world's religions.

We may begin our discussion of the undeniability of Nirvāṇa with the most explicit passage on the subject found in the Tipiṭaka, the Theravāda Buddhist canon.

There is, monks, that plane where there is no earth, water, fire, or air [the four great elements, i.e., matter]; no plane of infinite space, no plane of infinite consciousness, no plane of nothingness, no plane of neither-perception-nor-nonperception [the four supreme meditational absorptions]; not this world nor another world, neither moon, nor sun. There, monks, I say that there is neither coming nor going, no staying, no perishing and no arising. Indeed, it is not stable, not moving, and without any basis [for conceptualization]. This indeed is the end of unsatisfactoriness. . . . There is, monks, an unborn, not become, not made, uncompounded. Were there not, monks, this unborn, not made, uncompounded, there would be known no escape of the born, the become, the made, the compounded.

(Udāna, p. 80*)[2]

The reader may well wonder how it is that this passage, which makes only negative statements about Nirvāṇa, could possibly be regarded as exceptionally explicit. It is, however, the only passage in the Tipiṭaka that explicitly states that Nirvāṇa exists. According to the strict Theravāda position, this passage goes too far in doing so, for normally much care is taken to avoid associating Nirvāṇa with the world in any way. To say that Nirvāṇa is, or that it exists, is to put it in the category of the impermanent phenomena that constitute the unsatisfactory universe.

If the above passage is regarded as an argument for the *existence* of Nirvāṇa, it is certainly circular: Nirvāṇa, the cessation of unsatisfactoriness, exists, because if it did not exist there would be no cessation of unsatisfactoriness. We submit, however, that it is not such an argument. Instead, the passage *attempts to establish that Nirvāṇa is real.*

Given Buddhism's pessimistic evaluation of mundane existence, it is said that were it not for the possibility of release from the inexorable unsatisfactoriness of life in *saṃsāra* – the realm of endless birth, death, and rebirth – there would be absolutely no meaning or purpose in the infinite suffering of sentient beings. Unless one's suffering inspires an attempt to transcend suffering, it is held to be utterly pointless and meaningless. Suffering has meaning only insofar as it urges one to seek the spiritual release of Nirvāṇa. In this sense, Nirvāṇa is *the reality upon which all other realities depend and from which they derive their ultimate*

2 Our translations in this chapter follow the Pali Text Society and Sacred Books of the Buddhists series, or the footnoted translation, unless the citation is followed by an asterisk, which indicates our translation.

meaning. Nirvāṇa is not the ontological basis or origin of the universe. Nonetheless, mundane reality has a meaning only insofar as it is referred to the supramundane reality of Nirvāṇa. Nirvāṇa, however, is the very antithesis of the suffering and unsatisfactoriness that characterize all *saṃsāra.* For this reason, the preceding passage draws a radical contrast between Nirvāṇa and this mundane reality that is born, made and becomes, which is, in a word, impermanent. Even the most sublime mundane experiences, namely the several meditational absorptions, are in radical contrast with Nirvāṇa. The radical contrast between *saṃsāra* and Nirvāṇa excludes everything in our experience in terms of which we might conceptualize Nirvāṇa. It also excludes the notion of existence, because everything we encounter and refer to as existing changes and ultimately perishes. Cups and saucers exist. Nirvāṇa must be imagined in different terms.

The Udāna passage just quoted, then, does not urge *that* Nirvāṇa is but rather urges *what* Nirvāṇa is. What Nirvāṇa is, moreover, is necessarily conceived in negative terms. One can say only what Nirvāṇa is not. The fundamental characteristics of all that we experience in the mundane world are impermanence and unsatisfactoriness. All other characteristics are, from the Buddhist point of view, variations upon these themes. If Nirvāṇa is to be satisfactory, it must be permanent, but if it is permanent, it must be unlike anything we have ever experienced. If, indeed, it is unlike anything we have ever experienced, it cannot be expressed in the terms we use to describe our experiences. Attempting to express Nirvāṇa is said to be analogous to the attempt to describe sight to a person blind from birth.

Nonetheless Theravāda Buddhism makes two assertions that may be regarded as intellectual symbolism of the undeniability of Nirvāṇa. First, because desire can be isolated as the single root cause of all unsatisfactoriness, there is necessarily the possibility for the cessation of unsatisfactoriness, because this cessation would be accomplished by the removal of desire. Cessation of unsatisfactoriness is itself the minimum definition of Nirvāṇa. According to Buddhist reasoning, Nirvāṇa is undeniable because the unsatisfactoriness of existence has a cause. This unsatisfactoriness necessarily ceases when its cause is removed.

The things which arise from a cause,
Of these things the Tathāgata (Buddha) has stated the cause.
And of these (things) there is the cessation.
Such is the creed of the great ascetic.

(V 1:40)[3]

3 Translation follows Pe Maung Tin, *Buddhist Devotion and Meditation* (London: S.P.C.K. Press, 1964), p. 30.

The second assertion regarding the undeniability of Nirvāṇa is that this cessation of unsatisfactoriness cannot be described or conceptualized in verbal terms, all of which are appropriate only to the day-to-day realities that language has been concocted to describe. Being indescribable and inconceivable, Nirvāṇa, much like the Ātman-Brahman of the Upanishads, is undeniable. It is undeniable precisely because it is unaffirmable.

This basic position is augmented with a considerable amount of philosophical material critical of the reality of the mundane world. With regard to expression of the central spiritual reality of humankind, philosophical analysis that lessens the apparent undeniability of brute, material reality enhances the undeniability of an ultimate, nonmaterial reality. In this sense too, Nirvāṇa is *the reality upon which all other realities depend and from which they derive their ultimate meaning.* This Theravādin critique of apparent reality is eventually taken up in Mahāyāna Buddhism and elaborated along two lines by the Mādhyamika or "dialectic" school and the Vijñānavāda or "consciousness" school. The groundwork for both of these later developments in Buddhism is readily apparent in the older, but less philosophically sophisticated Theravāda texts, which we will therefore consider first.

The Theravāda texts themselves explain the observable impermanence of all phenomena as being due to their dependence upon causes and conditions. The texts reason that because all phenomena are impermanent, constantly changing, they are devoid of any abiding ontological essence that makes them what they are. Instead, things are what they are by virtue of a shifting collocation of causes and conditions, each of which is in turn dependent upon another collocation of causes and conditions. The material world appears substantial, but when examined analytically, it vanishes like sand running through one's fingers.

Let us consider, for example, a chair. In normal parlance we say a chair *has* legs, *has* a seat, *has* a back – as if a chair existed on its own and merely *possessed* these attributes. Actually, though, there is no chair apart from legs, a seat, and a back. Take away the back, and it is a stool. Take away the legs also, and a plank remains. Moreover, the remaining plank is not properly a "seat." It is merely a piece of wood. The legs, removed from the chair or stool, are no longer "legs"; they are sticks of wood. A stick of wood is a "leg" only in certain circumstances – namely, when it holds up a chair or table. In other words, just as "a chair" depends upon its components for its existence and definition as "a chair," so the components of the chair depend for their definition – as "legs, seat, and back" – upon their collocation in a particular configuration known conventionally as "a chair." Nonetheless, we speak and act as if chairs, legs, and so on were self-defined entities, when it may be shown analytically that chairs and legs, like all things, always depend upon other things which in turn are not self-defined either. Modern atomic physics provides particularly good illustrations of the component nature and resultant impermanence of all things. The ancient texts illustrate this doctrine with the well-known simile of the chariot, employed in the following passage by the Buddhist monk Nāgasena in a debate with the Greek king Milinda.

Then Milinda called upon the Yonakas [Greeks] and the brethren to witness: "This Nāgasena says there is no permanent individuality [no soul] implied in his name. Is it now even possible to approve him in that?" And turning to Nāgasena, he said: "If, most reverend Nāgasena, there be no permanent individuality involved in the matter, who is it, pray, who gives to you members of the Order your robes and food and lodging and necessaries for the sick? Who is it who enjoys such things when given? Who is it who lives a life of righteousness? Who is it who attains to the goal of the Excellent Way, to the Nirvāṇa of Arahatship? . . . "

And the venerable Nāgasena said to Milinda the king: "You, Sire, have been brought up in great luxury, as beseems your noble birth. . . . How then did you come, on foot or in a chariot?"

"I did not come, Sir, on foot. I came in a carriage."

"Then if you came, Sire, in a carriage, explain to me what it is. Is it the pole that is the chariot?"

"I did not say that."

"Is it the axle that is chariot?"

"Certainly not."

"Is it the wheels, or the framework, or the ropes, or the yoke, or the spokes of the wheels, or the goad, that are the chariot?"

"No, Sir."

"But is there anything outside them that is the chariot?"

And still he answered no.

"Then thus, ask as I may, I can discover no chariot. Chariot is a mere empty sound. What then is the chariot you say you came in? It is a falsehood that your Majesty has spoken, an untruth! There is no such thing as a chariot! You are king over all India, a mighty monarch. Of whom then are you afraid that you speak untruth?" And he called upon the Yonakas and the brethren to witness, saying: "Milinda the king here has said that he came by carriage. But when asked in that case to explain what the carriage was, he is unable to establish what he averred. Is it, forsooth, possible to approve him in that?"

When he had thus spoken the five hundred Yonakas shouted their applause, and said to the king: "Now let your Majesty get out of that if you can."

(Milindapañha, 25–7)[4]

In the Mādhyamika school of Mahāyāna Buddhism, the lack of self-definition of all phenomena is expressed as lack of self-existence

4 *Milindapañha*, trans. T. W. Rhys Davids as *The Questions of King Milinda*, vol. 1, Sacred Books of the East, vol. 35 (London: Oxford University Press, 1890), pp. 25–7. Reprinted, New York: Dover Publications, 1963, pp. 41–4.

(*svabhava*). This led the Mādhyamikas to formulate their well-known metaphysical doctrine of emptiness (*śūnyatā*). The less extreme form of Mādhyamika, the Svātāntrika, differs little from the implicit Theravāda position, holding that the conditionality and component nature of all phenomena entail their metaphysical emptiness. The extreme form of Mādhyamika, the Prāsaṅgika, sought to avoid even the doctrine of conditionality and interdependence, and attempted to establish emptiness on entirely dialectical grounds. Any statement concerning reality, they asserted, could be shown to be meaningless by careful analysis of its terms.

Consider, for example, the statement, "I go." This statement implies both an actor, a goer, and the action of going, as well as a distance traversed, a "gone over." There can be no goer, however, without the act of going. Nor can there be the act of going without a goer. Both the action and the agent, moreover, must necessarily refer to an object, a "gone over," which in turn is unintelligible without a goer and the action of going. Thus, even the simplest statement may be demonstrated to be nonsense, since none of its terms refer to anything that exists, other than as an imaginary construct dependent for its meaning on other equally imaginary constructs. This Prāsaṅgika argument is not a refutation of going as such. This would merely imply rest, which involves one who rests, an act of resting, and a place rested upon, each of which, again, is meaningless in and of itself. Instead, the refutation of going and a goer lays the groundwork for a thoroughgoing critique of all conceptual knowledge. The Prāsaṅgika Mādhyamika school applied similar arguments to any and all philosophical and doctrinal positions that came to their attention, including Buddhist positions. For their own part, they claimed not to hold any view whatsoever concerning the nature of reality. In the famous words of Nāgārjuna, recognized as the founder of the Mādhyamika school, "If I would make any proposition whatsoever, then by that I would have a logical error. But I do not make a proposition; therefore I am not in error."[5]

As a secular philosophy, such thought would be regarded rightly as skepticism of the most radical sort. It must be remembered, though, that Mādhyamika philosophy expresses the nonmaterial, nonsecular orientation of Buddhism. Whether the Mādhyamika dialectic is successful in its assault upon all possible points of view need not concern us here. For our purposes, what is important is that in refuting conceptualizations of apparent reality, Mādhyamika Buddhism attempts to establish the undeniability of the Buddhist expression of ultimate reality. True, Buddhism typically refuses to express in verbal terms this ultimate reality, but this is exactly the point of the Mādhyamika dialectic. It attempts to demonstrate

5 Nāgārjuna, *Vigrahavyāvartanī*, vs. 29. translation follows F. Streng, *Emptiness* (New York: Abingdon Press, 1967), p. 224.

that the only reality that cannot be denied is the reality that cannot be expressed or conceptualized, and this, moreover, is the only reality.

This argument resembles the Advaita Hindu approach to the notion of "that than which nothing greater can be conceived." According to Mādhyamika Buddhism too, the greatest conceivable reality is necessarily inconceivable. Although the Advaita and Mādhyamika conclusions in this regard are similar, their paths to this conclusion differ markedly. The Advaita assumes the necessity of an ultimate explanation of the universe and moves to the conclusion that this ultimate explanation is inexpressible. The Mādhyamika, on the other hand, starts with an examination of expressions of common, everyday "reality." In refuting these it points to an inexpressible reality that can be realized through Buddhist spiritual practices, essentially meditation. In essence, Mādhyamika Buddhism attempts to undermine our sensual, conceptual, and intellectual notions of reality and to compel us to resort to meditation and intuition.

A similar process of philosophical elaboration upon early Buddhist teachings accounts for the intellectual expression of the undeniability of ultimate reality in the second major branch of Mahāyāna Buddhism, the Vijñānavāda. Like the Mādhyamika, the Vijñānavāda assails the apparent undeniability of the mundane world in order to call attention to the undeniability of a spiritual reality. In order to accomplish this task, the Vijñānavāda emphasizes another general characteristic of Buddhism found in the Theravāda scriptures. According to these early scriptures, as noted previously, reality consists of a dynamic complex of causal and conditional relationships. None of these relationships is more essential than the interrelationship between consciousness and its objects. The Theravāda scriptures do not formulate an explicit metaphysical doctrine on the matter, but they note repeatedly that the nature of the perceiving mind affects perceived objects as much as the objects perceived affect the mind. As a familiar aphorism has it, "One person's trash is another person's treasure."

In the context of Buddhism, with its emphasis upon meditative introspection, such observations have far more than aphoristic significance. They indicate a fundamental property of reality. Reality is what we perceive, and what we perceive is affected by our minds. We do not see the world as it is, but rather as we see it. On the other hand, what we do experience obviously has an effect upon the nature of our minds. Violence in the home tends to create violent personalities. This interrelationship between the mind and objects of perception was incorporated into Buddhist doctrine at an early stage and subsequently elaborated considerably. It is most notably apparent in the doctrine of "conditioned arising," which seeks to illustrate the Buddhist theory of perception and integrate it with the theory of karma and rebirth.

The details of the theory of conditioned arising are far too complex even to summarize here. Suffice it to say that according to this integrated theory, the results of karma, both in this life and the next, can be regarded as actualization of the potential of the mind. A habitually violent mind tends to perceive reality as violent and on that basis to behave violently. By behaving violently, one creates further violence in the world one already perceives as violent. The circle is vicious and complete, and it is very difficult to determine what part of this violence resides in the objective world, and what part of it originates in one's own mind. Such considerations provide further incentive for meditation. The mental purification at which Buddhist meditation aims may be seen as conducive not only to spiritual welfare but also to immediate mundane welfare and welfare in future lives.

Because of its preoccupation with the practicalities of meditation, Buddhism has tended to concentrate upon the mental side of this interdependence between consciousness and its objects. This natural predilection for the mental aspect of reality eventually developed into a metaphysical alternative to the emptiness doctrine of the Mādhyamika. The Vijñānavāda, or consciousness school, proposed that whether or not there really is an external, material world, we have no way of verifying its existence. The only reality we know or can ever know is the reality that reaches us through our senses, and this is an internal, subjective reality. If one is philosophically rigorous, one must admit that the only reality about which we know or may ever know anything is a reality composed entirely of mental images. For example, all that one knows visually of a tree is the result of a tiny, inverted image on the back of one's eyeball, and even this image must be further translated in order to enter one's mind. The tree itself can never enter anyone's mind. The Vijñānavāda can thus argue that all of reality – as one can ever hope to know it – is consciousness only. Like the Mādhyamika dialectic, this philosophical argument has the effect, in the context of Buddhism, of devaluing the apparent material reality that immediately seems so undeniable.

Each of the three major branches of Buddhism – Theravāda, Mādhyamika, and Vijñānavāda – employs a critique of the apparent undeniability of the mundane world in its intellectual expression of the undeniability of its ultimate referent. These branches of Buddhism differ in doctrinal details, but their strategies concerning the expression of undeniability are similar and typically Buddhist. These strategies may be characterized as negative intellectual symbolism of the undeniability of an ultimate reality. By analyzing and devaluing the mundane world, they force one to look beyond it to a nonmaterial source of value. They drive one toward ultimate reality by driving one away from apparent mundane realities. The negative nature of this expression is typical of the general

Buddhist reluctance to conceptualize ultimate reality. Buddhism seeks to deny all that is deniable, leaving the undeniable to be discovered individually through spiritual enlightenment.

Spiritual Symbolism of Undeniability

Buddhism's spiritual symbolism of undeniability follows naturally from the Buddhist intellectual expression of the undeniability of the ultimately real. We suggested in our introductory chapter that spiritual symbolism of undeniability intimates an *appeal for personal consent to the inevitability of living with reference to the central spiritual reality of humankind*. The intellectual symbolisms discussed above urge one relentlessly toward just such personal consent. Buddhist philosophy thus shades into Buddhist spirituality. Buddhist philosophy may in fact be viewed as the servant of spirituality. It urges one in every instance toward recognition of the inevitability of orienting one's life with reference to a stable reality beyond the impermanent, empty, imaginary reality that is immediately apparent.

Buddhism augments its negative evaluation of mundane reality with an emphasis on the immediate advantages of the Buddhist spiritual path. The fruits of this path are held to be immediately apparent and beneficial. The intellectual propositions and moral prescriptions of the Buddhist path, moreover, submit themselves to – and in fact demand – verification by testing them in actual experiences. Most forms of Buddhism, excepting the highly devotionalistic sects which will be discussed later, insist that one must verify the intellectual teachings of Buddhism by testing them, critically reflecting upon them and observing the objective world and one's own mind to determine whether these teachings accurately describe reality. Without such verification, mere intellectual assent to Buddhist doctrines is held to be worthless. The following statement, attributed to the Buddha, illustrates this radical appeal *for personal consent to the inevitability of living with reference to the central spiritual reality of humankind.*

Just as wise men test (ostensible) gold by burning, cutting and rubbing (on a touchstone); my statements, O monks, should be accepted after examination and not out of respect (for me).

(Tattva-saṅgraha, vs. 3587*)[6]

Such testing of Buddhist truth claims is an integral part of Buddhist meditation. In its widest sense, meditation in Buddhism is denoted by the

6   Śāntarakṣita, *Tattvasaṅgraha*, ed. Dvarikadas Shastri (Varanasi: Baudha Bharati, 1968), 2:1115.

term *bhāvanā,* meaning "(mental) development." In this widest sense, the essential element of meditation is *sati, smṛti* in Sanskrit, meaning literally "remembering," but more fully translated by "mindfulness." Mindfulness meditation is not confined to something one does while sitting cross-legged and facing a wall. Instead one is urged to practice mindfulness throughout one's waking life, by being constantly and keenly observant of what is happening within one's own mind and in the world around one. The following passage from a major text on meditation, "The Establishment of Mindfulness," illustrates the ideal of constant mindfulness.

A monk, when he is walking, comprehends, "I am walking"; or when he is standing still, comprehends, "I am standing still"; or when he is lying down, comprehends, "I am lying down"; so that however his body is disposed he comprehends that it is like that. . . . And again, monks, a monk, when he is setting out or returning is one acting in a clearly conscious way; when he is looking in front or looking around . . . when he has bent in or stretched out (his arm) . . . when he is eating, drinking, chewing, tasting . . . when he is obeying the calls of nature . . . when he is walking, standing, sitting, asleep, awake, talking, silent, he is one acting in a clearly conscious way.

(M 1:56–7)

Such constant and keen observation will, it is held, eventually verify both the truth claims and the moral precepts of Buddhism. One will, for example, observe and internalize the impermanence of all phenomena. In the moral sphere it is held that if one observes one's behavior carefully, one will cease to do wrong. A Buddhist riddle illustrates this: Two Buddhists met on the road and in the course of their conversation discovered that one of them was going to the temple and the other to a brothel. When they had reached their respective destinations, the one in the temple had his mind on the brothel, and the one in the brothel had his mind on the temple. The question is "Which was the better Buddhist?" The answer, which illustrates the Buddhist emphasis upon mindfulness, is "neither one." A good Buddhist, when in the temple has his mind on the temple, and when in the brothel has his mind on the brothel. If, moreover, one were to be keenly mindful of a visit to a brothel – observant of one's own motivations and desires, the motivations and desires of the pimps and prostitutes, the multiple dishonesty, exploitation, and tragedy that characterize the entire situation – one would not go a second time.

Thus, with the appealing suggestion that one simply be mindfully observant at all times, Buddhism seeks to integrate one's entire life into its spiritual path. Most forms of Buddhism hold that if one merely agrees to be continuously mindful and to accept only what one has verified in one's own experience, one will naturally become correctly oriented in the Buddhist spiritual path. One will naturally begin to shun incorrect views and behavior and to adopt the views and behavior that lead ultimately to enlightenment. This process of gradually discarding the unwholesome and adopting the wholesome is, moreover, the only way to make spiritual progress. A Buddhist parable states, "As a palm tree grows, its lower branches naturally fall off, but one cannot force a palm tree to grow by ripping off its lower branches." Similarly, even if one were immediately willing to adopt all that Buddhism proposes and reject all that it opposes, one would still have to go through the gradual spiritual path of verification by mindfulness. Repressing or denying one's baser tendencies is as futile as ripping off the palm tree's lower branches.

I, monks, do not say that the attainment of profound knowledge comes straightaway. Instead, monks, the attainment of profound knowledge comes by gradual training, gradual doing, a gradual path. . . . Having heard *dhamma* [the Buddha's teaching] one remembers it. One tests the meaning of the teachings remembered. When the meaning is tested, the teachings are approved. There being approval of the teachings, aspiration is born. When aspiration is born, one makes an effort. Having made the effort one examines (its results). Having (thus) examined, one strives: Being thus resolute, one realizes for oneself the highest truth, and penetrating it by means of wisdom, one sees.

(M 1:479–80*)

To be mindful and to accept only what one can verify are the very basis of the spiritual path in most forms of Buddhism. The suggestion that a life based on these two principles will naturally become a spiritual life, whether true or not, is a notable use of spiritual symbolism to express the undeniability of an ultimate reality. It is not inevitable that one actually practice mindfulness and accept only what one can verify, but it is almost inevitable that one agree that these are sensible principles upon which to base one's life. Buddhism's spiritual expression of the undeniability of its ultimate referent exploits the inevitability of such assent by insisting that one observe these practical principles as part of one's spiritual path. Willingness to accept Buddhism on the basis of blind faith is not acceptable. Instead, Buddhism insists that its followers practice mindfulness and verify the teachings afresh in their own experience. By declaring these practical principles to be not only sufficient but also necessary for entrance upon the Buddhist spiritual path, Buddhism makes a radical appeal for *personal consent to the inevitability of living with reference to an ultimate spiritual reality.*

Moral Symbolism of Undeniability

Insofar as moral symbolism is concerned, our discussion of undeniability as expressed in the Hindu theory of karma and rebirth applies to Buddhism as well. The moral implications of the Hindu and Buddhist theories are exactly similar. The Buddhist doctrine of "no soul" (*anātman*), however, results in some unique dimensions in Buddhism's attempt to *expose self-contradictory behavior,* and thereby assert the *inevitability of living with reference to an ultimate spiritual reality.* The Buddhist theory of *anātman* or no soul is widely misunderstood and misrepresented, and therefore it requires a brief explanation.

According to Buddhism, mindful meditation focused upon the nature of one's own inner being will reveal that there is no abiding core of identity that can be construed as a soul. Instead, objective introspection, without preconceived convictions, will reveal a dynamic flux of interrelated components of consciousness – feelings, sensations, emotions, concepts, volitions, and so on. No matter how deeply one looks, according to Buddhism, one will never find a stable core of identity that could survive death, or for that matter that survives as the same thing from day to day or even from moment to moment. Emphatically, this is not to say that the individual human being does not exist, it is merely to say that the individual has no soul.

Many Western writers misinterpret Buddhism on this point, and many others make the even more egregious assertion that the aim of Buddhism is the grim task of destroying the soul. Obviously, one cannot destroy something that does not exist, and the considerably more lighthearted aim of Buddhism is simply to realize that like all other phenomena, one is oneself impermanent. At most, Buddhism seeks to destroy the *false idea* that one has a soul. Strictly speaking, though, Buddhist arguments refuting the concept of the soul are not seen to be primarily of theoretical value. Instead, the Buddhist refutation of the soul is intended to create an intellectual and spiritual environment conducive to *personal realization* of soullessness. Sustained pursuit of such realization requires considerable personal courage, for it requires that one confront one's radical mortality. This individual identity I strive so hard to protect is doomed. It will not survive death.

When I was an adolescent, I remember trying very hard to survive, but I did not survive. That young person – with all of his desires, opinions, emotions, aspirations, values – is gone, just as surely as if he were dead. He is nowhere to be found. At the moment I am here, but I am not he. Nonetheless, there is clearly some relationship between me as I am now and that even more confused adolescent. According to Buddhism, this relationship is a causal relationship, pure and simple, nothing more. The present configuration of physical and mental constituents that I call myself is nothing more than the momentary result of a long series of cause-and-effect relationships that are not strung together by any abiding core of identity. I am not the same as the people I have been in the past – in infancy, childhood, adolescence – and yet I am not altogether discontinuous from them either.

According to Buddhism, death and rebirth are merely a continuation of this ceaseless process of change based on cause and effect. When one dies, one's stream of consciousness, which has been manifest as many different personalities in this life, simply goes on to be manifest in yet another form. Only two things distinguish death and rebirth from any other two consecutive moments of life. One changes bodies, and one's memory is severely impaired, although not altogether eradicated. If one wishes to verify the theory of rebirth, the Buddhist texts contain detailed techniques whereby one may revive one's memory of past lives. If one is successful in these techniques, Buddhism holds that one will recognize that one has been – in each rebirth as in the different periods of one's present life – "not the same and not another," (*na ca sa na ca añño*) in classical terms. One's identity has changed, but one remains linked to past identities via an uninterrupted series of cause-and-effect relationships.

Buddhism holds not only that this account of the nature of the human being and of rebirth is literally true, but also that it is uniquely and supremely conducive to true morality by virtue of its power to *expose self-contradictory behavior.* We are concerned with this expressive power, not with the literal truth of the theory. According to Buddhism, it is not necessary to presume the existence of a soul in order to see that one's good and bad actions inevitably bear fruit. As in the Hindu theory of karma, most of these results are immediately apparent, if one is but mindfully observant. According to Buddhism, however, all incentive to immoral behavior ultimately resides in the mistaken notion of a permanent soul, an unchanging essence of individual identity. The concept of a soul is no mere philosophical speculation; it is a natural and ingrained aspect of human consciousness. In modern parlance, we might say that the notion of a soul is a naturally evolved biological survival mechanism. Buddhism contends that this most ingrained of concepts is responsible for all moral evil. It is only in the service of "I, me, and mine" that one is impelled to behave immorally. All cruelty, all deceit, all crime, and all war are perpetrated in order to protect and promote this illusory entity, the soul or self.

Moreover all envy, jealousy, rivalry, and hatred are based on falsely ascribing unchanging individual identity to others. If one hates another, what does one hate? Is it the body, the hair, the feelings, the emotions, the thoughts, the actions? If it is the thoughts, then one despises certain thoughts; if it is the actions, then one despises certain actions, not another person. If one despises certain thoughts, emotions, and actions in others, then one must despise them in oneself as well. This is the essence of

Buddhism's moral symbolism of the undeniability of an ultimate spiritual referent of human life.

"As I am, so are they. As they are, so am I." Comparing others with oneself, one should neither harm nor cause harm.

(Sn 705*)

Self-contradictory behavior is simply behavior one despises in others.

The foregoing discussion of Buddhism's moral symbolism of undeniability is based on Theravāda Buddhism. In Mahāyāna Buddhism, the Vijñānavāda and Mādhyamika schools developed somewhat different intellectual refutations of the concept of a permanent self, but it has remained axiomatic in Buddhism as a whole that to whatever extent I exist, others exist also, and that "as I am, so are they." This means that whatever I am able to verify by mindful contemplation of my own mind and my own existence is true of others as well. In my own mind and life, I can observe and verify that all greed, hatred, and delusion – the so-called roots of ill – stem from the false notion of a permanent self, and that these traits cause nothing but strife and suffering. Therefore, when one is the victim of these traits in others, one should be inspired to pity rather than to retaliate, for one's own sake as well as for the sake of others. Again, this preeminently moral attitude is not presented as a sentimental plea, but as an undeniable fact of life that can and in fact must be verified through mindful observation and contemplation.

Mythological Symbolism of Undeniability

Even though Buddhism characteristically insists that one base one's acceptance of Buddhism on verification in one's personal experience rather than upon faith in the infallibility of the Buddha, the Buddha is still widely regarded as a superhuman being. Intellectually inclined Buddhists often deemphasize belief in the superhuman status of the Buddha. Particularly when presenting Buddhism to a critical Western audience, they assert that the Buddha is regarded merely as a great teacher. Even before a critical audience, however, the widespread veneration of the Buddha need not be explained away if it is recognized as an aspect of Buddhism's mythological symbolism of the undeniability of an ultimate spiritual reality.

Seldom if ever has more mythology sprung up around a historical individual than around the Indian prince Siddhārtha Gotama, who eventually became the Buddha. The broad historical outlines of his life are fairly clear. He was born in approximately 550 B.C.E. to a ruling class family in northern India, in present day Nepal. In early adulthood, he left his home and family, like many young men of his day, to become a wandering ascetic in search of spiritual enlightenment. He joined the followers of at least two noted spiritual masters. Eventually he became dissatisfied with them and finally set out on his own to realize enlightenment. Sitting in meditation near present day Bodh Gaya in the modern Indian state of Bihar, he underwent a transformative experience that he regarded as final and complete enlightenment. At this point he became the Buddha or "enlightened one." After this enlightenment experience, as the Buddha, he began to deliver sermons and eventually attracted a large band of followers who helped spread Buddhism throughout northern India. After his death, his disciples, known as the Saṅgha or brotherhood of monks, continued to spread his teachings until Buddhism became the dominant faith of all East Asia.

Within a few centuries of the death of the Buddha, every aspect of his life had become thoroughly mythologized, and the mythology of the Buddha continued to grow over many centuries, fueled by the ideals and imaginations of the many different cultures in which Buddhism thrived. This rich mythology gave rise to a welter of artistic expressions of the indominable discipline, composure, and compassion of spiritual enlightenment depicted in the form of images of the Buddha and his most revered followers. These *images of serene power seek to express as irresistibility the undeniability of a spiritual referent of human life.* The irresistibility depicted is the passive irresistibility of the power of supreme patience rather than the dynamic irresistibility of overwhelming force. As a whole, these images attempt to portray the triumph of the immovable object over the irresistible force. The apparently irresistible force that is overcome is the force of ignorance and desire, which keeps beings embroiled in the potentially endless frenzy of suffering, frustration, defeat, and death that characterizes the realm of *saṃsāra*.

Like most art, Buddhist art must be allowed to speak for itself. Given an opportunity, a fine Buddha image expresses the Buddhist ideal of spiritual enlightenment self-sufficiently and inimitably. Nonetheless, some aspects of Buddhist iconography may be enhanced by an explanation of their mythological origins. Though it is somewhat arbitrary to categorize the subtle and mysteriously universal appeal of the Buddha image, it seems to fall most naturally in the category of mythological symbolism of undeniability.

Anyone who has seen a Buddha image will have noted several peculiar characteristics – elongated ear lobes, a bump on the crown of the head, a circle of hair between the eyes, and often wheel symbols on the palms of the hands and the soles of the feet. These are all iconographic representations of the "thirty-two major and eighty minor marks of the superman." Like Jesus' birth, the birth of the Buddha is said to have been presaged by

auspicious omens, and as in the case of Jesus, three wise men examined
the miraculous child. In the case of the Buddha, the focus of their attention was his possession of the major and minor marks of the superman.
According to Buddhist mythology, these marks foretold one of two
things: Either the child would become a *cakravartin* or "wheel turning"
monarch of the entire earth, or he would become the spiritual savior of
humankind. The child's father, being himself a political ruler of some
consequence, was understandably eager that his child should become
ruler of all the earth. Two of the wise men in attendance advised the father
that in order to ensure that his son would not be attracted to the spiritual
quest, the child would have to be shielded from any experience whatsoever of human suffering. As a result, the father is said to have built a
lavish pleasure palace in which to attempt to raise the child without any
contact with human suffering.

The futility of such a scheme is obvious, but mythology does not
recognize the constraints of the obvious, and it is said that the prince lived
completely shielded from human suffering until the age of twenty-nine.
At this point, the prince, driven by curiosity, contrived to escape from
the pleasure palace with the help of his best friend, his charioteer. On this
adventure, he experienced the so-called "four visions." He saw an ill
person, an old person, a dead person, and finally a wandering ascetic on
the spiritual quest. Horrified at the true nature of the human condition,
and yet astounded that the ascetic could maintain composure and serenity
in the face of such horror, the prince resolved to leave the palace forever
and himself become a wandering ascetic in search of spiritual enlightenment. He made his final escape with his charioteer and his favorite horse,
rode to the bank of a river, removed his princely garments, and swam
across. On the other side, he clothed himself in rags retrieved from a
rubbish heap and bade farewell to his friend and his horse. The horse died
then and there from a broken heart, and his charioteer returned to the
palace to announce the sad news.

This story illustrates, of course, the futility of attempting to avoid
suffering. It illustrates also the fundamental role of suffering in inspiring
human spirituality. This in itself is a mythological expression of the *irresistibility* of the claim of an ultimate spiritual reality to orient human life.
To return to the iconography of the Buddha image, however, all of this is
represented in the circle of hair between the eyes. The third wise man
who examined the miraculous prince realized that there was no way to
prevent the child from becoming the spiritual savior of humankind, because this circle of hair curled clockwise. If it had circled counterclock-
wise, the child would have become a "wheel-turning" universal monarch.
As things turned out, the child was destined instead to "turn the wheel of
Dharma," the all conquering wheel of truth.

If Prince Siddhārtha had been destined to be a wheel-turning monarch, at the appointed time a miraculous, jewel-encrusted wheel would have appeared to him and, once set in motion, would have led him irresistibly to dominion over all earthly political powers. As it is, his first sermon after becoming the Buddha is entitled "The Setting in Motion of the Wheel of Dharma," a wheel as irresistible as the wheel of universal dominion. Next to the Buddha image itself, the wheel is the most universal symbol of Buddhism. Thus, though *images of power expressing undeniability as irresistibility* are not readily apparent in the mainstream of Buddhist mythology and iconography, the predominant serenity of these aspects of Buddhism is imbued with an air of calm inevitability that overwhelms the most potent dynamism.

Desirability

In the long course of its development and spread, Buddhism evolved more dynamic, even fearsome, iconographic expressions of the many aspects of enlightenment and the path thereto. This exuberant iconography, however, remains peripheral to the more essential mythological expression epitomized by the serene Buddha image. These images of serenity and composure are, of course, powerful expressions of the desirability of the ultimately real. Buddhism's more dynamic images of power clearly may be regarded as mythological expressions of the undeniability of an ultimate reality. Before one can even begin to unravel Buddhism's complex iconography, however, it is necessary to move into the realm of the desirability of the central spiritual reality of humankind as expressed in Buddhism.

Spiritual Symbolism of Desirability

Many of the more fearsome images encountered in Buddhist iconography are actually representations of obstacles overcome and powers gained in the course of meditation and spiritual development. Many of the demons of Buddhist iconography actually represent the demons of one's own mind, the various aspects of greed, hatred, and delusion that torment the unenlightened. Many of the fearsome "guardian" deities represent the protection that spiritual development affords against these mental demons. Sword-wielding deities, for example, often represent the power of meditative concentration to "cut through" delusion. Though sometimes expressed iconographically in *images of power,* we regard as spiritual symbolism of desirability the various powers and protections said to accrue to one who practices the Buddhist path of meditation.

We noted that formal "cross-legged" meditation does not exhaust the Buddhist path of spiritual development or *bhāvanā*. Nonetheless formal meditation is regarded as an integral part of spiritual development in most forms of Buddhism. One's meditation practice may be merely a quiet time of reflection in the morning and evening. Meditation practice can become a rigorous discipline absorbing sixteen or more hours a day for weeks, months, or even years. In any case, meditation in Buddhism is regarded as a potent spiritual practice capable of radically transforming the mind and leading one to realization of one's ultimate potential as a human being. Meditation is therefore one of the most powerful forms of karma or action.

Like the results of other forms of karma, many of the results of meditation are held to be immediately apparent in this very life. This is another aspect of the Buddhist principle of verification discussed previously. One need not undertake meditational practice on faith, for many of its beneficial results accrue to the practitioner immediately. In the Theravāda scriptures, the "Sāmañña-phala Sutta," "Scripture on the Fruits of the Life of a Recluse," recounts the Buddha's answer when questioned concerning the practical results of sustained meditational practice. In addition to enumerating qualities such as composure, restraint, fearlessness in the face of danger, and mental alertness, the Buddha mentions many supernormal powers. At advanced stages of spiritual cultivation – where formal, "cross-legged" meditation is predominant – the practitioner is said to develop the ability to fly through the air, walk upon water, walk through walls, become invisible, or read other minds.

Normally, we in the West regard accounts of such feats as part of a religion's fanciful mythology. In Buddhism, however, these feats are held to be literal accomplishments accessible to any dedicated practitioner of meditation. This is particularly true of Tantric Buddhism, now associated primarily with Tibet. Tantrism also exhibits most notably Buddhism's iconographic depictions of the various supernormal powers said to be gained in the course of practicing the rigorous, formal meditation associated with advanced stages on the spiritual path of Buddhism.

For many if not most Westerners, such supernormal powers are simply preposterous. Many modern Buddhists attempt to accommodate the Western attitude by deemphasizing the miraculous element of Buddhism. Nonetheless, the fact remains that classical Buddhism accepts as a matter of course that such supernormal powers can arise in the course of meditational practice, and even in the face of modern skepticism, stories of miracles persist from the Eastern world in general, many of them from apparently reliable sources. In fact, each of the religions we have examined affirms in all seriousness that spiritual development can result in supernormal powers. For these reasons, we hesitate to sidestep the issue of miracles and the supernormal by relegating them entirely to the mythological dimension of religion.

We recognize that myths need not be factually inaccurate in order to be myths. Still, with regard to mythology, the literal truth or falsity of the events in question is not a real issue. The power of the narrative, didactic, or iconographic expression, regardless of its literal truth or falsity, is the essence of mythology. Although the miraculous plays a prominent part in the mythological dimension of religion, the supernormal is not confined to mythology, as is perhaps most readily apparent in Buddhism, which offers specific instructions for developing supernormal powers here and now.

The present authors have never encountered any phenomenon that we regard as supernormal. On the other hand, both of us have been party to serious accounts from trustworthy individuals of miraculous feats performed by spiritually developed individuals. We regard such accounts, whether verbal or scriptural, as spiritual symbolism of the desirability of the central spiritual reality of humankind. Such accounts *emphasize the personal benefits of response to an ultimate spiritual reality.* Accounts of miracles and the supernormal are *symbolic* because, in the context of religion as opposed to mere superstition, they are never ends in themselves. In the religious context, miracles and the supernormal, whether they occur or not, *point to and participate in a larger reality.*

This situation, though operative in other religions, is particularly evident in Buddhism. All forms of Buddhism prohibit or discourage exhibition of supernormal powers gained in the course of meditational practice. Such supernormal powers are regarded as signposts on the path to final enlightenment, as symptoms of spiritual progress toward the ultimate goal. To exhibit supernormal powers, it is felt, would tend to distort the true object of spiritual practice, which is realization of final enlightenment. Even the highest meditational states, the so-called *jhānas* such as the "sphere of infinite consciousness," are regarded as passing attainments, not to be cultivated for their own sakes and to be transcended as quickly as possible through continued progress toward ultimate enlightenment.

This simultaneous affirmation and negation of the value of supernormal events or experiences that may occur in the course of meditation reveals their symbolic nature. When one practices meditation for long periods of time, one may indeed experience the feeling that one has penetrated to a higher level of consciousness, or that one has become so light that one could fly through the air. Whether such experiences are valid in themselves is of no great consequence in Buddhism. On the one hand, they are affirmed in scriptures, and so if apparently supernormal experiences occur, they may be accepted as indications that one's meditational practice is progressing. On the other hand, the practitioner is urged to disregard any such supernormal experiences and to press on beyond them in meditational practice.

Thus Buddhism accepts the supernormal and the miraculous as a matter of course, and simultaneously dismisses both categories of events as potential distractions from the true goal of spiritual practice, the realization of final enlightenment and Nirvāṇa. In essence, Buddhism's spiritual symbolism of desirability seeks to take advantage of the inspirational value of the supernormal and the miraculous, and yet keep Buddhism aloof from a realm of spirituality that can degenerate into dissolute superstition and vain hocus-pocus.

The popular story of Kisāgotamī illustrates well the Buddhist attitude toward miracles and the supernormal. When Kisāgotamī's young son died, she became insane with grief and set out, carrying the dead body of the child with her, to find a medicine to revive him. Eventually, she approached the Buddha, who assured her that he could prepare such a miraculous medicine, but that it would require that she find for him one essential ingredient: a mustard seed from a family in which no loved one had ever died. In the course of her vain search for this mustard seed, she realized not only the futility of trying to bring her son back to life but also the universality of human suffering. As a result, she disposed of the dead body of her son, became a follower of the Buddha, and eventually realized supreme enlightenment. Even in such a popular story among the Buddhist masses, the issue of whether the Buddha could have performed the desired miracle remains unresolved. Even the restoration of life is merely a cheap trick in relation to the true aim of Buddhist spiritual development: the final alleviation of human suffering through the realization of enlightenment and Nirvāṇa.

Moral Symbolism of Desirability

Although Buddhists may speak of stages on the path to enlightenment, and enumerate various lists of higher and lower meditational attainments, Nirvāṇa itself is qualitatively different from any of these stages or attainments. Any meditational attainment, no matter how sublime, remains in the realm of *saṁsāra*, the impermanent realm of karma and its results. Realization of final enlightenment requires a radical break from the realm of *saṁsāra*, the treadmill of karma and rebirth. This radical break cannot be accomplished through karmic potential accrued in *saṁsāra*. Nonetheless, Nirvāṇa *defines desirable human conduct*. Without the possibility of spiritual liberation, the Buddhist vision of *saṁsāra* would be one of the most pessimistic world views ever conceived. Any ascent to rebirth in the more pleasant echelons of *samsāra*, such as a human birth or birth into one of the many heavens, will always be followed eventually by descent into the extremely unpleasant rebirths, as an animal or a denizen of one of the many hells. In any case, one will always be tormented, with only relatively brief respite, by impermanence and decay, illness, old age, and death.

One does not get any "closer" to Nirvāna by attaining a more favorable rebirth, particularly if one defines "favorable" in terms of wealth, power, and beauty. A truly favorable rebirth is one that provides a good foundation upon which to construct the diligent spiritual practice that may effect a radical break from *samsāra* and realization of final enlightenment. Truly good rebirths, then, are those that are conducive to spiritual practice that may result in the realization of enlightenment. Many apparently favorable rebirths, such as birth into a rich and powerful family, may well be highly unfavorable. Such a rebirth may result in wasting a human life in mindless dissipation and losing thereby the opportunity of another human rebirth. One could, of course, make spiritual advantages of wealth and power, but they can be the source of one's downfall. No human rebirth, then, is inherently good or bad; it depends always upon what is done with it. There is absolutely no security in *samsāra*.

Given this picture of *samsāra*, it is obvious that hope for a favorable rebirth is not sufficient motivation for moral conduct. It is true, of course, that many Buddhists are not fully impressed by Buddhism's negative attitude toward *samsāra* and are motivated by desire for a better birth. Buddhist doctrine, however, regards such motivation as foolish for two reasons. First, it is based upon a naive view of *samsāra*. *Samsāra* is unsatisfactory throughout, and cannot offer satisfaction of desire even in its most exalted realms. Second, because intentions are the essence of karma, apparently moral behavior motivated by fear of future suffering or desire for future benefit results only in minimally beneficial results. The following passage from the Theravāda scriptures illustrates the latter point.

Consider, Sāriputta, a self-seeking man, wrapt up (in the result), seeking reward, who gives a gift, thinking: "I'll enjoy this hereafter!" . . . Then consider one who gives a gift but is no self-seeker, not wrapt up in the result, seeking no reward, nor thinks to enjoy the fruit hereafter; yet gives thinking: "It's good to give!" . . . Verily, this is the reason, the cause, why one man's gift given in one way may become not great in fruit . . . (and) why given in such a way the gift may become great in fruit, great in profit.

(A 4:60–3)

The Mahāyāna philosopher Tsong-kha-pa of Tibet formalized the general Buddhist ideal of disinterest in the personal rewards of moral action in his teaching of three ascending levels of moral motivation: desire for a better rebirth, desire for spiritual liberation, and finally desire to bring about the welfare of others.⁷ This last level of motivation represents the Bodhisattva ideal of Mahāyāna Buddhism. According to this ideal, one should resolve, by taking the Bodhisattva vow, that upon realizing enlightenment one will renounce the realization of Nirvāṇa, thereby continuing to exist in *saṁsāra*, where one can work selflessly to lead other beings to Nirvāṇa. In encouraging renunciation of one's aspiration to realize Nirvāṇa, the Bodhisattva ideal in Mahāyāna Buddhism encourages Buddhists to *abandon self-interested morality* and to develop the Bodhisattva's *spontaneous regard for the welfare of others*. Mahāyānists typically criticize Theravādins for being selfish in accepting Nirvāṇa when enlightenment comes. The Mahāyāna claims, moreover, that as a result of this selfishness, the Theravāda practitioner does not realize complete enlightenment or final Nirvāṇa.

Such criticisms are unintelligible in the context of Theravāda Buddhism, which regards the realization of enlightenment and of Nirvāṇa as necessarily simultaneous and by nature complete and final. The realization of Nirvāṇa is not a matter of deliberated consent. Given the Theravāda concept of enlightenment and Nirvāṇa, the most one can do after realizing enlightenment is to teach the path to others until the end of one's final life in *saṁsāra*. Thus, Theravādins typically regard the Bodhisattva vow as laudable but unrealistic and misleading. Although Theravāda Buddhism does not encourage the Bodhisattva vow as such, it nevertheless *seeks to transform self-interested morality into spontaneous regard for the welfare of others*. The following well-known passages testify to this ideal in Theravāda Buddhism.

"As I am, so are they. As they are, so am I"; (thus) comparing others with oneself, one should neither harm nor cause harm.

(Sn 705*)

Just as a mother would protect her only child at the risk of her own life, even so one should cultivate a boundless heart toward all beings.

(Khp. 8; Sn 148*)

The primary means through which Theravāda Buddhism encourages such *spontaneous regard for the welfare of others* is a set of four meditations upon love, compassion, sympathetic joy, and equanimity. These

7 Tsong-kha-pa, *Lam-gyi rim-pa mdo tzam-du bstan-pa*, trans. as "A Brief Exposition of the Main Points of the Graded Sutra and Tantra Courses to Enlightenment," in *A Short Biography and Letter of Je Tzong-k'a-pa*, (Dharamsala, H.P., India: Translation Bureau, Library of Tibetan Works and Archives, 1975), pp. 42-3.

meditations, known as the *brahma-vihāra* meditations, encourage one to develop an equanimity of love, compassion, and sympathetic joy toward all people. That is to say, one should love all people equally, mourning with them in their sufferings and failures and rejoicing with them in their joys and achievements. These meditations proceed by attempting to extend first love, then compassion, then sympathetic joy to all people, starting with oneself. Realizing that "As I am, so are they," one accomplishes the final ideal of equanimity when one is able to extend this attitude without discrimination toward all people, first to oneself and to friends, then to casual acquaintances and finally to perceived enemies. Theravāda Buddhism thus encourages its followers to extend to others the same healthy regard one naturally has for oneself. Such cultivation of regard for others purifies one's mind of the three "roots of unwholesomeness," greed, hatred, and delusion, which Buddhism regards as the primary defilements of mind that prevent realization of enlightenment.

As we will show in the section on Buddhism's expression of the elusiveness of ultimate reality, this mental purification in itself cannot be regarded as equivalent to the realization of enlightenment or Nirvāṇa. The attitude of loving kindness toward others encouraged by the *brahma-vihāra* meditations, moreover, cannot be regarded as merely a self-interested means to gaining mental purification as an end. Instead, *replacing self-interest with spontaneous regard for the welfare of others* is an integral part of the mental purification that facilitates, but does not cause, realization of the summum bonum in Buddhism.

In both Mahāyāna and Theravāda Buddhism, moral behavior may be motivated initially by fear of karmic retribution and desire for enlightenment. However, both forms of Buddhism – Mahāyāna through the Bodhisattva vow and Theravāda through the *brahma-vihāra* meditations – *seek to integrate morality into larger, overall expressions of the meaning and purpose of human life. Both seek to minimize selfish motivations for good behavior by basing moral motivation on a free decision to attempt to realize an ultimate spiritual reality.* The *brahma-vihāra* meditations seek to minimize selfish motivation by making true regard for others an integral aspect of the mental purification that renders enlightenment possible. The Bodhisattva vow discourages self-serving morality by urging one to banish the thought of one's own realization of Nirvāṇa from one's mind. In each instance, such abandonment of self-interested morality is regarded as the only way to realize the erlightenment or Nirvāṇa.

The Bodhisattva's ambition to lead others to realization of the Nirvāṇa the Bodhisattva has rejected as an inferior goal appears self-contradictory. We will have occasion to examine further Mahāyāna Buddhism's ambivalent attitude toward the realization of Nirvāṇa, and to treat developments in the Mahāyāna notion of Nirvāṇa which make this ambivalence reasonable. For the moment, though, suffice it to say that the Bodhisattva's rejection of Nirvāṇa, like the Theravāda *brahma-vihāra* meditations, is an example of an aspect of moral symbolism of desirability, the aspect that *discourages self-interested motivation for good behavior and encourages spontaneous regard for others.*

This other-regarding nature of Buddhist morality is a fundamental aspect of Buddhism's overall expression of its ultimate referent. Nirvāṇa is the ultimately desirable, but it can be realized only through the cessation of desire. It is not to be sought ambitiously. This entails that moral conduct not be motivated either by desire for a saṁsāric reward or desire for Nirvāṇa. The essential aim of Buddhism is to eradicate desire, which is held to be the cause of all suffering. As in Hinduism, sophisticated Buddhist versions of the theory of karma picture its results as the actualization of habitual mental predilections rather than as rewards and punishments. Desire is the one mental predilection that Buddhism seeks most to eradicate. As a result, it is said that even desire for Nirvāṇa must also fade before Nirvāṇa may be realized. It is necessary from the Buddhist point of view that not only desire for a better rebirth but also desire for Nirvāṇa be deemphasized as motivations for morality. If Buddhist morality allowed itself to be based upon desire for Nirvāṇa, it would thereby encourage the innate predilection for desire, and this predilection, like other predilections, would become actualized in the future mental character of one so motivated. Paradoxically, though Nirvāṇa is ultimately desirable, ultimately it must not be desired.

Nonetheless, with regard to the aspect of moral symbolism of desirability that *defines desirable human conduct with reference to the ultimate desirability of an ultimate spiritual reality,* the concept of Nirvāṇa ultimately provides for all Buddhism the referent that orients morality and spiritual practice. Though Nirvāṇa is variously conceived in different forms of Buddhism, without some such fixed and changeless reference, even the most exalted status in *saṁsāra* could not be viewed as having true worth. Without such reference, the essential Buddhist moral norm of harming none and serving all loses its force. It is necessary that one's service to others be seen as creating in *saṁsāra* situations that conduce to liberation from *saṁsāra*. Otherwise, altruistic actions cannot be viewed as serving the true interests of either the beneficiary or the benefactor. Indeed, without reference to the changeless reality of Nirvāṇa, neither benefactor nor beneficiary could be seen as having any true interests to serve. For this reason, Mahāyāna Buddhism's deemphasis of Nirvāṇa as the goal of spiritual practice and morality does not constitute repudiation of Nirvāṇa as the ultimate criterion of desirability. Instead, Mahāyāna Buddhism reinterprets the meaning of Nirvāṇa in the course of developing Buddhism's initially sparse *mythological symbolism* of the desirability of its ultimate referent.

Mythological Symbolism of Desirability

The Theravāda scriptures place before the practitioner an idealized though not fully mythologized image of the historical Buddha, as well as a similarly idealized image of the *arhats*, the enlightened Buddhists of old. In the early stages of the development of Buddhism, such quasi-mythological expressions of the desirability of the ultimately real were no doubt sufficiently evocative for the largely monastic Buddhist community. Most of the lay and monastic followers of Buddhism in its early stages were directly involved with meditational practice and were no doubt convinced of the desirability of Buddhism's ultimate referent by the fruits of the spiritual path. In the realm of mythological expression of desirability, the small and elite Buddhist community of the early period seems to have been sufficiently inspired by the infrequent, quasi-mythological expressions of the desirability of the ultimate referent of Buddhism.

After Emperor Aśoka's conversion in the third century B.C.E., Buddhism rapidly became a mass religion and began to develop a more generally appealing mythological expression of the desirability of its ultimate referent. Although ritual had not been a part of the Buddhism taught in the Theravāda scriptures, when Buddhism became a mass religion in India, it developed an elaborate ritual and built temples in which to stage it. In Theravāda Buddhism, however, the Buddha himself is not considered an entirely appropriate object of worship. Although his image is found in every temple and in most Buddhist households, it is held to serve only as a reminder of the example set by the historical Buddha, not as an object of devotion. True, many Theravāda Buddhists do look to the Buddha more as a god than as an exemplar, but there is also widespread awareness that the Buddha, having utterly passed away never to be reborn, is an inappropriate object of worship.

For this reason, Theravāda Buddhism makes use of a number of originally Hindu deities in its devotional practices. Like their Hindu counterparts, these deities, with their widely varying characters and representations, appeal to the wide range of temperaments and immediate concerns of the masses. The Buddha himself stands serenely above this welter of deities, expressive of the remoteness and mystery of ultimate reality. Day-to-day concerns are brought before the deities much as minor concerns are brought to the attention of minor government officials. It is thought to be inappropriate to approach the Buddha with such concerns, much as it would be inappropriate to bring minor complaints before a king. An attitude of hushed and humble reverence supersedes the general clamor of temple worship when the devotee approaches the Buddha image. In most cases, in reverent silence the devotee will make an offering of incense, flowers, or an oil lamp. The devotee may chant a few memorized verses, usually from the Pāli *suttas* (sermons of the Buddha in the Theravāda canon), but ideally he or she should be primarily concerned with maintaining a pure, unselfish mind during the ceremony.

Theravāda temple Buddhism can be an appealing and evocative expression of the desirability of the ultimate referent of Buddhism, but it presents some conceptual inconsistencies. The deities worshiped are Hindu deities, and this poses problems for maintaining the identity of Buddhism in relation to Hinduism. Similarly problematic is the maintenance of the Buddha's unique status over and against Hindu deities. In general, Theravāda Buddhism maintains the attitude toward deities expressed in the Pāli scriptures. These scriptures do not deny the existence of the many deities, but they make it clear, in passages such as the following, that such deities do not represent ultimate reality or desirability. Instead, they share the status of unenlightened humans as slaves of the universal impermanence of *saṁsāra*.

Then, brethren, whatsoever *devas* [gods] there be, long-living, beautiful and blissful, long established in lofty palaces, when they hear the Norm-teaching of the Tathāgata [the Buddha], for the most part [Commentary: "except those *devas* in this world who are Āryan (Buddhist) disciples"] they become fearful, fall a-trembling and a-quaking, (and they say) "It seems, friends, that impermanent are we, and permanent we deemed ourselves. Unstable are we, it seems, and stable we deemed ourselves. Not to last, friends, it seems are we, and lasting we deemed ourselves. Verily, friends, are we impermanent, unstable, not to last, imprisoned in a person."

(S 3:85)

Although such an attitude toward the deities addressed in Theravāda temple Buddhism may serve to preserve the unique status of the Buddha, it reduces the power of such deities as mythological expressions of the desirability of Buddhism's ultimate referent. Moreover, it does not provide a foundation for appropriately Buddhist devotionalism or for specifically Buddhist mythological symbolism of the desirability of the ultimate referent of the religion. Considerations such as these help explain the development of certain characteristics of Mahāyāna Buddhism. In many ways, the development of Mahāyāna Buddhism may be seen as the development of appropriately and specifically Buddhist devotionalism that expresses mythologically the desirability of Buddhism's ultimate referent.

Mahāyāna Buddhism developed this appropriately Buddhist devotionalism around two specifically Buddhist figures, the Bodhisattva and the Buddha. In Mahāyāna Buddhism the Bodhisattva ideal is the primary expression of the general Buddhist moral principle of *regard for the welfare of others*. The Bodhisattva concept first appears, however, in the Jātaka Tales of Theravāda Buddhism, an extensive collection of fable literature concerning the previous lives of the Buddha. Theoretically, any achievement as great as that of single-handedly discovering the path to ultimate enlightenment must be founded upon numerous previous lives characterized by very good karma. The Jātaka Tales flesh out this theory by recounting stories from the Buddha's previous animal and human rebirths. As he is not properly referred to as "the Buddha" or "awakened one" before his enlightenment, he is called in these stories the Bodhisatta, Bodhisattva in Sanskrit, meaning literally "enlightenment being." Though not yet the Buddha, the Bodhisatta demonstrates already many of the qualities of a Buddha, most notably a selfless desire to serve others regardless of the consequences for himself.

Theravāda Buddhism, though regarding the Bodhisatta's motivation and actions as ideal, tends to consider these tales as fanciful, didactic children's stories. Mahāyāna Buddhism, however, turned to the concept of the Bodhisattva (using the Sanskrit term) for part of its moral and mythological expression of the desirability of its ultimate referent. If we who have little chance of attaining enlightenment in this life seek a model for our lives and our own search for enlightenment, surely no better model than the Bodhisattva can be found. The Bodhisattva was motivated exclusively by a desire to serve others, so if we are so motivated, each of us, like the Bodhisattva, will eventually become a Buddha. To be a Buddha, moreover, is better than merely to realize Nirvāna, because a Buddha guides countless other beings to enlightenment by teaching them the path. It is inconceivable, the Mahāyānists reasoned, that one who had dedicated countless lifetimes to serving others would vanish into Nirvāna soon after attaining enlightenment, just when there is greatest scope for truly serving others by continuing to teach. Thus, they reasoned, a being truly dedicated to service of others would postpone Nirvāna and continue to exist in *samsāra* to serve others. Such continuing enlightened service of others would constitute the best imaginable karma and would result in increasingly exalted rebirths, eventually to rebirth in the highest celestial realms wherein one would exert enormous compassion and power in the service of suffering beings everywhere. Such a being is an appropriate object of specifically Buddhist devotionalism. Bodhisattvas could replace the Hindu gods worshiped in early Buddhism.

Bodhisattvas are eloquently depicted in Mahāyāna scriptures as radiant beings seated upon jewel-encrusted thrones and surrounded by an entourage of celestial beings. As such they become powerful mythological expressions of the desirability of the ultimate referent of Buddhism. Like the Hindu pantheon, they appeal to a wide variety of temperaments. In addition to being objects of devotion, however, they are evocative visualizations of the outcome of one's own spiritual practice. Mahāyāna Buddhism urges its followers to begin immediately to be motivated by the same selfless desire to serve others that characterizes the Bodhisattva's motivation. Mahāyāna Buddhists usually take and repeatedly reiterate the "Bodhisattva vow," a promise to cultivate such motivation and to postpone their own realizations of Nirvāṇa until they have led countless beings to enlightenment. Thus, mythological depictions of the celestial Bodhisattvas may be seen as projections of oneself into a visualized state of perfection. Many of the visualization meditations common in Tibetan Buddhism make explicit the ultimate identity of the meditator and the visualized Bodhisattva. In this way, the original self-reliance of Buddhism is not violated by devotionalism. Ultimately these idealized mythological representations of Bodhisattvas are representations of the devotee in a perfected form. This compassion is the devotee's compassion; their help is the devotee's self-help. Devotion to them is devotion to the best in oneself. The great Tibetan teacher Tsong-kha-pa makes this point clear in a letter to one of his disciples.

You must continually keep in mind the fact that you have taken on the form of the meditational deity who represents that aspect of Full Enlightenment of Buddhahood to which you are karmically attracted. Also keep in mind that you are assuming this form in order to attain Buddhahood through it, to be able to liberate all living beings from their sufferings.[8]

Thus, the Bodhisattva concept combines mythological, spiritual, and moral symbolism in its expression of the desirability of an ultimate spiritual reality. Mythologically, it *depicts ideals evocatively,* in this case as the ideal hero. Spiritually, it *emphasizes the personal benefits of response to the ultimately real* by reminding one – through one's own personal Bodhisattva vow – that this mythological ideal is within the scope of one's own responsibility and grasp. Morally, as we have shown, it serves *to minimize selfish motivations for good behavior and to encourage spontaneous regard for the welfare of others.*

Intellectual Symbolism of Desirability

A question might be raised at this point concerning the difference between the celestial Bodhisattvas and the blissful gods. In Buddhism, both of them are thought to have attained their status through exceptionally good

8   Ibid., p. 51.

karma, and to exist within *saṃsāra*. Yet the gods' position is reckoned as insecure, not truly desirable, whereas the Bodhisattva figure apparently expressed legitimately the ultimate desirability of the ultimate referent of Buddhism. According to Buddhism, the ultimacy of the Bodhisattva's status derives from the realization of enlightenment. True, the decision to remain in *saṃsāra* must be regarded as volitional and thereby karmically efficient, and the continued compassionate service to human beings is also karmically efficient, resulting in continued celestial status. In the case of the Bodhisattva as opposed to that of the gods, the realization of enlightenment eternalizes the celestial status. The possibility of an eternalized heavenly status has the effect of diminishing the importance of Nirvāṇa as the ultimate norm of desirability in the Mahāyāna. In many ways, Dharma, rather than Nirvāṇa, becomes the ultimate referent of Mahāyāna Buddhism.

As noted in the introduction to this chapter, however, neither the Theravāda nor the Mahāyāna is without ambiguity in labeling the ultimate referent of Buddhism as either Dharma or Nirvāṇa. In the Mahāyāna, Nirvāṇa remains theoretically important as the ultimate goal of spiritual practice. Emphasis upon the Bodhisattva concept, however, has the effect of pushing Nirvāṇa into the background. Most often, the Bodhisattva vow is expressed as a promise to postpone one's Nirvāṇa until *all* sentient beings in the universe have been led to Nirvāṇa. In the context of the Buddhist world view, this has the effect of transforming Nirvāṇa into the equivalent of an infinitely distant eschaton. According to general Buddhist cosmology, whether Theravāda or Mahāyāna, there are in the universe infinite numbers of worlds inhabited by infinite numbers of beings. To lead all of them to Nirvāṇa is an infinite task. Hence, the Bodhisattva's realization of Nirvāṇa would seem to be postponed forever, to an eschaton when all beings would realize Nirvāṇa together. Theoretically, Nirvāṇa remains *ultimately* desirable. Construed as liberation for *all* beings, however, it becomes such a distant goal as to lose all urgency.

Nonetheless, the Buddha himself followed the Bodhisattva path and did realize final Nirvāṇa. He realized it, moreover, while there were still countless beings in *saṃsāra*. The Mahāyāna overcomes these and other dilemmas through a reinterpretation of what it is to be a Buddha and to realize Nirvāṇa. This reinterpretation may be seen as a substitution of the concept of Dharma, "truth," for Nirvāṇa as the central spiritual reality of Buddhism. In our terminology, *intellectual symbolism of desirability in Mahāyāna Buddhism identifies Dharma as the ultimate valuational norm, and thereby seeks to make other expressions of desirability reasonable.*

Theravāda Buddhism, of course, also views Dharma as being very much at the core of religious life. In the Theravāda, as in Buddhism as a whole, the essential meaning of Dharma is truth. It is also the term for the teaching of the Buddha, which is held to enshrine this truth. Most often, when the term is used in these senses, the two meanings are implied together. For example, an often repeated passage in the Theravāda scriptures describes Dharma as being, "eternal, verifiable, onward-leading, to be known individually by the wise" (M 1:265, etc.). Similarly, another well-known passage states that "whether or not Tathāgatas (Buddhas) arise, this world remains (the same, with) constancy of Dharma, normativeness of Dharma" (S 2:25–6*). The ring of ultimacy in such passages no doubt derives from the notion that to become a Buddha or an *arhat* (enlightened saint) by realizing Nirvāṇa also involves realizing the true nature of reality. One who reaches the ultimate goal according to Theravāda Buddhism realizes both Nirvāṇa, an eternal state beyond suffering, and Dharma, the eternal truth about the universe. Liberation as realization of Nirvāṇa and enlightenment as realization of Dharma occur together. In general, Theravāda Buddhism emphasizes realization of Nirvāṇa. This liberation is necessarily accompanied, however, by enlightenment, *bodhi*, "waking up" to the nature of reality as it is.

The Mahāyāna, on the other hand, emphasizes realization of Dharma and deemphasizes Nirvāṇa. This deemphasis is almost complete insofar as Nirvāṇa is regarded as the radical cessation of existence in *saṁsāra*. As we have noted, Nirvāṇa in this sense is removed to the infinitely distant future. It becomes an unrealizable eschaton so remote that it ceases to play any functional role in Mahāyāna Buddhism. Functionally, Dharma becomes the equivalent of Brahman in Advaita Vedānta, but *only* functionally. Intellectually, the expanded concept of Dharma addresses specifically Buddhist concerns and is worked out with purely Buddhist terms and concepts. The expanded concept of Dharma in the Mahāyāna is in no way to be imagined as a throwback to Upanishadic monism, which asserts a unitary metaphysical principle underlying and ontologically unifying discrete phenomena. The expanded Buddhist concept of Dharma, by contrast, is derived from the specifically Buddhist principle that all things are devoid of any metaphysical or ontological basis. This fundamental Buddhist principle of universal emptiness is stated concisely in Āryadeva's Four Hundred Verses.

Whoever sees (the true nature of) a single phenomenon sees (the nature of) all things. The emptiness of one is the emptiness of all.

(Catuḥśatakam, vs. 191*)

Both the Mādhyamika and Vijñānavāda forms of Mahāyāna Buddhism regard metaphysical emptiness as ultimate truth, as Dharma. Thus, given the concept expressed in the previous passage, it is possible to assert that Dharma is present in its entirety in each and every thing. All things manifest Dharma, but in a different way than all things manifest Brahman for the Vedāntin. For the Vedāntin, Brahman is the metaphysical basis of all things, whereas the Dharma present in all things is thought to be the absence of any metaphysical basis. Ultimately, Dharma is emptiness (śūn-yatā).

In its expression of the desirability of its ultimate referent, Mahāyāna Buddhism makes a further identification – in addition to the identity of emptiness and Dharma – and that is the identity of Dharma and Buddha. Mahāyāna Buddhism came to regard the essential Buddha not as a human being but as the omnipresent truth (Dharma) manifest in all things. To emphasize this distinction, Mahāyāna Buddhism refers to the Dharma-kāya or "truth body" of the Buddha as opposed to the Nirmāṇa-kāya or "physical body" of the historical Buddha. In this connection, there is a well-known story of a traveling Zen monk who stopped into a roadside temple to spend the night. Immediately upon arriving, he spat on the Buddha image on the altar. His host asked, "Why did you spit on the Buddha?" the Zen monk answered, "Kindly tell me where I could spit without spitting on the Buddha." In illustrating the concept of the om-nipresent Dharma-kāya Buddha, we will expose the bulk of Mahāyāna Buddhism's *intellectual symbolism* of the desirability of its ultimate refer-ent. To highlight the specifically and appropriately Buddhist character of this expression, it will be necessary to make occasional references to the Theravāda.

The Theravāda scriptures record the story of the monk Vakkali, who, on his deathbed, desired to glimpse the Buddha before he passed away. The Buddha – who is consistently portrayed in the Theravāda scriptures as resisting the development of a personality cult centering upon himself – consented, but regretted his disciple's behavior, saying, "Vakkali, whoever sees Dharma, sees me. Whoever sees me, sees Dharma" (S 3:120*). In the context of Theravāda Buddhism, the intent of such a statement is clearly that it is more important to one's spiritual well-being to practice the Buddha's teachings (Dharma) and thereby see truth (Dhar-ma) than it is merely to see the Buddha. When considered in conjunction with the Buddhist doctrine of the eternality of Dharma, however, such statements by the Buddha suggested to some Buddhists that the Buddha could be regarded as eternally present, even after his final passing away, which Theravāda Buddhists regard as final and utter extinction from saṁsāra. If, however, the Buddha remains present in saṁsāra, a new understanding of Nirvāṇa is required. The great Mahāyāna philosopher Nāgārjuna expressed this new understanding in his doctrine of the identi-ty of saṁsāra and Nirvāṇa.

There is no distinction of saṁsāra from Nirvana.
There is no distinction of Nirvāṇa from saṁsāra.

(Mk #25.19*)

This doctrine is a rejection of the Theravāda concept of the radical duality of "this world" (samsāra) and the "other world" (Nirvāṇa). Nirvāṇa and samsāra become two sides to the same reality, the same Dharma, a concept that allows the Mahāyāna to render its devotionalism intellectually reasonable. Everywhere one looks there is truth, Dharma. The question is whether one sees it. If one sees it, one sees Buddha. In technical terms, one sees the Dharma-kāya or "truth body" of the Buddha. By seeing the truth, one realizes enlightenment, bodhi, and thereby becomes a Buddha, "an enlightened one." In becoming an individual Buddha, one automatically shares in the Dharma-body of the universal Buddha. Thus, like the Buddha himself, anyone who has achieved enlightenment may say of oneself, "Whoever sees me sees the Dharma." One becomes an embodiment of the eternal truth that is present everywhere at all times, waiting to be seen by those who exert themselves in the spiritual path. And yet, like everything else in the universe, even prior to enlightenment, one already is such an embodiment of eternal truth, for the truth is eternally present in all things, even ignorant beings. Nothing really transpires in the realization of enlightenment. In becoming a Buddha, one merely awakens to the fact that all along one has been participating, like everything else in the universe, in the Dharma-body of the Buddha. Samsāra is Nirvāṇa, thoroughly and at all times.

When the Bodhisattvas face and perceive the happiness of the samādhi [meditative absorption] of perfect tranquillization, they are moved with the feeling of love and sympathy (for other beings) owing to their original [Bodhisattva] vows. . . . Thus, they do not enter Nirvāṇa. But the fact is that they are already in Nirvāṇa because in them there is no rising of discrimination concerning all things.

(Lk #80)

Further on in this passage the event of enlightenment is compared to a man who is dreaming that he is drowning and by his struggle to save himself wakes up. The waking state is, of course, analogous to enlightenment. From the perspective of waking, one sees clearly that there was no drowning, no water, and no struggle. Nothing really changed, except that one woke up. In the dream, these things seemed real and important, but from the perspective of waking, they are illusory. Similarly, when one realizes enlightenment, when one wakes up to Dharma, one sees simultaneously that nothing has really changed, but that what one saw previously was illusory.

It is like a man crossing a stream in a dream. For instance, Mahāmati, suppose that while sleeping a man dreams that he is in the midst of a great river which he earnestly endeavors with all his might to cross himself; but before he succeeds in crossing the stream, he is awakened from the dream, and being awakened he thinks: "Is this real or unreal?" He thinks again: "No, it is neither real nor unreal."

(Lk #80)

In this context, the historical Buddha may be regarded as something like a dream lifeguard. Actually, the historical Buddha was part of the dream of the nonenlightened state. There was no individual called the Buddha, no renunciation, no bodhi tree, no enlightenment and no passing into Nirvāṇa. There is only the eternal Dharma, which may be viewed in the deluded state as saṁsāra or in the enlightened state as Nirvāṇa.

From the point of view of the deluded state, the Bodhisattva's rejection of Nirvāṇa, considered alongside the Buddha's realization of Nirvāṇa, may appear problematic. From the point of view of enlightenment, however, there are no such problems. In appearing to reject Nirvāṇa and remain in saṁsāra for the sake of others, the Bodhisattva is in reality only an awakened being who reaches over to shake into wakefulness other beings who remain asleep. When one shakes and calls out to one who is sleeping, these actions may initially be manifest to the sleeper in terms of his or her dream. In this dream, one may perceive oneself being buffeted about by waves and hearing one's name called by a potential rescuer on the same ocean. One wakes, only to find oneself being shaken and called by a friend standing by the bed. Similarly, one might perceive the Buddha's realization of Nirvāṇa as a vanishing from saṁsāra, or the Bodhisattva's rejection of Nirvāṇa as a remaining in saṁsāra. In reality, though, the Bodhisattva remains in saṁsāra only in the sense that one's awakened friend remains in one's dream by shaking one and calling out one's name. One imagines in the dream that there is a rescuer on the ocean calling one, just as one imagines that there are Bodhisattvas remaining in saṁsāra to save one. Actually, there is only the eternal Dharma-kāya, which, as it were, shakes its sleeping constituency and calls to them to wake up.

Similarly, the Buddha's apparent vanishing from saṁsāra is also only an appearance. It is only another illusory manifestation of the Dharma-kāya in a form to which deluded beings can relate.

The Tathāgata who so long ago was perfectly enlightened is unlimited in the duration of his life; he is everlasting. Without being extinct, the Tathāgata makes a show of extinction, on behalf of those who have to be educated.

(Sp #15)

Both the Buddha's apparent vanishing and the Bodhisattva's apparent remaining in saṁsāra are instances of the important Buddhist concept of upāya or "skill in means." The great compassion of the Buddhas and Bodhisattvas would be useless in leading others to enlightenment if it were not for the skillful means they employ to entice and cajole even the most deeply deluded beings out of their slumber. The concept of *upāya* appears in germinal form in the Theravāda scriptures, where the Buddha declares that no doctrine, including his own, is ultimately valid (M 1:134–5 etc.). All doctrines merely approach the truth more or less effectively. In some cases, it may be necessary to employ an inferior teaching in order to reach an inferior audience, and in all cases, one must express oneself in terms comprehensible to one's audience. This notion may be seen as in essence recognizing the need for effective expression of the desirability of a religious ultimate. In Mahāyāna Buddhism the concept of *upāya* was expanded into a theory of the nature of the interaction of the Dharma-body of the Buddha with the illusion of *saṁsāra*. As such, it allows for a large variety of appeals to people of varying backgrounds and abilities for recognition of the desirability of a spiritual orientation in life. These appeals, of course, may be mythological, spiritual, or moral in addition to intellectual, but the doctrine of *upāya* itself is an intellectual expression of the desirability of the ultimate referent of Buddhism that integrates and *renders reasonable all other such expressions.*

Buddhism made extensive use of this strategy as it moved beyond India to spread across the whole of the Eastern world, thus becoming one of the most successful missionary religions in history. Everywhere it spread, Buddhism adapted itself to the existing culture and religion it found there. Chinese, Japanese, and Tibetan deities became Buddhas and Bodhisattvas, all construed as expressive of the compassionate workings of the Dharma-kāya Buddha. From a Buddhist point of view, the entire history of Buddhism may be regarded as the elaboration of *upāya*, as the unfolding of the vast variety of compassionate skillful means necessary to urge different types of people toward liberation and enlightenment.

The Buddhist notion of *upāya* is thus functionally similar to the notion of the *ishṭa-devatā* in Hinduism. It allows for a widely appealing presentation of the desirability of an ultimate spiritual reality. Similarly, Dharma plays the same functional role as Brahman in Hinduism. In Hinduism the various deities all focus upon and express Brahman, the ultimate reality beyond expression. So too, for Buddhism, all the Bodhisattvas and Buddhas, gods and doctrines are *upāyas*, skillful means of pointing to the Dharma beyond expression or comprehension.

In some worlds, the Bodhisattva Mahāsattva Avalokiteśvara assumes the form of a Buddha to teach the Dharma to beings. In other worlds, he teaches in the form of a Bodhisattva. For some beings he teaches in the form of a Pratyekabuddha; for others he appears in the form of an ordinary disciple, or in the form of Brahma or Cakra or a minor deity. For those who are to be converted by a demon, he teaches in the form of a demon, or in the form of Iśvara or Maheśvara or a great king, or a goblin, or some other deity. Thus is the Bodhisattva Mahāsattva Avalokiteśvara endowed with incalculable qualities.

(Sp #24)

Elusiveness

The perceptive reader will have sensed that the foregoing discussion of Buddhism's expression of the central spiritual reality of humankind demands resolution in a treatment of the elusiveness of the ultimate referent of Buddhism. Every Buddhist expression of the ultimately real is accompanied by a disclaimer. The apparently resulting indecisiveness of Buddhism is in fact a consistent recognition of the *freedom and responsibility* that the spiritual dimension of human life entails. More than any of the religions we have examined, Buddhism emphasizes this freedom and responsibility in its expression of the elusiveness of the ultimately real.

Intellectual Symbolism of Elusiveness

In Theravāda Buddhism, intellectual symbolism of the elusiveness of ultimate reality is elegantly straightforward. We have already noted that according to the "creed" of Buddhism:

The things which arise from a cause,
Of these things the Tathāgata (Buddha) has stated the cause.
And of these (things) there is the cessation.

(V 1:40)

Anything that arises as a result of a cause is destined to pass away. Nirvāṇa is eternal; it does not pass away. Hence Nirvāṇa cannot have a cause. One may work diligently to bring about the cessation of ignorance and desire, but one may not bring about the realization of Nirvāṇa. This final realization is quintessentially elusive. The conditions for the realization of Nirvāṇa may be fulfilled, but the event itself cannot be caused. For this reason, Buddhists generally prefer to speak of "realization" of Nirvāṇa rather than "attainment" of Nirvāṇa. The texts themselves speak of the *sacci-karaṇa*, the "making real" of Nirvāṇa. That Nirvāṇa cannot be caused is not merely a matter of philosophical consistency, for one of the subtlest desires is said to be the desire for enlightenment. Even this subtle desire must be abandoned. As a well-known Buddhist maxim states, "Enlightenment ambitiously sought will never be gained."

Theravāda Buddhism employs both intellectual and spiritual expressions of the elusiveness of its ultimate referent to urge its followers to abandon the futile ambition to *attain* Nirvāṇa. Instead one should concentrate humbly upon self-improvement and let the *realization* of enlightenment come in due course. In the Theravāda, as well as Buddhism in general, recognition of the elusiveness of the ultimately real is a spiritual necessity as well as a philosophical necessity. Beyond the Theravāda, however, Buddhism's intellectual expression of this elusiveness becomes considerably more complex. Examination of this expression brings us to the heart of some of the most abstruse aspects of Mahāyāna thought.

We have shown that, for the Mahāyāna, insofar as the truth is everywhere, Buddha is everywhere. In this sense, everything in the universe is Buddha. To those unfamiliar with Buddhism, such statements sound equivalent to the Hindu assertion that all is Brahman. Indeed, the two respective identifications – all is Buddha and all is Brahman – play analogous roles in Buddhist and Hindu mythological expressions of the desirability of their respective ultimate referents. The philosophical presuppositions and reasonings behind the Buddhist identification of all things with the Buddha, however, are specifically Buddhist and render Buddhist "monism" radically different from Hindu monism. Buddhism's intellectual expression of the elusiveness of the ultimately real comes to the fore when one considers the philosophical underpinnings of the Mahāyāna mythological identification of ultimate truth with the Buddha.

One of the most prominent characteristics distinguishing early Buddhism from similar currents in orthodox Hinduism is the Buddhist refusal to posit an ontological ground of being. This metaphysical skepticism has remained operative in most if not all subsequent forms of Buddhism. When the concept of a universal Buddha emerged in the course of the development of Buddhist devotionalism, the Buddhist intellectual expression of this universal retained the metaphysical skepticism of early Buddhism. In monistic Hinduism, the statement "all is Brahman" implies the intermediate statement "all is one." In other words, "all is one in Brahman." Mahāyāna Buddhism's declaration that "all is Buddha" implies neither the unity of all things nor their ontological grounding in a metaphysical absolute. The statement "all is Buddha" indicates instead that ultimate truth, the Buddha, resides in its entirety in each *individual* thing. Elucidation of this situation requires that we examine two related but divergent streams of Buddhist thought: that which culminates in Mādhyamika Buddhism and that which culminates in Vijñānavāda Buddhism. The headwaters of each of these streams are found in the Theravāda scriptures.

The philosophical basis of Mādhyamika Buddhism is the doctrine of *śunyatā,* "emptiness." According to this doctrine, the ultimate truth about all things and each individual thing is that they are ultimately empty of any self-existence (*svabhava*). The Mādhyamika holds that careful analysis of any phenomenon, whether objective or subjective, will reveal its metaphysical emptiness, its lack of grounding in anything permanent. In the Mādhyamika branch of the Mahāyāna, the Buddha as ultimate truth represents precisely this emptiness, this lack of any metaphysical basis. All things are the Buddha in the sense that each and every thing is utterly empty of self-existence, utterly devoid of metaphysical basis. Having located the Buddha in all things, as part of its mythological and intellectual expression of the desirability of its ultimate referent, Mādhyamika Buddhism employs the same concept as an expression of the elusiveness of this ultimate referent. It does this by declaring that the omnipresent Buddha represents universal emptiness. The Buddha – the truth that we seek – is everywhere; yet when found it is not found, for there is nothing to find. To seek and to find nothing is to find the true Buddha.

15. Those who describe in detail the Buddha, who is unchanging and beyond all detailed description – those, completely defeated by description, do not perceive the Tathāgata [the Buddha].
16. The self-existence of the Tathāgata is the self-existence of the world. The Tathāgata is without self-existence (and) the world is without self-existence.
(Mk #22.15–6)

According to our definition, *intellectual symbolism attempts to make the elusiveness of ultimate reality reasonable*. To render reasonable the doctrine of the emptiness of all phenomena, Mādhyamika Buddhism resorts to two lines of argument, the Svātāntrika and the Prāsaṅgika, both of which may be discerned in an incipient form in the Theravāda scriptures.

The Svātāntrika school expanded upon the doctrine of impermanence, which in the Theravāda scriptures is of central importance as the philosophical basis of the first noble truth, universal unsatisfactoriness. In the Theravāda scriptures, the argument for the impermanence of all phenomena rests on the argument that all things are results of causes and conditions that are themselves caused and conditioned. Anything that arises dependent upon causes and conditions lacks its own essence and must necessarily pass away when the conditions of its existence are no longer fulfilled. Eventually, deficiency of necessary conditions is inevitable. Everything we can observe is in a constant state of change and motion, and therefore all things are impermanent, including ourselves. The Svātāntrika school expands upon this basic notion of essencelessness and impermanence to establish the Mādhyamika doctrine of metaphysical emptiness. In terms of the example of the chair cited previously, whereas the Theravāda merely wanted to establish the impermanence of component things, the Svātāntrika wanted to establish the nonexistence of component things, in this case a chair. The Svātāntrika argument becomes, in effect, a philosophical justification of the basic concept of Mahāyāna devotionalism, for the emptiness of all things is itself ultimate truth (Dharma), is itself the ultimate, Dharma-kāya Buddha.

The Prāsaṅgika school was not satisfied with this positive demonstration of universal emptiness. The source of its dissatisfaction resides in an urge to express what we call the elusiveness of the central spiritual reality of humankind. Emptiness, the Prāsaṅgikas hold, cannot be comprehended or expressed through a mere philosophical theory. Instead, emptiness represents the failure of all theories to capture truth. True, all phenomena are empty of self-existence, but the causal mechanism whereby the Svātāntrika school seeks to establish this emptiness is itself merely an empty figment of the imagination. To prove their point, the Prāsaṅgikas offer a detailed refutation of the concept of causation, which seeks to show that it is impossible to maintain that things are caused by themselves, caused by another, caused by both or by neither.

The Prāsaṅgikas approached the doctrine of emptiness through another prominent stream of Buddhist thought, one that emphasizes the inexpressibility of ultimate truth. Again, the headwaters of this stream of thought are apparent in the Theravāda scriptures. At several points these early scriptures refer to the Buddha's refusal to answer certain questions. When confronted with these questions – essentially, "Is the universe finite or infinite? Does it have an origin or is it beginningless? And does one who has realized Nirvāṇa exist or not exist after death?" – The Buddha is said to have remained silent, refusing to affirm any of the alternatives (S 4:400–402). Elsewhere, the Buddha explained this silence as follows:

[To affirm any of these alternatives] is going to a (speculative) view, the scuffling of views, the fetter of views; it is accompanied by anguish, distress, misery, fever; it does not conduce to turning away from, nor to dispassion, stopping, calming, superknowledge, awakening, nor to *nibbāna* [Nirvāṇa]. I, Vacca, beholding this is a peril, thus do not approach any of these (speculative) views. . . . Vacca, going to "speculative view" – this has been got rid of by the Tathāgata.

(M 1:486)

The silence of the Buddha on such occasions became a recurrent theme in Mahāyāna Buddhism. Symbolizing the inexpressibility of emptiness, the Buddha's "noble silence" became a fundamental Buddhist expression of the elusiveness of the ultimately real. Many Mahāyānists, in fact, consider this silence to be the Buddha's most important statement. They regard his verbal teachings as *upāyas*, skillful teaching methods tailored to the varying abilities of his audience, employed provisionally to lead them to the point where they can understand the Buddha's ultimate silence.

It is said by the Blessed One that from the night of the Enlightenment till the night of the Parinirvāṇa [the passing away of the Buddha] the Tathāgata in the meantime has not uttered even a word, nor will he ever utter; for not speaking is the Buddha's speaking.

(Lk #61)

In expressing emptiness, the Prāsaṅgika school in particular focused single-mindedly upon the provisional nature of all truths in an attempt to convey the inexpressibility of ultimate truth. In so doing, it emphasizes the elusiveness of the ultimate referent of Buddhism. It must be remembered, though, that the Prāsaṅgika dialectic is not philosophical skepticism for its own sake. Instead, it is an integral part of Buddhism's overall expression of its ultimate referent. Emphasizing the elusiveness of Buddhism's ultimate referent through its dialectic, the Prāsaṅgika school simultaneously buttresses Buddhism's mythological expression of the desirability of this referent by illustrating the all-inclusive domain of emptiness, the ultimate nature of the Buddha. The Prāsaṅgika notion of emptiness also strengthens Buddhism's expression of the undeniability of the ultimately real by illustrating that not only all objects, but also all ideas collapse under analysis and give way to an inexpressible reality standing silently behind them in every case. One may truly see in all things the serene, silent Buddha described in the Vimalakīrti Sūtra:

The Tathāgata is neither generosity nor avarice, neither morality nor immorality, neither tolerance nor malice, neither effort nor sloth, neither concentration nor distraction, neither wisdom nor foolishness. He is inexpressible. He is neither truth nor falsehood; neither escape from the world not failure to escape from the world; neither cause of involvement in the world nor not a cause of involvement in the world; he is the cessation of all theory and all practice. He is neither a field of merit nor not a field of merit; he is neither worthy of offerings nor unworthy of offerings. He is not an object, and cannot be contacted. He is not a whole, not a conglomeration. He surpasses all calculations. He is utterly unequaled, yet equal to the ultimate reality of things. He is matchless, especially in effort. He surpasses all measure. He does not go, does not stay, does not pass beyond. He is neither seen, heard, distinguished, nor known. He is without any complexity, having attained the equanimity of omniscient gnosis. Equal toward all things, he does not discriminate between them. He is without reproach, without excess, without corruption, without conception, and without intellectualization. He is without activity, without birth, without occurrence, without origin, without production, and without nonproduction. He is without fear and without subconsciousness, without sorrow, without joy, and without strain. No verbal teaching can express him. "Such is the body of the Tathāgata and thus should he be seen. Who sees thus, truly sees. Who sees otherwise, sees falsely."[9]

The second major branch of Mahāyāna Buddhism, the Vijñānavāda or "consciousness school," builds upon early Buddhism's analysis of consciousness to give intellectual expression to the doctrine that all reality, whether subjective or objective, is consciousness only. For the Vijñānavāda, as for the Mādhyamika, ultimate truth, Buddha, may be characterized as emptiness. Rather than the analytical philosophical approach of the Mādhyamika, however, the Vijñānavāda employed an analysis of the relationship between consciousness and its objects to establish the emptiness of all things.

We have noted already the Theravāda doctrine that consciousness and its objects are mutually interdependent. The Vijñānavāda expanded upon this perceptual theory and concluded that all reality is known only as mental images. Indeed, there may be an independently existing external world, but we have no hope of discovering its existence or anything at all about its nature. All we can know about reality is confined to the content of a stream of mental images which is unique in each individual mind. We experience this internal stream of images as an enormous external universe in which we live and move as subjects. In most cases we uncritically assume that there really is such a universe and that it is the same for others. The purpose of meditation is to focus the mind upon the actual basis of experience, the actual mental images in one's own mind.

When this is accomplished, the Vijñānavāda maintains, one sees that both the objective universe and the subjective mind originate from the imaginary bifurcation of a simple stream of mental images. These mental images, in themselves, are neither subjective nor objective, neither substantial nor nonsubstantial, neither material nor immaterial, neither conscious nor nonconscious. This stream of images is held to constitute reality itself, but as such it cannot be perceived, for to perceive it is to persist in the imaginary bifurcation of the nondual stream of images. As the great Vijñānavāda philosopher Vasubandhu wrote:

27. As long as he places something before him(self), taking it as an (objective) basis, saying: "This itself is the mental image only," so long he does not abide in that (mental image) alone.
28. But when cognition no longer apprehends an object, then it stands firmly in consciousness only, because where there is nothing to grasp there is no more grasping.

(Trimsikā, vs. 27–8)

9 *Vimalakīrtinirdeśa Sūtra*, trans. Robert Thurman, as *The Holy Teaching of Vimalakīrti* (University Park: Pennsylvania State University Press, 1976), p. 92.

The commentary by Sthiramati upon this letter verse reads:

Where there is an object there is a subject, but not where there is no object. The absence of an object results in the absence also of a subject. . . . It is thus that there arises the cognition which is homogeneous, without object, indiscriminate and supramundane. The tendencies to treat object and subject as distinct and real entities are forsaken, and thought is established in just the true nature of one's own thought.

Vasubandhu's famous treatise ends with two verses that extol meditative absorption in consciousness-only as the supreme reality, Dharma-kāya Buddha.

29. It is without thought, without bias, and is the supramundane cognition. . . .
30. This is the element without defilements, inconceivable, wholesome and stable, the blissful body of liberation, the Dharma-body of the great sage.
(Trimsikā, vs. 29–30)[10]

Thus, the Vijñānavāda, like the Mādhyamika, seeks to render the doctrine of the omnipresent Buddha intellectually reasonable and at the same time to express the elusiveness of the ultimate reality thus established. Like the Mādhyamika again, the Vijñānavāda avoids asserting the metaphysical unity of the universe. For the stream of mental images referred to is held to be unique and independent in each individual being. The character of empirical reality is uniformly the same, it is a mere stream of mental images, but ultimate reality does not consist of the ontological unification of discrete entities in an overarching metaphysical absolute.

Each of the three major branches of extant Buddhism, in its own characteristic way, *attempts to make the elusiveness of ultimate reality reasonable*. According to the Theravāda, Nirvāṇa cannot be the result of a cause or causes, for if it were, it would be like all other effects, impermanent by virtue of its dependence upon causes. According to the Mādhyamika, even to seek ultimate reality is to make emptiness into an object and thereby to miss the mark entirely. As Nāgārjuna said:

Emptiness, having been dimly perceived, utterly destroys the slow witted. It is like a snake wrongly grasped or (magical) knowledge incorrectly applied.
(Mk #24.11)

The Vijñānavāda, much like the Advaita Vedānta school of Hinduism, shifts the focus of intellectual symbolism of elusiveness from the futility

10   Translation throughout follows Edward Conze, ed., *Buddhist Texts through the Ages* (Oxford: Bruno Cassirer, 1954; reprint, New York: Harper & Row, 1964), pp. 210–11.

of the action of seeking to the impossibility of finding the ultimately real while remaining in any meaningful sense a subject. The Advaita scheme depicts the successful seeker of truth as being absorbed into the discovery, whereas the Vijñānavāda scheme pictures the seeker as necessarily nullifying his or her subjective status in the course of realization of ultimate reality.

Given the emphasis in each of the major branches of Buddhism upon self-conscious intellectual expression of the elusiveness of the ultimately real, there is in Buddhism a universal suspicion of both the validity of doctrine and the effectiveness of spiritual practices as such. All doctrines are inadequate, and all practices are provisional. All forms of Buddhism applaud the following advice, from the Laṅkāvatara Sūtra, not to look at the finger when someone points at the moon.

Let son or daughter of a good family take good heed not to get attached to words as being in perfect conformity with meaning, because the truth is not the letter. Be not like the one who looks at the finger-tip. For instance, Mahāmati, when a man with his finger-tip may be taken wrongly for the thing pointed at; in like manner, Mahāmati, the people belonging to the class of the ignorant and simple-minded, like those of the childish group, are unable even unto their death to abandon the idea that in the finger-tip of words there is the meaning itself, and will not grasp ultimate reality because of their intent clinging to words.

(Lk #76)

The Theravāda parable of the raft expresses this same suspicion of doctrines and spiritual practices by pointing out the absurdity of using a raft to cross a river and then, out of attachment, carrying it around on one's back.

Similarly, monks, the Dhamma [Dharma] I teach is like a raft, for crossing over, not for burdening. You, monks, who understand that the Dhamma is like a raft, should give up even good things, all the more bad things.

(M 1:135*)

Spiritual Symbolism of Elusiveness

Statements such as the preceding passage merge intellectual symbolism into spiritual symbolism of the elusiveness of the ultimate referent of Buddhism. They point to a radical discontinuity between the spiritual practices that lead to enlightenment and enlightenment itself, whether this enlightenment be conceived as realization of Nirvāṇa or as realization of Dharma. If, as Buddhist intellectual symbolism declares, Nirvāṇa cannot be caused and emptiness cannot be grasped, the actual role that the spiritual practices of Buddhism play in the realization of enlightenment is ambiguous. This led to tension in Buddhism between the so-called sudden and gradual theories of enlightenment. Though different forms of Buddhism are associated with one theory or the other, it is misleading to speak of sudden and gradual schools of Buddhism, because this tension crosses sectarian boundaries.

In general, Theravāda Buddhism emphasizes a gradual, cumulative path to enlightenment. It denies emphatically, however, that the realization of Nirvāṇa can be regarded as the result of an accumulation of merit, wisdom, and meditational proficiency. The Theragāthā and Therīgāthā, Poems of the Monks and Poems of the Nuns, contain many accounts of a spontaneous, unexpected realization of enlightenment, inexplicably brought about by some apparently trivial event.

113. Why do I, possessed of virtuous conduct, complying with the teaching of the teacher, not obtain quenching? (I am) not slack, nor puffed-up. . . .

115. Then taking a lamp I entered my cell. Having inspected the bed, I sat on the couch.

116. Then taking a needle, I drew out the wick. The complete release of my mind was like the quenching of the lamp.

(Therīgāthā #113–16)[11]

Whether enlightenment is realized gradually or suddenly or both or neither is not our concern here. The point is that records of such events in the scriptural tradition of Buddhism are examples of spiritual symbolism of the elusiveness of the ultimately real. Such accounts point to a *missing link in Buddhism's scheme of salvation*, and yet they *encourage sustained discipline despite the elusiveness of the ultimately real*. They indicate that though one may not see light at the end of the tunnel, it may appear suddenly and unexpectedly just around the next bend. They remind one that others too have held firm in their spiritual convictions and practices without knowing precisely how or when they would come to fruition, or indeed what would be the nature of that fruition. The Zen monk Chōkei is said to have uttered the following ecstatic verse when he unexpectedly realized enlightenment while rolling up a window shade.

How deluded I was! How deluded indeed! Lift up the screen and come see the world! "What religion believest thou?" you ask. I raise my *hossu* (scepter) and hit your mouth.[12]

11 *Therīgāthā*, trans. K. R. Norman as *The Elders Verses* II, (London: Pali Text Society, 1971), See also verses 48–50, 77–81, 213–23, and *Theragāthā*, verses 13, 49–54, 267–70, 271–4, 299–302, 312–19, 325–9, 405–10, 459–65.
12 D. T. Suzuki, *Essays in Zen Buddhism*, series I, (1949; London: Rider, 1949; 1973), p. 249.

Similarly, the utterly ordinary event recorded in the following haiku is said to have triggered the enlightenment of the great Zen poet Basho.

'Tis an ancient pond,
A frog leaps in –
Oh, the sound of water![13]

Such passages are symptomatic of a general emphasis in Mahāyāna Buddhism upon sudden enlightenment. Buddhism's most widely familiar spiritual expressions of the elusiveness of the ultimately real are without doubt Zen Buddhism's *kōans*, insoluble riddles such as "What is the sound of one hand clapping?" and *mondos*, apparently nonsensical exchanges between master and student such as the following.

When at Demboin, Baso used to sit cross-legged all day and meditating. His master Nangaku Yejo, saw him and asked:
"What seekest thou here thus sitting cross-legged?"
"My desire is to become a Buddha."
Thereupon the master took up a piece of brick and began to polish it hard on a stone near by.
"What workest thou on so, my master?" asked Baso.
"I am trying to turn this into a mirror."
"No amount of polishing will make a mirror of the brick, sir."
"If so, no amount of sitting cross-legged as thou doest will make of thee a Buddha," said the master.
"What shall I have to do then?"
"It is like driving a cart; when it moveth not, wilt thou whip the cart or the ox?"
Baso made no answer.
The master continued: "Wilt thou practice this sitting cross-legged in order to attain *dhyāna* [absorption] or to attain Buddhahood? If it is *dhyāna*, *dhyāna* does not consist in sitting or lying; if it is Buddhahood, the Buddha has no fixed forms. As he has no abiding place anywhere, no one can take hold of him, nor can he be let go. If thou seekest Buddhahood by thus sitting cross-legged, thou murderest him. So long as thou freest thyself not from sitting so, thou never comest to the truth."[14]

Many *mondos* are not this explicit, but one clear intent, even of *mondos* as obscure as the following, is that neither erudition nor even spiritual practices are sufficient to bring about enlightenment.

13 Ibid., series II (1953; London: Rider, 1972), p. 235.
14 Ibid., series I, p. 236.

A monk asked, "All things are said to be reducible to the One, but where is the One to be reduced?" Chao-chou answered, "When I was in the district of Ch'ing, I had a robe made that weighed seven *chin*."[15]

Zen monks meditate upon these *kōans* and *mondos* for months, even years, seeking *satori* (enlightenment) in their solutions. Obviously, the "solutions" sought are not intellectual comprehensions. They are spiritual insights into the ineffable nature of reality in general. *Kōan* practice seeks to empty the mind of preconceptions and thereby open it to a spontaneous realization of enlightenment. These *mondos* and *kōans* may be regarded as spiritual symbolism of the elusiveness of the ultimately real. Their paradoxical nature calls attention to the *missing link* in even the apparently self-reliant spiritual practice of Zen Buddhism.

Despite Mahāyāna Buddhism's emphasis on sudden enlightenment, and consequent deemphasis of the gradual path to enlightenment, it is tacitly understood that though enlightenment does not come about because of spiritual practices, it does not come about without them either. It must be remembered that the previous passages representing Zen Buddhism occur in the context of a strict, lifelong regimen of constant meditation and self-discipline. The following account of the enlightenment of the Buddhist saint Asaṅga, from Tāranātha's *History of Buddhism in India*, illustrates the necessity of long years of spiritual practice to set the stage for the unexpected instant of enlightenment. In this passage, enlightenment is depicted mythologically as a vision of the Buddha Maitreya.

In a cave of the Gur-pa-parvata, which is mentioned in the scriptures as the Kukkuṭapāda-parvata, he spent three years propitiating Ārya Maitreya. But he felt disheartened by the absence of any sign (of success) and came out (of the cave). He noticed that in the course of a long time the stones (of a narrow crevice) were worn out by birds' wings, though these wings touched the stones only when in the morning the birds, which had their nests on the rocks, went out in search of food and once when in the evening they returned to their nests. "So, I have lost assiduity" – thinking thus, he continued the propitiation for three more years.

Similarly, he came out again. Noticing the stones eroded by drops of water, he propitiated for another three years and again came out. This time, he saw an old man rubbing a piece of iron with soft cotton and saying, "I am going to prepare fine needles out of this. I have already prepared so many needles by rubbing iron with cotton." And he showed a box full of needles.

So he propitiated for three more years. In this way twelve years passed by; but he saw no sign of success. Disappointed, he came out and went away.

In a city he came across a bitch, infested with worms on the lower half of her body, furiously scratching her wound. The sight made him full of compassion.

15 Ibid., series II, p. 94.

He thought: "If these worms are not removed, the bitch is going to die. But if removed, the worms are going to die. So I am going to place the worms on a piece of flesh cut from my own body."

He brought a shaving razor from the city called Acintya [Inconceivable], placed his begging bowl and staff on a sitting mat, slashed the thigh of his own body and, with his eyes shut, stretched his hands to catch the worms. Failing to reach the worms, he opened his eyes and saw there neither the worms nor the bitch. He saw instead *bhaṭṭāraka* Maitreya with the halo of *lakṣaṇas* and *vyañjanas* [auspicious marks and manifestations]. To him he said with tears flowing from his eyes:

"Oh my father, my unique refuge,
I have exerted myself in a hundred different ways,
But nevertheless no result was to be seen.
Wherefore have the rain-clouds and the might of the ocean,
Come only now, when, tormented by violent pain
I am no longer thirsting?"

(Maitreya) answered,

"Though the king of the gods sends down rain,
A bad seed is unable to grow
Though the Buddhas may appear (in this world)
He who is unworthy cannot partake of the bliss."

"I have been throughout present near you," (continued Maitreya) "but remaining under obscurations as you did by your own *karma*, you failed to see me. The obscuration of your sin is now removed by the accumulated power of your previous repetition of the charm [mantra] along with your present great compassion as expressed in the rigorous form of cutting off the flesh of your own body. That is why you can now see me. Now, take me up on your shoulder and carry me to the city to show me to the people there."

When he was being thus shown, others saw nothing. Only a woman wine-seller saw him carry a pup. As a result, she later became enormously rich. A poor porter saw only the toes. As a result, he reached the stage of *samādhi* [meditational absorption] and attained *sādhāraṇa-siddhi* [supernormal powers].[16]

Passages such as the foregoing illustrate the convergence of meditational and devotional Buddhism in symbolizing spiritually the elusiveness of ultimate reality. Like the Dharma that the meditator seeks to realize, Maitreya Buddha is said to have been constantly with Asaṅga. Again, like the meditator, Asaṅga was unable to realize the object of his spiritual practice only because of a subtle blockage in his own perception. To remove this blockage, the Zen practitioner ardently contemplates an insoluble *kōan*, which is thought to empty the mind of the preconceptions that prevent one seeing reality as it is. Similarly, Asaṅga is said to have resorted to repetition of a mantra, a short formular prayer, to open his

16 Tāranātha, *Rgya-gar chos-'byung*, trans. Lama Chimpa and Alaka Chattopadhyaya as *History of Buddhism in India* (Simla, H.P., India: Indian Institute of Advanced Study, 1970), pp 156–8.

mind to enlightenment. That devotional practice in Buddhism is not mere mechanical repetition of formulas is emphasized by exaggerating the compassion that must develop in the course of one's spiritual training. The saint Asaṅga is depicted as having been so thoroughly compassionate that he would slice flesh off his own body to avoid harming even a maggot.

Few could even imagine themselves spending twelve years alone in a cave, much less cutting the flesh from their bodies to feed maggots. Nor, we suggest, do passages such as the foregoing really intend to bring about such exaggerated forms of self-sacrifice in their readers. Instead, by positing an ideal, they point out the inadequacy of our own efforts and successes at developing and perfecting our best qualities. For some, this in itself *encourages sustained discipline despite the elusiveness of the ultimately real.* It is not surprising, however, that others find such ideals daunting rather than inspiring. For these, the focus of devotional Buddhism's expression of the elusiveness of ultimate reality is shifted from deities as meditational devices to deities as saviors. Thus, devotional Hinduism's monkey-hold and cat-hold theories of salvation are paralleled in Buddhism by the "self-power" and "other-power" theories of salvation.

The other-power theory of salvation is most prominent in Pure Land Buddhism, which, instead of enlightenment, promises its followers rebirth in the Pure Land paradise of Amida (or Amitābha) Buddha. The other-power that is thought to bring about one's salvation is the Bodhisattva vow of Amida to lead all beings to salvation. According to Pure Land Buddhism, absolute reliance upon the saving power of Amida's vow is the only means of salvation, which eludes human effort altogether. Access to this saving power is thought to be gained through constant verbal and mental repetition of the *nembutsu,* the formular prayer or mantra, "Homage to Amida Buddha." Though the other-power orientation of Pure Land Buddhism differentiates it radically from self-reliant Zen Buddhism, in some ways the repetition of and concentration upon the *nembutsu* is analogous to the *kōan* practice of Zen. Those Zen Buddhists who are sympathetic toward Pure Land Buddhism typically regard the *nembutsu* as a sort of *kōan,* a mental discipline that empties the mind of preconceptions and allows the spontaneous realization of enlightenment. Pure Land Buddhists insist, however, that their discipline in practicing the *nembutsu* is none of their own doing. Instead, as is illustrated by the following touching passage dictated by an aged, illiterate woman to her son, such apparent discipline is the work of the other-power of Amida Buddha.

It was because of my blindness and powerlessness that the Dawn came upon me through the power of Oya [Amida]. How grateful I am now! *Namu-amida-butsu!* [Homage to Amida Buddha!] I was utterly blind, and I did not know it. How shameful to have thought I was all right! The *Nembutsu* I uttered, I thought, was my own. But it was not; it was Amida's call. How grateful indeed I am! *Namu-amida-butsu!*[17]

Regardless of whether the *nembutsu* works on the basis of self-power or other-power – indeed, regardless of whether it is effective at all in bringing about either enlightenment or salvation – it is an example of spiritual symbolism of the elusiveness of the central spiritual reality of humankind. On the one hand, the reliance of *nembutsu* practice on other-power highlights the *missing link* in Pure Land Buddhism's scheme of salvation. On the other hand, the same practice *encourages sustained discipline despite this missing link.*

Moral Symbolism of Elusiveness

Reliance upon other-power in Pure Land Buddhism is also a notable example of moral symbolism of the elusiveness of the central spiritual reality of humankind. All forms of Buddhism, like Hinduism, *admit that good behavior, good karma, in itself is insufficient for personal perfection.* All forms of Buddhism recognize in the moral component of their respective schemes of salvation the same *missing link,* which also characterizes spiritual symbolism of the elusiveness of the ultimately real. In Pure Land Buddhism, this *missing link* becomes a chasm symbolizing and emphasizing the inadequacy of human effort to realize or even approach ultimate reality. Even the saint Shinran, founder of a major branch of Pure Land Buddhism, was moved to make the following declaration of his utter intellectual, spiritual, and moral inability to bring about his own salvation.

As for me, Shinran, there is nothing left for me but to receive and believe . . . that we are saved by Amida merely through the utterance of the *Nembutsu.* I am entirely ignorant as to whether the *Nembutsu* is really the cause of Birth in the Pure Land, or whether it is the *karma* which will cause me to fall into hell. I will have no regrets even though . . . by uttering the *Nembutsu,* I should fall into hell. The reason is that, if I could become Buddha by performing some other practice and fell into hell by uttering the *Nembutsu,* then, I might feel regret at having been deceived. But since I am incapable of any practice whatsoever, hell would definitely be my dwelling anyway.

(Tanni Shō #2)[18]

---

17 D. T. Suzuki, *Collected Writings on Shin Buddhism* (Kyoto: Shinshū Ōtaniha, 1973), p. 79.
18 *Tanni Shō,* trans. Ryōsetsu Fujiwara (Kyoto: Ryukoku University Translation Center, 1966), pp. 19–20.

With the following remarkable example of symbolism of the elusiveness of the ultimately real, Shinran further emphasized the inability of human beings to realize personal perfection through morality.

> Even a good person is born in the Pure Land, how much more so is an evil person! However, people in the world usually say, "Even an evil person is born in the Pure Land, how much more so is a good person." At first sight this view seems to be reasonable, but it is contrary to the purport of the Original Vow, of the Other-Power. The reason is that, as those who practice good by their self-power lack the mind to rely wholly on the Other-Power, they are not in accordance with the Original Vow of Amida. However, if they convert their minds from self-power and trust the Other-Power, their Birth in the True Land of Recompense is assured.
>
> Amida made His Vow out of compassion for us who are full of evil passions, and who are unable to set ourselves free from *saṁsāra* by any practice. Since the purpose of His Vow is to have evil persons attain Buddhahood, the evil person who trusts the Other-Power is especially the one who has the right cause for Birth in the Pure Land. Hence, the words, "Even a good person is born in the Pure Land, how much more so is an evil person." Thus the Master said.
>
> (Tanni Shō #3)[19]

Such passages, of course, do not encourage evil behavior in followers of Pure Land Buddhism. On the contrary, virtuous behavior and good deeds are encouraged so long as they are not regarded as rendering one deserving of salvation. Instead, moral behavior is regarded as an expedient for developing true faith in the saving power of Amida's vow.

> Various good deeds and numerous (spiritual) practices, when performed with Sincere Mind and Aspiration, all, without exception, serve as the expedient good for attaining birth in the Pure Land.
>
> (Jōdo Wasan #63)[20]

Bad behavior, on the other hand, is bad not because it renders one less deserving of salvation, but because it hinders the practice of devotion to Amida.

> The *Nembutsu* of Amida Buddha's Original Vow, for evil beings with perverted views (especially denial of the effects of *karma*) and arrogance, is extremely difficult to believe and retain. Of all difficulties nothing is more difficult than this.
>
> (Shōshin Ge, lines 41–4)[21]

19 Ibid., pp. 22–3.
20 Shinran Shōnin, *Jōdo Wasan*, trans. R. Fujimoto et al. (Kyoto: Ryukoku University Translation center, 1965), p. 95.
21 Shinran Shōnin, *Shōshin Ge*, trans. Daien Fugen (Kyoto: Ryukoku University Translation Center, 1961), p. 26.

Notably in these passages, *morality defines itself with a reference to a spiritual reality,* though clearly *good behavior in itself is insufficient for personal perfection.*

Theravāda Buddhism, Zen, and in fact most forms of Buddhism other than the Pure Land, urge self-reliance in moral discipline. All forms of Buddhism, however, emphasize that moral behavior alone will not win enlightenment or Nirvāṇa. This emphasis urges Buddhists to abandon desire for Nirvāṇa as well as fear of karmic retribution as motivation for moral behavior, though such desire and fear may be appropriate in the early stages of the path. Instead, Buddhism encourages its followers to incorporate moral motivation – essentially regard for the welfare of other beings – as an integral part of the larger concern with purifying the mind of greed, hatred, and delusion, the roots of unwholesomeness. Mahāyāna Buddhism effects this incorporation by emphasizing the Bodhisattva path of service to others. Theravāda Buddhism accomplishes the same thing through the *brahma-vihāra* meditations, which urge one to develop, as an integral aspect of mental purification, an equanimity of love, compassion, and sympathetic joy toward all people. Neither the Bodhisattva path of compassion and service nor the *brahma-vihāra* meditations can properly be regarded as means to an end. On the contrary, they are an integral aspect of the end itself, that end being the mental purification that opens the mind to enlightenment. Strictly speaking, enlightenment itself may not be regarded as an end brought about by means, for it eludes any and all means. Instead, mental purification – which facilitates but does not bring about enlightenment – is the end of the means enshrined in the various forms of Buddhist morality and spirituality. In this way, Buddhism's spiritual and moral symbolisms of the elusiveness of its ultimate referent converge, *encouraging sustained discipline despite the elusiveness of the ultimately real,* and pointing out that *though morality defines itself with reference to an ultimate spiritual reality, good behavior, even with the best motivation, is insufficient for personal perfection.*

Mythological Symbolism of Elusiveness

Mythological symbolism providing illustrations of the elusiveness of the ultimately real abounds in Buddhism. It is particularly apparent in Mahāyāna Buddhism, which generally places more emphasis on mythological expression than does the Theravāda. Still, Theravāda scriptures also occasionally express the atmosphere of awe and mystery that surrounds enlightenment, Nirvāṇa, and Buddhahood.

When the Exalted one died, the venerable Ānanda, at the moment of his passing away from existence, uttered this stanza:

Then was there terror!
Then stood the hair on end!
When he endowed with every grace –
The supreme Buddha – died!

(D 2:157)

During the first several centuries of Buddhism, when the Theravāda was predominant, no images of the Buddha appear to have been made. Instead, one finds depictions of an empty throne under a *bodhi* tree, reminding the beholder of the mysterious nature of enlightenment and the elusiveness of the ultimately real.

In the Mahāyāna, numerous accounts – like the story recounted of Asaṅga's twelve years of practicing austerities in a cave – seek to *illustrate the elusiveness of enlightenment.* A common theme in such accounts is an eventual discovery by the seeker that the object of the quest has been with him or her all the time. The following passage recounts one of the many trials the aspirant Naropa encountered while searching for his guru Tilopa.

When he had come to a narrow footpath that wound between rocks and a river, he found a leper woman without hands and feet blocking the path. "Do not block the way, step aside," (he said). "I cannot move," (she answered). . . . Although he was full of compassion, he closed his nose in disgust and leaped over her. The leper woman rose in the air in a rainbow halo and said:
    Listen, Abhayakīrti [Naropa]:
    The ultimate in which all become the same
    Is free of habit-forming thought and limitations.
    How, if still fettered by them,
    Can you hope to find the *Guru*?
At this the women, the rocks, and the path all vanished and Nāropa fell into a swoon on a sandy plateau. When he recovered consciousness he thought: "I did not recognize this to be the *Guru*, now I shall ask anyone I meet for instruction." Then he got up and went on his way praying.[22]

Naropa goes through eleven other similar trials, encountering his guru in such unlikely forms as a vermin-invested dog and a man torturing his parents. Finally, when he is on the verge of suicide, there appears an old man in cotton trousers whom he recognizes to be Tilopa.

Having found his guru, Naropa's lot does not improve immediately. His guru starves him, beats him frequently, forces him to leap off buildings, and makes him pick hopeless fights and thereby get beaten within an inch of his life. Naropa himself, after persevering through all this appar-

---

22   Translated by Herbert V. Guenther, *The Life and Teaching of Naropa* (London: Oxford University Press, 1963), p. 30.

ently pointless cruelty, and realizing enlightenment, is said to have been fond of hunting deer with hounds while engaging in sex with his consort. Records of such antinomian behavior on the part of Buddhist sages is clearly not to be taken literally. Instead, accounts of Buddhist gurus violating and commanding their disciples to violate the most cherished norms of Buddhist morality and spiritual practice are mythological hyperbole emphasizing the elusiveness of the ultimately real. Such accounts serve to highlight the inadequacy of morality and spiritual practices for realization of enlightenment.

Such mythological tales of aspirants undergoing and gurus meting out extreme physical hardships no doubt reflect in part the psychological difficulties encountered in attempting to discipline the mind through meditation. Let anyone who doubts such psychological difficulties attempt for only one hour the rudimentary Buddhist meditational exercise of sitting motionless and concentrating single-mindedly upon the point where the breath touches the nose. In the course of such an exercise, all but the purest of heart will find themselves confronted with some of the ugliest and most disappointing aspects of their own minds. They will not be able to maintain concentration, but will think of food, sex, petty annoyances and triumphs in their jobs and social lives. In the course of a week long meditational retreat, they would find themselves mentally rehearsing orgies, fist fights, and humiliatingly triumphant tirades against perceived adversaries.

Such psychological difficulties encountered in the course of meditation seem to suggest that the mind by its very nature is the opposite of the ideal that Buddhism encourages. This seemingly insurmountable difficulty is expressed and resolved mythologically in the tale of the Buddha's encounter with and victory over Māra's hosts on the night of his enlightenment. This encounter with the hosts of Māra, the Buddhist equivalent of Satan, is a common theme in Buddhist mythology and iconography. The following account comes from Aśvaghosha's Buddhacarita or Life of the Buddha, regarded by many as the greatest epic of Sanskrit literature. It too *illustrates the elusiveness of the ultimate referent of Buddhism.*

1. When the great sage, the scion of a line of royal seers, sat down there, after making his vow for liberation, the world rejoiced, but Māra, the enemy of the good Law, trembled. . . .

18. Then as soon as Māra thought of his army in his desire to obstruct the tranquility of the Sākya sage, his followers stood round him, in various forms and carrying lances, trees, javelins, clubs and swords in their hands. . . .

25. Some, as they ran, leapt wildly about, some jumped on each other; while some gambolled in the sky, others sped along among the treetops.

26. One danced about, brandishing a trident; another snorted, as he trailed a club; one roared like a bull in his excitement, another blazed fire from every hair.
27. Such were the hordes of fiends who stood encompassing the root of the *bodhi* tree on all sides, anxious to seize and to kill, and awaiting the command of their master.
28. Beholding in the beginning of the night the hour of conflict between Māra and the bull of the Sākyas, the sky lost its brightness, the earth shook and the quarters blazed and crashed.
29. The wind raged wildly in every direction, the stars did not shine, the moon was not seen, and night spread forth still thicker darkness, and all the oceans were troubled. . . .
53. The deer and the elephants, giving forth cries of distress, ran about and hid themselves, and on that night, as if it were day, the birds on all sides fluttered about, screaming in distress.
54. But although all beings shivered at such howls of theirs, the sage, like Garuḍa at the noise of crows, neither trembled nor quailed.
55. The less the sage was afraid of the fearsome troops of that array, the more was Māra the enemy of the upholders of the Law, cast down with grief and wrath. . . .
72. As he of the flower-banner fled away defeated with his following, and the great seer, the passion-free conqueror of the darkness of ignorance, remained victorious, the heavens shone with the moon like a maiden with a smile, and there fell a rain of sweet-smelling flowers with water.

(Buddhacarita #13)[23]

The mythology of Buddhism lives not only in literary works such as the foregoing, but also in the visual arts of painting and sculpture. The subtler aspects of Buddhist aesthetics may therefore be regarded as mythological expression of the elusiveness of the ultimately real. To be sure, nonmythological Buddhist art forms such as Zen painting, flower arrangement, and gardening also express subtly the elusiveness of ultimate reality, omnipresent and yet hovering inexpressibly and tantalizingly just beyond the ken of our senses and intellects. Somewhat arbitrarily, we choose to treat the aesthetics of Buddhism under the heading of mythology, partly because it allows us to conclude our examination of Buddhism with one of the most moving examples of the concrescence that we urge among religions. The following is an appreciation by the Christian monk Thomas Merton of the Buddhist sculptures hewn in the living rock of Gal Vihara, at Polonnaruwa, Sri Lanka.

The path dips down to Gal Vihara: a wide, quiet hollow, surrounded with trees. A low outcrop of rock, with a cave cut into it, and beside the cave a big

23 Aśvaghosha, *Buddacarita*, trans. E. H. Johnston (1936; Delhi: Motilal Banarsidass, 1972), pp. 188–202.

seated Buddha on the left, a reclining Buddha on the right, and Ānanda, I guess, standing by the head of the reclining Buddha. In the cave, another seated Buddha. The vicar general, shying away from "paganism," hangs back and sits under a tree reading a guidebook. I am able to approach the Buddhas barefoot and undisturbed, my feet in wet grass, wet sand. Then the silence of the extraordinary faces. The great smiles. Huge and yet subtle. Filled with every possibility, questioning nothing, knowing everything, rejecting nothing, the peace not of emotional resignation but of Mādhyamika, of *śunyatā*, that has seen through every question without trying to discredit anyone or anything – *without refutation* – without establishing some other argument. For the doctrinaire, the mind that needs well-established positions, such peace, such silence, can be frightening. I was knocked over with a rush of relief and thankfulness at the *obvious* clarity of the figures, the clarity and fluidity of shape and line, the design of the monumental bodies composed into the rock shape and landscape, figure, rock and tree. And the sweep of bare rock sloping away on the other side of the hollow, where you can go back and see different aspects of the figures.

Looking at these figures I was suddenly, almost forcibly, jerked clean out of the habitual, half-tied vision of things, and an inner clearness, clarity, as if exploding from the rocks themselves, became evident and obvious. The queer *evidence* of the reclining figure, the smile, the sad smile of Ānanda standing with arms folded (much more "imperative" than Da Vinci's Mona Lisa because completely simple and straightforward). The thing about all this is that there is no puzzle, no problem, and really no "mystery." All problems are resolved and everything is clear, simply because what matters is clear. The rock, all matter, all life, is charged with Dharmakāya . . . everything is emptiness and everything is compassion. I don't know when in my life I have ever had such a sense of beauty and spiritual validity running together in one aesthetic illumination. . . .

The whole thing is very much a Zen garden, a span of bareness and openness and evidence, and the great figures, motionless, yet with the lines in full movement, waves of vesture and bodily form, a beautiful and holy vision.[24]

Such openness to and perceptiveness of religious sentiments other than one's own – evident in exceptional individuals such as Thomas Merton – provide an ideal that world theology must aspire to engender on a wider basis. In pursuit of this ideal, we now turn to an examination of Middle Asian and Western theism as exemplified by Judaism, Christianity, and Islam. We recognize that the foregoing brief treatments of Hinduism and Buddhism have not been exhaustive of Eastern spirituality, and that these treatments may have raised more questions than they have answered. From the standpoint of practicality, however, we cannot at present hope to accomplish more than broadly stroked sketches of a representative sample of expressions of the central spiritual reality of humankind.

24 *The Asian Journal of Thomas Merton*, ed. Naomi Burton et al. (1968; New York: New Directions, 1975), pp. 233–6.

CHAPTER FIVE

Judaism and the Central Spiritual Reality of Humankind

The spirituality of Middle Asia and the West has found expression pre-eminently in four monotheistic religions: Judaism, Christianity, Islam, and Baha'i. These four religions are governed by two presuppositions that differ radically from the regulative presuppositions of Hinduism and Buddhism. All of these monotheistic religions presuppose, first of all, that ultimate reality is a single, sovereign, conscious Will who has no antecedent and no need for assistance from any other source, and who creates, governs, and provides for every other reality whatsoever. They suppose, secondly, that this ultimate Will has singled out the human phenomenon to receive special attention, communication, and favor from the divine Will, thus giving humanity a unique status among the vast array of other creations.

Each of the four monotheisms has developed its own distinctive symbolic systems to express these presuppositions. We have chosen to examine the symbolic expressions worked out by Judaism, Christianity, and Islam, and to exclude Baha'i for the compelling reason that neither of the present authors has done primary research in that religion. We note in passing, however, that Baha'i, in its public professions, has been more hospitable toward religions with *non*theistic and *a*theistic presuppositions than have the other three monotheisms. Typically, representatives of Judaism, Christianity, and Islam have used their own basic assumptions to categorize and prejudge other religions without taking recourse to factual information. This arbitrary and absolutist procedure has come necessarily under criticism and review to some extent in all three of these religions because a vast amount of verifiable information about other religions has been accumulated and it defies doctrinaire and facile categorization.

Judaism, whose antecedents reach back approximately to 2000 B.C.E., is the oldest of the world's living monotheisms and is the primal ancestor of the other three. The later three originated in such a relation to Judaism that they have to acknowledge that Judaism founded ethical monotheism in the world and that the Judaic paradigm continues to serve as a guiding principle in their respective versions of it. Each of these later monotheisms has found itself compelled, by history and other circumstances, to explain its own version of God's singularity and unity in reference to the *ethical* monotheism of Judaism and to justify its own existence independent of Judaism. In these respects at least, Judaism's monotheism remains indispensable for understanding Christian, Islamic, and Baha'i monotheism.

Judaism states its constitutive monotheistic formula in a verse from its scripture, "Yhwh is our God, [and] Yhwh is one" (Deuteronomy 6:4). The letters *Yhwh* transliterate a four-letter Hebrew word that the Judaic tradition coined and has used exclusively as a proper name to designate its God, forbidding that it ever be pronounced. In addressing or referring to Yhwh orally in Hebrew and when reading the scriptures where this word is written, Jewish people utter the word *Adonai* in place of the word *Yhwh*. When using English in these circumstances, they use the English translation of *Adonai*, which is *Lord* or *the Lord* and which, for persons unfamiliar with Judaism, tends to obscure the fact that it substitutes for the proper name of the Judaists' God. We ask our readers to keep themselves reminded as they read this chapter that *the Lord* is the proper name and that God is the title that Judaism uses for the Reality that it holds to be ultimate: "The Lord is our God, [and] the Lord is one." From their beginning, the Jewish people have recognized that other peoples have ascribed godhood (sovereignty) to various realities and that some people have considered each of the multiplicity of gods to be a part of a single Deity or a member of a category of divine beings. While recognizing the fact that humanity has many gods and rationalizes their plurality and relation to each other, religious Jews have affirmed that the Lord alone is *their* God, that the Lord alone is worthy of being reverenced as sovereign by anyone, and that the Lord is one and indivisible. Because, according to Judaic conception, the Lord's reality is not divisible and because the Lord has no offspring, the presence and sovereignty of the Lord is not to be confused with anyone or anything else that claims or is claimed to be ultimate and sovereign. Therefore, nothing can be more important to any human than to know and do what the Lord requires. According to Judaism's understanding, the Lord has created Judaism expressly for the purpose of making this known to the rest of the world's peoples.

Unlike its three monotheistic descendants, Judaism has always been the religion of, and for, a single ethnic group. This group is known today as the Jews, but its selfsame ethnic line can be traced and distinctively identified, under a succession of different names, to a date very near to 2000 B.C.E. Historians identify them first as the Apiru or Habiru whom we call the Hebrews. They were a new group formed from the Semitic people who inhabited the long Fertile Crescent, which borders the Arabian Desert from Egypt to Babylonia. This new group consisted of craftspeople and herders who became known and feared for their periodic raids on caravans and isolated settlements along the Crescent. Their descendants were the Israelites who established a theocracy in the hill country and coastlands of the eastern end of the Mediterranean Sea. These Israelites produced a literature that became scripture for all subsequent generations of this ethnic line. That scripture, the Tanakh, is also known as the "Old Testament" section of the Christian Bible. Modern day Israelites call themselves *Yehudim* or Jews and, scattered among numerous nations, they number only 18,000,000 worldwide, six million having been murdered by Hitler in the Holocaust.

Throughout their continuous history these people have carefully protected their ethnic integrity. In recent times, as Jewish people, they have effectively monitored their identity, generally allowing that a person is Jewish only if born of a Jewish mother or initiated ritually into Jewish existence. Being or becoming a Jew in this ethnic sense is the necessary precondition for anyone who wants to practice Judaism, that is, the Judaic religion. This religion is addressed to all Jewish people as such, but practicing the Judaic religion is not a requirement for Jewish ethnic identity. In the modern period of Jewish history vast numbers of Jews have denied the validity of any religious claim and have chosen not to be identified with the Judaic religion. In order to designate those Jews who do practice the Judaic religion, or who at least identify themselves with it, we will use the term "Judaists," thus following a suggestion made by Raphael Loewe and Jacob Neusner.[1] To avoid repetition of tedious detail, we will ordinarily use the term "Judaism" or "Judaic religion" when referring to this religious tradition at all points of its history, and we will use "Judaists" to refer to its adherents in every period.

Although monoethnic, Judaism is a *world* religion. For nearly half of Judaism's approximately four thousand years of history, Judaists and other Jews have been compelled by political force and circumstances to "transcend," to live beyond, the land of Judaism's origin and to survive while dispersed among the peoples of other lands. After the reestablishment of the state of Israel in 1948, numerous Judaists and nonreligious Jews have chosen to live as citizens of nations other than Israel. Living for centuries in forced exile from their Mediterranean homeland and living more recently in countries of their choosing, Judaists have learned that

---

1   Raphael Loewe, "Defining Judaism: Some Ground-Clearing," *Jewish Journal of Sociology* (London) 7, no. 2 (December 1965): 153–75, and Jacob Neusner, *The Way of Torah: An Introduction to Judaism*, 4th ed. (Belmont, Calif.: Wadsworth Publishing Company, 1988), chap. 3.

the Judaic religion lends itself to authentic practice everywhere and that it invests their lives with its special transcendent meaning irrespective of their geographical location. In this significant sense, then, Judaism is a *world* religion. Communities of observant Judaists exist all over the globe, and their members participate responsibly and influentially in the civil societies of the whole world. These communities are living evidence that Judaism can both survive and thrive in a variety of social systems and national settings and that it can generate its own subculture in existing cultures variously based.

Judaism is a *world* religion in another significant sense. Whereas Judaism makes an effort to enlist only Jews to practice its rites, it relates its message of ethical monotheism to all human beings in two ways. Its definitive conviction and perpetually defining principle, "The Lord is our God, [and] the Lord is one," means, according to Judaist exposition, that "in the end of days" this singular and undivided Lord will subdue all the centers of power that have pretended to sovereignty or to which humans have mistakenly ascribed sovereignty and that all humans, not merely Jewish humans, will be made accountable to this one Lord. Furthermore, apart from the cultic and ritual requirements that the Lord's revelation imposes on the Jews as Jews, the major content of that revelation is a body of ethical instruction that Judaists direct toward the ethical education and moral improvement of all humankind. By its own understanding of its special revelation, Judaism exists for the sake of the moral edification of all humanity. It assumes the obligation to communicate the Lord's universal ethic to humanity – through Judaists who act it out in their moral conduct and demonstrate it in their public contribution to the analysis, criticism, and resolution of human problems. Judaists consider it their divinely given lot to live their lives before the one Lord for the sake of the whole of humanity. Only this sense of divine assignment to improve the quality of all human life can adequately account for the disproportionately large achievements made by this numerically small people in all fields of human learning, in all the arts, in all aspects of the search for equal rights and justice, and in all the ministries to human need.

Judaic existence is quintessentially a life of deeds, which means observing the commandments the Lord has revealed. These revealed instructions derived with consistent logic from the single constitutive belief that the Lord is categorically the only Lord, is one and undivided, and relates to Judaists as their God. Apart from this one stupendous belief Judaism is not a religion of doctrines to be subscribed to, and even assent to this regulative belief does not hold priority over doing the deeds prescribed by the Lord. The rabbis in antiquity quoted the Lord as saying, "Would that [my people] forsake me and do my commandments, for by observing my instruction [*Torah*] they will come to know me" (Pesikta Kahana, 15).

This emphasis upon divinely given instruction, obedience thereto, and consequently membership in a community of the faithful is a theme that runs through each of the monotheisms to be discussed in the remainder of this book. Emphasis, deemphasis, or reinterpretation of one or another of the essentially Judaic themes – revelation, obedience, and community – provide Christianity and Islam with their distinctive expressions of a monotheism fundamentally Judaic in origin and character. The ways in which these monotheistic religions deal with these three common themes render these religions, as a group, distinct from the eastern religions we have considered thus far, but these ways do not preclude integration into our scheme of undeniability, desirability, and elusiveness.

Undeniability

Spiritual Symbolism of Undeniability

In the actual development of the Jewish child's Judaic identity, learning to behave Judaically precedes intentional belief in the Lord's oneness. This emphasis upon moral conduct might incline one to assign primacy to moral symbolism. We will consider Judaic spiritual symbolism of un-deniability first, however, because the presupposition of every aspect of Judaic religion is belief in the one, undivided Lord whose ethical Will makes human morality possible and necessary.

Judaism expresses an obvious and unambiguous spiritual symbolism of undeniability merely by reciting the Shema, which Judaists regard to be their constitutive charge. The Shema proclaims both the Lord's unity and the ethical demand that follows from that unity.

Hear, O Israel, the Lord is our God, the Lord alone. You must love the Lord your God with all your heart and with all your soul and with all your might.

(Deuteronomy 6:4–5)[2]

This proclamation addresses all Jews (alias Israel) with the imperative to collect every part of their life into a unified response of love to the Lord their God. In this way Jews can become Judaists, that is to say, they can become Jewish persons who seek to fulfill their humanity by willingly obeying the Lord. Judaism holds, however, that even those Jewish individuals who do not respond to the Lord in the wholeness of love live out their lives in reference to the reality of the one Lord: They are free to ignore the Lord's presence and neglect the Lord's instruction, but they cannot remove themselves from the audience to whom the Shema is ad-

2   Jewish Publication Society translation of the Torah (Philadelphia, 1962). All other scripture quotations in this chapter are our own translations unless otherwise stated.

dressed. Thus the Shema *appeals for the consent of every Jewish person to the inevitability of living the entirety of her or his life in reference to the Lord.* When Jews read the Shema in scripture, privately or in public worship, and when they recite it in rituals of regular or Holy Day services, the Shema is a spiritual symbol asserting the Lord's undeniability. When Judaism goes on to explain that the Lord, the God of Judaists, is the only Lord and that all humans are therefore finally and decisively accountable to this one reality, this explanation becomes *a symbolic appeal for universal assent to the inevitability of all humans living in reference to a central spiritual reality.* Judaism declares, in other words, that the Lord – whom Judaists address and refer to as *"our* God" but not usually as *"our* Lord" because they do not regard the Lord to be one and ultimate for them alone – is the central spiritual reality of all people. Other peoples may acknowledge now some reality other than the Lord to be their God (sovereign), but these other realities can have only temporary sovereignty at most. The Lord alone, the Judaists assert, is the author and governor of the whole world and will be the final judge of all the peoples of the world. By intended inference, then, Judaism asserts *the universal human necessity of giving assent to humanity's central spiritual reality.*

It is important to note well that the Shema claims exclusivity only for the Lord's being who "He" is – that is, for Yhwh's being the only reality that is Yhwh and for Yhwh's being nothing except Yhwh. The Shema does not assert, and Judaism does not otherwise claim, that Judaists have either exclusive access or most favored relation to the Lord. About itself Judaism claims to have been founded by the Lord for a purpose bound up with the mystery of the Lord's purpose for all human history. Judaism locates its origin in a covenant event that the Lord putatively initiated with the original Judaic ancestors. In that event the Lord covenanted or pledged to be present with these people and their posterity in perpetuity. The words of that covenant neither limit nor specify all the ways in which the Lord may choose to be present. They do specify that the Lord will be present, always at the Lord's own initiative and on the Lord's own terms. The Hebrew name (Yhwh) of the Lord was coined from a verb form and was probably intended to mean "I will be present as I will be present," indicating the Lord's independence in defining the manner and terms on which the divine presence will be given at any particular time and place. The several scriptural accounts of this covenant and its renewal can be summarized to form the following composite of its assertions and promises: "I am the Lord. I have brought you out of anonymity and have delivered you from slavery in Egypt. I will be present with you and your descendants on my own terms. I will be your God and you shall be my people, and through you I will bless all the peoples of the earth" (cf.

Genesis 12:1–3; Exodus 2:23–5, 19:1–6, and 34:1–8, and Deuteronomy 29:1–14). Transparently these covenant assertions and promises express *the inevitability of this people's living with reference to the Lord.*

Judaists of different generations have tried to determine the reason why they were chosen to receive from the Lord both the special revelation of his identity and a guarantee of his unfailing, bonded presence with them. They considered and promptly rejected, for example, the suggestion that they were either the most righteous or otherwise the greatest of all the peoples; they concluded that the Lord chose them because he loved them for reasons known only to the Lord (Deuteronomy 4:7ff., 7:6ff., and 9:4ff.). They have tried also at various times to ascertain the purpose that the Lord intends them to serve as a distinct but numerically small people among all the other peoples and nations of the world. They have asked themselves repeatedly, "What specifically is the blessing the Lord wants us to be or to provide to all the other peoples?" They have never found convincingly clear and satisfying answers to these inquiries, and therefore they do not claim ordinarily to comprehend why they were chosen by the Lord or to know what special blessing of the Lord they are transmitting to the world's other peoples. Nevertheless, Judaists have understood all along that their being elected, however inscrutably, by the Lord and that their being the recipient of the Lord's irrevocable pledge and irremovable presence, mean at least what Moses promulgated as the first of the Lord's commandments to this people: "I am the Lord your God. . . . Therefore you shall have no other gods besides me" (Deuteronomy 5:6–7). Whatever other service they may render wittingly or unwittingly to humanity in general, Judaists are certain that they are under mandate to render a credible witness to the Lord's right to a monopoly on sovereignty over all peoples, not merely over the Jewish people. Their knowledge of the Lord's dominion, based on their experience of the Lord's covenant, requires, they say, that they witness to the Lord's singularity, indivisibility, initiative, impartiality, and ethical demand. Even to acknowledge that this witness is required of them is to express *the human necessity of assenting to a central spiritual reality.*

Because of their preoccupation with the command that the Lord alone be their God, Judaists have always had to reckon with the competitive reality of other gods, that is, with contenders for ultimate sovereignty. The fact and issues of religious pluralism are as old as Judaism. As we mentioned earlier, it has been an inescapable fact in Judaic experience that there are numerous realities that human beings will both acknowledge and organize themselves to honor as sacred and sovereign. That is what Judaism means by the word "god": whatever humans identify, worship, and serve as sacred and sovereign. In this sense, literally any reality is capable of being given the status of god, and John Dewey, in his book, *A Common Faith*,[3] opined that probably everything that human beings have ever experienced or even imagined has been apotheosized by some person or group somewhere at sometime. In any case, the mass of realities known to have been called god were sufficient to convince Dewey that the word "god" has no permanent and distinctive content. Judaism has acknowledged from its beginning that god making is a common characteristic of humankind. Therefore a double meaning is intended when its scriptures state that only a fool can say in his heart, "There is no god" (Psalm 14:1). Everybody acts at sometime as if there is a sovereign referent, and everybody who has a sovereign has a god. Judaism knows that every acknowledged sovereignty claims a total attitude from its subjects and makes a definitive difference in their lives. The reality of these gods – the fact that they demand a total attitude and make a conclusive difference in peoples' lives – provokes Judaism necessarily into being a comparative, contrastive, and competitive religion. As a religion under charge to have no gods other than the Lord and under constraint to witness to the sole, indivisible, righteous, unshared, and ultimate sovereignty of the Lord, Judaism constitutes an unrelenting and contrasting challenge to any religion that ascribes sovereignty to any reality other than the Lord, or which appears to divide or modify the Lord's own sovereignty, as in the case of Christianity with its triune designation of Father, Son, and Holy Spirit.

While Judaism never asserts that there is only one god, it always asserts that there is only one Yhwh (the Lord), that Yhwh alone is ultimate and that Yhwh alone, therefore, has the right to be everybody's god or sovereign.[4] Judaic scriptures inveigh against other people as well as Judaists who apotheosize either humans themselves or the works of their hands, the powers or processes or parts of nature, the political power embodied and wielded by human individuals and groups, the products of human reason, or any other contingent reality. The scriptural narratives, legislation, prophets, and psalmists alike disparage "all the gods of the peoples" as "prostitutes," "vain things," "things of naught," and "imaginations of their own evil hearts" (cf. Exodus 34:16 and Jeremiah 10:14–15) while extolling the Lord as "God Almighty," "the God of Gods," "the King of kings," "the King of the universe," and "the Lord of Lords" (cf. Genesis 21;23 and Deuteronomy 10:17; 2 Kings 19:15–19; and Daniel 10:17). Rather than quote numerous passages from the polemical and apologetic

3 John Dewey, *A Common Faith* (New Haven, Conn.: Yale University Press, 1934).
4 Cf. C. J. Labuschagne, *The Incomparability of Yahweh in the Old Testament* (Leiden: E. J. Brill, 1966).

literature of Judaism in order to illustrate Judaism's case for the Lord's superiority, we will sketch a version of what Manfred H. Vogel[5] has called Judaism's "normative" theological view. This view has never been authorized by any official body of Judaists nor formulated into a creedal statement, but the specifics that we will sketch are essentials to be found in the distinctive theological constructions of each of the four periods of Judaic history: Biblical, Rabbinic, Medieval, and Modern. With our sketch of this view we conclude our demonstration of Judaism's spiritual symbolism of undeniability.

The standard Judaic view maintains that the Lord's identity is characterized by at least eight revealed attributes. According to this Judaic perspective, the reality of the Lord is *sovereign, one and unique, living, spiritual, self-revealing,* and *ethical, creating and guiding history* as well as *creating and governing nature.* The term "sovereign" serves as the substantive for the other seven qualifying terms and phrases because it defines essentially what is meant when one says that the Lord is *God.* By sovereignty Judaists mean the Lord's intentional exercise of the ultimate power that inheres in the sheer transcendent and independent reality of the Lord. Exercised in the creation and governance of all other realities, the Lord's power is characterized by its originality, freedom, and goodness and by the righteous manner of its administration. It is power directed toward goals that are "right in the sight of the Lord" (Deuteronomy 13:18). The Lord is not bound or restrained or guided by any higher, equal, or subordinate will, law, or power. All other realities are definitively related and finally accountable to the Lord for the simple but profound reason that the Lord has made them so according to the divine power and purpose. As the *one and unique* Sovereign (God) of all realities, the Lord's reality and unicity are incomparable. As the sole and undivided reality of this kind, the Lord does not share the integrity of divine unity or the exercise of divine sovereignty with anyone or anything else. One ultimate Lordship is regnant at all places and at all times throughout the cosmos. This solitary Sovereign is the *living* Lord and as such is aware, volitional, communicative, and responsive and holds the power to give life to others and to take it away.

As *spiritual,* this living Lord is immaterial and has the power to create, to be present, and to evoke personal presence from human spirits. Exercising that power, the Lord conceives, initiates, and fulfills purposes that comprehend both material and immaterial realities. In other words, the Lord demonstrates spirituality or inventive initiative by creating and administering both nature and history. Long before they identified the Lord

5   Cf. Manfred H. Vogel, *A Quest for a Theology of Judaism,* Studies in Judaism (Lanham, Md.: University Press of America, 1987), p. 3.

as Creator and absolute ruler of the whole universe, ancient Judaists credited the Lord with *creating and guiding human history.* They reasoned that the Lord, by becoming present to the human spirit, evokes personal responses of limited creative freedom from human beings and thus "creates" or occasions freedom in human beings. The divine freedom initiates and sustains encounters with the divinely given human freedom. These encounters with the Lord create the conditions in which humans are enabled to be present and to conceive, initiate, and bring to fulfillment limited purposes of their own – in other words, to participate as agents in their own existence and destiny. These powers to be present, creative, and responsible make up what Judaists call the human spirit. They regard human history to be constituted of the responses that the human spirit makes to the Lord's spiritual presence. As living spirit the Lord communicates with humans as living spirits. Humans can know the Lord because the Lord engages them in *self-revealing* activities. In certain meetings of the divine and human spirits, the *ethical* character and instruction (Torah) of the Lord become specially disclosed. In these revelatory acts the Lord is seen to exhibit in the supreme degree the same morality that these revelations demand of human beings. These special acts that make up "the history of revelation" occur within the context and sequence of ordinary history and manifest the relevance of the Lord's justice and mercy to all human relationships. From the perspective of this Judaic understanding, all history consists of human responses to manifestations of the Lord's ethical presence, which humans often neglect to recognize for what it is.

In their own ordinary and revelatory history, Judaists early on concluded that the Lord *governs nature,* using it to convey divine judgment and grace to humans. It was late in the development of their covenant relation with the Lord, however, before Judaists drew the further inference that the Lord *created* the whole natural universe. They had never expressed doubt about the Lord's effective control of nature and all of its powers, but for some reason they were slow to attribute the creation of nature to "their" God. Since at least the eighth century B.C.E., however, the image of the Lord as creator has been not simply axiomatic in Judaic piety and theology; it has been the image comprehending all the other characteristics of the Lord.

We submit that the Judaists who communicate this perception of the Lord are *making an appeal for personal consent,* not only from Jews and Judaists but from humanity universally, *to the inevitability of living with reference to the ultimate spiritual reality,* which they identify as the Lord their God. This Judaic portrait of the Lord argues both for *the undeniability of the central spiritual reality of humankind* and for *the necessity of a world theology.*

Moral Symbolism of Undeniability

Judaism's moral symbolism of the Lord's undeniability is the necessary counterpart of the spiritual symbolism we have just discussed. According to the logic of the Shema, a radical moral demand arises when a person acknowledges the incomparable reality, sovereignty, and unicity of the Lord. This logic and the radical character of the moral demand become more evident when one reads the Shema as we translate it here, selecting English words and phrases more for their ability to convey meanings equivalent to the original Hebrew than for their aesthetic felicity:

Hear, O Israel, the Lord is our God, and the Lord is one. Therefore you must love the Lord your God with all your heart and mind and will, and with all your consciousness and with all your might.

(Deuteronomy 6:4)

From this translation it becomes apparent that Judaism's monotheism is not only a *radical* monotheism. It is a radical *ethical* monotheism, and its radical ethical demand is the duty of a radical and total love, which, by *exposing self-contradictory behavior, discloses to Judaists the inevitability of living with reference to the Lord.*

Elaborating the logic of the Shema, Judaism argues that those who know that the Lord is one and righteous are obligated to make their own lives one and righteous by loving the Lord with every part, aspect, and power of their individual being. Quite obviously love is understood here to be something more than emotion. It can be reasonably demanded; therefore it has to be an intentional act of the will rather than a fortuitous sentiment. It has to be initiated at will, at one's own discretion or pleasure.

Based on the usage of a number of words in Judaic scripture one can determine a basic and fairly precise definition of "love" in Judaism. For Judaism love is the movement of the human will that integrates a person's powers, into a focused intention of affectionate, other-regarding goodwill and that steadfastly expresses this intention toward a specific recipient in order to establish and sustain a reciprocal relation of affectionate goodwill. Once the Lord's reality and sovereignty are affirmed and the duty of an integrated response of total personal love has been assumed, the rest of Judaism concerns moral behavior. From that point on, Judaism is a matter of doing the morally right deed in specific human situations rather than affirming right beliefs. There are no other articles of belief to be confessed, and there is no further preoccupation with love itself. Love is the motive for Judaists' behavior; it is not a disposition they are encouraged to evoke for its own sake or to be sentimentalized romantically. A

Jew becomes a Judaist by sustained acceptance of the Shema's constitutive instruction to will with one's whole individual life those righteous deeds that the Lord has revealed to be required of Jews. Judaism expects Jews to make this total personal response not once or occasionally or even at certain regular intervals, but literally around the clock and routinely with every breath a person takes and in every act of mind, mouth, and body as long as the person lives.

Judaism is, then, a total way of living human life, a way that is called *Torah*. Over its long history the Judaic people have accumulated a large corpus of scripture and tradition, all of which they call *Torah*. For them the word *torah* means instruction that the Lord has revealed. They use it to mean everything that their people have learned about the Lord's way with and for humanity and which can now be studied and practiced. A large portion of the Torah consists of laws and commandments, both ethical and ritual. Judaists welcome these instructions as specifications of *what* love should do in the various occasions and relations of their lives. Another portion of this inheritance instructs Judaists *how* to observe all these commandments. Judaists refer to these prescriptions as *halakhah*, which means literally a way of *walking* and, by inference, the proper way of observing the rules and regulations prescribed in the Torah for those seeking to make their life one and righteous. Outside observers tend to perceive and describe Judaism pejoratively as "a legalistic religion," which burdens its adherents with the obligation to observe strictly no less than 613 moral and ritual laws. Judaists themselves, however, welcome their accumulation of commandments and guidelines, all of which they designate by the English word "Law," and they consider as righteous that person "who delights in the law of the Lord" and therefore "meditates on it both day and night" (Psalm 1). Living one's life under the discipline of Torah, Judaists continue to say, brings the joy of expressing one's love of God.[6]

Judaists reverse the terms of the Christian slogan and say with integrity and gratitude, "The Law fulfills love." They can say this because they consider that the Torah's commandments and prescriptions enable them to give disciplined expression to that radical, total, and rigorous love evoked when one comes to know and willingly to accept the Lord's right to sovereignty. Few if any Judaists would boast or even make the claim of exemplifying the fullness of such love. On the other hand, few would hesitate to admit, if asked, that it is a demanding love that impels a Judaist toward faithful observance of the commandments and that faithful observance of the commandments gives love a generous expression, which is satisfyingly consistent with the revealed unity and character of the Lord.

6 Cf. esp. Neusner, *The Way of Torah.*

The ethical demand imposed on Judaists does not allow them to be content with an individualistic morality. It is not merely the individual Judaist who is summoned to become one and righteous. Judaists are individual members of a people whose *collective* reality also has a divine calling to become one and righteous. The commandments of the Torah require individual behavior that strengthens the Judaic community, and a Judaist is said to serve and please the Lord best by being intentionally joined with other Judaists in behavior that promotes the godly unity and goodness of the community.

Behold how good and how pleasant it is when brothers dwell together in unity!

There the Lord pronounces his blessing, life forevermore.

(Psalm 133:1)

Judaism's conscience will not let its sense of responsibility stop at the borders of the Judaic community. The commandment to "love one's neighbor as oneself" extends beyond Judaists to include the "outsider who sojourns" among Judaists (Leviticus 19:18, 33–4). Since about 70 c.e. the Jewish people have been dispersed among the nations of the world, compelled to live in spatial proximity to sundry peoples. This experience has impressed upon them that their commandment intends that they reach out, in the neighborly behavior of mercy and justice, to all people in an effort to build community with them. The burden of this exacting duty is mitigated for Judaists by their conviction that the Lord himself – "who created the earth . . . and gives breath *to all of its people*" – "trains" the Judaic people for the kind of righteous work that liberates humankind for community:

I am the Lord.
I have called you for righteousness.
I have taken you by the hand and trained you.
I have given you to be a covenant to humankind,
   a light to the nations,
   to give sight to the blind,
   to bring captives out of prison,
   out of dungeons where they are confined in darkness.

(Isaiah 42:5–6)

The moral symbolism of Judaism illustrates all that we said in Chapter One about the force of nonmaterial motivations in *commending necessary behavioral assent* to the undeniability of *the central spiritual reality* that is conceived in terms of ultimate good. With the righteous character of the Lord as its highest good, and with *the nonmaterial motivation* of love as its incentive for moral behavior, and with the Torah – in its universal applicability – as the medium and measure of consistent ethical behavior, Judaism's moral symbolism has a built-in necessity to *expose self-contradictory behavior* and thereby to *disclose the inevitability of living with reference to the Lord.* The following psalm by an ancient Judaist exemplifies this symbolism ideally:

O how happy is the person
  who does not walk in the counsel of the wicked,
  nor stand along the way taken by sinners,
  nor sit in the seat of the scornful;
but who delights in the law of the Lord
  and meditates on this law day and night.
He is like a tree
  planted near running water;
  it yields its fruit in its season,
  and its leaves do not wither.
In all that he does, he prospers.

The wicked are not like him;
  they are like chaff which the wind drives away.
Therefore the wicked will not survive
  in the judgment,
nor sinners in the congregation
  of the righteous,
because the Lord sustains the way
  of the righteous,
but the way of the wicked vanishes.

                                                   (Psalm 1)

Intellectual Symbolism of Undeniability

In the Judaic construction of the human situation, the Lord's self-revelation is the most convincing reason for believing in what the philosophers refer to as "the existence" of God. For this reason intellectual symbolism of the undeniability of God is not given top priority in Judaism. There is no authority higher than the Lord that can compel belief in the Lord, and, except for its self-revelations, the Lord's reality transcends all human processes of knowing:

Inquire of the Lord while he is present,
call upon him while he is near. . . .
For my thoughts are not your thoughts
and your ways are not my ways,
  says the Lord.

For as the heavens are higher than the earth,
so are my ways higher than your ways
and my thoughts higher than your thoughts.

(Isaiah 55:6, 8–9)

Judaism *experiences* the reality of the Lord God in the covenant relation that the Lord initiated and established. That covenant creates and sustains the relational reality expressed in either of two phrases: "the Lord, God of Israel" and "Israel, the people of the Lord." Even in these two phrases used to describe the covenant relation, one can see that Israel derives its corporate identity from being "the people *of the Lord*" while the reality of the Lord exceeds, and is not contingent upon, being "the God *of Israel*." In this relationship the Lord's reality is more certain than the reality of Israel's corporate identity, an identity wholly contingent upon the Lord's bonding to this people. Judaists have typically used terms of intimate personal relation to describe the kind of knowledge of the Lord they derive from this relation. Their scriptures, for example, use the same word *yada*, to know, when referring to sexual intercourse and to the Lord's bonded presence with the people of Israel: "Adam *knew* his wife Eve and she conceived and bore him Cain" (Genesis 4:1), and "You only have I *known* of all the families of the earth" (Amos 3:2).

Despite this emphasis upon "knowing God" through existential relation, intellectual symbolism of the undeniability of a *central spiritual reality* has a significant place in Judaism. Judaism has always given mind and reason an exalted role in working out the responsibilities concomitant with revelation. We have already noted the Shema's command to love the Lord with all one's mind. The prophets and psalmists in the Tanakh (Scriptures) support their inspirations with direct appeals to the mind, "aiming to demonstrate the operation of God's law and love in ways accessible to human reason."[7] Jeremiah, among other prophets, appeals to the orderliness of nature and to the inexorability of the Lord's laws in nature and in human life (5:22–9). Readers should examine Deuteronomy 13:26, Jeremiah 23:25–40, and Ezekiel 33–4 to see that rational tests are offered for distinguishing true prophecy from false. One psalmist exclaims, "The heavens are telling the glory of the Lord, and the firmament proclaims his handiwork" (Psalm 19:1). Another psalmist observes that only a fool (an "empty headed person") can say sincerely that "there is no God" but that "a wise person applies its mind to God" (Psalm 14:1–2 and 53:1–2).

In ancient biblical times, some Judaic people were successfully tempted to break away from the cult of the Lord and worship the gods of other

---

7   Samuel S. Cohon, *Jewish Theology* (Assen, the Netherlands: Koninklijke Van Gorcum, 1971), p. 152.

nations. The Judaic prophets appealed passionately to the rational judgment of these apostates, arguing that the Lord's reality is the only reality worthy to be humanity's God. The oracles of Jeremiah are typical of all prophetic reasoning in the Tanakh. In chapter 10 of his prophecies, Jeremiah argues literally that "the Lord is the *true* God" and that the gods of the other nations are "false." He says that the Lord is "the living God and the everlasting King" who has the destiny of all nations in his discretion because he "made them all" and made Israel his "heir." Jeremiah elaborates this theme of the Lord as creator. "It is he who made the earth by his power, put the world in place by his wisdom, and stretched out the heavens by his understanding." By stark contrast, Jeremiah reasons, the gods of the other nations "cannot speak"; because they are made by "craftsmen" and "smiths," that is by "skilled men," they "cannot walk" and have to be "carried" by men. They are "stupid and foolish" and their "instruction," like the material from which some are made, is "wood." No one should be awed by them for "they have no power to do harm or good." Indeed, they are "a work, a delusion," "worthless" and "false": "there is no breath in them." Jeremiah's reasoning amounts to an argument that the Lord is *the central spiritual referent for all humankind*, not merely that for the Judaic people, and that he is *the reality upon which all other realities depend and from which they derive their ultimate meaning*.

After the Temple was destroyed in 70 C.E., authority in Judaism was assumed by the sages, known and revered as rabbis. Some of these taught that the authority of the prophets' inspiration – direct and immediate communication with the Lord – had passed to the searching minds of the sagacious rabbis. In any case, these sages emphasized the role of reason in coming to understand and observe Torah. According to them, Torah is a matter of *learning*: something to be *taught* rigorously and *studied* thoroughly in order to be *observed* strictly for the hallowing of one's life in relation to the Lord and other humans. In this holy life of study and practice, mind and reason have a preeminent role but they remain at the service of revealed instruction from God. For the rabbis the "existence" of the Lord was axiomatic and required no proof. In fact, the rabbinic literature known as the Talmud has no Hebrew word for atheist. Its word *min* signifies someone who denies the sovereignty, providence, and justice of the Lord rather than one who denies the Lord's existence or reality. In the Talmud it is said that those who make such denials of the Lord will develop a disregard for the moral commandments of the Torah even as those who begin by disregarding the commandments ultimately deny both the divine origin of the moral laws and the sovereignty of the Lord (Tos. Shebvot 3.6 and Sifra Behukotai 3). Also in the Talmud, one Pseudo-Jonathan, commenting on Genesis 4:8, represents Cain, who murdered his own brother, as a man who espoused the philosophy that "the world was not created in mercy and is not governed in mercy" and that "there is no judgment or judge, no other world, no reward for the righteous and no punishment for the wicked." Many such references in the Talmud indicate that the rabbis dealt with practical atheism, the disregard of moral and ritual observance, rather than outright doubt about the root principle of Judaic faith. There is nonetheless some rudimentary speculation in this rabbinic literature concerning the existence of God. A Rabbi Isaac resorts to the argument from design when he explains how Abraham, without being taught by anyone, reasoned his way to God:

It is like a man who was traveling from place to place and saw a palace all lighted up. As he reflected, "Is it conceivable that this palace is without a caretaker?", the owner looked out and said, "I am the caretaker of the mansion." So with Abraham. As he wondered, "Is it conceivable that the world is without a caretaker?", the Holy One, blessed be He, looked down and said to him, "I am the Master of all the universe."[8]

Similarly, in answering a heretic's skepticism about the world's having a creator, Akiba appealed to the analogy of human craftsmanship. "As the house attests the existence of the builder, a coat of the weaver and a door of a carpenter, so the world testifies to its creator" (Midrash Temura, end). It is said that the Emperor Hadrian asked Rabbi Joshua the direct question, "Does God exist?" The rabbi reportedly answered, "Would you say that this world is without a guide?" (Yalkut Shimeoni). These forms of appeal to the argument from design and the cosmological argument are only intimations of speculative reasoning, but they do certify the rabbis' recognition that affirmation of the Lord God's reality deserves to be made with a mind that is convinced by reason.

Thoroughgoing skepticism and ideological atheism eventually did become an option and problem for the community of Jews living in the Hellenistic culture of Alexandria, Egypt. Philo, a Judaic theologian and Hellenistic philosopher who lived in Alexandria at the beginning of the first Christian century, sought explicitly to refute intellectual challenges to the root principle of Judaic faith. He undertook to develop an understanding of Judaism's Lord God in the light of Platonic, Aristotelian, and Stoic thought, and to show that belief in the Lord's revealed reality can survive critical investigation made by rigorous minds. To this end he constructed reasoned arguments for the existence of God and inaugurated Judaism's long and distinguished tradition of speculative philosophy. Identifying God ontologically as the One "to whom alone existence be-

8   Gen. R. 39.1, cited by Harry Wolfson, *Philo: Foundations of Religious Philosophy in Judaism, Christianity, and Islam* (Cambridge, Mass.: Harvard University Press, 1947), 2:77, n. 22.

longs,"[9] Philo developed both a cosmological and a teleological argument on the assumption that the *existence*, but not the essence, of God can be known "from created things by virtue of a process of reasoning."[10] On the basis of these arguments and a third drawn from the nature of the human psyche (an inanimate and irrational universe could not have generated from itself a being that is both animate and rational), Philo concluded that human intelligence can discern with reasonable certainty that God exists and that God is the First Cause and the efficient ground of all that is and will ever come to pass. For Philo the revealed Lord alone is God; therefore, this reasoned case for the existence of God constituted for him an intellectual demonstration that *the Lord God is real and is the reality upon which all other realities depend and from which they derive their ultimate meaning.*

In the medieval West. Judaism encountered again the remonstration of a robust Greek thought, which, transmitted by Islam, aroused among Judaists a strong sense of religious obligation to corroborate the truths of revelation by the resources of the human mind and to demonstrate the existence of the Lord on the grounds of irrefutable reason. The doctrine of *creatio ex nihilo*, the creation of the universe from nothing, had now become an axiom of Judaic theology as well as a buttress to piety. The philosopher, Saadia ben Joseph Gaon (882–942), took as his starting point, a teaching he believed to be derived from revelation, "All things were created and the Lord created them *ex nihilo*." To confirm by reason this truth of revelation, Saadia developed a cosmological argument incorporating arguments from Aristotle and the Islamic philosophic speculations called the Kalam. Maintaining that the material substance of the world had to have had a beginning, Saadia's argument required reason to deduce that all material beings derive from the immaterial God, a deduction, he observed, that agrees with the teaching of Judaic scripture: "Before the mountains were brought forth or ever thou hadst created the world, from everlasting to everlasting thou art God" (Psalm 90:2). Amusingly Saadia points out the self-evident impossibility of demonstrating the process of creation ex nihilo: To do this one would have to become the creator instead of a creature.

Judaic philosophy reached its zenith in the mind and work of Maimonides (Moses ben Maimon, 1125–1204) who has been called "the greatest single figure in medieval Judaism in both philosophical and halakhic scholarship."[11] Maimonides refrained from the conventional Judaic method of deducing the existence of God from the belief in creation out

9 Philo, *Moses*, 1.14.75.
10 *Legum Allegoria* 3.33.100–3.
11 Steven T. Katz, *Jewish Ideas and Concepts* (New York: Schocken Books, 1977), p. 306.

of nothing, recognizing that there is a risk in basing Judaism's constitutive claim (the Shema) on such an unprovable belief. Intellectually honest thinkers, he wrote, must concede that the question of the world's creation or eternity cannot be settled "with mathematical certainty."[12] He chose to make his own rational demonstration of God's existence on the assumption of Aristotle's hypothesis of the world's eternity. As a Judaist, he did not subscribe to this hypothesis but used it heuristically to show the rational credibility of religious belief in God's reality.

Maimonides developed four cosmological arguments to demonstrate the existence, unity, and incorporeality of God. He based two on motion, a third on potentiality and actuality, and a fourth on possibility and necessity. "In a sense they are different forms of the same argument, based on (1) the universality of causation, on (2) the impossibility of infinite regress, and on (3) the fact that each compound substance consists of matter and form."[13] It is a matter of historical import that Thomas Aquinas, born some twenty years after Maimonides' death, restated these four arguments and added another to form his "five ways of knowing" that God exists. Maimonides, having developed his four arguments on the basis of Aristotle's "*opinion*" that the universe is eternal, then presented philosophical arguments to prove that the doctrine of *creatio ex nihilo* is superior to the doctrine of an eternal universe.[14]

At the beginning of the *Mishneh Torah*, Maimonides explains that the *existence* of God is an article of faith that every Jew is obligated to believe and which is "the great root [*hashoresh hagado*] upon which everything else depends." In this explanation Maimonides gives a succinct statement of his third argument for the necessary existence of God:

The foundation of all foundations and the pillar of the sciences is to know that there is a Prime Existent who produced everything in existence, and that all beings in heaven and on earth and in the intervening space do not exist save through the reality of His existence. If it could be imagined that He does not exist, then nothing else could exist. On the other hand, if it should be imagined that everything beside Him did not exist, He alone would still exist and He would not cease because of their removal. For all existents depend upon him, but He, the Blessed One, is not dependent on them, not on any one of them. This is what the prophet said: "The Lord God is the *true* God." He alone is truth (reality) and nothing else possesses a reality like His.[15]

12   *Moreh Nebukhim*, 1, 71 (trans. Schlomo Pines, *Guide of the Perplexed*, Chicago: University of Chicago Press, 1963, pp. 175–84).
13   Cohon, *Jewish Theology*, p. 184.
14   *Moreh Nebukhim*, 2.
15   Quoted from Cohon, *Jewish Theology*, p. 191.

Here Maimonides expresses the reality of Judaism's Lord God in terms of necessary existence and assigns to all other realities a derived and dependent status wholly contingent on the reality of the Lord God.

From this survey it is evident that Jewish philosophy has made an impressive effort to demonstrate that Judaic belief in the Lord's reality can withstand the scrutiny and remonstrations of reason and that the Judaic mind can excel in the rigors of speculative philosophy. While philosophical argumentation concerning the existence of God is not an integral feature of Judaism, the foregoing material shows that Judaism has made significant use of intellectual symbolism to demonstrate the intellectual credibility of its revelation. This symbolism asserts that *the Lord, the God of Judaism, is real and is the reality upon which all other realities depend and from which they derive their ultimate meaning.*

Mythological Symbolism of Undeniability

Because Judaism holds that the Lord is the ultimate source of all power, its mythological symbolism of undeniability asserts that the Lord's dominion is unshared, unchallengeable, and unlimited. Judaism's scriptures present numerous examples of this kind of symbolism. *Employing images of power* to depict the Lord as the sole creator of all that exists and as the unchallengeable sovereign who administers both nature and human history with irresistible providence, the writers of Judaism's Bible *express undeniability as irresistibility.*

We mentioned previously that, in the development of their definitive concept of God, Judaists were slow to ascribe creation of the natural universe to the Lord, even though they claimed from the beginning that the Lord enlists nature's powers at will to effect his purposes. Creation was a significant theme in the religious world of Judaism's origin. The mythologies of ancient Judaism's neighbors dealt with creation extensively. The early Judaists themselves, however, held a skeptical attitude toward mythologies. They tended to consider the mythological world to be imagined rather than merely imaginatively described. The Judaists focused their own imagination and all their other cognitive powers on history in their effort to know, believe, understand, and speak about the Lord. They were convinced that the Lord is immediately and mightily involved with human events to direct them irreversibly in a linear succession toward the goal of his immutable purpose. Subsequent generations of Judaists received as canonical this twofold bias: negatively against a world mythologically posited and described, and positively toward history as the place where the Lord is present and active continually in ways that are humanly perceivable. Consequently, Judaism has never shown any appreciable interest in developing a distinctive mythology of the Lord's reality and activities. However, it has always recognized that the reality of the Lord transcends historical experience and requires a symbolic representation that enlarges upon the data of human experience and exemplifies what we call mythological symbolism.

When Judaists did eventually appropriate the notion of creation, they reconceptualized it to conform both to their belief in the Lord's exclusive dominion and to their preference for the historical over the mythological. They construed creation to be a complex of initial acts with which the Lord originated the conditions necessary for human existence and inaugurated human history. Strictly speaking, Judaism's well-known story of creation in the first chapter of Genesis does not present the notion of creation out of nothing. The earliest-known explicit statement that Judaism's God created out of nothing seems to have been written toward the end of the second century before the common era:

I implore you, my child, to look at the heavens and the earth and see everything that is in them and recognize that God, in making all those things, did not use anything that already existed.

(2 Maccabees 7:28)

Scholars think that the Genesis story of creation was given its present form in the sixth century before the common era. This story construes creation under the image of God's having ordered an undifferentiated chaos into a systematized cosmos. It relates that God began this work on chaos in the solitude of his singularity, receiving neither advice, consent, aid, nor opposition from any other source. Prior to God's creative word, this story knows of no other power or reality except the primeval chaos, and it knows of no combatant resistance offered by that chaos to God's effort to give it structure. Here the power of God's word is utterly efficacious. God has only to utter the simple command, "Let there be" and the actual results correspond to the specifications of God's expressed command: "And God said, 'Let there be light'; and there was light, and God saw that the light was good" (1:3–4). The Genesis story recounts a succession of six such daily utterances with which God breathtakingly commanded the entire universe into the reality of an interrelated system. Before taking a rest "from all the work which he had done in creation" (2:3), "God saw everything that he had made, and behold, it was very good" (1:31).

As a developed theme, creation is presented in only one other place in Judaism's Bible. Psalm 104 extols the unsurpassable greatness of the Lord's unassisted wisdom and power in creating the universe and in directing its daily operation. We call the reader's attention to the reference to Leviathan in this psalm. Leviathan (Lothan) was a mythological monster who figured in Canaanite creation myths and was familiar to the ancient Judaists. In the myths he appears as a belligerent sea monster who battles against the creative and integrative forces of the good deities and who therefore symbolized a volitional primeval chaos. In sharp contrast, the imagination of the Judaic psalmist, awed by the immeasurable power of the Lord God, reduces the mythical Leviathan to the Lord's plaything. The psalmist pictures Leviathan as a sea animal that the Lord created to romp amusingly in the vast expanses of ocean also created by the Lord. Indeed, for this psalmist, everything that exists owes its reality and reason for existence to the intention and wisdom of the Lord, *the irresistibility of whose power* over creation boldly exhibits his *undeniability.*

O Lord my God, you are truly great, clothed in majesty and glory, and wrapped in a robe of light.

You stretched out the heavens like a tent and laid the beams of your abode on their waters. Making the clouds your chariot, you ride on the wings of the wind; you use the winds as messengers and flames of fire as servants.

You fixed the earth on its foundations so that it never can be shaken. You wrapped it with the deep as with a robe and the waters lay above the mountains. At your rebuke the waters fled; at the sound of your thunder they rushed away, flowing over the mountains and down into the valleys to the place you appointed for them. You fixed a boundary which they must not pass so that they may never again cover the earth.

You make springs gush forth in the valleys and their water to flow between the hills. The wild beasts all drink from them, the wild asses quench their thirst. The birds of the air nest on their banks and sing among the leaves.

From your lofty abode you water the mountains, and the earth abounds with the fruit of your effort. You make grass to grow for the cattle, and plants for the use of humans so that they get provisions from the soil – wine to gladden their hearts, oil to make their faces shine, and bread to sustain their strength.

The trees of the Lord get plenty of rain, those cedars of Lebanon which he planted. In them the birds build their nests and on the highest branches the stork makes her home. On the high mountains the wild goats have their haunts, and the badgers hide among the boulders.

You have made the moon to mark the seasons; the sun knows when to set. You bring darkness on and night comes; all the beasts of the forest come out: young lions roar for their prey seeking their food from God. When you make the sun rise, they go back to their lairs to lie down, and humans go forth to their work to labor until dusk.

O Lord, your creations are countless. By your wisdom you have made them all. The earth is filled with your creations. There is the vast immeasurable sea, teeming with innumerable things, living things both great and small, and ships sail there, and Leviathan, whom you made for your amusement, plays there.

All these creatures depend on you to feed them regularly; what you give to them they gather up; when you open your hand, their hunger is satisfied. When you hide your face, they suffer; when you take away their breath, they die and return to dust. When you send forth your Spirit they are created, and you renew the face of the earth.

Biblical writers symbolize the Lord's unshared sovereignty even in the way they use the Hebrew verb *bara'*, create. By using *bara'* with the Lord God as its exclusive subject, these writers assert that the Lord holds a monopoly on a certain category of actions. They use its primary synonym – *asah,* do or make – interchangeably with *bara'* to describe the Lord God's unique creative acts (Genesis 1:7, 16, 25, e.g.), but they use *asah* commonly also with humans as its subject. As the sole subject of *bara'*, the Lord is said to have *created* the universe ("the heavens and the earth," Genesis 1:1 and Isaiah 45:18), humankind (Genesis 1:27, Isaiah 45:12, Psalm 89:47, and Deuteronomy 4:32), the individual human (Ezekiel 21:35, Malachi 2:10, and Ecclesiastes 12:1), the divisions of labor ("the producer" and "the destroyer," Isaiah 45:16) and the people Israel as a nation (Isaiah 43:7). We learn also from this literature that the Lord continues to create (*bara'*) independently and distinctively. It is said that the Lord *is creating* "a new thing" (Jeremiah 31:22 and Isaiah 48:6–7), "a clean heart" (Psalm 51:10), righteousness and salvation (Isaiah 45:8), and that in the future the Lord *will create* a new condition in nature (Isaiah 65:17). By using *bara'* solely to indicate the creative actions of the Lord, the biblical writers subtly assert the Lord's unshared responsibility in the creation of all realities, and thus asserting the Lord's *irresistibility,* they express symbolically *the undeniability of the central spiritual referent of humankind.*

The Judaic Bible attributes to the Lord permanent, unchallengeable control over the vast reaches and intricate processes of the physical cosmos he has created. With the wisdom and purpose that occasioned creation in the first place the Lord daily commands each part of the universe's system to do what he created it to do (Job 38–9). For example, with daily dependability he evokes dawn and dusk (38:12; cf. Amos 4:13, 5:8) and gives breath and spirit to humans. He gives and withholds rain (Deuteronomy 11:13–17), bestows the fruits of the soil (Hosea 2:10–12), and gives progeny to humans and beasts (Deuteronomy 7:13 and Jeremiah 31:12). The greatness and reality of the Lord's power enables him to effect these blessings without himself being involved in the process.

Similarly, the Bible distinguishes the Lord's reality from phenomena of the storm with which it frequently associates him. The Lord's presence with the storm and his transcendence of each of its accompanying phenomena are emphatically stated in the biblical account of Elijah's temporary lodging in a cave on Mount Horeb:

Behold, the Lord passed by, and a great and strong wind rent the mountains and broke in pieces the rocks before the Lord, but the Lord was not in the wind. And after the wind, there was an earthquake, but the Lord was not in the earthquake; and after the earthquake there was a fire, but the Lord was not in the fire; and after the fire, there was a soft whisper. . . . And the Lord said [to Elijah], "Go . . . anoint Hazael to be king over Syria, and Jehu . . . to be king over Israel."

(1 Kings 19:11–12, 15)

Another biblical story of the Lord and a storm on a mountain is central to Judaism. It recounts in mythological images of power a visit reputedly made by the Lord to Mount Sinai where he met Moses and gave him the commandments that the Lord intended to be observed by every generation of Judaists:

There were thunders and lightnings, and a thick cloud upon the mountain, and a very loud trumpet blast, so that all the people who were in the camp trembled. . . . And Mount Sinai was wrapped in smoke, because the Lord descended upon it in fire . . . and the whole mountain quaked greatly . . . . and the Lord called Moses to the top of the mountain . . . and spoke all these words, saying, "I am the Lord your God who brought you out of the land of Egypt, out of the house of bondage. You shall have no other gods besides me."

(Exodus 19:16, 18, 20 and 20:1–3)

These biblical accounts of the storm-associated theopanies at Mount Horeb and Mount Sinai do not depict the storm as a sheer display of brute force. The storm's power-filled phenomena are rather warrants for the undeniable presence and irresistible purpose of the Lord. In company with the storm, the Lord becomes manifest to implement his righteous will, which, in these two instances, was respectively to make assignments for national leadership and to give instruction for his chosen people.

Bringing the origin and operation of the natural world under the solitary and uninterrupted dominion of the Lord was a predictable and credible achievement of the ancient Judaic imagination. It was merely the extension of the previously formed and tenaciously held Judaic conviction that the Lord governs human history with irresistible providence. Ancient Judaists reasoned that nature, in all of its magnitude and with all of its intricacies, posed less of a challenge to their belief in the Lord's autarchy than did history. They observed that whereas nature in general obeys the Lord's intention with either inanimate or instinctive compliance, human beings are able to act intentionally, even to neglect and oppose the Lord's intentions:

The Lord has spoken: "I have reared and brought up a people, but they have rebelled against me. The ox knows its owner, and the ass its master's crib; but Israel, my own people, shows neither knowledge nor discernment."

(Isaiah 1:2–3)

Even the stork in the sky knows the time to migrate, and the turtledove, swallow and crane keep the season of return; but my people do not know the ordinances of the Lord.

(Jeremiah 8:7)

Humans, as understood in this Judaic biblical perspective, are able to act intentionally because the Lord has created them with freedom and fated them to exercise it. Merely to be human places one under the necessity of identifying options, choosing one of them, and acting upon it. Under this concept, then, humans are capacitated to learn the Lord's instructions for human life and to recognize that they should obey those instructions, but because their freedom is genuine, albeit finite, they may choose not to learn the Lord's instructions or, having learned them, not to obey them, and to pursue rather their own self-defined course of action. Since the biblical mind believes that the Lord himself designed human existence with this built-in, obligatory prerogative, it will not allow that the august sovereignty of the Lord will supplant or even curtail the necessity for a human to make its own choices and to act upon them.

Biblically construed, history comprehends the actions of both the human and the divine will. In this coincidence of two independent volitions, however, the Lord's will is seen to prevail irresistibly, yet without compromising the finite freedom of human beings. Because the Lord is one of its participants, history exceeds the range possible for human finitude alone, and within this larger dimension the Lord is able to utilize the effects of human initiatives as causes in his own immediate and ultimate purposes. The biblical story of Joseph illustrates this. Joseph, a member of a family in Palestine, was the youngest of several brothers. He evoked the extreme jealousy of his elder brothers and they contrived to dispose of him. They succeeded by selling him into slavery in faraway Egypt. Circumstances in Egypt favored Joseph "because the Lord was with him, and whatever he did, the Lord made it prosper" (Genesis 39:23). Eventually, Joseph became the Pharaoh's most trusted staff member and held power second only to Pharaoh himself. Meantime, famine having overtaken Joseph's family back in Palestine, his father sent the brothers to Egypt to seek relief supplies. They had to present their petition to Joseph, whom they did not recognize but who recognized them and sent them home loaded generously with supplies. On another occasion, when the brothers returned to Egypt, Joseph identified himself and, seeing their utter dismay, said to them, "Now do not be distressed or reproach yourselves for having sold me here, for God also sent me here, ahead of you, in order to help save lives" (45:5). Later, after their father had died, the brothers again became manifestly fearful that Joseph would retaliate. Joseph spoke to reassure them and his reassuring words constitute the Bible's paradigm description of the way the Lord uses human intentions and their fulfillment to accomplish his own purpose: "Do not be afraid. Is it for me to take God's place? You meant to do me harm, but God meant it to do good, to achieve his immediate purpose of helping many people to stay alive" (50:19–20). This story asserts that the intentions of the brothers were allowed to run their full course and hence to become acts of harm to Joseph, and it asserts that the Lord was able to use the very same humanly willed, evil acts to bring about his own purpose to help many people at that time. By depicting the Lord's powerful providence as unimpeded by the acts of human volition, the Joseph story *expresses undeniability as irresistibility.*

As related in Judaism's Bible, the Lord administers the actions of all the nations in the same way that he managed events in the Joseph story. While honoring the finite independence of each nation, the Lord takes the actions they initiate for their own purposes and uses those actions to accomplish *irresistibly* his own purpose for humankind. For example, with reference to an international conflict between the powerful Assyrian nation and the tiny nation of Israel, the biblical prophet Isaiah maintained that the Lord was using Assyria's arrogant aggression to give Israel a punishment it deserved. Isaiah quoted the Lord as saying:

Ah, Assyria, the rod that I wield in my anger,
    the staff of my fury!
I send him against a godless nation,
    and I command him to march against
      the people of my wrath,
to spoil, plunder and trample them
    down like mud in the streets.
But this is not what he intends,
    this is not what he has in mind.
He intends only to destroy,
    to demolish nation after nation.

                                         (Isaiah 10:5–7)

Isaiah added his own comment,

When the Lord has finished all that he wants to do on Mount Zion and on Jerusalem, he will punish the king of Assyria for his own arrogance and haughty pride.

(Isaiah 10:12)

For the biblical writers and for Judaism generally, it is axiomatic that the Lord governs the historical outcome of every nation and of the whole world. Understandably, however, Judaism focuses on the Lord's governance of the Israelite people. Both its Bible and its rituals spotlight the special history that has resulted from the Lord's exercise of sovereignty over this Israelite or Jewish people with whom, they believe, he has sustained a special, permanent bonding. The central event of this special history is the *exodus* or deliverance of the Israelite ancestors from cruel slavery in Egypt. According to accounts preserved in the Bible and commemorated in rituals celebrated by Judaists to this day, the Israelites had lived and toiled for "four hundred and thirty years" (Exodus 12:40) in merciless bondage to a succession of Egyptian Pharaohs when an entire generation attempted an escape. Pursued by Egyptian military forces equipped with chariots, fine horses, and finely trained charioteers, the Israelites became trapped on the shores of the Red Sea. The Bible's mythological description of what happened next is used ritually to sculpture the Jewish ethnic self-consciousness of every Judaic boy and girl:

The Lord drove the sea back by a strong east wind all night, and turned the sea bed into dry land. With the waters divided so that they formed a wall on the right and a wall on the left, the Israelites marched through the sea on dry ground. The Egyptians followed in pursuit – all the Pharaoh's horses, chariots and horsemen – far into the sea . . . . The Lord looked down on the Egyptian army . . . and threw them into a panic by clogging their chariot wheels and making them difficult to turn . . . and the sea returned to its accustomed flow. . . . The waters flowed back and covered all of the Pharaoh's army, the chariots and the horsemen. . . . Not so much as one man was left alive. . . . Thus the Lord saved Israel that day from the hand of the Egyptians. . . . And Israel saw the great work which the Lord did against the Egyptians, and the people feared the Lord, and they believed in the Lord.

(Exodus 14:21–31)

This same event is mythologically described in the Book of Deuteronomy. It instructs all ethnic descendants of those delivered by the Lord from Egypt to perpetuate in solemn ritual the memory of the exodus, and it charges these descendants to profess that the Lord accomplished the Israelites' deliverance by "the terrifying power" of his "mighty hand and outstretched arm":

You shall solemnly recite before the Lord your God: "My father was a wandering Aramaean who went down to Egypt with a few relatives and sojourned there until they became a great, powerful and numerous people. The Egyptians mistreated and humiliated us; they coerced us into cruel slavery. Then we cried to the Lord the God of our fathers for help. The Lord listened to us and saw our affliction, our misery and our oppression; and so the Lord brought us out of Egypt with the terrifying power of a mighty hand and an outstretched arm, and with signs and wonders.

(Deuteronomy 26:5–8)

The narrative (Haggadah) of the annual Passover ritual commemorates the exodus as the event in which the Lord, in effect, *created* a people, Israel, out of slaves who, in the chaos of their Egyptian bondage, were no people. This ritual narrative calls upon all Jewish persons to identify themselves imaginatively as personal participants in the Egyptian slavery and in the deliverance from it, and to acknowledge and proclaim that it was the Lord who accomplished this miracle of justice and mercy for the entire ethnic lineage:

In every generation each Jew should regard himself as though he personally went forth from Egypt. . . . It was not only our forefathers whom the Holy One, praised be he, redeemed from slavery, but us also did he redeem together with them. . . . Therefore, we should thank and praise, laud and glorify, exalt and honor, extol and adore God who performed all these miracles for our fathers and for us.[16]

The supreme manifestation of the Lord's unshared sovereignty and irresistible providence is eschatological, which means that it is envisioned for the time of the *end*, the time when all resistance yields to the matchless power of the Lord's righteous will. The biblical concept of eschatology went through stages of development, but the conviction that impelled that development remained consistent. That is the conviction that history must come to an end in two senses. The matchless power of the Lord guarantees that history will end with a victory for the Lord, and the immutable righteous character of that power necessitates that history eventuate in a state of affairs ordered unconditionally by his righteousness. As the Israelites saw history, the Lord directs the careers of

Israel and all other nations and peoples toward the fulfillment of his own designs. Neither the success nor the failure of the nations' own intentions makes a decisive influence upon the fulfillment of the Lord's designs. Indeed, human achievement in any sense does not fulfill the Lord's intentions for history, and human sin cannot prevent the Lord from accomplishing what he intends for history immediately and ultimately.

Envisioned especially by biblical prophets, the *end* time will be "the Day of the Lord," the time when the Lord will "get his way." On that "day," the prophets anticipate, the Lord will make a universal and irrevocable judgment upon all nations, including Israel (Isaiah 2:10–17, Amos 5:18–20, and Zephaniah 1:1–18). That judgment will terrify the wicked as the Lord "sweeps away everything from the face of the earth" – "man and beast . . . birds of the air and fish of the sea" (Zephaniah 1:2–3). As part of this judgment, the Lord will allow the cosmos to revert momentarily to the primeval chaos ("waste and void") that it was prior to his original creative action (Jeremiah 4:23–6). Then the Lord will demonstrate his power in a display of constructive actions. He will "create new heavens and a new earth," which will be appropriate for those who are to enjoy salvation, and the former heavens and earth "shall not be remembered, or come to mind again" (Isaiah 65:17). The new earth will be lushly fertile (Amos 9:13 and Joel 3:18), and there will be no alternation of day and night or of seasons. The animal world will be unpredatory and devoid of enmity and rivalry (Isaiah 11:6–8). For the humans who have qualified to live in the new realm and age, life will be continuous with their godly life in history – relieved, of course, of all sinful disruptions. In human relations on the new earth there will be universal peace because

the mountain of the house of the Lord
shall be established as the highest mountain

. . .

and all nations shall flow to it,
and the multitudes shall come and say:
"Come, let us go up to the mountain of the Lord
. . . that he may teach us his ways
and that we may walk in his paths."

(Isaiah 2:2–3)

This envisioned eschatological demonstration of the Lord's power to prevail and to provide according to his righteous will and purpose completes Judaism's *mythological symbolization of undeniability expressed in images of the Lord's irresistibility*. It also leads quite naturally into a discussion of Judaism's symbolization of the Lord's desirability.

Desirability

In Judaism's symbolic expressions, the Lord's power to prevail is never expressed merely to overpower. It is expressed always to effect some purpose intended by the Lord. Inferring from its perception of the Lord's participation in history, Judaism claims that all of the Lord's purposes are good because they are demonstrably directed toward the immediate and long term well-being of humans. In this view, even when the Lord acts to punish persons or nations, it is seen to be action intended to redirect them for their best interest and for that of all concerned. Therefore Judaism's symbolisms of *desirability* represent the Lord's Presence in history as *the ultimate valuational norm and the source of humanity's supreme personal benefit*, which, according to Judaism, is humanity's salvation.

Intellectual Symbolism of Desirability

Judaism's intellectual symbolism of desirability straightforwardly *identifies the Lord's revealed Presence in history as the ultimate valuational norm which makes all other expressions of desirability reasonable*. Regarding history as the Lord's breaking through to the ordinary world of everyday human experience, the Judaic mind ideally concentrates its powers on identifying the Presence of the Lord in human experience and demonstrating its supreme desirability. Ideally also, this mind does not think of itself as able to break through to a level of reality beyond the ordinary world. For its knowledge of the Lord, the devout Jewish mind accepts as its fate total dependence upon what the Lord self-reveals and teaches in the course of human affairs. It esteems the Lord's self-given Presence as the supreme expression of desirability accessible in human experience, and it considers faithful observance of the Lord's teaching (Torah) as the way to keep oneself mindful of the Lord's Presence and fit to enjoy it. However, the Lord's being present for the edification of his people, which is the quintessence of his desirability, depends entirely on the Lord. People can seek the Lord, meet and be with the Lord, only because the Lord makes his Presence available.

We noted previously that Judaism considers the exodus of its ancestors from Egypt to be the defining center of its existence. In the Bible's narrative account of that exodus, the Lord, explaining his name, tells Moses that *Yhwh* means "I will be what I will be," or, less philosophically phrased, "I will be present as I will be present" (Exodus 3:14). This explanation, of course, denotes the utter self-determination, freedom, and sovereignty of the Lord, but it also indicates the assured ubiquity of the Lord's Presence. We are told later in this narrative that Moses pitched a tent, which he called the Tent of the Presence, and that "everyone who sought the Lord would go out to the Tent of the Presence" (33:7). Once Moses went there and requested intimate knowledge of the Lord's reality. He prayed, "Show me your glory," which is tantamount to saying, "Make your Presence visible to me." The narrative relates that the Lord answered,

I will make all my goodness pass before you, and in your hearing I will pronounce my name Yhwh; and I will be gracious to whom I will be gracious, and I will have mercy on whom I will have mercy. But you cannot see my Presence, for no human can see me and live.

(33:18–20)

The Lord's answer reiterates the independence and freedom of the Lord's reality and goes on to assert that the Lord remains invisible even when he manifests his Presence. Philo interpreted this answer to mean that humans can know the reality, but not the essence, of the Lord.[17] Surely it means, at least, that humans can identify the Lord's Presence and discern its character by the goodness (which includes his justice), graciousness, and mercy that it manifests in human affairs.

In the Bible the Presence of the Lord is thought to be ubiquitous:

Where could I possibly flee from your Presence?
If I ascend to heaven, you are there!
If I make my bed in Sheol [the region of the deceased],
    you are there!
If I take wings to the birthplace of the morning
    or dwell beyond the western sea,
even there your hand will meet me
    and your right hand will uphold me.

(Psalm 139:7–10)

The characteristics of the Lord's Presence – goodness, justice, and mercy – are paired consistently with each other, in varying combinations throughout the biblical literature. Here we need only to illustrate that they are used together to distinguish the character of the Lord's Presence and thereby to express symbolically its utter *desirability*. In the account of the Lord's proclamation to Moses at Mount Sinai, prior to giving the Ten Commandments, the Lord identifies mercy and justice as primary characteristics of his reality and makes mercy and justice the basis of the covenant he intends to contract with Moses' people, the Israelites:

The Lord, the Lord, a God compassionate and gracious, slow to anger and abounding in steadfast love and faithfulness, extending steadfast love to the thou-

17 Wolfson, *Philo*, 2:86–89.

sandth generation, forgiving iniquity and transgression and sin; yet who does not withhold punishment, but visits the iniquity of the fathers upon the children and the children's children, unto the third and fourth generations.

(Exodus 34:6–7).

Tradition has continued to remember that the Lord demonstrated his mercy by redeeming the Israelites from their slavery in Egypt and making a covenant with them: "When Israel was a child, I loved him, and out of Egypt I called my son" (Hosea 11:1). Likewise, tradition reminds this people that the Lord continually reveals his justice by punishing the Israelites when they fail to uphold their obligation to observe the covenant: "You only have I known of all the families of the earth; therefore I will punish you for all your iniquities" (Amos 3:2).

As portrayed in the Bible, the Lord's mercy and justice are evident and central throughout his covenant relation with Israel. At a time when Israel was thought to have broken faith with the Lord, one of her prophets spoke oracles in which the Lord promised to keep faith with his own covenanted justice and mercy: "I will punish [Israel]. . . . I will betroth you to me forever . . . in righteousness and justice, in steadfast love and mercy" (Hosea 2:13, 19). Because the Lord is thus perceived to have "betrothed" his Presence to Israel "forever" and because the Presence of the Lord is good, steadfastly loving Israel and mercifully apportioning justice to Israel and other nations, biblical prophets argued that it is reasonable for the Israelites to seek to imitate the character of the Lord's Presence and to pursue this as a realizable aspiration. An oracle in the Book of Micah summarizes the reasoning of a whole generation of eighth-century B.C.E. prophets on Israel's obligation to imitate the Lord:

He has showed you, O human, what is good.
What the Lord requires of you is this:
   to act with justice
   to love steadfastly with mercy and
   to walk humbly before your God.

(Micah 6:8)

The notion that the Lord's Presence is Judaism's priceless treasure finds clear and emphatic expression in postbiblical rabbinical writings. The rabbis used the term *Shekhinah* to designate the Presence of the Lord in the world. Some, like the followers of Rabbi Ishmael, thought that "the Shekhinah is everywhere."[18] Quite generally *Shekhinah* refers both to the Lord's being present simultaneously in all parts of the world and also to

18 Cohon, *Jewish Theology*, p. 218.

any particular manifestation of this Presence when it becomes apparent at a given place. According to rabbinical teaching,

Even those special places and objects which God imbues with an extra holiness by His presence — such as the torn bush in which He revealed Himself to Moses, or Mount Sinai, or the Tabernacle in the wilderness — in connection with which the term *Shekhinah* is most often used, teach us that no place is devoid of His presence: neither the lowliest of trees, nor the barest of mountains, nor a wooden sanctuary.[19]

Although assuming the Lord to be present everywhere, the rabbis thought the *Shekhinah* to be preeminently apparent in the affairs of Israel since Israel is his agent in the world. Because Israel sinned, however, its relation to the *Shekhinah* was disrupted and the Temple, where the *Shekhinah* had always been present, was destroyed. Some rabbis held that the destruction of the Temple caused the *Shekhinah* to repair to heaven, but other rabbis maintained that the *Shekhinah*, always faithful to the Lord's covenant, had remained with sinful Israel and would go with this people even into exile among the nations and would return with them when they were brought back.

The rabbis preserved also the notion that the Lord's people should imitate the Lord's behavior except that they were careful to reserve the exercise of ultimate judgment to the Lord. They expressed no restraints on human acts of mercy, however. "Be like [the Lord]. Just as he is gracious and merciful, so you also should be gracious and merciful."[20] Rabbi Hama bar Hanina urged his people "to walk after the attributes of [the Lord]":

Just as the Lord clothes the naked, so you shall clothe the naked. Just as He visits the sick, so you shall visit the sick. Just as the Lord comforts the bereaved, so you shall also comfort the bereaved.[21]

The thought here is not simply that "the actions of the Lord served the rabbis as ideals of conduct": It means that the person whose behavior reflects the character of the Lord's actions "merits having the *Shekhinah* dwell with him."[22]

In its Bible and rabbinical teachings, then, Judaism asserts unequivocably that the Lord is *the ultimate valuational norm* for human character and conduct. Judaism makes its own ethical ideals *reasonable* by identify-

19   Katz, *Jewish Ideas and Concepts*, p. 80.
20   Mekh. Shivah 3. cf. Wolfson, *Philo* (1947), 1:194.
21   Sota 14a; cf. Wolfson citation in previous note.
22   Cohon, *Jewish Theology*, p. 219.

ing them with the Lord's attributes and as requirements stipulated by revelation from the Lord. In this way Judaism employs intellectual symbolism of the desirability of the central spiritual reality of humankind. It compels its constituency to reflect on the desirability of an ultimate referent whose property is always to act mercifully with justice and whose power to prevail in its purpose is uncontestable.

Spiritual Symbolism of Desirability

The Lord's revealed Presence and instruction hold a much greater significance for Judaism than its intellectual symbolism of desirability can communicate. Judaism further expresses this significance in a spiritual symbolism that, consistent with our definition, *emphasizes the personal benefits of responding to the Lord's revealed Presence and instruction.* For the most part, Judaism has defined the ultimate personal benefit as one's participation, "at the end of days," in the redemption of the ethnic whole. According to the opinion held widely among the rabbis,[23] neither individual nor corporate redemption can take place without the other, and both are made possible by the prevenient, provident, and purposeful mercy of the Lord. The regnant concept here holds that the redemption of individual Judaists will occur as a part of this people's corporate redemption "at the end of days."

For Judaism, salvation includes all of the Lord's action: creation, revelation, and redemption. Judaism considers each of these to be a "saving act," and it considers everything the Lord does in relation to these to be salvific work. Accordingly, with *creation* the Lord made human life and gave it a freedom that obligates the human person to act as an agent in its own destiny, choosing and pursuing a purpose that either pleases or displeases the Lord. With *revelation* the Lord singled out the Judaic people, specially bonded his Name and Presence to them and instructed them in the holy life they covenanted to live here and now in a relation constituted of the Lord's overriding will and their own free and conscious assent. As this Judaic reasoning goes, the Lord established a saving relation with all people by their creation and a covenant relation with the Judaic people by his revelation. With *redemption* "at the end of days" he will overcome all opposition that has been exerted against the saving purpose he has demonstrated in creation and revelation, and he will fulfill

---

23 In a controversy between Rabbi Eliezer and Rabbi Joshua, Rabbi Eliezer held that the national redemption of Israel will not happen until appropriate individual repentance has taken place (Babylonian Talmud Sanhedrin 97b). Maimonides ruled in favor of Rabbi Eliezer over Rabbi Joshua. Cf. Maimonides' ruling (Hilkhot Teshuva 7.5), holding decidedly that individual repentance is prerequisite to national redemption.

his general obligation to all those whom he created and his special obligation to those with whom he covenanted. For Judaists themselves, salvation does not wait for the Lord's consummating and universal work of redemption at the time of the end. Their Bible assures them that they are already "a people saved by the Lord" (Deuteronomy 33:29). Therefore, for them in the here and now of history, salvation is a matter of maintaining a proper attitude toward the Lord's revealed Presence and instruction. That attitude, which can "restore the joy of salvation" to even the vilest sinner, is specified repeatedly in scripture and rabbinical teaching as repentance. The following quotations are typical:

Create in me a pure heart, O God,
   and give me a new and steadfast spirit.
Do not cast me away from your Presence
   or take your holy Spirit from me.
Restore to me the joy of your salvation
   and grant me a spirit that sustains it.

O Lord, God of my salvation, save me
   from punishment by death. . . .
My sacrifice, O God, is a broken spirit;
A broken and contrite heart, O God,
   you will not despise.

        (Psalm 51:10–12, 14, 17; emphasis added)

They asked Wisdom, "What is the sinner's punishment?" She replied, "Misfortune pursues sinners" (Proverbs 13:21).

They asked Prophecy, "What is the sinner's punishment?" She replied, "The soul that sins, it shall die" (Ezekiel 18:4).

They asked Torah, "What is the sinner's punishment?" She replied, "Let him bring a guilt offering and it shall atone for him."

They asked The Holy One, Blessed be He, "What is the sinner's punishment?" He replied, *"Let him repent and it shall atone for him."*

        (Jerusalem Talmud, Makkot, 2,6; emphasis added)

It should be noted that repentance is rendered necessary by sin, which is a willful breach in the relation previously covenanted with the Lord, a deliberate living away from the Lord. "Repentance is not a process by which one makes initial entry into the Grace of God and enjoys the benefits of his Mercy, but rather a means by which one is *restored* to that proximity."[24] It is conventional Judaic wisdom that every person sins (1 Kings 8:46) and therefore needs to repent: "There is not a righteous person in the whole world who does [nothing but] good and never sins" (Ecclesiastes 7:20). Nevertheless, there is assured mercy with the Lord for every repentant person:

Let the wicked forsake their way,
  and the unrighteous their thoughts;
let them return to the Lord,
  that he may have mercy on them,
and to our God, for he will
  abundantly pardon.

(Isaiah 55:7)

The sinner's repentance and restoration is not a private, individualistic phenomenon. A Judaist is an individual belonging to the community of the Lord's people. That people is considered as a single or corporate person. "One's individual identity is discovered through membership in that people."[25] The individual Judaist has a corporate existence, and, in the words of Hillel, Judaism admonishes these individuals, "Do not separate yourself from the community" (Avot 2:5). Therefore, restoration to the Lord after individual repentance includes being restored to responsible participation in the Lord's covenanted people. The reconciling effect of repentance by an individual Judaist is guaranteed specifically by the Lord's immutable fidelity to the covenant he made with the Judaic people as a people. The individual Judaist has the benefit of the group's claim on the Lord. Reflection on the Lord's eagerness to forgive and to restore a repentant individual or nation is itself an incentive to repentance. Scripture reminds the Judaists that if they sin so grievously that the Lord's punishment scatters them "among the nations," they will nevertheless "return" because the Lord's covenanted mercy and fidelity will neither destroy nor lose them:

You will return to the Lord your God and you will obey his voice. Because the Lord is a merciful God, he will not forsake you nor destroy you nor forget the covenant with your fathers which he swore to them.

(Deuteronomy 4:30–1)

24 Rabbi David Rose, "To Be Jewish throughout the Centuries: Salvation and Redemption in Traditional Jewish Theology," *Face to Face: An Interreligious Bulletin,* Anti-Defamation League of B'nai B'rith, 14 (Spring 1988): 8.
25 Robert L. Cohn, "Sainthood on the Periphery: The Case of Judaism" in *Sainthood: Its Manifestations in World Religions,* ed. Richard Kieckhefer, (Berkeley: University of California Press, 1988), p. 45.

As they understand salvation, Judaic people do not have to wait to be saved by some further intervention of the Lord such as the final redemption "at the end of days." For their life in the present world, their salvation consists in the reconciliation that is effected when the Judaist, with sincere repentance, solicits pardon from the merciful Lord who is eager to restore the errant sinner. To be restored and sustained "in front of the Lord," to be living in "ever-renewed communion"[26] with the Lord, is, for Judaists, nothing other than *realized salvation*. The poetic piety of the Psalms, urging sinners to return to the Lord, proclaims the conviction that the restored person enjoys, already in this life, everything that is good and desirable:

I sought the Lord and he answered me.
   He delivered me from all my fears.

This wretched man called out to the Lord
   who heard him and saved him from all his troubles.

Taste and see how good the Lord is,
   and how happy it is to take refuge in him!
Revere the Lord, you who are his holy people,
   for those who revere him shall not want for anything.
The irreverent suffer want and go hungry,
   but those who seek the Lord lack no good thing.

(Psalm 34:4, 6, 8–10)

The twenty-third Psalm describes the completeness of the devout person's present life with the Lord. Like a shepherd, the Lord "leads" his followers "in right paths," "renews [their] life" and "relieves" their fears, even the fear of death. Reflecting on the amplitude of the Lord's shepherding providence for his follower's preservation, protection, comfort, and joy, this pious Judaic poet exclaims,

Surely [the Lord's] goodness and mercy shall follow me
   all the days of my life,
and I shall dwell in the house of the Lord
   as long as I live.

(23:5–6)

The presently experienced Presence and response of the Lord is, for the psalmists' piety, salvation actualized under the conditions of mortal life: "I thank you that you have answered me and have become my salvation" (118:21).

26 Pinchas H. Peli, "Individual Repentance in the Jewish Theological Tradition," *Face to Face: An Interreligious Bulletin*, Anti-Defamation League of B'nai B'rith, 14 (Spring 1988): 22.

Emphasizing, as it does, the necessity and incomparable present *personal benefit of responding to the Lord with repentance*, Judaism makes a spiritual symbolization of the Lord's utter desirability. In turn, this symbolic expression of the Lord's supreme desirability points to the desirability of humanity's ultimate spiritual referent.

Moral Symbolism of Desirability

From our review of Judaism's intellectual and spiritual symbolisms of desirability it will have become obvious already that the Lord *defines desirable human conduct* for Judaists. Granted that intellectual symbolism has identified the Lord's revealed actions as Judaism's ultimate valuational norm and that spiritual symbolism has emphasized the personal benefit of imitating the Lord's actions and "walking" steadfastly in his ways, statutes, and commandments, Judaic moral symbolism of desirability necessarily counsels that *imitation of the Lord's ethical attributes* is the virtue leading to the highest human good. The Lord, it is thought, exhibits in perfection the morality that his will requires his people to imitate. The same revealed Reality that constrains Judaists to worship also commands them to behave like the Lord. By emphasizing that piety and morality are inseparable and that Judaic people have the capacity and the obligation to behave like the Lord, Judaism's moral symbolism *integrates its ethical precepts into its larger, overall expression of the meaning and purpose of human life*. Because this moral obligation is defined, imposed, and supervised by the will of the Lord, it serves to *minimize selfish motivation for good behavior*.

Since the time when Moses gave Israel the Lord's commandments, human reason has had neither the prerogative nor the need to determine what is good. All Israel should know that the Lord is the author, revealer, and supervisor of all moral law. There is no other source of moral law than the moral will of the Lord, and in the stipulations of the Covenant he "has shown what is good and what [he] requires" (Micah 6:8) of his people. Having reminded his people that the Lord's gracious redemptive dealing with them is the basis of the behavior that his covenant commandments require of them, Moses counseled his people,

Now, Israel, what does the Lord your God require of you, but to revere the Lord your God, to walk in all his ways, to love him, to serve the Lord your God with all your heart, mind and will, and with all your consciousness, and to keep the commandments and statutes of the Lord which I command you this day for your good?

(Deuteronomy 10:12–13)

Having been shown by the Lord's actions and having been instructed in the revealed Torah what is good, the nation Israel and the individual

Israelite are capable at any time of doing what the Lord requires. Neither the Bible nor rabbinic Judaism knows any "failing in man whether collectively or as an individual which requires special Divine Intervention and which cannot be remedied, with the guidance of Torah, by man himself."[27] Scripture says that the Lord has given the "book of instruction [*toroth*]" to the Judaic people so that they "may do *all* the words of this instruction," and it goes on to say that the Lord's commandment – that this people keep *all* of the commandments in this book – "is not too hard." It requires something they can actually do by their own volition: "Turn to the Lord with all your heart, mind and will and with all your consciousness. . . . *you can do it*" (Deuteronomy 29:29; 30:10, 11, 14, emphasis added). This notion of the human capacity to turn at will from sinning to fulfilling the Lord's requirements is expounded by Isaiah, the eighth century B.C.E. prophet. Speaking as the mouthpiece of the Lord, Isaiah said,

"Wash yourselves; make yourselves clean;
remove your evil deeds from before your eyes;
cease to do evil,
learn to do good;
seek justice, correct oppression;
defend the fatherless, plead for the widow."

"Come, now, let us reason together,"
says the Lord.

"Though your sins be like scarlet,
they shall be as white as snow;
though they be red like crimson,
they shall become like wool.
If you are willing and obedient,
you shall eat the good of the land;
but if you refuse and rebel,
you shall be devoured by the sword,
for the mouth of the Lord has spoken."

(Isaiah 1:16–20)

Like the biblical view of humanity's ability to turn itself to the Lord once the Lord has revealed the way, rabbinic Judaism knows of no human impediments that would prevent the human from doing in the first place what the Lord requires, or from returning (*teshuvah*) by its own will, whenever it wishes, from sin to the Lord and the Lord's way. This returning or repentance is a person's independent act, and it is the person's

27 David Flusser, "Atonement," *Encyclopedia of Judaism* (New York and London: Funk and Wagnalls, 1901–6), vol. 2.

repentance itself that effects reconciliation with the Lord. It is said in the Babylonian Talmud that "the sinner who repents is on a level which the innocently righteous cannot reach" (Berachot 346) and that when the sinner's repentance (*teshuvah*) is motivated from love – and hence not from fear of punishment or hope of reward – it transmutes past sins into deeds of righteousness (Yoma 86b). This is a notable example of the use of moral symbolism of desirability *to minimize selfish motivation for good behavior.*

According to the rabbis each human has an inclination to good (*yetzer tov*) and an inclination to evil (*yetzer ha-rah*). The former inclines one to follow the best that one knows, and for the Judaist the best that one can know is the *mitzvot*, the commandments or good deeds revealed, specified, and required by the Lord. The inclination to evil, however, prompts a person to behave selfishly and hence to neglect the Lord's *mitzvot*. Nevertheless, the human person always determines which inclination it will express and is therefore never beyond the point of returning to a right relationship with the Lord. Maimonides maintained that every person is free to become as "righteous as Moses" or as "unrighteous as Jeroboam," an infamous king (Mishneh Torah Teshuvah 5:2). The human person has the capacity both to discern that the Lord's *mitzvot* are more desirable than selfishly motivated deeds and to recognize that one has the power to do the *mitzvot*, and each person has the moral obligation to act out one's good inclination, which naturally correlates with the *mitzvot*. When one does choose to do the Lord's *mitzvot*, one *transforms self-interested morality into spontaneous regard for the welfare of others* because the Lord's *mitzvot* have as their objective the well-being of the whole community in which the individual Judaist participates.

Judaism's moral ideal for the individual is the *tsaddik*, the righteous person who endeavors earnestly to perform all that the Lord's Torah requires for sanctifying every aspect of life. Judaism offers this as an ideal to which any Jew can realistically aspire. In light of what we have just said about the transmuting power of repentance, we can understand how Judaism holds that even the wicked person who repents can become a *tsaddik*. The goal of the righteous person's holy living is to contribute to the sanctification of the Judaic people as a whole, not to guarantee one's own individual salvation. The ethical imperatives embodied in the *mitzvot* do not intend to lead to self-centeredness but to participation in the holy community. The earnest individual Judaist "walks in the ways of the good and keeps to the path of the righteous" (Babylonian Talmud, Baba Mesia 83a) in order to make holy the whole life of the entire community. The whole Judaic way of life is a commandment, a *mitzvah*, and therefore every aspect of life is a proper target for sanctification. This image of the *tsaddik*, who seeks to reflect in his behavior *the desirable human conduct defined by the Lord,* symbolizes the *desirability* of the Lord because it *integrates into Judaism's overall expression of the meaning and purpose of human life* the ethical aspects of the Lord's reality and revelation.

Mythological Symbolism of Desirability

In the three preceding sections we have shown that Judaism addresses symbolic expressions respectively to the Judaic mind, will, and conscience, asserting that the Lord is the *summum bonum* and appealing for the appropriate human response. Judaism further expresses the supreme desirability of the Lord in the mythological symbolism with which it appeals directly to the human imagination. Mythological symbolism of desirability, it will be remembered, *depicts abstract ideals evocatively in concrete images.*

The biblical story of the Garden of Eden at the beginning of the world is generally well known. This story describes the Lord's generosity and attention to detail in preparing an ideal world for the idyllic life of the first human couple, Adam and Eve. The Lord spared nothing in arranging for the needs, comfort, and pleasure of the man and woman. The story shows also the avarice with which Adam and Eve, indulging their evil inclination, corrupted life in the Garden. Judaism has made far less of this myth than have the makers of Christian doctrine. In the Talmud, rabbinic thinkers identified the Garden of Eden as the realm in which the Lord gives the righteous their reward following their death. The Jewish person known or thought to be dying is therefore encouraged to pray,

I acknowledge, O Lord my God, and God of my fathers, that my healing and my death are in Your hands. May it be Your will that You heal me with a perfect healing. But if I die may my death be an atonement for all the sins, transgressions, and iniquities which I have committed before You. Grant me my portion in the Garden of Eden, and let me attain the World to Come which is destined for the righteous.

(Shulchan Arukh, Yoreh Deah 338)

Holding that every person becomes at death what one's own discipline or desire has made of that person, the Talmudic rabbis described vividly the sufferings that the wicked will experience in the fires of *Gehinnom* and the ecstasies the righteous will enjoy in the Garden of Eden. The spiritual meaning of all that imagery is specified in passages, such as the following, which picture the righteous dead transfixed in undisturbed joy in the Presence of the Lord:

The world to come is not like the present world. The world to come does not have in it eating or drinking or procreation or business dealings or jealousy or hate or competitiveness. Only the righteous, sitting there with their crowns on their heads, enjoy the radiance of the Shekhinah.

(Berakhot 17a)

The imagery of such passages is intended to evoke the conviction that a permanent place in the infinitely desirable Presence of the Lord is worth all of the rigors and deprivations involved in living a disciplined, righteous life.

In an investigation of the category of sainthood with respect to Judaism, Robert L. Cohn describes three "ideal types that Judaism commends for emulation." He comments that "it is these ideals, rather than flesh-and-blood human beings, on which most Jewish aspirations have focused."[28] Judaism respects its worthy flesh-and-blood individuals, but it does not hold them up as examples in an effort to inspire desirable human behavior. Moses, for example, is the premier human person in this religion's entire history. He was the human leader in the Israelites' escape from Egypt. Scripture says that he "talked" directly with the Lord, that he received from the Lord the tablets of commandments and transmitted them to his people and that he was a prophet "whom the Lord knew face to face" and the like of whom "has not appeared since in Israel" (Deuteronomy 34:10). Maimonides, in the face of Christian claims for Jesus and Islamic claims for Mohammed, wrote into his creed the affirmation that Moses was "the father of all the prophets that came before him and that followed him" (article 7, Perek Halect). Even so, Judaism does not exhort, "Be like Moses!" Enoch, an idealized ancestor alleged to have lived "three hundred and sixty-five years," is celebrated in scripture as one who "walked with God and was not, for God took him" (Genesis 5:21–4). The wording of that statement powerfully suggests that Enoch successfully fulfilled the Lord's *halakhakic* ("walking") requirement, yet tradition does not enjoin Judaists to imitate Enoch. When Judaism tries to evoke desirable human behavior, it appeals to three ideal figures constructed by pious Judaic imagination. These three ideal types are the *tsaddik*, the *talmid hakham*, and the *hasid*.

We have already made reference to the *tsaddik*, the person who, earnestly seeking to do everything that the Lord's revelation requires, is the very reason for the creation of the world. "The world exists for the sake of a single *tsaddik*, as it is written, 'The *tsaddik* is the foundation of the world' (Proverbs 10:25)" (Babylonian Talmud, Yoma 38b). The *talmid*

28 Cohn, "Sainthood," p. 44.

hakham, the second ideal figure, is the person who consecrates his life to the perennial study of the Torah. This figure is considered to be "the premier ideal of Jewish piety" on the grounds that, according to rabbinic legend, "God too studies Torah" and therefore, "by applying his mind to Torah, the *talmid hakham* imitates God."[29] The third ideal is the *hasid,* the person who loves the Lord so single-mindedly that the character and action of his own life literally reflect the Lord's unbounding love, mercy, and generosity. Until the Hasidic movement began in the eighteenth century, "the title *hasid* was given to lone individuals, not to a social group."[30] Though ruggedly individualistic, the *hasidim* "were understood as part of their communities and were not organized into exclusive pietistic conventicles."[31] Because each of these three figures *depicts evocatively a concrete image of an ideal aspect* of the Lord's character, each serves to symbolize *the ultimate desirability* of the Lord.

The epitome of Judaism's mythological symbolism of *desirability,* however, is its myth of being Israel, the holy people. Israel, according to Bible and tradition, is a people, a social phenomenon, whom the Lord created differently from the way he creates other nations and social groups, and with Israel the social reality the Lord has bonded his own reality in an everlasting covenant. "Covenantal peoplehood," Rabbi Monford Harris has written, is Judaism's "classical category" and "the basic premise of Jewish self-understanding."[32] Rabbi Harris went on to point out, for example, that from the point of view of the book of Genesis itself, the main event in that book's account of creation is not the creation of the majestic cosmos or the creation of humanity. Rather the main event occurs in chapter 12 where the Lord makes the promise – and begins to fulfill it – to form a new people out of Abram (Abraham) and his posterity.[33] Everything before chapter 12 – the creation of the universe and humanity, the expulsion of Adam and Eve from the Garden of Eden, the world-engulfing flood and the survival of Noah's family, the confusion of humanity's language and the scattering of humanity over the face of the earth – is preparation for the creation of Israel, the Lord's people. Likewise, "from chapter 12 throughout Genesis, everything is involved with the coming into being of this people."[34] It is not too much to say that everything else in the Bible is concerned with Israel's being the Lord's people. Other nations appear in the story, but it is Israel's story. Within the development of Israel's story the Lord's sovereignty is declared and "shown" to prevail over all the other nations, but as far as those nations

29 Ibid., p. 59.   30 Ibid., pp. 62–3.   31 Ibid., p. 63.
32 Monford Harris, "Israel: The Uniqueness of Jewish History," in *Rediscovering Judaism,* ed. Arnold Jacob Wolf (Chicago: Quadrangle Books, 1965), p. 81.
33 Ibid., pp. 86ff.   34 Ibid.

are concerned, the Lord's sovereignty over them remains largely an "unrecognized sovereignty."[35] The Lord has compassion also for the people of all other nations and a purpose for them, but these peoples' recognition of the Lord's favor awaits the final "day of the Lord." Prophetic writers in the Bible describe that "day" as a time when the Lord will fulfill the promise he made to Israel at the time of its creation:

I will make you into a great nation and I will bless you. . . . and all the families of the earth shall bless each other through you.

(Genesis 12:2, 3)

An oracle of Isaiah anticipates a "day" when the Lord will "make himself known" (Isaiah 19:21) to all the world's peoples, represented under the names of Israel's two perennial and powerful foes, Assyria and Egypt; when all peoples will "acknowledge and worship" the Lord and will participate in a universal community of worship, and when the Lord will bless each people separately, addressing each with a term of endearing intimacy:

When that day comes there will be a highway between Egypt and Assyria, and Assyrians will come to Egypt and Egyptians to Assyria, and the Egyptians and Assyrians will worship together.

When that day comes Israel will be a third partner and will be a blessing at the center of that world which the Lord will bless, saying, "Blessed be Egypt my people, and Assyria the work of my hands, and Israel my legacy.

(Isaiah 19:23–5)

Until that day comes, however, Israel will remain "a people that lives apart and is not reckoned as are other nations" (Numbers 23:9). Israel's existence, character, and mission derive solely from the Lord's intention, promise, and command. Israel exists and is special, the Bible states, because the Lord created it a people out of no people, redeemed it later from its oblivion in Egyptian bondage, and set it apart to imitate and reflect his character.

You shall be holy because I the Lord your God am holy. . . . I will make my abode among you. . . . And I will walk among you and will be your God, and you shall be my people. I am the Lord your God who brought you forth out of the land of Egypt.

(Leviticus 19:2, 26:11–13)

35   Ibid., p. 90.

Moses explained to Israel that it became a people separated (holy) for the Lord solely because the Lord "set his love upon" Israel and "chose" it:

You are a people holy to the Lord your God. Out of all the peoples on the face of the earth, the Lord has chosen you to be his legacy people. It was not because you were more numerous than any other people that the Lord set his love upon you, for you were the least numerous of all the peoples. It is because the Lord loves you and keeps the oath which he swore to your fathers, that he brought you out [of Egypt] with the strength of his hand.

(Deuteronomy 7:6–8)

As the Lord's "legacy" to the nations of the world, the very peoplehood of Israel has been understood by many Judaists to be a priesthood: "You shall be a kingdom of priests and a holy people" (Exodus 19:6). Discerned by prophetic vision and described in the Bible, the service to be rendered by this "priestly community" is "a universal mission."[36] One prophet declared that the Lord has "bequeathed" Israel "as a covenant to humanity" to be "a light to the nations, to give sight to the blind [and] to bring captives out of prison" so that the Lord's "salvation may reach to the ends of the earth" (Isaiah 42:6, 7, and 49:6). Identified as the Lord's priestly people and a legacy for the salvation of the nations, Israel symbolizes the Lord's own reality and utter desirability. The phenomenon called Israel, this historically real and eschatologically idealized people, *points beyond itself to the reality of the Lord's ultimate purpose and utter desirability and participates in that reality* as a priest in history of the Lord's saving intentions for all humankind. This myth of Israel's existence and priesthood epitomizes Judaism's mythological symbolism of desirability. In Judaism's own self-understanding, the *concrete image* of Israel the people of the Lord *points to and depicts* the Lord as the *summum bonum* of all Jews in history, be they Judaists (religious) or not, and of all peoples eschatologically. With this mythological symbolism of desirability, Judaism contributes to world theology a distinctively Judaic, monoethnic claim that there is a single, *central spiritual reality* for all humankind and that this reality is *supremely desirable*.

Elusiveness

The elusiveness of humanity's central spiritual referent is transparent in all symbolic expressions of Judaism's ultimate referent. In those Judaic expressions of the Lord's undeniability and desirability that we have just described, the Lord's unsearchable otherness, independence, and freedom are inherent and obvious. Humans know about the Lord what the Lord gives them to know. For example, creation, history, revelation, salvation,

36 David Polish, *Israel – Nation and People* (n.p.: KTAV Publishing House, 1975), p. 45.

and eschatological redemption are represented as gifts from the Lord, gifts that were conceived, actualized, and presented at the independent discretion of the Lord alone. Furthermore, the Lord's selection of Israel, now the Jewish people, to be the special recipient of these gifts and to be the Lord's witness concerning these gifts, was a choice made by the Lord's wise, unprompted love. The reason for this choice is known only to the Lord's wisdom whence it originated. *That* the Lord "loved" Israel in a distinctive way is affirmed by the Judaic tradition; *why* the Lord loved Israel this way remains for Judaism a matter of speculation. Like all other humans, Israel had no virtue or power of its own that could compel the Lord's attention and partiality or persuade him to disclose the reason for his selection of Israel.

As symbolized in Judaism, the Lord's reality transcends all constraining accountability except to itself. Humans may complain about the Lord and to the Lord, but they cannot compel the Lord. According to the Judaists' own records, they have complained frequently to the Lord, particularly about the disparity between the self-revealed justice of the Lord and the apparent injustice of some of the Lord's actions in Judaic history. Abraham, the founding patriarch of the Judaic tradition, set the example of challenging the integrity of the Lord's claim to act justly. Exercised by the prospect that good people would be killed by a divine act proposed for the punishment of the wicked people of Sodom, Abraham admonished the Lord, saying, "Far be it from you to kill good and bad together. . . . Shall not the judge of all the earth do what is just?" (Genesis 18:25). Even though courageous in challenging the Lord, Abraham used language that acknowledged the inevitability of living in reference to "the judge of all the earth." Abraham's challenge actually exemplifies, then, Judaism's perception that, irrespective of Judaists' own moral sensibilities, the Lord's reality is, and remains, independent, wholly other, and free. Self-evidently knowledge of such reality *eludes* the unaided powers of human cognition. From this viewpoint, therefore, human beings, lacking their own means of gaining knowledge of the Lord's reality, are at the mercy of the Lord's discretion to self-disclose that reality. That the otherwise inaccessible and incomprehensible reality of the Lord does in fact self-reveal is, for Judaism, the preeminent illustration of its elusiveness. Elusiveness is, however, integral to and manifest in all of Judaism's symbolic expressions of the Lord, and for that reason, in this section, we need only to illustrate it further and to make a brief, specific description of it.

Mythological Symbolism of Elusiveness

In addition to the "gifts" of creation, history, revelation, salvation, and eschatological salvation, Judaism has an extensive mythological symbolism that *illustrates the elusiveness of the Lord.* This mythological expression begins with the ineffable personal name of the Lord. That name, as we have indicated before, is YHWH. Its very meaning, "I will be present as I will be present," indicates to Judaists the Lord's use of personal, independent discretion in encountering humans, participating in their affairs, and, with the overarching sovereignty of his will, making the evil they do serve the good he intends.

For Judaists, the sovereignty of the Lord's independent judgment is nowhere more evident than in the sheer survival of this people despite the tyrannies to which history has subjected it. Enslaved by Egypt, conquered and humiliated successively by the empires of Assyria, Babylonia, Greece, and Rome, deprived of its own national existence and exiled in fragments among other nations for two millenia, and, most recently, hideously targeted for extinction by Hitler's Nazi regime, this people has survived repeatedly, always with "its own spiritual impulses intact."[37] Now, "standing over the grave of [its] most recent oppressor,"[38] the Jewish people are witnessing the rebirth and growth of Israel as an autonomous national entity. Reflecting on the survival of the Jewish people and the rebirth of their nation, present day Judaists recall the opinion expressed about Israel by an ancient gentile prophet, Balaam. That outsider, contemplating the miracle of Israel's escape from Egypt, concluded that Israel "is a people that dwells alone and is different from other nations" (Numbers 34:9). David Polish, a past president of the Central Conference of American Rabbis, commented in 1975, "Israel appears to have been selected to endure *as Israel.*"[39] He continued, "Israel has a course in history which is altogether different from that of other peoples. Israel defies the deterministic rules of history, which insist that every civilization undergoes a process of rise, decline and death."[40] One of the present authors heard the late Karl Barth, a Christian theologian, say, "The only demonstrable proof of the existence of God is the survival of the Jews."

The elusiveness of the Lord, understood as the Lord's utter independence and wholly otherness, forms a central theme in Judaism's biblical, rabbinic, and philosophical literature. We cited earlier the classical biblical passage that states that the Lord's reality transcends all unaided human processes of knowing:

My thoughts are not your thoughts
and your ways are not my ways,
    says the Lord.
For as the heavens are higher that the earth,

37 Ibid., p. 51.   38 Ibid.
39 Ibid., p. 50.   40 Ibid., p. 51.

so are my ways higher than your ways
and my thoughts higher than your thoughts.

(Isaiah 55:8–9)

Rabbinic thought also pondered the difference between the Lord's ways and human ways:

Come and see how different are the ways of God from the ways of human beings.
(Mekilta, Vayasa 1)

Not like the attribute of the human is the attribute of God.

(Megilla 14a)

In the medieval period, Maimonides analyzed and described philosophically the Judaic concept of God. In that philosophical description Maimonides made a categorical distinction between the reality of the Lord and the reality of every other living being. He stated that humans

must be taught that God is incorporeal; that there is no similarity in any way whatever between him and his creatures; that his existence is not like the existence of his creatures; that his life is not like that of any living being, nor his wisdom like the wisdom of the wisest men; and that the difference between him and his creatures is not merely quantitative, but absolute (as between two individuals of two different classes). . . . Anything predicated of God is totally different from our attributes; no definition can comprehend both; therefore his existence and that of any other being totally differ from each other, and the term existence is applied to both homonymously.

(*Moreh Nebbukhim*, 1, 34)

Maimonides did not originate a new idea of God. He made an exposition of the philosophical inferences of a notion already and always pervasive in Judaism: The Lord is the Lord, and the human is the human. Throughout the Judaic tradition the Lord and the human are regarded as two distinct realities that, as Jacob J. Petuchowski once observed, "never merge, neither by an apotheosis of man, nor by an 'incarnation' of God."[41] They meet and communicate, but never merge. Their meeting is possible because the Lord has the capacity and interest to bring about the meeting. In the communication that transpires in these meetings, the inscrutable otherness and independent will of the Lord's reality, which otherwise utterly *eludes* unassisted human powers, becomes known to Judaists at least under the conditions of human understanding. These

---

41 Jacob J. Petuchowski, "The Dialectics of Reason and Revelation," in Wolf, *Rediscovering Judaism*, p. 29.

self-motivated revelations that the Lord makes to the covenant people and to individuals *illustrate* preeminently Judaism's mythological expression of the Lord's elusiveness. This paradox extends into Judaism's intellectual symbolism of elusiveness, for it is the Lord's revelations that make the Lord's elusiveness *reasonable*.

Intellectual Symbolism of Elusiveness

The concept of revelation is basic to Judaism's intellectual expressions of elusiveness. It is from the Lord's own self-revelations that Judaists have learned both that the Lord's reality is unsearchable and that this inscrutability is *reasonable*. Because the Lord is "Spirit" and humans are "flesh," the Lord's reality is said to "hide" itself from human knowing (Isaiah 3:13, 45:15). According to Judaic wisdom, however, when the Lord elects to reveal, human cognition cannot elude it:

Can you search out the deep things of God?
Can you find out the limit of the Almighty?
It is higher than the heights of heaven
   – what can you do?
It is deeper than Sheol
   – what can you know?

When he passes through, he may do it without
   anyone knowing,
If he makes it known, who can fail to see him?

                              (Job 11:7–8,10)

We have already seen that Judaists, the remnant of Israel, understood themselves to be a people to whom the Lord has chosen to self-reveal. From the content of those revelations, Judaists claim to learn that the Lord's reality differs infinitely and qualitatively from human reality. Given that categorical distinction between human being and the Lord's being, human knowledge of the Lord's inscrutable reality is made possible, and its *elusiveness* is made *reasonable*, only because the Lord, for whom all realities are searchable, seeks out the human and self-reveals. According to this gestalt of concepts, the Lord, while remaining the Lord, self-reveals to humans who, remaining humans, become acquainted with the Lord and responsible for the knowledge the Lord makes known to them.

Judaism's biblical and talmudic literature emphasize the personal character of the Lord's revelation. In the Bible one reads frequently that the Lord "appeared unto," "spoke to" and "visited" individuals (Adam, Noah, Abraham, Moses, the prophets) and Israel as a whole, and that certain humans "have seen the Lord" or "have heard the word of the Lord." These revelations confront humans with the reality and the demands of the Lord. In them the Lord "makes Himself known . . . and He also reveals the commandments."[42] The Bible represents these revelations as having the sole purpose of developing communion between the Lord and humans. They are perceived to occur in a manner that calls upon the recipient of revelation to make a *personal* response of prayer and ethical obedience, and this perception prompted the biblical mind to conceptualize the Lord as a living, humanlike person. Of course the Bible never refers to the Lord with the epithet person for the very simple reason that the Hebrew language of the Bible had no words that were equivalent to our English words person, personal, or personality. The notion was there, however, and is expressed vividly in the biblical literature. The Bible takes for granted everywhere that the Lord communicates with humans in the same terms that one human addresses another. Just as one human person reveals his or her heart and mind to another human person through speech and other acts, so the Lord is thought to reveal the divine heart and mind to Israel and individual Israelites through utterances, visions, and other actions.

According to biblical thinking, then, the Lord, addressing human powers of understanding, has communicated to humans a knowledge of the divine reality and a body of instruction on the way of life that pleases the Lord – the way of justice and mercy. Although conceptualizing the Lord anthropomorphically as a rational, self-determining, and ethical being, most minds contributing to biblical literature tended to understand that the Lord's thoughts and ways were not theirs and that the Lord's behavior cannot always be comprehended strictly in terms of what humans presently regard to be reasonable. Given the revealed knowledge of the Lord's infinite and qualitative distinction from humans, biblical thinkers found it *reasonable* enough that such an incomprehensible reality would reveal to humans its life and a way for their salvation.

The talmudic rabbis and the medieval Jewish philosophers concurred with the biblical view that the Lord's revelation makes the Lord's elusiveness reasonable. For both these groups, the Sinai revelation is the definitive revelation of the Lord. The rabbis enlarged the scope of that revelation to include the Oral Law, the accumulation of interpretations of scripture that arose over the centuries from the need to apply the written commandments to circumstances of changing times. They remained faithful to the biblical prototype of revelation, speaking, on the one hand, of the revealing of the Lord's presence (*gilluy shekhinah*), which evokes personal and group communion with the Lord, and, on the other hand, of

42 Ibid., p. 31.

the Lord's giving guidance (*mattan torah*), which calls for ethical observance. For the rabbis, this comprehensive revealed Torah was the primary and normative datum. They assigned to reason a role that functioned wholly within the framework of revelation as the student and servant of revelation.

For Jewish medieval philosophers such as Saadia Gaon, Judah Halevi, and Moses Maimonides, the respective roles of reason and revelation were more complex. They considered reason to be also an authoritative means for establishing "truth and certainty."[43] Nevertheless, these philosophers regarded the revelation to Moses and Israel at Sinai to give more truth, or at least to give it more efficiently, than reason is capacitated to give. In any case, the revelation at Sinai is an already established fact that reason does not have to find and prove. It therefore constitutes the presupposition and starting point of Jewish philosophizing. Reason, in other words, needs to seek to understand the content of the Sinai revelation. Saadia Gaon allowed that reason should be the final arbiter of the contents and meaning of that revelation. Judah Halevi maintained that there is nothing in the Judaic revelation that contradicts reason or is antirational, but that reason itself cannot grasp the knowledge that evokes worship of the Lord, and that is precisely the aim of revelation. Saadia Gaon antedates Pascal's observation that the God of philosophical speculation is not the God whom people worship. Maimonides also maintained that there can be no real conflict between reason and revelation. He argued that the Lord, who is revealed to be one and ultimate and who has created humans with the power of reason, cannot be the source of a real contradiction. Maimonides held, therefore, that Bible passages whose literal meaning "can be refuted by proof must and can be interpreted otherwise."[44]

There is a bias that runs throughout Judaism's accounts of the Lord's revealing acts and its reflections on these revelations. This bias is the assumption that whatever the Lord thinks or does will be rational, and it is inferred from the Lord's self-identification at Sinai as a compassionate God whose actions are just and merciful. Judaists assume, therefore, that when humans are allowed to know the Lord's purpose for any divine act, they will be able to acknowledge it as a *reasonable* purpose and action. Judaism has found in its own experience with the Lord, however, that, on several occasions when it has sustained catastrophe, the Lord's part and Presence in the catastrophe was ambiguous at best and irrational at worst. The Lord seemed to be either absent, eclipsed, or hidden during these catastrophes. Nevertheless, Judaists as a people have not "given up on" the Lord despite the elusiveness of the divine Presence and purpose in

43   Saadia Gaon, *Sepher Ha-Emunoth Veha-De'oth*, Introduction.
44   *Moreh Nebukhim*, 2.25.

these catastrophes.[45] This fact – Judaism's call for sustained fidelity to the Lord when there seems to be no rational theological explanations for the Lord's action – is elaborated in Judaism's spiritual symbolism of elusiveness, which we consider next.

Spiritual Symbolism of Elusiveness

Consistent with the model we described in Chapter 1, Judaism's spiritual symbolism of elusiveness *encourages sustained discipline despite the elusiveness of the Lord* especially in times of catastrophe. This encouragement is based on and typically harks back to the definitive period in Judaism's history: Israel's *endurance* of four hundred years of enforced slavery under the tyranny of pharaohs in Egypt, *the Lord's intervention* to direct and guarantee Israel's escape and the *survival* of this people. To Merneptah, a pharoah shortly after the exodus, it appeared that Israel's existence was ended. Around 1220 B.C.E., on a stele recording his victory over the Libyans and describing the reduced straits of other peoples in his region, Merneptah wrote, "Israel is laid waste; he has no more seed" (Merneptah Stele, line 55).

That obituary was inaccurate, of course. Israel survived, and Israel has continued to survive, but in a historical existence that has alternated between annihilation and renewal. The survival of Israel and its descendants, the Jews, is a compelling fact, especially for outsiders. For Judaists, David Polish says, the history of their "destruction and resurrection" is "a continuous recapitulation of the original slavery and deliverance."[46] Speaking as an insider, Polish comments, "Every exile has been Egypt. Every tyrant has been Pharoah. Every deliverance has been the first deliverance enlarged."[47] Polish follows this comment with a bit of Judaic lore that relates that "Pharoah stands at the gates of hell and says to the new tyrants as they enter: 'Fools, why couldn't you learn a lesson from me?'" From Judaism's long history of "destruction and resurrection," we have selected two instances to illustrate this religion's efforts to *encourage sustained discipline despite the elusiveness of the Lord* as demonstrated in this people's catastrophes.

We must give a brief historical background for the first of our illustrations, which is the Babylonian exile of the Jews. From the time of the exodus to 722 B.C.E., Israel lived in regular ritual remembrance of the miraculous deliverance from slavery in Egypt. Its leaders referred to that delivery as a birth and as a creation. During those five centuries a monarchy developed out of a confederacy of twelve separate tribes. Each of

---

45 Cf. Robert Cohn, "Biblical Resposes to Catastrophe," *Judaism* 35 (1986).
46 Polish, *Israel*, p. 51   47 Ibid.

those tribes became a distinct political unit in the Israelite monarchy. In 722 the Assyrians captured and carried away into oblivion ten of Israel's twelve political units, and then repopulated the captured territory with imported people. With ten of the monarchy's units annihilated by Assyria, only Judah and tiny Benjamin were left as the remnant of Israel's united monarchy. Benjamin's identity was soon obscured, and eventually swallowed up, by Judah. Judah's capital city, Jerusalem, was considered inviolable because it housed the Temple, which had been the center of worship for all Israel and was a symbol of the Lord's covenant with this people. Then, in 587, catastrophe struck Judah. The Babylonians, assisted by "the people of Edom" (a country to the southeast of Judah), conquered Judah, destroyed and plundered Jerusalem, and forced Judah's leadership and a large number of its people into exile in Babylon.

The Jews exiled in Babylon could have been traumatized into oblivion by this shattering blow to their beliefs in the inviolability of Jerusalem (Zion) and in the Lord's covenant to be effectively present with them. They seemed to be reduced to nothing but memories, further humiliations, and vindictive resentments. One of their psalmists immortalized the sad reality of those three possessions:

By the rivers of Babylon we sat down
    and wept
  when we remembered Zion.
There on the willow trees we hung
    up our harps,
    for there our captors demanded songs
      from us,
    and our tormentors, mirth, commanding,
      "Sing us one of the songs of Zion!"

How could we sing the Lord's song
  in a foreign Land?

If I forget you, O Jerusalem,
  let my right hand wither away.
Let my tongue cling to the roof of
    my mouth
    if I do not remember you,
    if I do not set Jerusalem
    above my highest joy.
Remember, O Lord, against the
    people of Edom
  the day of Jerusalem's fall,
When they said, "Down with it,
    Down with it,
    down to its very foundations!"

O Babylon the devastator,
　　happy the one who repays you
　　for all that you have done to us!
Happy shall be the one who
　　　seizes your children
　　and dashes them against the rock.

(Psalm 137:1–9)

Realistic observers could have credibly surmised that Babylon's deities had defeated the Lord, that Jerusalem had never been inviolable, that the Lord's covenant with Israel had been more imagined than real, and that exiled Judah would become extinguished Judah. Instead, despite its desperate circumstances and the ambiguity of the Lord's role in letting this happen to Judah, exiled Judah held on tenaciously to its faith and embarked vigorously on a program of religious activity that committed Israel's several traditions to writing, collected the writings of its prophets, and produced a priestly version of the Torah, among other literary accomplishments. There in exile, the religious leadership of Judah kept the people reminded of *the inevitability of living their lives in reference to the reality of the Lord* and *encouraged* the people to *sustain faithfulness (discipline) despite the Lord's elusiveness.* More than one prophetic mind in the exilic period (586 to 544 B.C.E.) suggested that the Lord brought about this exile *for some additional reason* than the mere exercise of retributive justice for Judah's sin. We cite one of these prophets who, claiming to see that the exile was coming to an end, *encouraged* his people to *sustain discipline* with assurances of the Lord's reasonable judgment and constructive sovereignty:

Comfort, comfort my people,
　　says your God.
Speak tenderly to Jerusalem
　　and tell her
that her term is over,
that her penalty is paid,
that she has received from the
　　Lord's hand
double for all her sins.

(Isaiah 40:1–2, emphasis added)

This prophet reported having heard the Lord announce that "for a long time I have held my peace, have kept still and restrained myself, but now I will cry out." And the burden of the Lord's communication was the plight of the exiled Jews:

This is a people robbed and
    plundered,
they are all of them trapped in
    holes
  and lost to sight in prisons,
carried off as spoil with none to
    rescue,
as prey with none to say,
  "Give them back."
Hear this, all who will,
listen and give heed to what I say:
Who gave away Jacob to the spoiler,
  who gave away Israel for prey?
Was it not the Lord?
Against him they sinned,
in his ways they would not walk,
and his law they would not obey.

(Isaiah 42:22–4)

Here Isaiah reminds his audience that in Judaic understanding the freedom of Judah and the freedom of its oppressors are both allowed to run their complete but finite course, and that the Lord, without abridging the freedom of either party, exercises the overarching divine sovereignty and judgment. The exilic prophet goes on to assert confidently that the divine sovereignty will soon command Babylon to give back the captives:

I will say to the north, "Give them
    back,"
  and to the south, "Do not withhold
    them.
Bring back my sons and daughters
    from afar,
  bring them back from the ends of
    the earth.
Bring back every one who is called
    by my name,
  all whom I have created, formed
    and made for my glory."

(Isaiah 43:6–7)

The prophet has a message for exiled Judah in the interim prior to the Lord's intervention to renew them:

You are my witnesses, says the Lord,
  my servants whom I have chosen

to know me and to put faith in me
  and to understand that I am He.
There was no god formed before me,
  and there shall be none after me.
I am the Lord, I myself,
  and besides me there is none who can deliver.
I myself have made it known
  – not some alien god among you – and
  you are my witnesses, says the Lord.
I am God, and henceforth I am He.
There is none who can take away
  what my hand holds,
  and what I do, none can hinder.

(Isaiah 43:10–13)

By reminding the exiles that they are who they are, the Lord's witnesses, because the Lord is who the Lord is, the sole sovereign of the universe, the prophet *encouraged* the exiles to *sustain discipline* despite their inadequately explained exile.

The other instance we have selected from Judaism's history of "destruction and resurrection" is "the rebirth of [this] people out of the ashes of the Holocaust."[48] The horrendous plan of Hitler systematically and finally to exterminate the Jewish people is universally known. We do not presume to review Hitler's "success" in extinguishing six million Jewish lives in ways so cruel, perverse, and humiliating as to confound human imagination and elude adequate description in words. It is, however, the "ways" of the Lord in the Holocaust that eludes all human powers of understanding. For all theistic-minded humans, the elusiveness of the Lord in the Holocaust defies theological explanation. For the Jews, the Holocaust has threatened to supplant the exodus from Egypt as the defining center of their existence in history. Martin Buber, arguably Judaism's most sensitive and influential interpreter in the twentieth century, exclaimed, "How can we say in the presence of Auschwitz, praise God for he is good, for his mercy endures forever?"[49] Other Jewish commentators like Rubenstein[50] were prepared to say that there can be no God for Jews after Auschwitz.

The most poignant and characteristically Judaic spiritual symbol of elusiveness that we know to have come out of Judaists' response to the Holocaust is an apocryphal story. This story relates that a group of rabbis were holding a trial of the Lord for having allowed the Holocaust to happen. They had argued their case against the Lord for many hours

48   Ibid., p. 76.
49   In ibid., p. 54.   50   Ibid.

when one of their number interrupted the proceedings to say, "Brethren, it is time for prayers." Whereupon, the story goes, the rabbis adjourned the proceedings and all filed out to the place for prayers.

Moral Symbolism of Elusiveness

We have seen that in Judaism's radical ethical monotheism the Lord *defines morality*. When this is understood it becomes evident that *good behavior is insufficient for what the Lord requires* for human salvation. A Midrash quoted in the introduction to this chapter makes the point. It has the Lord say, "Would that [my people] forsake me and do my commandments, for *by observing my Torah they would come to know me*" (Pesikta Kahana, 15). The point is that the revealed Torah does not become separated from the commanding Presence of the Lord. Therefore, when humans appropriate it and observe it they do so necessarily in relation to the commanding divine Presence. They cannot fulfill the Lord's requirements for salvation apart from the divine Presence because there is no Torah apart from the Lord's commanding Presence. According to Judaic interpretation, the Lord's purpose in giving the divine Presence together with the divine commandments is to enable humans to "come to know" the Lord, and that means to sustain an interpersonal relation with the Lord. There can be, then, no Judaic moral life that is cut off from the worship of the Lord and is still acceptable to the Lord. Worship and moral conduct belong together in Judaism, because the Lord's commanding Presence and the Lord's commandments come together in the Lord's revelations.

Emil L. Fackenheim, on whose study of "revealed morality" our discussion here largely depends, has argued that "the authentic revealed morality of Judaism" manifests "the essential togetherness" of (1) "a divine commanding Presence which never dissipates itself into irrelevance" and (2) "a human response which freely appropriates what it receives."[51] In the logic of this moral construction, the Lord, while remaining the Lord, and Judaists, while remaining human, accomplish a oneness of wills without abridging either the Lord's otherness or the sacrosanct freedom of the human response. The *otherness* of the Lord's commanding Presence is "starkly disclosed" in the pristine moment of the Lord's first overture to humans. "In that moment there are as yet no specified commandments but only a still unspecified divine commanding Presence,"[52] which addresses the individual with the unconditional de-

---

51   Emil L. Fackenheim, *Encounters between Judaism and Modern Philosophy* (New York: Basic Books, 1973), p. 44; cf. also Wolf, *Rediscovering Judaism*, p. 64.
52   Ibid., p. 45.

mand of the Shema: "Therefore you must love the Lord your God with all your heart, mind and will, and with all your consciousness, and with all your might." When the Lord first encountered Abraham, for example, Abraham was given no finite content that he might evaluate and appropriate in the light of familiar standards. When one is addressed in pristine moments of encounter with the Lord's commanding Presence, "there can be no mistaking this initial voice for one already familiar, such as conscience, or reason or 'spiritual creativity.' "[53]

Likewise Judaism maintains that, in the primal moment of encounter with the Lord, the human will is free to appropriate without the conditions of fear or hope the unspecified command of the Lord's commanding Presence. This freedom is more than the opportunity to accept or reject specific commandments for personal benefit or for their own sake. It is "nothing less than the freedom to accept or reject the divine commanding Presence as a whole, and for its own sake – that is, for no other reason than it is that Presence."[54] This is not an autonomous freedom that might offer a person numerous options. It is rather the freedom to do nothing other than to accept or to reject the Lord's commanding Presence. In giving the human this option, the Lord's Presence paradoxically forces upon the human the necessity of making that free choice. It does not force the human *to accept* the Lord but to make the choice. That choice itself is not conditioned. The human either accepts or rejects the Lord's commanding Presence "for no other reason than that it *is* that Presence." At this moment – when the gulf between the Lord's otherness and human reality is most "starkly disclosed"[55] – the human person who accepts the Lord's commanding Presence accepts the Lord's will as that person's own. This entails in consequence nothing less than acceptance of the specific commandments that the Lord reveals.

Judaism construes these commandments to have intrinsic value and to be permanent once they are revealed. They become Torah and have their own identity, but that does not render the Lord's Presence irrelevant to them. The Lord gives the Torah when humans are ready to receive it, and the act of receiving that Torah occurs in an encounter with the Lord's Presence. Furthermore, as Judaists understand it, the revealed morality of the Torah imposes a three-term relationship involving the person, the Lord, and the person's neighbor. The Lord does not become, then, an external sanction behind the commandments but remains a participating Presence in every moral relationship.

Referring to the summary of the commandments in Michah 6:8, Fackenheim observes that "there is no humble walking before God unless it

---

53 Ibid.
54 Ibid., p. 46   55 Ibid., p. 45.

manifests itself in justice and mercy to the human neighbor, [and] there can be only fragmentary justice and mercy unless they culminate in humility before the Lord."[56] To be performed acceptably to the Lord, moral commandments must be performed by taking one's neighbors seriously in their own right and by taking the commandments seriously as demanded by the Lord. Both the commandment and the neighbor possess intrinsic value because the Lord has revealed them to be so. For this reason, in the Judaic scheme of ethical monotheism, performing the commandments for their own sake *only* – which is to say, *good behavior* by itself – *is insufficient for personal perfection* or acceptability before the Lord. The Lord is not rendered obsolete or irrelevant by the intrinsic value of the commandments or by the intrinsic value of human persons and their neighbors. Rather the Lord becomes disclosed through all intrinsic values as their ultimate source.

56   Ibid., p. 49.

CHAPTER SIX

Christianity and the Central Spiritual Reality of Humankind

Christianity takes its name from Jesus, the historical figure whose followers call him "Christ." Jesus Christ is the governing symbol for the reality Christians call God. The followers of Christ were first called "Christians" at Antioch of Syria about twenty years after his death. Antioch had a mixed population made up mostly of Greek-speaking Gentiles. When some of Jesus' followers fled to Antioch, following their persecution in Jerusalem, they preached his gospel not only to the colony of Jews living there but also, and effectively, to the Gentiles. Preaching in Greek, these missionaries referred to Jesus with the Greek term "Christos" (God's "Anointed One") rather than with the Hebrew "Messiah." Thereby they identified Jesus' gospel as universal and launched their religion upon its global mission. Since then – in the several Eastern Orthodox Churches, the Roman Catholic Church, and the varieties of Protestant Christianity, and at various times over the last twenty centuries in sundry cultures on all continents of the planet – Christianity has been and remains characterized by one, original, originating, irreducible, and permanent datum: Jesus Christ. In whatever place, time, and form one may find and examine Christianity in past or present history, one will find Jesus Christ to be its defining and unique constituent.

Christianity's intellectual, mythological, spiritual, and moral symbolic expressions for God combine and explicate Jesus Christ as the governing symbol for everything properly called Christian. A preliminary examination of some salient details of Christianity's constitutive symbol will facilitate understanding of our discussion of the derivative symbolic expressions of the Christian God.

Christianity began almost two thousand years ago as a small sect among the Jews of Palestine, a territory located at the easternmost end of the Mediterranean Sea. The Roman Empire had administered Palestine politically since 69 B.C.E. and had organized the territory into three discrete units: Galilee, Samaria, and Judah. Galilee, the northernmost of the three political units, was populated predominantly by Jews. Samaria, the middle political division, was populated by the racially mixed Samaritans, whom the Jews generally despised. Judah, the southern division, was populated almost exclusively by Jews, the conspicuous exception being the Roman administrators and their military cohort.

The Galilean Jews estranged themselves religiously from the Judean Jews by seeking divine guidance more through immediate communication with God than through study and practice of the Torah (instruction) prescribed in their five books of sacred law. Sometime between 6 and 4 B.C.E., Jesus was born to a Jewish family in Galilee and grew up in the Galilean city of Nazareth. He spent his youth and early adulthood in historical obscurity. About the year 27 of the common era, however, he entered history as an itinerant religious preacher and teacher. In something like an inaugural address at the synagogue in Nazareth, Jesus stood up and read from the scroll of the prophet Isaiah:

The Spirit of the Lord is upon me.
By virtue of that, he has anointed me to
    preach good news to the poor;
He has sent me to proclaim freedom
    for prisoners
and recovery of sight for the blind,
to release the oppressed,
to proclaim the acceptable year of the Lord.

(Luke 4:18–19)[1]

Having read this scripture, Jesus identified himself as the messenger whom it proclaimed: "Today this scripture has been fulfilled in your hearing" (4:20).

Claiming henceforth the authority of "the Spirit of the Lord," Jesus inspired others to regard him as the Son of God. He referred to God publicly as "my Father" and addressed God intimately in prayer as "Father." Speaking to his contemporaries he referred to God as "your Heavenly Father" and urged them to convert to a filial relation to God. Eventually, a small group of followers gathered around Jesus, more out of personal attachment to him than out of profound understanding of his message, and he instructed them to think of themselves, with him, as children of God.

Through the power of such simplicity, involving as it did a reconceptualization of God's relation to humans, Jesus alienated himself, and

---

1 In this chapter we have given our own translation of passages quoted from the Bible unless otherwise indicated.

consequently his community of followers, from the Jewish community in Judah. It must be emphasized at the outset, however, that Jesus did not introduce a new deity. Indeed, Jesus' image of God, and that of all Christianity subsequent to him, perpetuated the eight characteristics previously identified as fundamental to the notion of God in Judaic scripture and tradition. Jesus and all Christianity to the present have sustained the ancient Judaic perception of God as *sovereign, one and unique, living, spiritual, self-revealing* and *ethical, creating* and *guiding* human history as well as *creating and governing* nature. Jesus accepted also as axiomatic the Jewish teaching that God creates human history by being present to human beings in ways that occasion their freedom. It is in response to God's presence that humans conceive, initiate, and bring to fulfillment purposes of their own. In other words, God enables humans to participate as agents in their own existence and destiny by evoking their powers to make themselves present to God and each other and to be creative and responsible. These powers make up what Christians call the human spirit.

Mindful of the uncompromising sovereignty of God in the Judaic image, Jesus characterized God as the Heavenly Father who, with fatherly concern and care, governs both human history and nature in a fatherly manner. In his personal prayers Jesus addressed this sovereign God directly as "Father" rather than using the conventional evocative of Jewish prayers, "King of the Universe." He taught his followers to pray thinking of themselves as God's children in every sense and therefore to say,

Our Father in heaven,
  let your name be hallowed,
    your kingdom come and
    your will be done
      on earth as in heaven.

(Matthew 6:9–10)

By identifying and characterizing as "fatherly" the motivation, manner, and intention of the King of the Universe, Jesus transformed the image of the relation in which God stands to humans from that of king and subjects, or judge and accused, to father and children. The Kingdom of God is a family. This image of filial relation was not altogether new to Jesus' contemporaries, but it was not common and it had never been worked out in the detailed and consistent image that Jesus developed.

In Jesus' time many Palestinian Jews, both Galilean and Judean, held a centuries' old hope that God would someday choose and anoint a King of the Jews who would establish for God, the King of the universe, a kingdom of righteousness on earth. They referred to this long-expected, divinely appointed person as "the messiah," a title that translated into

Greek as *Christos* and much later into English as Christ. The Jewish hope for the coming of this messiah included the expectation that the messianic kingdom would be a political kingdom that would replace the foreign rulers in Palestine and bring about a peaceful accord among all the nations of the earth.

According to the New Testament account, Jewish religious leaders instigated the charge that Jesus was claiming to be the messianic "King of the Jews," and the Roman authorities accepted this charge and authorized the death of Jesus by crucifixion. Within the few hours between his arrest and crucifixion, so the story goes, Jesus was betrayed by several of his friends and condemned by both religious and secular bodies. In spite of treachery by religious leaders, betrayal by friends, and miscarriage of justice by judicial authorities, Jesus – in his last living moments, dying in agony and anguish – is recorded as having prayed aloud, "Father, forgive them, for they do not know what they are doing. . . . Father, into your hands I commit my spirit" (Luke 23:34, 46).

Remembering these words, probing and pondering their meaning, Jesus' followers, from the time of the crucifixion itself to the present, have extolled his death as his ultimate act of filial obedience to God his Father. They have seen it as Jesus' voluntary self-sacrifice, a sacrifice in which Jesus unconditionally gave up being Jesus in order to be the obedient Son revealing the Fatherhood of God. At the same time Christians have regarded Jesus' death as a sacrifice that God, in accord with the fatherly character that Jesus depicted in his sonship, graciously accepted as a full and sufficient atonement for the sins of the whole world.

By the way he died, then, as well as by the way he lived and preached, Jesus recharacterized the image of God he inherited from Judaism. Simultaneously he redefined the image, role, and meaning of the title Christ. When adequately understood, to say that Christianity began as personal attachment to Jesus is to say that Christianity began as *a different way* of understanding, relating to, and serving the same God whom the Jewish people and their ancestors had understood, related to, and served for centuries.

As the movement centering upon the person of Jesus Christ developed, it became known as *Christianity*, in recognition of the centrality of Jesus Christ in this new religion that had developed within the Jewish sectors of Palestine. Like Buddhism, Christianity was to prosper beyond rather than within the location of its origin. In its first centuries of rapid expansion and throughout its span of twenty centuries to the present, Christianity has expressed itself in diverse forms, reflecting the various cultural environments in which it took residence and from which it took nurture. Despite this diversity, the permanent characterizing factor of Christianity in its varied forms has not been a certain set of beliefs and practices, a specific mode of worship, or a single world view. Rather, the constitutive factor in Christianity in all its forms and at all times has been the person of Jesus Christ, regarded as the definitive self-revelation that God *began* in Jesus of Nazareth long ago and continues in the resurrected, living Jesus Christ.

The Christian term for this twofold – begun and *continuing* – historical revelation is "God in Christ." It will become evident in our analysis of Christianity's various symbolic expressions that, for Christians, the sum and substance of God's revelation in Christ may be summarized in the phrase *righteous selfless love.* Christians regard God's love revealed in Christ as *selfless* because they assert that God is without self-reference and therefore seeks always the well-being and happiness of others. They regard it as *righteous* because it is undeviatingly and therefore dependably what it claims to be: impartial and good willed. Christians identify this righteous selfless love, manifest historically as "God in Christ," as the supreme source of evidence for the *undeniability, desirability,* and *elusiveness* of humanity's common central spiritual reality and as the standard for all other evidential claims. In particular, the historical character of the revelation of God in Christ generates and governs all of the Christian symbolization of the central spiritual reality of humankind. As will become clear in the discussion that follows, Christianity's preoccupation with divine love revealed in history emphasizes and conflates *spiritual* and *moral* expressions of Christianity's ultimate referent. Wherever either spiritual or moral symbolism is identifiable in Christian communication, the other is expressed also, either explicitly or implicitly. Through this primary spiritual – moral symbolism, Christianity's historical revelation orders and informs its mythological and intellectual expressions. For this reason, we consider spiritual and moral together rather than separately in the following account of Christianity's expression of the undeniability of the central spiritual reality of humankind.

Undeniability

Spiritual–Moral Symbolism of Undeniability

In its conjoined spiritual–moral symbolism of God's historical revelation in Christ, Christianity makes its primary expression of the undeniability of humanity's central spiritual reality. When interpreted in light of the Christian concept of the revelation of God in Christ, all human history simultaneously *calls for personal consent to the inevitability of living with reference to a central spiritual reality* and *discloses this inevitability by exposing self-contradictory behavior.*

It is necessary to examine the Christian concept of history at the outset of this discussion. Revelation of ultimate reality through the history of a human person contrasts markedly with Hindu cosmogonic monism and Buddhist systems of rational doctrine. Both of these religious orientations gain their insights into ultimate reality without reference to history as such. Of course, the respective Hindu and Buddhist grasp of ultimate reality occurred to humans in time. Furthermore, these disclosures have been transmitted and elaborated by other humans with the consequence that they have a history of their own, a discernable continuity over a period of time. But history is not regarded in Buddhism and Hinduism as the source of the truths set forth in these two perspectives. Neither is it regarded as the instrument of their transmission nor the key to their understanding. Indeed, both Hinduism and Buddhism assign a negative value to historical existence. In sharp contrast, for Christians all valid revelation occurs within history and appeals to history in a radical sense. Though quite different from the perspective met with in Hinduism and Buddhism, Christianity's distinctive perspective nonetheless clearly attests the *undeniability of the same central spiritual reality.*

For Christians, the revelation of God in Christ occurs not merely *within* history; it occurs *as* history, as a series of concrete historical events. Revelation is itself a historical datum, interwoven within the movement of world history. In any revelation, as we use this term in critical and technical studies of religions, something that has been hitherto unknown concerning ultimate reality becomes known through the instrumentality of some divine being or extraordinary human. In examining any account of revelation, one wants to know, in addition to the content made known, how the deity or extraordinary human made this disclosure and by what means ordinary humans receive it. In the Christians' understanding of their own revelation, God communicated through the medium of a human person in that person's own history, and other humans are able to receive this communication only through their participation in history. Revelation in the Christian context is itself a historical event that cannot be separated from or properly considered apart from history. Christians believe that at one definite point in time and in a specific geographical location, the human life, words, works, and death of Jesus the historical person became the self-disclosing communication of the character of God. There and at that point in time in Jesus the historical human, Christians believe, this sovereign God made a free entry into human history without interrupting or contravening the normal flow of historical events. This revelation came not as a dazzling sight to be seen, or as a radically new doctrine to be believed, but as a historical datum, a personal overture creating the necessity of a responding personal decision that, whether accepting or rejecting the offer, makes a significant difference in the decider's own personal and public history.

In the context of Christianity the divine–human encounter, mediated by Christ, reveals the central spiritual reality to humankind in a personal relationship; it reveals also the personal and religious nature of history itself. In this context history is seen to be amenable to God and compatible with God's self-communication. In the Christian story, it was not necessary for God to alter the way history happens or to interfere with history's regular sequential flow in order to make the divine self-revelation possible, fluent, understandable, and ample. Jesus' followers discern him to be a free moral person whose very own genuinely human flesh, psyche, and spirit gave historical presence to the reality of God. To them God's presence and participation in the human phenomenon became apparent in Jesus' own decisions and actions. His followers observed that Jesus made decisions in a characteristically human manner and acted them out, but he was different in that he decided consistently in reference to and in favor of an ultimate spiritual reality. By his sustained awareness of God and prepossessing deference to God, Jesus made his followers aware of God's presence and character and of the human necessity to make decisions for or against God's intentions for them. These followers and successive generations of Christians took this insight and drew out its implications. Human decisions, made for or against God, are the source of human acts that make up what we call history. All history, not just Christians' history, is thus identified to be a spiritual–moral phenomenon, created when free (*spiritual*) and responsible (*moral*) human persons act out their decisions for or against the ultimate referent of their lives. Inescapably, human beings are historical and are history makers. They live, decide, and act in relation to an ultimate reference, wittingly or unwittingly, cooperatively or uncooperatively. The spiritual–moral symbolism of undeniability in Christianity urges that human beings have no other option than to live as decision makers in reference to an ultimate spiritual reality. Only by deciding in favor of this ultimate reality does one live as an accountable participant in history.

Humans do not need a special revelation to inform them that their historical existence is bounded and is lived at every moment in reference to the mystery of accountability. Humans have the natural capacity to transcend themselves sufficiently to know that they cannot be convincingly the center of their own existence and that their own achievements and civilizations cannot permanently satisfy human aspiration and serve as the end or fulfillment of history. Humanity's unaided common sense can perceive that historical existence is self-evidently contingent: It is not self-sufficient and self-contained, and its meaning and possibilities for fulfillment are not inherent and self-evident. Quite without a divine revelation of the identity of history's mysterious referent, humans as such have an existential obligation to decide what to do with their finite historical existence and to consider the consequences – to themselves and to others – of their actions. Accountability inheres in historical existence. *Responsibility* (what one does with the finite freedom one actually has) rather than *finitude* (what one cannot do because of *limited* power, knowledge, and freedom) is the definitive characteristic of humans in their historicity.

According to Christianity, God's self-impartation in Christ explains the mystery of the moral and spiritual accountability inherent in historical existence by identifying God in Christ as the *ultimate referent* for all human decisions and actions. According to Christianity, this mystery is not merely the situation that human history in itself is incomprehensible without recognition of some referent of accountability. The mystery involves further the fact that humanity as such, prior to any revealed knowledge of God, is subject already to the salvific intention of God. Christianity holds, because it thinks Christ discloses, that the divine love has always wanted for humans, individually and totally, nothing less than that they exercise their freedom in history with a view to their temporal and eternal well-being, which is to say their salvation. Here history receives a positive value. It is seen here to be in fact the only means by which humans either realize or forfeit their fulfillment. According to this reasoning, decisions and their consequences refer willy-nilly to God and therefore bear decisively on one's present and eternal well-being. All history is either salvation history or its antithesis. When identified thus as unavoidably decisive for salvation, history itself *appeals self-evidently for personal consent to the inevitability of living with reference to a central spiritual reality common to all humanity* and *exposes the self-contradiction* of trying to live unaccountably to ultimate reality by living with reference to oneself or something else less than ultimate reality.

Christianity depicts this imperious, grave, and urgent character of human historicity in a succinct proclamation: To live once only in history, accountable to God, choosing one's own eternal future, is every human's fate. "Now is the time of salvation" (2 Corinthians 6:2) is both a consolation and a warning to the effect that all persons decide their own destiny within one limited lifetime by the fundamental disposition they manifest toward God as an inevitable and ultimate referent. Although Christian symbolic expression is rich with metaphors of a personal life that continues after death, Christianity has held that this one present mortal life is decisive. Only within the span of this one lifetime does a person have an opportunity to develop a disposition acceptable for eternal life with God. Because each person gets only one opportunity, historical existence is either the hope or the despair of every human being. On this assumption, Christianity makes an urgent appeal to humankind individually and collectively to work out its historical existence and eternal destiny in cooperation with God's will as revealed in Christ.

The *historical* character of the revelation of God in Christ, including the historical way Christians experience and express it, integrates a complex of other Christian axioms. This *historical* revelation is also *theocentric, christonormative,* and *person-aimed.* Like the historical axiom, these other four Christian axioms affirm, through their respective spiritual–moral postulates, *humanity's common and central spiritual reality.*

The historical revelation of God in Christ is *theocentric,* postulating that God alone is absolute. Though expressed in history and indissolubly associated with history, the Christian concept of revelation identifies a spiritual reality that transcends history and indeed all other realities.

Christianity recognizes two kinds of reality: the reality that is God and the reality that is subject to God. "The Christian believes," said St. Augustine, "that nothing exists save God himself and what comes from him."[2] The reality of God is holy, existing by its own principle of unmitigated independence, and that makes it fundamentally different from and unfathomable by all other reality. All other reality is secular, which means that it is dependent and transitory. According to Christianity, holy and secular are qualitatively different but not moral antagonists. Although the secular world as such, being dependent and transitory, differs categorically from the holy God, it is compatible with the holy God. It is good and therefore compatible with God, according to Christianity's mythological concept of Creation, because the "supremely and immutably" good God created all things whatsoever so that "each single created thing is good, and taken as a whole they are very good" in that together they make up a secular world of "admirable beauty."[3] According to such reasoning the secular world becomes profane, opposed to God, when humans construe and use it as if it or they were not relative to God. Only when humans profane the secular world does the holiness of God become morally antagonistic toward the world, and then only toward its profanation, not toward its being dependent and transitory. At all times, however, God's holiness, Christians maintain, is categorically distinct from all other reality. Christians do not claim precise and full knowledge of God's holiness, but maintain that God has informed them repeatedly in their scriptures that, because God is Holy, the reality of God must never be confused with anyone or anything else – neither with some part, power, or aspect of human life, nor with part or all of other historical or natural realities. In reference to all other realities, God is literally always *other than* and sovereign. We will show later on that, for Christianity, the elusiveness of God consists more in this qualitative *otherness* than in God's remoteness.

2 Enchiridion, 3.9, in *Augustine: Confessions and Enchiridion,* newly translated by Albert C. Outler and published as volume 7 of The Library of Christian Classics (London: SCM Press, 1955).
3 Ibid., 3.10.

According to Christianity, the reality of God, who is always *other than*, revealed its own reality in Christ. Christians see that self-revealed reality to be sovereign freedom and righteous selfless love. Thus present in Christ, God became and remains accessible to humans in their history, making it possible for them to have a personal, participatory relationship with God. In this relationship the human person remains human and God remains *other than* human. In becoming present to humans in their history, God transcends divine otherness without deprivation of divine otherness. God's transcendence is not restrained by divine otherness or inhibited from becoming God's immanence. Christians assert that through Christ humans have access to a reality entirely unlike their own. God self-communicates so humanly in Christ that humans are able to recognize the wholly other divine reality and to grasp and evaluate its meaning for their existence and destiny. In asserting the presence of God in Christ, however, Christianity does not assert that God ceases to be God. The divine reality remains free and independent of historical existence and inaccessible to rational comprehension, though present to both. The transcendent God does the revealing in Christ, and Christ is not to be understood as an independent center of divine will. All the revealing in Christ and all its concomitant saving work are God's activity: "All this is from God, who through Christ reconciled us to himself . . . that is, in Christ God was reconciling the world to himself" (2 Corinthians 5:18, 19). Christ himself, like history itself, is relative to God, who alone is absolute. On the basis of the conviction that it is God who is "in Christ," Christianity, since its fourth century, has affirmed that Christ participates in the absolute character of God and that his revealing and saving activity are relevant transhistorically.

Christianity's theocentricity bears the undeniable implication that Christians should regard (1) all human experience of God, including fellowship with God in Christ, as relative; (2) all concepts of God, including all Christian concepts of God in Christ, as relative; (3) all witnesses to God, including the witness of the Christians' Bible, doctrines, and testimonies, as relative; and (4) Christianity itself, as a cumulative human response to God in Christ, as relative – in each instance, *relative to God*. The historical revelation of God in Christ is so indisputably theocentric that Christians are bound to take the universality of human finitude in earnest, acknowledging and accepting all human experiences, insights, judgments, and formulations as tentative. This theocentricity challenges every insinuation of absolutism on the part of any person, group, institution, or power, including especially Christians and the church. It calls all absolutist pretensions into question by making humanity, culture, history, the world, and even the revelation of God in Christ itself relative to God whose reality exceeds all that is revealed in Christ. When consistent with their notion of God's sovereign freedom and righteous selfless love as revealed in Christ, Christians should not prescribe any limits to the scope of divine reality and revelation.

Christians of most persuasions readily acknowledge these days that the history of Christianity fails to demonstrate a consistent deference to theocentricity. The reason for this failure is that Christians in general have taken God's revelation in Christ to be final and decisive for all human existence and destiny. Failing to give preeminent attention to the theocentric character of this revelation, however, they have concluded typically that their Christian religion is absolute and that all other religions are relative to it. With few exceptions, they have held, therefore, that Christian response to God is the only acceptable, saving response for all humans. With this mind-set most have had little inclination to consider the possibility that the revelation may evoke numerous differing but saving responses, that God may have approached humanity in a number of saving ways, or that Christianity may be only a phase of religious history that God will supersede by calling forth some other religion. When analyzed, however, the monopolistic Christian claim, like every other human claim, contradicts the Christian theocentric axiom that God alone is absolute. The Christian religion is rendered provisional by the very revelation to which it is a response. One may reasonably claim that because the revelation in Christ is God's revelation it is permanent and unconditional. One may not claim credibly, however, that this revelation exhausts the reality of God. Nor may one argue validly that any particular response to it has sacrosanct finality.

Christianity's affirmation of uncompromising theocentricity does more than relativize all human and therefore all Christian existence, perception, and conceptualization. It positively asserts that all humanity is accountable to the same ultimate referent, the same central spiritual reality. It regards God's self-communication in Christ to be intended for humans universally, and it facilitates this communication by its own worldwide missions, which seek to present Christ to all the human world. On the one hand, this missionary witness asks humans without exception to give *personal consent to the inevitability of living with reference to God in Christ*. On the other hand, this same witness acknowledges the uncontestable sovereignty of God and thus affirms the *undeniability of a common central spiritual reality for all humanity*. Correlatively, by holding every human person and group accountable to a common absolute referent, Christianity's theocentric witness *exposes the self-contradiction* of those Christians and all other persons and groups who pretentiously try to absolutize their own existence, experience, or interpretation. Thus again Christian expression points beyond its particularity to *the central spiritual reality common to humanity universally.*

Christianity represents the *historical, theocentric* revelation of God "in Christ" as also *christonormative*. Because its ultimate referent is God, this historical revelation is considered *theocentric*. It is considered *christonormative* because God revealed historically in Christ is definitive for Christian understanding and decisive for Christian response to God. The distinction between the suffixes *-centric* and *-normative* explicates Christianity's explanation of the relation of Jesus Christ to the total reality of God. The very earliest Christian theological assertions specify the "special sense" in which God was present in Jesus. They say that the *eternal Son of God* came into human existence in the man Jesus, a unique divine–human reality embodying coincidentally the full presence of God's reality and the full presence of a real and actual human being. This explication of Jesus Christ's relation to God has prevailed as Christianity's official estimate of Christ, withstanding other interpretations that either overstated the divine reality and understated the humanity or overstated the humanity and understated the divine reality present in Jesus Christ. It becomes apparent in the mainstream interpretation that Jesus Christ the person represents the *normative* aspect of the quintessentially *theocentric* faith of Christianity. He gives human presence to the reality of God. Because the reality of the Son of God participates in God's reality, the Son poses no challenge either to the holy character or the absolute status of God in Christianity.

Jesus himself initiated this christology in his own seminal statement,

All things have been entrusted to me by my Father; and no one knows who the Son is except the Father, or who the Father is except the Son and those to whom the Son chooses to reveal him.

(Luke 10:22)

Jesus depicts here an intimate relation between the Father and himself that goes beyond the usual messianic designations current in his day. The grammatically absolute phrase, *"the* Son," indicates a relationship between Jesus and the Father that no other human has. These considerations configure the image of a unique Father–Son companionship between God and Jesus, with Jesus the Son cast in the singular role of revealing the Father.

What Jesus expressed seminally about his filial relation with God, his apostles developed explicitly in their estimate of Jesus' significance for humankind. They proclaimed that this human person who had lived and ministered among the Jewish people of Galilee and Judah is *the eternal Son of God* who has been associated with the Father in heavenly life from all eternity, in the divine work of creating the universe and history, and, most recently, in the historical work of effecting the salvation of humankind first through the people Israel and now through Christ and his church. For them it was evident that *the Word of God* – which represents both the revelatory and saving reality of God – had entered into human existence as the human person, Jesus of Nazareth conceived as the Son of God. To them *the Truth of God* that Jesus made present and effective was not a law to be observed, not an item of information to enlarge their knowledge about God, and not a teaching whose lessons they should learn. The Truth of God that these apostles saw revealed in Jesus was the very person of Jesus. They believed that in his personal relationships with them he made known the saving reality of God. His teaching and deeds of mercy and miracle evoked from them and others questions about his personal identity: "Who gave you the authority to say and do these things?" and "Who then is this, that even the winds and waters obey him?" and with similar astonishment, "Who except God alone can forgive sins?" (cf. Matthew 21:23, Luke 20:2, and Mark 2:7). The apostles concluded that God's Son–Word–Truth became incarnate in the human person they knew as Jesus for the sole purpose of effecting through his interpersonal relationships humanity's salvation, *from* sin *to* eternal life with God. This Christology finds explicit statement in the well-known New Testament passages of John 1:1–18, Colossians 1:15–20, and Hebrews 1:1–3. Communicated from the apostolic communities, these christological statements explicate for all Christians one unalterable standard for understanding Christ's relation to God: The Son of God, who is genuine eternal deity but not the entirety of God's deity, entered fully into the one human person of Jesus in order to make the saving reality of God personally known, accessible, and effective to all other human persons.

In 325 C.E. official representatives (bishops) of Christian congregations throughout the world met in Nicaea and formulated a creedal statement of this apostolic interpretation of God in Christ and voted to make it officially binding on all Christians. In 451 at Chalcedon, in a council even more representative of the whole Christian world, the bishops reaffirmed the creed formulated at Nicaea and the obligation of all Christians to affirm it. The christological clause in the Nicaean creed states,

[I believe] . . . in one Lord Jesus Christ, the only-begotten Son of God, begotten of the Father before all worlds, Light of Light, very God of very God, begotten not made, being of one substance with the Father; by whom all things were made; who, for us humans and our salvation, came down from heaven and was incarnate by the Holy Spirit of the Virgin Mary, and was made human; and was crucified also for us under Pontius Pilate; he suffered and was buried and the third day he rose again, according to the scriptures, and ascended into heaven.

From the standpoint of this apostolic and conciliar explication, it is evident that the historical revelation of God in Christ is *theocentric* precisely because it is *christonormative*. Jesus Christ is the personal center at which the saving reality of God becomes personally present and accessible to all other human persons. Christ embodies God's intention and initiative to effect humanity's salvation from sin to eternal life.

Identified in this way as God's provision for the eternal well-being of humans universally, Christ speaks to the universal human necessity of affirming meaning and purpose in one's life as a whole and thereby points not merely to the Christian experience of God revealed in Christ but also to humanity's common experience of the *undeniability of a central spiritual reality*. In his appeal for personal collaboration with God and in the human faith he evokes, Christ *exposes the self-contradiction* and self-destructiveness of "unfaith," of not wishing and working for the eternal well-being that he asserts that God wants for all humanity.

The fourth axiom in Christianity's interpretation of the historical revelation of God in Christ has been indicated already in our discussion of each of the other axioms. Christianity aims its interpretation of each of them toward the human person. According to this interpretation of the *historical, theocentric,* and *christonormative* revelation of God in Christ, the righteous selfless love of God aims expressly to provide the present fulfillment and eternal salvation *for human persons*. In its exposition of this axiom Christianity articulates its most poignant spiritual–moral *appeal for personal consent to the inevitability of living with reference to humanity's central spiritual reality,* and likewise it develops its clearest spiritual–moral *exposure of self-contradictory behavior.*

Christianity is regularly referred to – favorably by its adherents but pejoratively by some of its critics – as a supremely personal religion. We must be clear about what Christians in the mainstream mean when they describe God and their religion as personal and, more pertinently, what Christian teaching means when it makes the human person's salvation the goal of God's revealing work in Christ.

Admittedly some Christians do understand, worship, and otherwise relate to God under the image of a person,[4] but to do so is not required by Christian scripture. Neither the Old nor New Testament applied this word "person" to God, though their use of "Lord" and "Father" to refer

---

4　In the nineteenth and twentieth centuries, under the influence of Immanuel Kant, some individual theologies represented God as a Person. Kant had distinguished nature, which is ruled by physical law, from personality, which is ruled by moral law. This distinction enabled certain theologians to maintain a place for God in spite of crowding from modernity. Paul Tillich has made a trenchant criticism of representing God as a Person (cf. his *Systematic Theology* [Chicago: University of Chicago Press, 1951], 1:245), but George W. Forrell has argued that reference to God as "person" "does tell how [God] meets us" and "guards against" pantheistic and polytheistic misunderstandings of God as the "Supreme Being" even though admittedly it does not characterize the reality or "form" of God as such (*The Protestant Faith* [Englewood Cliffs, N.J.: Prentice-Hall, 1960], pp. 87–8).

to and address God invites the imagination to personalize its concept of God. Christian scripture intimates and doctrine teaches that because the reality of God surpasses all that humans mean by "person," God has the capacity to effect reciprocal relations with human persons. In other words, God is not a Person, but God is certainly not *less than* a person. We observed previously, in the second chapter, that *personal* is not a universally attested characteristic of *humanity's central spiritual reality*. Because of the Christian's personal experience of God we must register here the further observation that *apersonal* and *impersonal* also do not meet the test for universality. Even so, after this observation is duly registered, it must be attentively noted and remembered that the Christians' personal experience of God revealed in Christ does not require that Christians conceive of God as a Person.

Christian doctrine holds that Jesus was a human person and remains so in the enlarged reality of his resurrection. It holds further that, in a different meaning of the word "person," Jesus Christ the Son of God is the second of three Persons (Father, Son, and Holy Spirit) in the one Godhead. In its formulaic phrases, "three Persons in one Godhead" and "God in three Persons," Christianity has intended that "Person" indicates one or another of three distinct subsistences in the one reality called God. Even those readers who are not familiar with the theological nuance of the philosophical word "subsistence" will understand that it does not refer to a person in our modern psychological sense. In the confessional phrases for the Holy Trinity, "Person" does not refer to a separate center of divine will, and "God in three Persons" does not describe three individuals having interpersonal relations among themselves. We make this reference here to the doctrine of the Trinity only to point out that Christianity formally teaches that the full reality of God is neither a Person nor three independent personalities. Because God becomes accessible to Christians through the medium of personal relationship with Jesus as a fully human being, they quite properly use such phrases as "the personal God" and "God's personal revelation." Likewise, they characterize their religion as intrinsically personal because they think that the revelation of God in Christ evokes from them a personal response, which, in turn, prompts them to address and refer to God with personal pronouns (you, he, who). Their use of these phrases and pronouns, however, does not constitute a valid basis for conceiving of God as a Person, even though it has often had this effect in general reflection.

The *person-aimed* character of God's revelation in Christ inheres in the revelation itself and identifies human beings as the ones to whom God is sending unbounded and unbinding goodwill. Yet, in these very persons whom God intends to benefit, God's love meets its most tenacious opponent, the human self, which represents the antithesis of God's love.

As appraised by Jesus and subsequent Christian reflection, the human person in his or her natural state exists in bondage to consuming interests of the self. This is the essence of Christianity's doctrine of original sin. "All have sinned and failed to attain what pleases God" (Romans 3:23). All people are sinners preoccupied with *self;* they are *self*-indulgent sinners, *self*-pitying sinners, *self*-righteous sinners, or some combination of these. In many ways it is true to say that Christianity's only empirically verifiable doctrine is this doctrine of original sin. Sin is "original" in that it cannot possibly have derived from God; it is "sin" because it preoccupies itself with self-serving interests. The denial of original sin is "empirically falsifiable" because a self-defense offered for one's selflessness is self-evidently self-contradictory. Christianity holds that humans in their natural human state want what pleases themselves individually, define their personal fulfillment individualistically, invest interest in the common welfare only in accord with their vested self-interests, and consequently hold distorted notions about what would be ultimately good for themselves or others. Christian reflection developed a complex but not universally accepted theory explaining how humans became self-preoccupied, but that theory of original sin is not needed to make credible the Christian contention that every human person is the consenting participant in self-preoccupation and needs to be saved from it by a radical reform of personality.

While realistic about this self-centeredness of human persons, Jesus and his followers have claimed to be realistic also about the possibilities for the reign of God's benevolence in a person's life. Having identified himself as God's Son, Jesus announced that he had come expressly "to call sinners to repentance" (Luke 5:32) because "it is the Father's good pleasure to give" eternal life to any and all who repudiate the rule of self in their lives (Luke 12:32). According to the New Testament narratives, Jesus' own exemplification of selfless love inspired some of his contemporaries to conclude that God is not too exalted to be loved and that humans are not too self-consumed to be converted from their inherent selfishness. These narratives relate that he ameliorated the self-centered human situation, first by his modest success in inspiring some of his contemporaries to supplant their self-referenced motivation with appreciation for God's generous regard, and then by charging his church to perpetuate, implement, and universalize that appeal. Those who were persuaded by Jesus found themselves in a paradox of personal freedom, obliged to choose either to remain in their self-identity or to identify their lives selflessly with Jesus in the rule of God's selfless love. Jesus distinguished the options plainly and depicted the respective consequences vividly for anyone who would consider becoming his follower: "If anyone wants to become my follower, let one abandon one's self and . . . begin to follow me"

(Matthew 16:24). This saying merits further explanation. Most standard translations render the independent clause as "let him [or, he must] deny himself and . . . follow me" (cf. the King James Version, the Revised Standard Version, and the New International Version). This rendering lends itself easily to the erroneous suggestion that Jesus asked people merely to give up the satisfactions they would really like to enjoy. The Jerusalem Bible gives a more accurate approximation of the meaning of the original Greek as well as the Latin text: "If anyone wants to be a follower of mine, let him renounce himself . . . and follow me." The Greek text calls clearly for the exclusion of the self altogether, or, better stated, it calls for "the affirmation that the self is nothing, that it has no claims and no values."[5] In another saying, the harshness of which perplexes most Christians still, Jesus called explicitly for the unequivocal exclusion of the self: "If a person comes to me and does not repudiate [literally, *hate*] its own father and mother, and wife and children and brothers and sisters, and indeed its very own self, that person cannot be my disciple" (Luke 14:26).[6]

Jesus' insight into the perverse reality of the self suggests close analogy with the Buddha's *anatta* (no self) doctrine, but the history of Christian thought has not educed a doctrinal concept and teaching that adequately captures Jesus' insight. Rather, Christian thought and preaching throughout history have represented Jesus' insight generally as distinguishing between a "false" or "lower" self and a "true" or "higher" self, or between selfishness and unselfishness, and have encouraged privation of the "unworthy" or "worldly" self rather than eradication of the very notion of the self.

Jesus made no such distinctions between a lower and a higher or an unworthy and a worthy self. He conceded no validity whatsoever to the self and declared that it should be dispossessed completely, not merely dislodged from the center of personal life or deprived of some desired enjoyments. In Jesus' teaching the only self is an evil self. It is evil because it pretends to reality, but, being inherently self-deceptive and self-consuming, it cannot fulfill itself. Because the self defies fulfillment, self-love cannot be love at all. It is lust, the sheer desire to satisfy the insatiable, unrealizable self. It contradicts love: It excludes, alienates, neglects, and destroys. Self-love is a self-destructive reality that *makes a difference* in persons' lives only by usurping the rightful place of love. Love is constructive power that unites and fulfills human persons by displacing the mind's self-references. Jesus called upon his contemporaries to renounce

5 *The Jerome Bible Commentary*, 2:92.
6 Cf. Matthew 10:37, where the absolute sense of Luke's version is lost in a comparison: "The person who loves father or mother . . . son or daughter *more than* me is not worthy of me."

the self irrevocably and to convert to a personal identity and a pattern of morality that are referenced whole-mindedly to God and neighbor.

The apostle Paul grasped and affirmed Jesus' total repudiation of the self. Describing his own conversion and Christian life, Paul professed, "Now I can live for God. *I* have been crucified with Christ, and *I* no longer live but Christ lives in me" (Galatians 2:19b–20a). In his instruction to the Christians in Rome, Paul contrasted the outcome of two alternative behavioral orientations that epitomize the Christian expression of *the inevitability of living with reference to a central spiritual reality* and the inherent *self-contradiction* of attempting to do otherwise. "Sin pays off with death, but God freely gives eternal life in Jesus Christ our Lord" (Romans 6:23). Echoing Jesus undistortedly, Paul went on to exhort the Romans to make the enlightened choice of serving God instead of self.

My brothers and sisters, I beg you, consider God's merciful providence and worship him in a way that befits thinking beings. Make an offering that is truly pleasing to God by consecrating your entire living person to him. Do not acquiesce in the ways of this world, but let your consecrated mind transform your behavior so that you truly demonstrate what God wants, which is the good, the well-pleasing and the perfect.

(Romans 12:1–1)

Even though the Christian tradition has not developed a thoroughgoing doctrine of no self, it has sustained Jesus' appeal for conversion from self to selflessness, and it has been clear in identifying this as a fundamental change in personal orientation from self-will to God's will. It has maintained that conversion is possible on the ground that when someone is encountered by Christ's appeal made through the church, that person becomes existentially free, having the option and the capability to choose orientation to God and thus a new personal identity. It has insisted that this conversion is necessary for finding purpose and ultimate meaning for one's own life and for making sense of life as a whole. With equal insistence, the Christian tradition has held that, given this spiritual opportunity, anyone presented with it has the moral obligation to prefer and accept it. Christians have used a variety of names and phrases for this conversion including being born again or second birth, spiritual birth, regeneration, renewing the mind, and becoming a new creature, a new being, or an authentic person. By all of these phrases Christians designate the same fundamental remotivation that they consider necessary to bring about a Christ-like mode of personal behavior.

Up to this point our discussion of the *person-aimed* revelation of God in Christ might suggest an individualistic concept of the Christian person.

On the contrary, mainstream Christian teaching rejects all individualistic concepts outright and straightforwardly; it holds rather that the term "Christian person" excludes both "private individual" and "collectivistic group." From this point of view, a proper personal response to God's selfless love could never be that of an individual disengaged from responsible relations to others; nor yet that of a collective expressing the will of the group but neglectful of the free, independent intention of the individual. Christian response to God's love must always be *interpersonal*, that of an individual responsibly relating to other persons. Jesus reiterated and designated as preeminent the Jewish scriptural commandment which enjoins, "Love the Lord your God with all your mind, heart, and will, and with all your consciousness, and with all your strength" (Deuteronomy 6:5, cf. Mark 12:30, Luke 12:27, and Matthew 22:37), meaning "Devote your entire personal existence to loving God." Lest anyone think that loving God could be a private affair between an individual and God, Jesus commended as "self-same" to the "greatest commandment" another injunction from Jewish scripture, "Love your neighbor as yourself" (Leviticus 19:34; cf. Matthew 22:39). In the light of his thoroughgoing repudiation of self-reference, Jesus probably intended this latter directive to mean "Love your neighbor instead of your self." In still another saying Jesus made accord with one's neighbor the proof of one's understanding that loving and worshiping God can never be an entirely private and individual matter. "If you are at the altar making your offering and there remember that another person has something against you, leave your offering there before the altar. First go and be reconciled to that person and then come and make your offering" (Matthew 5:24). One's relation with God comprehends all the other relations that one has. Acceptable worship of God requires that a person be in a state of love and peace with all acquaintances, including especially those who have a specific grievance. A person's relation with God is thus regarded as inseparable from one's interpersonal human relationships. Jesus pressed this point by designating neighbor-regarding love as the hallmark of God-like character and by requiring that his followers exercise peacemaking goodwill toward their enemies. "Love your enemies and pray for those who persecute you, and in that way demonstrate that you have the character of your Heavenly Father who makes his sun to rise on the evil and the good, and sends rain on the righteous and the unrighteous" (Matthew 5:44–5). Jesus' model of godly character allows no individualistic piety. A person stands before God as an individual in accountable relation to other such persons.

According to Christianity, Jesus' founding of the church consummated his revelation of God's love, manifested the essentially incorporative power of this love, and provided in perpetuity for the historical implementation of this love's design to culture human persons for eternal life.

At the very beginning of his public ministry, simultaneous with his earliest preaching, Jesus carefully formed a community for those identifying with him in his filial relation with God. He chose twelve apostles to constitute the nuclear and perpetuating unit of this family of God, thus defining his mission as a corporate activity that exceeded and would extend beyond his own physical presence and which he envisioned to supersede the Jewish religious community (Israel or "the People of God"). At his last meal with these twelve, just prior to his arrest, trial, and crucifixion, he said to them, "You are the persons who have stayed with me throughout my trials. Therefore as my Father appointed a kingdom to me, I now appoint a kingdom to you so that you may eat and drink at my table in my kingdom, and you will sit on thrones to judge the twelve tribes of Israel" (Luke 22:28–30). Because Jesus founded the church in and through these twelve apostles and deputized them to transmit his provision for salvation to the ends of the earth "until the end of the world" (Matthew 28:16–20), the church from its beginning has claimed its "apostolic" succession to be its legitimating characteristic. Its scripture, sacraments, doctrine, and teaching have their status as such because they can be shown clearly to be essentially those that the apostles formed and transmitted.

For Christian thought as for Jesus, the church exists for the salvation of persons everywhere. In Christian experience, conceptualization, and idiom, person and church are mutually inclusive and mutually dependent. Each is necessary for the other's existence and neither is separable from the other. Together they constitute what is meant by the axiom, the revelation of God is *person-aimed*.

Given the mutually dependent relation of Christian *person* and Christian *church*, and given the Christian presupposition that every human person needs to, can, and ought to be saved by God in Christ, there is meaningful insight and consistent logic in St. Cyprian's widely and heatedly debated statement that "outside the church there is no salvation" (*extra ecclesiam nulla salus*).[7] The *historical, theocentric,* and *christonormative* revelation of God in Christ aims specifically for the salvation of human persons and institutes the church to effectuate this universally.

The implications of Christianity's spiritual–moral message for our study of the undeniability of humanity's central spiritual reality should now be clear and poignant. Christianity insists that all human persons are naturally self-centered and therefore self-destructive. It insists also that everyone encountered by Christ and his church has the spiritual possibility (that is, the divinely given, once forever opportunity) and the moral obligation to become a person approved and prepared by God for

7 Cyprian, *Epistle*, 73:21.

eternal life. In this spiritual–moral message Christianity makes a three-fold witness to *the undeniability of God* and, thus by implication, to the *undeniability of the central spiritual reality of humankind*. First, it *attests the human necessity of affirming meaning and purpose in life as a whole* with its claim to solve the mystery of historical existence by making it possible for persons to participate here and now in the life of the church, which symbolizes eternal life. This portrays historical existence as consisting essentially of the freedom with which God has endowed human persons to transcend themselves and to love God and their neighbors. Second, Christianity *appeals for personal consent to the inevitability of living with reference to humanity's ultimate central spiritual reality* by setting forth a clear concept of the ideal Christian person. Such a one is never only a private individual, but always an individual organically related to the fellowship of Jesus' disciples and correlated to the needs of every human person. This constitutes the paradigm of personal fulfillment by appealing to humankind generally and to individual humans specifically to seek this fulfillment through personal response to Christ. Third, by showing the inevitable self-destructiveness of a self-interested life, Christianity *exposes the self-contradictory nature of sin* (i.e., selfish behavior) and so *discloses the inevitability of living accountably to the ultimate spiritual referent of humankind*.

Intellectual Symbolism of Undeniability

Christianity has produced a prodigious and richly varied intellectual witness that impressively attests the undeniability of the central spiritual reality of humankind. The apex of this achievement is usually identified with the celebrated systems of theology and theological philosophy developed by Augustine (354–430) and, during the Middle Ages, by such scholastics as Anselm of Canterbury (1033–1109) and Thomas Aquinas (1225–74). Whatever the apex, the intellectual enterprise itself has been coextensive with the existence of Christian faith. From the beginnings of Christianity the apostolic leaders definitively charged believers to use their minds to inquire intellectually into the revelation of God in Christ. They did not, of course, intend to bring the divine activity before the judgment of human reason, but rather to attempt to understand, worship, and serve God better. Jesus commanded his followers, "Love the Lord your God with all your mind" (Matthew 22:37); the apostle Peter, discussing the nature and responsibility of the Christian's life, admonished Gentile Christians in Asia Minor to "be prepared at all times to give a reasoned defense" of their faith in Christ (1 Peter 3:15) and the Apostle Paul exhorted the Christians at Rome, saying, "Worship [God] in a way that befits thinking beings. . . . Let your consecrated mind transform your behavior so that you truly demonstrate what God wants, which is the good, the well-pleasing, and the perfect" (Romans 12:2). Impelled by such apostolic charges, the Christian church has felt compelled to produce an intellectual symbolism of undeniability that faithfully clarifies and elaborates the revelation for Christians themselves and vindicates it to others.

We considered at some length, in Chapter Two, the Christian arguments for the existence of God and need not rehearse them here. The prominent debate over atheism and theism attempts to determine by reason whether God is. This debate, in which mostly Christian theologians have argued the case *for* the existence of God, tends to obscure the fact that symbolism of undeniability in Christianity is not, and cannot be, solely an attempt to establish the undeniability of a reality called God. Instead, a distinctively Christian intellectual symbolism of undeniability must offer reasoned explication and defense of the fundamental Christian position that what is revealed historically in Christ is undeniably God's reality and is decisive for the salvation of humans universally.

This fundamental Christian position does not require that Christians regard the revelation in Christ to be God's only revelation. Indeed, as Christians reason, the historical revelation of God in Christ indicates that revelation – a disclosure made by the divine reality itself – is the only means by which humans can have any knowledge of God. Because the reality of God's love revealed in Christ "surpasses all human knowledge" (Ephesians 3:10), they reason that all unrevealed reality of God is humanly unknowable. This does not necessarily imply that the revelation in Christ is God's only revelation. It indicates rather that all human knowledge of God has to have been communicated by God, because God's reality so differs in kind from human reality that it is inaccessible to unaided human faculties of knowing. Humans must leave the unrevealed reality of God (*Deus absconditus*), the majesty and nature of God in itself, "unexplored," as Martin Luther said, because God "has not willed that it be dealt with by us."[8] John Calvin advised that since God's unrevealed majesty "exceeds the capacity of human understanding," humans should "adore" it rather than try to "investigate" it.[9] Generally eschewing speculation about God's undisclosed reality and holding that this utterly other reality can be known only to the extent that it makes itself known, Christians hold that other symbolizations of ultimate reality are authentic and continuous with Christ insofar as their content is expressed or inherently intimated in Christ's revelation. Christians accept, for example, that that God made a series of specific revelations "by the prophets"

8 *Weimar Ausgabe*, XVII, 685.
9 *Instruction in Faith*, trans. Paul T. Fuhrmann (Philadelphia: Westminster Press, 1949).

(Hebrews 1:1) in the particular history of Israel and the Jews before Jesus. Christians regard those revelations to be the integral antecedent of God's continuing historical revelation in Christ.

Similarly, Christian thinkers, with rare exception, have taken for granted the validity of all general evidence for God's reality and have held that Christ's historical revelation serves to make explicit what the general evidence intimates concerning the character and purpose of the reality of God. They are predisposed to defend primarily the gospel's assertion that it was really God who was revealed in the historical Jesus and to assert that what God revealed specifically and locally there has a universal aim and validity. They also accept as given, however, that God has revealed divine reality in a general way to humans universally in their commonly shared natural world. This commonly shared evidence has the force, Christian teaching holds, of rendering every human person accountable for knowing that God is, is ultimate, and is therefore worthy of reverence and thanks. For Christians, then, this general revelation, though deficient, has sufficient power of persuasion to establish that God *is real and is the reality upon which all other realities depend and from which they derive their ultimate meaning.*

Christian intellectual symbolism of undeniability always presupposes and sometimes makes explicit use of this *general* revelation to clarify and strengthen its advocacy and defense of the *special* revelation in Christ. The apostle Paul, Christianity's first missionary to Gentile people and in the enterprise its first apologetic theologian, set the Christian precedent of approving and resorting to general revelation when communicating the Gospel. The New Testament recounts three notable instances in which Paul made recourse to general revelation: Acts 14:15–17, Acts 17:26–31, and Romans 1:18–32. We will look carefully at the second of these, Paul's sermon to philosophers at Athens, the city whose very name symbolized Greek learning and piety.

In Athens, Paul preached the gospel "in the synagogue" to Jews and their monotheistic sympathizers. "In the marketplace" he preached to any of the predominantly Gentile public who would listen, and he debated and argued with any who would participate. Some philosophers had heard him "preaching about Jesus and the resurrection" and a number of them had sarcastically called him "a propagandist for some outlandish gods," the same accusation which had been leveled earlier against Socrates (Plato, *Apology*, 24b, and Xenophon, *Memorabilia*, 1.1.1), their own incomparably intellectual compatriot. Cynical and bemused, but curious still, this group of philosophers invited Paul to join them for private discussion. Paul did not shrink from this audience, which promised to be intellectually skeptical about the idea of a gospel and personally indifferent to its reality. Given Paul's conviction that the gospel is God's power to effect salvation in any who have faith, Paul was confident that the Gospel contained an explanation of life worthy of consideration by the human mind as such. For our purposes it is even more important to note that Paul was confident that a cogent case can and should be made for Jesus' gospel of salvation. He considered it worth a try to advocate *evangelical* monotheism to the sophisticated philosophers of Athens. Monotheism they already knew about, but *evangelical – meaning based upon and supporting the gospel of Jesus* – they did not yet know. Paul's acceptance of their invitation indicates that he believed in the intellectual validity of the gospel and in the Christian's obligation to make an intellectual case and appeal for the position that what is revealed in Christ is undeniably God's reality and is undeniably decisive for the salvation of humans universally.

So Paul accompanied the philosophers to the Areopagus where they inquired closely of him. Thinking that his religion might be esoteric, they asked, "How much of this new teaching which you were speaking about are we allowed to know? Some of the things you said seemed startling to us and we would like to find out what they mean" (Acts 17:19–20). So Paul responded with a sermon, which the New Testament has preserved in the following carefully crafted but compacted digest.

Men of Athens, I see that you are painstakingly thorough in everything religious, for as I walked around observing your places of worship I came upon an altar inscribed: To An Unknown God. Now, then, this God whom you already worship as something unknown is the one whom I am making known to you by preaching.

The God who made the world and everything in it and who is the Lord of heaven and earth does not make his home in shrines made by human hands nor depend on human hands for anything. He can never be in need of anything because it is he who gives life, breath, and everything else to everyone. Out of one single stock he made every race of humans so that they could inhabit the whole earth, but he fixed an allotted time for each people and the boundaries of its habitation. God did this so that all peoples could seek the true God and, if they grasped for him, succeed in finding him. Yet he is not removed from any of us in reality, since it is in him that we live and move and have our reality. As some of your own poets have said, "We are his offspring."

Being then God's offspring ourselves, we ought not to think that the divine being looks like something which a human has designed and shaped in gold, silver, or stone. Having overlooked such occasions of human ignorance in the past, God is now telling everyone everywhere that they must repent, because he has set a day when he will judge all of the earth's inhabitants with righteousness by a man whom he has appointed and certified publicly by raising him from the dead.

(Acts 17:26–31)

Because this is a tightly compacted digest, we will unpack it exegetically in the following paragraphs.

Paul introduced his sermon good humoredly. The philosophers had sarcastically charged him with sounding like "a propagandist for some outlandish gods." He reciprocated their sarcasm with the taunt that he had personally observed the Athenians to be "painstakingly thorough" in all religious matters, and he cited as an example, not some sophisticated aspect of Greek philosophical monotheism but one of their sacred monuments, "an altar inscribed: To An Unknown God." He followed this with the ironical and paradoxical announcement that "the one" whom they already knew and worshiped "as something unknown" was the gospel's God whom he would now make known to them through preaching. Turning then to present *evangelical* monotheism seriously, Paul proclaimed that God had been unknown to the Athenians hitherto only because they had not wanted to seek according to directions and evidence that God has put there in the natural and human orders and made readily knowable by any human mind. Paul introduced each of his sermon's three points with an idea familiar already in some current of Greek philosophical theology. He referred first to God as creator, a concept common to Greek, Jewish, and Christian thought, and added to this still other details of the Christian concept (vv. 24–5). The God "who made the world and everything in it" and sustains these creations in a relation contingent to himself – the "Lord of heaven and earth" – exceeds the reality of his creator-governor relation to the universe. He is himself an utterly incontingent reality who "can never be in need of anything." The huge contingent universe – which includes humans who are aware of it and of their and its contingency – exists at all only because there is this unconditionally independent God "who gives life and breath and everything else to everyone."

Having thus begun with the panoramic but contingent universe whose reality implies the incontingent reality of God, Paul narrowed the focus of his second point (vv. 26–7) to the human phenomenon. Though also contingent, the existence of humankind intimates, in its structured limitations and possibilities, a common, discernible divine purpose for human life. Paul's point of departure here was the explanation that the unity of humankind, a topic made familiar already to Athenian audiences by the Stoics, derives from God's threefold gift to humanity: a common origin, a common historical destiny, and common resources with which to fulfill that destiny. Paul declared that God had created from "one single stock" the various ethnic groups, each with its separate locality and distinctive history, for the express purpose of enabling all ethnic groups everywhere to "seek the deity" successfully. Paul characterized this common purpose of all humanity as a search, as a "grasping for God" by following the evidence of his reality and way in the order that he structured into natural and historical existence. In his third point (vv. 28–9), Paul alluded to the sixth-century (B.C.E.) Greek poet, Epimenides, and quoted the third-century Cilician poet, Aratus, to assert that God is never removed from any human being since every human being is an "offspring" of God and therefore every human being should know that God is not something that human imagination has conceived or human hands have shaped. Paul argues here that every person is capable of knowing not only that God transcends all material realities and is creator and governor of the cosmos, including the human families; he argues further that every human being is sufficiently provided to come to know that God has created it specifically to be God's offspring. Any person's ignorance of its responsible relation to God is therefore culpable.

In his conclusion (30–1) Paul turned his evangelical reasoning into an appeal for *personal consent to the inevitability of dealing with the God of the gospel.* He observed that hitherto God had been generously forbearing with humanity's culpable ignorance, "but now" that the gospel was being preached with its provision of salvation, God was "telling everyone everywhere that they must repent." Repentance, which means changing one's mind to accept God's salvation, was needed immediately, Paul urged, because God had set a date for all the world to be judged by Jesus whose righteousness God had publicly accredited "by raising Jesus from the dead."

This sermon admirably illustrates both a Christian appeal to general revelation and a Christian argument for an intellectual continuity between the God who can be known in general revelation and the God revealed specifically in Christ. Even more significantly for our discussion of symbolic expression, it makes an intellectual appeal, presents a reasoned position, for the validity of God's special revelation in Christ. Paul builds his argument around original sin, repentance, and judgment day. Original sin and judgment day are often considered irrational, even demented, notions. We will later show that Christianity itself uses these as *mythic* images in its mythological symbolism of undeniability. We are not at all concerned here to evaluate the literal truth or falsity of these notions. We wish to show only that Paul has stated a reasoned argument for Christ's special revelation of God, using these three notions of original sin, repentance, and judgment day. In the following paragraph we draw out the logic of his argument and supply some clarifying details.

Paul reasons that there is objective, though deficient, evidence in nature for the reality of God. The reality of God thus evidenced is insufficiently known for clear conceptualization; therefore special revelation is necessary. God's special revelation in Christ confirms what Paul calls elsewhere creation's evidence "to the eye of reason" for God's invisible reality, eternal and beneficient power, and identity as deity (Romans 1:20). Humans are obviously undeserving of their place in creation: they neither had nor did anything to deserve being created at all. They certainly have not used their experience to make themselves deserving of inclusion in that destiny of eternal life that God planned and has now proffered in the special revelation in Christ. This destiny of eternal life is not empirically demonstrable, but it is not an unreasonable or irrational hope. Many people intuit an afterlife destiny that renders their present life meaningful and purposeful (as we have argued in Chapter One). Two of Paul's Christian doctrines, original sin and the necessity for repentance, symbolically express the possibility of persons *becoming* worthy now of eternal life beyond death, and they are therefore optimistic doctrines. Similarly, judgment day, the third doctrine in Paul's argument, provides a point of reference, an endpoint, in relation to which all individual lives and history as a whole become meaningful and purposeful. The symbolic expression of judgment day conforms, then, to the widely held, if not universal, conviction that people's lives and all events in history are somehow part of a meaningful pattern. In this way, then, Pauline reasoning directs an appeal to the intellect for acknowledgment that God revealed in Christ is *the ultimate referent upon which all other realities depend and from which they derive their meaning.*

Following Paul's presentation to the philosophers at Athens (and also his reasoning in the New Testament Book of Romans), all distinctively Christian intellectual symbolism of undeniability is evangelical monotheism. It aims primarily to persuade people to acknowledge not merely that there is a reality called God. It aims rather to convince people that the reality called God is being revealed in Christ and that their salvation depends on their letting this revelation transform their lives. Instructed by Paul's evangelical reasoning, Christian witness characteristically argues that all humans at all times have had both ample evidence and means to know God accountably, that all humans have intentionally misused the means and misconstrued the evidences for knowing God's reality, and that all humans in consequence of their deprived knowledge of God have degenerated into an irreversible self-preoccupation. Those three arguments are only the preface, however, to evangelical reasoning that aims to persuade human minds to acknowledge that the reality of God really was in Christ in order to enable humans to become partakers in the life of God's eternal love rather than to suffer eternal perdition. Although we cannot use the space here to demonstrate it, we must report that we have found this same evangelical argumentation in our examination of the church's rational constructions of Jesus the eternal Son of Humanity, of Jesus the eternal Logos of God, and of the distinction between prototypical Adam (from whom all humans descend and die) and the prototypical Christ (in whom all humans are made alive and enabled to choose eternal life). All of these reasoned constructions, we have found, argue that what is revealed historically in Christ is undeniably God's reality and has decisive bearing on the salvation of every human being. These constructions are continuous and consistent with Paul's evangelical monotheism in that they, too, constitute a symbolic expression of the intellectual *undeniability of a central spiritual reality for all humankind.*

Mythological Symbolism of Undeniability

Christianity's mythology is in essence the cosmology it constructs by historicizing the universe. This historicization of the cosmos further illustrates the governing role of spiritual–moral symbolism in this religion. Christianity's mythological symbolism of undeniability depicts the entire universe under the image of a series of acts that develop the benevolent purpose of God for humankind. This has the effect of both bolstering and instantiating moral symbolism. It communicates a single solicitous message: The ultimate power ordaining and ingenerating the whole cosmic process is the irrepressible selfless love that God demonstrates historically in Christ and whose purpose will inevitably succeed. This message of the ultimate *irresistibility of God's love* is itself a spiritual–moral appeal for *personal consent to the necessity of living with reference to God in Christ.*

Christian mythological images originate quite naturally in reflections on the limitless reaches of God's love, which is believed to have been amply demonstrated in human history. Paul, writing out for Roman Christians a delineation of the love of God manifested in Christ, was moved to a doxological reflection. A brief excerpt from that reflection will recall its gist and serve to introduce here the mythological innovations that occur in worshipful Christian reflection.

What shall separate us from the love of God in Christ? Shall tribulation or distress or persecution or famine or nakedness or peril or sword? . . . in all these things we more than conquer through him who has loved us. For I am certain that neither death nor life, neither angels nor demons, neither things present nor things yet to come, nor powers, neither height nor depth, nor anything else in all creation, will be able to separate us from the love of God which is in Jesus Christ our Lord.

(Romans 8:35, 37–9)

By evocative reflections like this, concatenating reason, imagination, and emotion, the Christian mind forms mythical images that relate Christ's love to the entire cosmos and urge that it is invincible throughout the universe.

Early in the development of the Christian tradition, preachers and teachers reconceptualized the universe, using images that reflect the sovereignty of God's Christly power. Their cosmology is not exhausted in the Old Testament stories of Creation, but those stories are included in the Christian cosmology. The specifically Christian concept of the universe is to be found in its incipient and determinative form in the sermons and letters of the New Testament, which depict a cosmic "historical" process ordained and originated by God's magnanimous love expressly to ingenerate realities that differ from God. Because of its own character, God's selfless love "does not seek its own reality' (1 Corinthians 13:5) as its beloved; rather it produces the universe that is not God but is real and, with its distinctive glory, is itself admirable and able to sustain conscious beings who are capable of receiving and responding to God's selfless love. Christian mythology divides cosmic history into three "periods": Creation, human history, and the End. Each "period" is held to illustrate a distinctive actualization of God's love for humankind. Each period is held to have been made without asking human consent and therefore to be experienced by humans as *irresistible grace*.

Although presented in a linear sequence with human history, Creation and End are not chronological periods of measurable duration that are subject to investigation. They are mythic images of meaning, elongating into the unresearchable reaches of the past and future reflections of the Christians' historical experience of Christ as the transmitter of God's love power. A proper analysis of Creation and End will not proceed, then, by asking such historical questions as when or whether they happened. A more compatible inquiry will ask what this "event" or period means for Christianity and how this meaning is a consistent inference from Christian experience. Our interest and discussion here center on the meanings that Christians have inferred, whether rightly or wrongly, and which proclaim through the mythological symbols of Creation and End that God's love is undeniable because its actions are unforestallable and its purpose sure to succeed. To state it otherwise, the Christian symbols of Creation and End *express undeniability as irresistibility.*

As an image of Christian meaning, Creation expresses symbolically the sovereignty of God's selfless love, the unnegotiable givenness of the world with sinful humanity and the saving Christ in it, and the irrevocable answerability that human beings have to God for their entire finite life in the world. Creation is a single Christian symbol that integrates these three realities so as to reveal and represent what humans experience as "the present." For Christians, Creation "(*the* Beginning" rather than "*a* beginning") is first of all a happening in "the present," and "the present" is infinitely more than the point of transition between what has already been and what is yet to be. *The present* is, as Albert C. Outler says, "the locus" where the human person "becomes 'present' in its true mystery of freedom, identity, and power to love."[10]

10 Albert C. Outler, *Who Trusts in God* (New York: Oxford University Press, 1968), p. 48.

Creation happens in the present when a person becomes aware that its own reality and all the possibilities and meanings in human history as well as all the fixed and changing forms and processes of nature are provided by the dynamics of God's sovereign love. The Christian symbol of Creation intends to evoke in others an awareness and conviction that present reality is something good, which God's sovereign goodwill is making to happen right now. It means that any human, in any given instant of consciousness, can be present at the Creation, because any given moment of consciousness can become the beginning of one's own personal createdness in the world that God's love is always making. Under this image Creation is not some event that literally initiated a temporal beginning of the cosmic process. Creation is continuous and changing and everything that happens, everything that comes into existence, happens "in *the* Beginning" (Genesis 1:1). This is not to propose that everything happens all at once. *The* Beginning is the continuum within which God gives a distinctive temporal beginning to each new finite reality through Christ's creative agency (John 1:13).

As *the* Beginning in this sense, Creation does not pretend to be a scientific explanation of the origin and chronological development of the universe. The Christian doctrine intends to say that however the universe has happened, it is the continuous consequence of the same selfless love that God demonstrates historically in Christ. The distinctive quality of that love is to direct its power away from its own reality and to create and provide for other realities. Creation exhibits the qualitative difference between God's reality and all other realities. God's creative love "naturally" makes the complex of forms and processes that we call the natural world and cares for it in continuance. It also makes human subjects who have the power and freedom to participate in God's caring for the world or to exploit the world. Because it is selfless, God's sovereign love shares its power and freedom with humans and thus sacrifices its omni*potence*. Because it is selfless, God's love remains forever sovereign and therefore omni*competent*[11] despite the finite freedom with which it has endowed humans. Its omnicompetence guarantees that nothing in all creation will be able to prevent the eventual fulfillment of its purpose for the world and humanity. The omnicompetence of God's love is itself an *image of power that expresses God's undeniability as God's irresistibility.*

In its mythological representation of cosmic history, Christianity has not ignored the partially successful resistance that human beings exert against the designs of God's creative love. Christian mythology describes humanity's universal inclination to resist and to deceive God as something

---

11 Herbert H. Farmer first suggested the term *omni-competence* in his book *God and Man* (New York: Abingdon Press, 1947), pp. 130–1.

acquired and highly original, as an aberrant individualistic use of the freedom that God has given to humanity. It refers to this adventitious disposition as the Fall of Humanity, and it regards this culpable aberration with measured seriousness by condemning it in the phrase "the Creation and Fall of Humanity."

Like the myth of Creation, the myth of the Fall depicts a reality far larger than a single episode of defiance in the life of the very first human. It embraces every human person's experience of resisting the overtures of God's goodwill with one's own will to pursue self-defined satisfactions and purposes. The Fall symbolizes then, the effective power that humans have in their finite freedom and which they use to frustrate the purposes of the very God who gave them their existence and freedom. The obverse of "the Fall" is "the Redemption," which expresses mythologically that the frustration of God's will by humans will eventually fail. In the historical reality of Jesus Christ, God's love has irresistibly made provision for the rescue, regeneration, and eternal life of every "fallen" human. Mythologically represented, redemption through Christ is an act or event that – though it happened in the life, crucifixion, death, and resurrection of the historical Jesus – God makes contemporaneous with and effective for every human person who has ever lived or ever will. Early Christians imagined that Christ, after his death, visited the realm of the dead and preached the gospel so that all persons who died prior to Christ's historical revelation could and did have access to redemption through Christ. By 359 C.E. this conviction became an article in Christian creeds,[12] summarized briefly in the words "he descended into hell."

Creation, Fall, and Redemption are Christian images of the indomitable power of God's omnicompetent love, and they give mythic expression to Christianity's quintessential conviction. Taken together as a "historical" narrative they assert that, irrespective of the time or manner in which realities appear in the causal order of the universe, and irrespective of the disruptions and delays that human freedom causes, one God, through divine selfless love, *undeniably and irresistibly*, makes, sustains, and, when needed, regenerates everything that is made in order to move the whole cosmos forward to its predetermined end.

Christianity clearly proclaims the End, the actual fulfillment of the purpose of God's love, to be inevitable. From a consistent Christian perspective the time when the End will occur is unpredictable. God's selfless love must realize its End by ways that are consistent with God's own independence, freedom, and aim and which are respectful of the finite identity, freedom, and power to love that God has appointed to

---

12 Cf. the article, "Descent of Christ into Hell," in *The Oxford Dictionary of the Christian Church*, 2d ed. (Oxford: Oxford University Press, 1974), p. 395.

human beings. Coherent Christian teaching does not and cannot claim to know the whole bearing or grace of love, which is to say, all of the ways that love will act to achieve its End. It does claim to know already through Christ that God's love always behaves courteously and that it never makes its way by coercion or deceit. To be sure, superficial and/or politically motivated Christian minds, in every generation of Christians, and politically motivated minds in some cases, have set schedules for the End, and popular Christian preaching has characteristically imagined its own self-serving details of the End. There is no warrant in the New Testament or any other part of Christianity's deposit of faith for such scheduling and specification of the End. In Christianity's canonical and accepted myth of the End, symbolic images proclaim the assured expectation that God's love will both fulfill its purpose and terminate the grace period within which humans can influence their destiny by the use they make of their finite freedom.

The End, like the Beginning and the Redemption, is an action that God's love makes through Christ. The End consists of the Last Judgment, the assignment of destinies, and the unmitigated reign of God. Jesus gave Christianity its seminal vision of the Last Judgment and the assignment of destinies. Toward the end of his life, as the account in Matthew gives it, Jesus related to his disciples and apostles the following narrative in which he refers to himself as "the Son of Humanity" and "the King," two titles for the Christ's role in the final administration of God's love toward humans:

When the Son of Humanity comes in his glory, escorted by all the angels, he will take his seat on his throne of glory and all human beings will be assembled before him. Then he will separate the humans into two groups, as the shepherd separates sheep from goats. He will put the sheep on his right and the goats on his left. Then the King will address those on his right and say,

Come, you have my Father's blessing:
Inherit the kingdom prepared for you at the
    creation of the universe.
For I was hungry and you gave me something to eat.
I was thirsty and you gave me something to drink.
I was a stranger and you welcomed me.
I was naked and you clothed me.
I was ill and you took care of me.
I was in prison and you came to visit me.

Then the righteous will respond to him and ask,

Lord, when did we see you hungry and give you food,
    or thirsty and give you something to drink?

And when did we see you a stranger and welcome you,
    or naked and clothe you?
And when did we see you sick or in prison
    and come to care for you?

And the King will answer them, "I will tell you the truth. Whatever you did for one of the least of these my kindred, you did for me."

Next he will address those on his left and say,

Depart from me. You have earned your doom:
Pass away into the eternal fire prepared for
    the devil and his demons.
For I was hungry and you gave me nothing to eat.
I was thirsty and you gave me nothing to drink.
I was a stranger and you did not welcome me.
I was naked and you gave me no clothes.
I was ill and in prison and you ignored me.

And they also will ask, "Lord, when did we ever see you hungering or thirsty, or a stranger or naked or ill or in prison and did not minister to you?"
And he will answer them, "I will tell you the truth. Whatever you neglected to do for one of the least of these, you neglected to do for me."
And these uncaring persons will pass into eternal punishment, but the caring into eternal life.

(Matthew 25:31–46)

According to this mythic preview, at the time of the End Jesus Christ the Son of Humanity will come "in his glory," an identity so unmistakably recognizable and manifestly credentialed that the unrighteous as well as the righteous of all ages, gathered in universal assembly, will address him as "Lord." He will make a final, destiny-determining judgment upon each human being's life by asking and answering himself concerning each person, "What did you do and neglect to do *for me?*"

That standard, *"for me,"* would be the supreme instance of self-centeredness were Jesus, who is the standard and Judge, not also understood to be the very same agent through whom God's selfless love has created the universe, revealed itself historically, and provided for the redemption of every fallen human. In neither creation nor revelation nor redemption does God's selfless love require that humans make the person of Jesus the object of their loving. To have required that would have contradicted the message of selfless love and discredited Jesus as its messenger. Jesus makes that very point in his story about the End. In the End, at the Last Judgment, the people to whom Jesus assigns an eternal presence with God are people who never had any notion that they were ministering to "the Lord" when they were caring uncalculatingly for people in distressed human circumstances. Jesus demonstrates that his inquiry concerning what a person had or had not done *for him* translates into this: Did you spend your life in selfless caring for other humans in their human needs? Jesus exalted the humanity of every other human person by equating it with his own humanity: "Whatever you did or neglected to do for even the least of these my human kindred, you did that for me." By the very same equation Jesus ascribed Christhood to every human being. Each person's humanity had capacitated it to love as well as to be loved. In virtue of that capacitated humanity alone, every human person who ever lived has had the power and calling to participate in and contribute to the eternal mission of the Christ of God *without even knowing who the Christ is*. This is such a radically revolutionary notion that Christian symbolisms – spiritual–moral, intellectual, and mythological – have not dared to elaborate it systematically. Yet Jesus' story of the End aims self-evidently to shed light on humanity's present existence before God who is its End as well as its Beginning. The story intends to recruit as many people as possible to accept and esteem every human person as a bearer of the real presence of Christ and to participate in the work of Christ. Those who assume this attitude and who behave accordingly will, obviously, have nothing to fear from the Last Judgment at the consummation of the cosmos. Though not emphasized in traditional Christian thought, the radical, all-inclusive universalism of Jesus' own understanding of the End is a remarkable and unprecedented attempt to express the seeming paradox of *love* offered and received as *irresistible power*. In this unique way, Christianity's *mythological symbolism of undeniability* employs *images of power* – albeit paradoxical images of power – *to express undeniability as irresistibility*.

Jesus made a final point in the story of the End just recounted. It is less radical but equally important. When the grace period for human freedom runs out, when Christ has exhausted all of the initiatives of love, if there still be people who have persisted in their resistance to loving and being loved selflessly, they will be given the destiny they have invented: eternal exemption from God's love. Even into that eternal banishment they will go by the irresistible and unalterable grace of God's love. God's selfless love, which establishes a person in individual freedom, will not revoke that freedom even if the person uses it against God. While God's omnicompetent love wills that all human persons be saved, it also wills that all human persons have inviolable freedom. That means that eternal perdition is a real possibility.

Mainline Christian interpretation has not formally pronounced whether any specific individuals will in fact exercise their right and power to reject God's love forever. The purpose of Jesus' story of the End, like that of the Christian doctrine of hell, is not to provide that kind of advance information about a terminal End. It seeks rather to induce people to live caringly right now by showing that a person who lives uncaringly creates hell for others now and for the person's own ugly self eternally. The way a person lives leads inevitably to either the good End that God wills or the bad End that an uncaring person wills and God permits. By retelling Jesus' story of the End, Christians create for their audiences occasions that make personal history. The story presses for faith, for a definitive personal decision to seek for one's own personal reality what the divine reality wants: the achievement of selfless loving. In this way Christianity's mythological symbolism of undeniability reinforces and reasserts Christianity's primary spiritual–moral appeal by showing that a person lives by choice toward one or the other of the two destinies that God has fixed.

In Paul's theology after the Judgment and the assignment of destinies, Christ "having conquered every rule and authority and power" will "hand over" the universe to God and will then subject himself to God "in order that God be *all in all*" (1 Corinthians 15:24, 28; emphasis added). Christian imagination is discouraged from trying to explore what the reality of God is prior to or after God's act of cosmic genesis, redemption, and fulfillment. This imagination does acknowledge and adore the undeniability of that reality, and it does this in images that celebrate God's sheer independence and irresistible magnanimity. One of the authors of this book recently heard a folk preacher say in his pastoral prayer, "We praise you, God, for being God all by yourself without any help from anybody." Another clergyman, John Mason (1645–94) in the Church of England, lyricized the same independence and characterized it as a "great and good" generosity. Ever since it was written, Mason's prayer hymn has enabled other Christians with little or much imagination of their own to sing mythic images which praise the sheer factuality of God's being God:

Thou wast, O God, and thou wast blest before the world began;
Of thine eternity possessed before time's hour glass ran.
Thou needest none thy praise to sing, as if thy joy could fade;
Could'st thou have needed anything, thou could'st have nothing made.

Great and good God, it pleased thee thy Godhead to declare;
And what thy goodness did decree thy greatness did prepare.
Thou spak'st, and heaven and earth appeared, and answered to thy call,
As if their maker's voice they heard, which is the creature's all.

To whom, Lord, should I sing but thee, the maker of my tongue?
Lo, other lords would seize on me, but I to thee belong.
As waters haste into their sea and earth into its earth,
So let my life return to thee from whom it had its birth.

With these and thousands of other images of praise, Christians illuminate the sheer Godhood of God's independent reality by imagining that the defining principle of God in the act of being God, before and after the cosmos, is the same love that characterizes God in the act of being present historically in Christ.

Christian mythology, we may summarize in concluding this section, expresses *the undeniability of humanity's central spiritual referent* as a great paradox. It depicts God's creation and governance of the cosmos, including its phenomenon of free human beings, *in concrete images of the irresistible power* of God's uncoercive selfless love. Reflecting retrospectively, Christian imagination reasons what must have happened if the remote origins of nature and history are to be made intelligible by what God reveals through Christ and expects from humans in the present. Reflecting prospectively, which is to say eschatologically, Christian imagination predicts what must be the outcome of the present world in which the presence of the love of God in Christ is inescapable and the freedom of human beings is irrevocable. Christianity characteristically maintains that God's provident love endows human persons with power, dignity, and privilege either to receive the gift of God's presence and to reciprocate it with their own presence or to reject God's presence and to withhold their own presence from God. The future of such a present world will predictably be either the heaven of infinite possibilities that selfless love creates, or the hell that occurs whenever and wherever and only if selfless love is excluded.

Desirability

As in the case of *undeniability*, the Christian concept of God's historical revelation in Christ governs all of Christianity's symbolic expression of *the desirability of the central spiritual reality of humankind.* For Christians it is not enough to say that the ultimate valuational norm is God. They regard God to be absolute as well as ultimate and therefore unknowable by humans – who are relative and contingent – except as God makes God's reality accessible for human knowing. God does this definitively in Jesus Christ, according to Christian discernment, and therefore Christians deem it necessary to say that *God revealed historically in Jesus Christ* is *the ultimate valuational norm from which all other realities derive their value.* All Christian symbolism of desirability emphasizes that a person's engagement with Jesus Christ is an engagement with God's own ultimate and supremely desirable reality. Because Christianity's intellectual symbolization of desirability seeks to demonstrate the fact and illuminate the character of God's presence in Jesus Christ, and because the other three Christian symbolizations of desirability presuppose that God's reality actually is present in Jesus Christ, we will describe the intellectual symbolism first, even though in practice Christians normally place priority upon spiritual and moral symbolisms.

Intellectual Symbolism of Desirability

Christian intellectual symbolism identifies Jesus Christ as *the ultimate valuational norm and seeks thereby to make other expressions of desirability reasonable* by depicting him as the one in whom the reality of God is present, revealed, and instituting God's definitive purpose for human beings. Sometimes Christians acclaim Jesus as *Emmanuel,* which means literally God-is-with-us. Always, in referring to Jesus, they mean that in him God is present with human beings as their companion and Savior, forgiving their sins and endeavoring to purify their minds so that they can love more perfectly and become both happy and good now and eternally. John Wesley, the eighteenth-century folk theologian, expressed the conviction of all Christians when, in his dying words, in reference to Jesus he said, "The best of all is, God is with us." It is the quintessence of being Christian to hold that God was, is, and will be present in Jesus Christ to do all that is presently and eternally best for humans, and that God's being present in this way is the highest good that humans can know and desire.

Jesus himself initiated the intellectual symbolization of this conviction by using the title "the Son of Humanity" to describe himself and his role in humanity's final accountability to God. He appropriated this title from the Jewish apocalyptic books of Daniel and Enoch.[13] In that literature the Son of Humanity is a divine being who is with God prior even to the creation of the world. After the world's creation, he remains hidden beside the throne of God where he waits for the time when God will send him into the world to reign sovereignly over all the world and finally, in an assembly of everyone who has ever lived in the world, to pronounce God's judgment on each of them. Jesus claimed for himself all of the majesty and prerogatives of this apocalyptic Son of Humanity: "All things have been given over to me by my Father" and "all authority in heaven and on earth has been given to me" (Matthew 11:26 and 28:18). However, Jesus gave these divine entitlements the surprising, paradoxical meaning of *serving love.* He represented himself as God's servant Son of Humanity who did not own even "a place to lay his head" and who had not come "to Lord it over" humanity or to make his importance felt by requiring others to serve him. He said that he had come rather "to serve others" by literally "giving his own life" to suffer deprivation, pain, hu-

13 Cf. esp. 1 Enoch 48:2ff.; 61:8; 62:7, 13–14; 69:25ff.; and Daniel 7:13–14.

miliation, and death in God's plan to rescue humans from their sin and selves and to recruit as many persons as possible for eternal life with God (Matthew 8:20 and 20:25, 28). In his earthly career as the Son of Humanity, Jesus conducted his dominion as a service to the whole human family. In rendering this ministry he identified his own putatively divine Humanity with the humanity of every person in every condition of human existence, and he imputed to each human person the honor, responsibility, and mission of his own Humanity. Anticipating that this ministry would lead him along a path of successive sufferings, even possibly to persecution and death, Jesus forewarned that any who would follow the Son of Humanity should be realistic, not sentimental, about the rigors and risks of a love that abandons self to serve others.

For all his humility, vicarious suffering, and eagerness to share honor and responsibility, Jesus did not attempt to conceal the divine authority he regarded as being his by virtue of his being the Son of Humanity. It was a paradoxical authority. Its sole power to command compliance was the cogency of the aims of a love that serves human need. Jesus appealed to this authority when he violated such highly respected religious conventions as observing the Jewish Sabbath in favor of helping hungry people to get food. He exercised this authority, his followers believe, to incapacitate disease and reverse infirmity, to eradicate demons, to forgive sins, and to define the issues of life and death here and now. He announced that he would use the Son of Humanity's authority at some appointed future time to make for God the final judgment upon each person's practice or neglect of serving love. Accordingly, at that time he would assign each a destiny either to be with or without God for eternity. He characterized that act of making final judgment as an expression of serving love, since it will honor even the right for any to enter eternal perdition if they have directed their moral life toward it (Matthew 12:8, 9:6, and 25:31–46).

By identifying himself as God's eternal Son of Humanity – the one to whom all humans are finally accountable for the character and conduct of their lives – Jesus initiated Christianity's intellectual symbolism of desirability. In presenting himself as God's *servant* Son of Humanity, Jesus was declaring that God's *ultimate valuational norm* was present *in* him, and therefore *with* his contemporaries, as the actual power and standard of God's saving, serving love. By identifying God's *ultimate valuational norm* as the serving love of God that he embodied and was manifesting, Jesus stipulated in effect that his historical actualization of this love *makes other expressions of desirability reasonable.*

Although Christians did not adopt Jesus' practice of identifying and describing himself with the title "Son of Humanity," they have universally reaffirmed his identification of himself as the bearer, revealer, and demonstrator of God's other-serving, vicariously suffering, and eternally saving love. Christian symbolization of this identification expresses and intends to evoke the twofold conviction: (1) that the historical and resurrected Jesus manifests among humans the real presence and power of that aspect of God's reality which God has consecrated to effect human salvation and which God therefore wants and enables humans to know, and (2) that the effective presence of this salvific reality of God in Jesus should be, self-evidently, humanity's highest value and supreme desire.

One such expression of this conviction is the Christians' universal use of the title "Christ" to acclaim, address, and confess Jesus. Jesus' first followers appropriated this title from their Jewish heritage, as we noted in the introduction to this chapter. The Jewish contemporaries of Jesus, politically oppressed by Roman occupation forces, held the firm, devout, and patriotic belief that God would eventually intervene to restore a kingship and political independence to the Jews. They expected that God would single out and anoint one of their own young men to become their savior-king (*mashiah* in the Hebrew language, and translated properly as either Messiah or Christ) and to vindicate their religion to the whole world. This young ruler-Christ, commissioned by God and invested with some of God's own prerogatives, would go forth from Jerusalem into the entire world to rebuke and destroy godless nations, to reprove sinners everywhere, and to persuade all the people of all the remaining nations that the righteousness that he proclaims and demonstrates is the supremely desirable righteousness of the absolute God.

Christians claimed for Jesus the title, office, and prerogatives of the Jewish Messiah-Christ, but they found it impossible to maintain credibly that the historical Jesus was the political and military savior-king of Jewish expectation. Jesus himself had made this impossible by the things he said and did during his earthly life. He made no attempt to deliver the Jewish people from political servitude or to gather his own followers into a political entity. Indeed, he emphatically rejected a political definition of his career and of God's kingdom, which he thought himself to be inaugurating in human history. In a story describing the beginning of Jesus' career, Satan is said to have offered Jesus sovereignty over "all the kingdoms of the world,"[14] an offer that corresponded closely to the Jewish messianic hope. In this story Jesus rebuked Satan and characterized the offer as a calculated temptation to idolatry. Toward the end of his actual life, after his arrest, Jesus was interrogated by Pilate, a Roman official, who asked directly,

"Are you the King of the Jews?" . . .

Jesus answered: "My kingdom is not one of this world's kingdoms. If mine were one of this world's kingdoms, I would have had forces fighting to prevent my arrest by the Jews. But that is not my kind of kingdom."

14 Matthew 4:8–9.

To this Pilate responded, "So, then, you really are some kind of a king?" Jesus replied: "It is you who call me a king. The reason I was born and came into the world is to give evidence for the truth. Anyone who wants the truth will listen to what I have to say." Pilate asked rhetorically, "Truth? What is it?" and went out to speak again to the Jews.

(John 18:33, 36–8)

By deliberate choice and public declaration Jesus categorically rejected the political and military role of the Jewish savior-king. Nevertheless, he was crucified on the charge of trying to become that very monarch. After his death and resurrection his apostles persisted in calling him the Christ, but they let Jesus' own words and demeanor govern their redefinition of the meaning of that title and hence all the rest of their religion. Their revised concept of the Christ excluded the military–political aspect and included a justification for his being executed on a false charge. The apostles held that Jesus' significance consists essentially in his manifest demonstration of God's self-denying, other-serving, saving love. They reasoned that God had consented to Jesus' crucifixion as a would-be political messiah precisely because Jesus was self-evidently innocent and because his acceptance of death under these circumstances would demonstrate publicly that self-denying love never retaliates and always serves even when it can do nothing more than forgive its persecuting enemies.

Notwithstanding the position taken by Jesus and the apostles whom he appointed to direct the church, some of Jesus' devotees even to this day have clung to the belief that the resurrected Jesus will return as a supernatural person to reign politically as Christ over a world empire and hence to fulfill Jewish expectations. Christianity's history exhibits egregious instances in which Christian leaders and followers, lusting to seize or maintain political power for the church, have envisioned and extolled a Christ who wields political power.

Because the apostles received their office and authority directly from Jesus, Christians as such are bound by apostolic teaching, and so the apostolic image of Christ is officially definitive for all Christians. This normative image is formed by a consistent combining of what the earthly Jesus said and did and what Christians perceive that God continues to do with him in the reality of his resurrection. In this normative image of Christ, the resurrected Jesus does not reign over a political body and does not administer God's saving righteousness through political structures and systems. Instead, the resurrected Jesus generates his own implementing structure, the church, which is a familial rather than a political entity. In his resurrected reality, "raised beyond death into a life continuous with God's saving activity,"[15] Jesus participates in the church family as its

15   John Hick, *God and the Universe of Faiths* (London: Macmillan, 1973), p. 112.

head, that is, as its central dynamic and governing influence. Through the church's fellowship, liturgy, and ministries of mercy, the resurrected Jesus seeks to mediate to humans universally the presence of God's saving love, which wills to deliver them from the servitude of sin and self and to enfranchise them in the freedom and life of God's eternal kingdom.

Christ, apostolically and officially defined for Christians, is a symbol of the real presence of the saving power of God's love. When Christians address, acclaim, and confess Jesus as the Christ, they intend both to express and to elicit the conviction that Jesus manifests God's *saving* reality, that aspect of God's reality that God wants and enables humans to know for their own eternal salvation and which is therefore the highest good that they can possibly know. Identified thus as the presence of God's saving reality, Jesus Christ becomes *the ultimate valuational norm from which all other realities derive their value and which makes other expressions of God's desirability reasonable.*

Christians make a similar intellectual symbolization of desirability when they use the other christological titles *in conjunction with* Christ. They do this with Lord, Savior, Son of God, and the Word, among others, in order to indicate that Jesus manifests the real presence of the absolute God. We will illustrate this with a brief account of the association of Lord with Christ in Christian usage.

At first Jesus' disciples addressed him as Lord in the sense of "Teacher" or "Learned Sir," saying, for example, "Lord, how many times shall I forgive my brother who sins against me?" or again, "Lord, teach us how to pray" (Matthew 18:21 and Luke 11:1). By the time of his first resurrection appearance, the apostles used this title to acclaim him as the messianic savior-king: "Lord, do you at this time restore the kingdom to Israel?" (Acts 1:6). They believed and emphasized that it was God who had "raised Jesus up" from the dead and had *"made* him both *Lord and Christ"* (Acts 2:32, 36). They elaborated[16] this into the definitive Christian assertion that God had exalted the resurrected Jesus to the status of deity and that God had bestowed on him the title and name "the Lord" (Philippians 2:11). The Lord is God's very own name and title in the Christians' heritage from Judaism: "Hear, O Israel, the Lord is our God. The Lord is one. Therefore, love the Lord your God with all your heart, mind, and will, and with all your consciousness and with all your might" (Deuteronomy 6:4–5). For Christians this does not mean that God transferred the divine sovereignty to the resurrected Jesus or divided it in order to share it with Jesus. It means for them that Jesus Christ himself is God's

---

16 Cf. Oscar Cullmann, *The Christology of the New Testament,* rev. ed. (Philadelphia: Westminster Press, 1963), p. 236, and Ethelbert Stauffer, *New Testament Theology* (New York: Macmillan, 1956), p. 114.

own manifestation of lordship, that he is God in God's exercise of divine sovereignty. There is one God who is both "Father" and "Lord":

For us there is one God, the Father, *from* whom all things come and *from* whom we exist, and one Lord, Jesus Christ, *through* whom everything was made and *through* whom we exist.

(1 Corinthians 8:6: emphasis added)

[The Lord Jesus Christ] is the demeanor of the invisible God, and he is the antecedent of all creation because everything – visible and invisible, in heaven and on earth – was created in him . . . everything was created *through* him and *for* him. He is prior to all things and in him all things hold together. He is head of the body, the church. He is its origin, the first to return from the dead, in order to become supreme in everything, *since by God's own preference, the consummate reality of God chose to dwell in him,* and through him to reconcile to itself all things, whether things on earth or in heaven, making peace through the blood of his crucifixion.

(Colossians 1:14–20; emphasis added)

As Lord, then, Jesus Christ is regarded as God in God's exercise of sovereignty – prior to creation in the formation of creation's purpose, in the creative process itself, and subsequent to creation in the constant providential care of all created things. In the providential care of creation the Lord Jesus Christ is regarded as God exercising the divine sovereignty to hold all things together; to reveal to humans the divine reality, its purpose for their existence and its plan for their eternal happiness; to originate and head the church and to reconcile all things to the divine reality. Christians intend to identify all of this with Jesus Christ when they pronounce upon anyone their highest blessing, "The Lord be [present] with you." They appeal to Jesus as being the very presence of God's sovereignty when they invoke him with the standard liturgical preface to prayer: "Lord, have mercy. Christ, have mercy. Lord, have mercy." They explicitly confess Jesus to be the consummate reality of God – present, revealed, and effective for human salvation – when they affirm the statements of the eucharistic creed:

We believe in *one God*, the Father Almighty, maker of heaven and earth, and of all things visible and invisible. And [we believe] in *one Lord*, Jesus Christ, the only begotten Son of God, begotten of the Father before all worlds . . . very God of very God, begotten, not made, being of one substance with the Father; by whom all things were made; and who, for us humans and for our salvation, came down from heaven, was incarnate . . . and was made human and crucified for us . . . he suffered and was buried and after three days he rose again.

(Nicene Creed, emphasis added)

Whenever Christians say that Jesus Christ is Lord they intend to assert and evoke the twofold conviction that he is God's sovereign reality, present among humans for their salvation, and that he is therefore the consummately desirable reality for human knowing and benefit:

At the name of Jesus every knee should bow, in heaven and on earth and under the earth, and every tongue should confess that *Jesus Christ is Lord*, to the glory of the Father.

(Philippians 2:10–11, emphasis added)

This use of Lord and other christological titles to identify God's presence in Jesus exemplifies Christianity's rich intellectual symbolization of the unsurpassable desirability of God's being present and revealed historically in Christ for humanity's salvation. We will merely mention and identify three further examples of this symbolism.

By now even readers hitherto unfamiliar with Christianity will have sensed that the Christian mind preoccupies itself with the image of God's reality being present in history as a human person, as a genuine historical agent, in order to influence the course of history from the inside. Christians have been thoroughgoing in developing and expressing the symbolism of this "inhistorization"[17] of God. They have elaborated a doctrine of the incarnation of God, by which they mean that the reality of God transcended itself and became the human flesh and person of Jesus of Nazareth. Incarnate as this human person, God was quintessentially historical and able to be present *with* other human persons and present *for* them. The doctrine of the incarnation thus represents a "self-transcendence of transcendence itself," whereby God as the *ultimate valuational norm* becomes meaningfully present to humans in such a way that *other expressions of desirability* may be effectively evaluated with reference to a humanly accessible *ultimate standard*. After Jesus' death the apostles extended the notion of the incarnation to the church. They symbolized the Christian community as the body of the resurrected Christ and each church member as part of Christ's resurrected body. Understood in this way, the church exists in history, through the organic community of its respective members, as the continuing, visible presence of God in Christ, to carry on and to carry out the saving project that God inaugurated with Jesus.

In addition to the doctrine of incarnation and the church, a third symbolization of God's inhistorization in Christ is the church's central act of worship, the eucharistic meal of bread and wine known variously as the Mass, the Eucharist, the Lord's Supper, and Holy Communion. This

17 H. H. Farmer, "The Bible: Its Significance and Authority," in *The Interpreter's Bible*, vol. 1 (Nashville: Abingdon Press, 1952?), p. 6.

liturgical meal is a sacrifice of thanksgiving for the benefits of Jesus' death. By accepting without resistance the undeserved, violent death inflicted on him by his enemies, Jesus is regarded as having rendered to God and all humanity a free, unstinting service, which, for Christians, demonstrates publicly and permanently that God's love forgives its offenders without any exception whatsoever and that the reign of such love is invincible. The sacrificial meal consists of very ordinary, physical bread and wine, which, when consecrated by Christians meeting in the Name of Jesus, are believed to make Christ present as a reality to the worshiping people and to enable them to appropriate the benefits of his meritorious death. In the Christian understanding, God's relentless will to save humanity becomes perceptibly present and specific in the Eucharist. In the eucharistic act, this particular tangible, visible congregation of faithful worshipers (the Church) becomes a "sign which does not simply point to a grace and salvific will of God that may exist somewhere, but *is* [itself] the tangibility and permanence of this grace and of salvation."[18]

With these and many other symbolic expressions, Christianity asserts that God's sovereign, saving reality is present in Jesus Christ and his church in order *to be with* human persons in their history in order to effect their eternal salvation. Revealed thus, *God in Christ is the ultimate valuational norm from which all other realities derive their value,* and with this claim Christianity makes an intellectually symbolic witness to *the desirability of the central spiritual reality of all humankind.*

Spiritual Symbolism of Desirability

Christianity maintains that God's historical presence in Jesus Christ and subsequently in the Christian church aims expressly to effect the salvation and eternal well-being of human persons. This historical presence itself is regarded as the *ultimate spiritual reality* vouchsafed to humankind. Therefore practically all Christian communication *emphasizes the personal benefits of response to its ultimate spiritual reality,* the presence of Christ in history. Thereby, virtually all of Christianity exemplifies spiritual symbolism of the desirability of a *spiritual reality* conceived as *central and ultimate for humankind.* There is, however, one Christian symbol, *the kingdom of God,* that stands for all the personal benefits that accrue to those who respond to God's historical presence in Christ. Those who welcome God's being present with them in Christ are said to have submitted to *the kingship of God* and to have become heirs of *the*

---

18 Karl Rahner and Herbert Vorgrimler, *Theological Dictionary* (New York: Herder and Herder, 1965), p. 155.

kingdom of God. The kingdom or reign of God signifies, of course, God's exercise of sovereign dominion in the eternal realm and in the operation of the cosmos. For Christians it has the further special meaning of being all the good that God will do for human persons who are willing to receive it, beginning right now and continuing forever. In other words the kingdom of God symbolizes the Christian goal of human life, both individual and social, in the present world and in the world to come. For this reason, it will serve as the focus of our discussion of spiritual symbolism of desirability in Christianity.

For Christians, the kingdom of God – the effective reign of the power of God's love in the lives, relations, and actions of free human persons – is inseparable from Jesus and his church. Jesus arrested attention by announcing publicly that God's time had come in the human world and that God's sovereign power, present in Jesus' person, words, and deeds, would begin its effective reign in the world of human freedom. Because the sovereign power of God intends the salvation of human persons, Jesus proclaimed its reign to be the most precious possession possible for human beings. He said that any person who perceives the kingdom's true, inestimable value will unhesitatingly give up any human relationship, any limb or organ of body, and any obligation that prevents or impedes one's admission into and participation in the reign of God. He told his disciples that God had begun the process that will make the kingdom accessible universally, but only as a gift and only as God gives it. "It is the Father's good pleasure to give you the kingdom" (Luke 12:32). As the agent of God's kingdom, Jesus is depicted as exercising its authority and manifesting its powers by forgiving sins, curing the diseased, exorcising demons, and calling all people to change the fundamental option of their lives from self-service to God's selfless, other-serving love. Whether Jesus actually performed miracles of exorcising demons is, of course, immaterial to our present purposes. The point is that such stories constitute part of the Christian concept of the institution of the kingdom of God, the predominant Christian *spiritual symbol of desirability.*

In further inauguration and implementation of God's reign in the human world, Jesus enlisted and trained disciples in the kingdom's life and mission, demonstrating in his own life that the way of the kingdom's power is personal acceptance of struggle, suffering, sacrifice, and death for the salvation of human beings. To perpetuate and universalize the offer of God's kingdom, the manifestation of its powers and the recruitment and training of its disciples, Jesus formed the church, the community of the kingdom's disciples. Through the church, Christians believe, the resurrected Jesus administers in perpetuity all of those ministries of God's reign that the historical Jesus instituted. We have already observed that

Jesus rejected all suggestions that he use political power and political institutions. He formed the church as the proper institution for the exercise of God's dominion in human affairs.

According to Christianity, the primary personal benefit of being with God in Christ and in the fellowship of the church is the forgiveness of one's sin – the release from obsession with self – and the freedom to grow in the perfecting of one's own loving through fellowship with God and other humans. It is axiomatic in Christianity that the reign of God's love in a person's life in the church demands that a person strive to love as perfectly, as selflessly, as God loves. This is the clear meaning of Jesus' injunction at the end of his discourse on the impartial, uncalculating character of God's loving: "Therefore, you must be perfect [teleioi, undivided, single-minded, whole-hearted] as your heavenly Father is perfect" (Matthew 5:48). That demand would be absurd were it not for the Christian conviction that the resources for human perfection in love are the infinite resources of God and that the perfecting work itself is done by God. God does this work only in receptive human persons, however, and so Jesus encouraged his followers to do everything possible to become receptive to the perfecting work of God's righteous, selfless love. He exhorted them to "hunger and thirst" for it, to make it the imperious option of their life, to pray fervently for it, saying, "Our Father in heaven, let your kingdom come, and let your will be done, on earth as it is in heaven" (Matthew 5:6, 6:33, and 6:9–10). This ideal of human perfection, beginning here and now, is of course Christianity's preeminent representation of the *personal benefits of response to an ultimate spiritual reality.*

Because the perfection or integration of a person's life into love is regarded as a work that God alone accomplishes, Jesus' injunction that humans be perfect in loving as God is perfect in loving – like the commandment to love God with all of one's reality – is an injunction to receive the kingship or reign of God's love in one's life. Christians aspire for this character of God's kingship in their personal lives when they pray some version of the church's collect for purity:

Almighty God, unto whom all hearts are exposed, all desires known, and from whom no secrets are hid: Cleanse the desires of our hearts and the thoughts of our minds by the inspiration of thy Holy Spirit, that we may perfectly love thee and each other and thus worthily magnify thy holy name, through Christ our Lord. Amen.

As God's gift to those who respond favorably to God's historical presence in Christ, the kingdom of God is a spiritual symbol of desirability that subsumes virtually all other such symbols in Christianity. In terms of the present scheme, it single-mindedly *emphasizes the present and eternal benefits* to be derived by persons who respond to the reign of God's sovereign love that is present and proffered in Jesus Christ and the church.

The kingdom of God signifies for Christians that the same God who reigns unchallenged "in heaven," whose omnicompetence guarantees the outcome of all of humanity's personal and social history, is immediately present in Christ and the church and is offering to exercise the sovereignty of divine love right now in the lives of freely consenting persons. Those who receive this reign of God's love accept a responsible participation in the worship and work of the church, which is the community and fellowship of all those who honor the kingship of God. Members of this historical community are not regarded as subjects or citizens, but rather as members of God's family. Jesus himself once said that "those who do what my Father wants are my family" (Matthew 12:50). Members in this historical family of God's fatherly kingship are believed to enjoy already here on earth a foretaste of eternal beatitude, of God's saving acceptance and perfecting love. This theme of the presently accessible foretaste of eternal salvation is one we have noted repeatedly in the spiritual symbolisms of the religions we have examined. For believing Christians, the kingdom of God is the supremely desirable alternative – both now and for eternity – to self, sin, and damnation. The reign of God's love does not seek something for God; it has as its end rather the immediate and eternal blessedness of human beings.

Moral Symbolism of Desirability

The kingdom of God is also Christianity's primary moral symbol of desirability, a fact that further illustrates the inseparability of the spiritual and the moral in Christian symbolic expression. In Christian symbolism of the ultimately real, the reign of God's love, giving reality and meaningful order to the universe and to a person's life in the fellowship of the church, is at once God's supreme gift and God's supreme moral demand. In our discussion of the kingdom of God as Christianity's primary spiritual symbol, we noted that its highest personal benefit is regarded to be the gift of being present with God, beginning now, in God's eternal reign of love. The reception of this gift carries with it, for Christians, the personal obligation to strive to love as selflessly as God loves. The morality of God's love, regnant in the person and activity of Christ, could not reasonably be conceived of as seeking anything for God. Rather, God's love in Christ is conceived as acting with pure, spontaneous regard for the present welfare and eternal blessedness of human beings. This demonstration of the reign of God's love in Jesus Christ constitutes the center of Christianity's dynamic matrix of authentic humanity, personal identity, and moral responsibility. It is therefore the Christian's permanent gauge of moral growth. Defined from Christ's exemplification, humanity becomes authentic in those human beings who freely and gladly receive into their lives the reign of God's selfless love and consequently experience a personal transformation in which *self-interested morality is studiedly transformed by selfless regard for the welfare of others.*

Christians maintain that this personal transformation – generally gradual, sometimes sudden – gives one a new and certain personal identity. It becomes clear, they say, that a human being is a person singled out to be loved by nothing less than ultimate reality itself, and that ultimate reality, acting through Christ, does this solely for the person's own immediate and ultimate good, which is that person's growth in uncalculating goodwill. Granting that a human being consents freely and gladly to be this person in whom the love of God works its selfless order, that person becomes capacitated and inspired to integrate everything belonging to its own identity – mind, will, body, and strength – in a single-minded regard for the welfare of others. Most Christians confess that the *transition from self-interested morality to spontaneous regard for others* requires a long stint of strictly disciplined cooperation with God's regenerating love.

All Christians agree that it is every Christian's unnegotiable responsibility to seek to grow in grace, to be receptively and responsively present with God's loving presence in Christ, until *spontaneous regard for others* becomes one's fundamental motivating option. The foundational documents of Christianity depict this responsibility as a special kind of demand that can be fulfilled only when a person freely wants to fulfill it. This demand arises not as a duty externally imposed or as an indebtedness to God. It arises as a personal desire and *free decision* to respond in gratitude for the presence of God in Christ. Genuinely Christian morality is conducted, then, as thanksgiving and has no place for *fear of punishment or expectation of reward.*

In practice, Christian preaching, teaching, and evangelizing have resorted often to the sanctions of fear of damnation in hell and the reward of salvation in heaven to promote desired behavior. Nevertheless, the Christian gospel repudiates fear and reward in the very core of its message. It will be recalled that the word "gospel" means "good news" and that Jesus used it to designate his good news that God's kingship forgives sin and regenerates sinners so that they can *freely decide* to initiate their own behavior of *selfless regard for others.* The New Testament prefaces one of its accounts of Jesus' birth with an angel's announcement,

Do not be afraid, for I bring you good news of great joy which shall be for all the people: Today in the city of David there has been born to you a savior who is Christ the Lord.

(Luke 2:10–11)

Jesus himself instructed his original disciples and, through their apostolic witness, all of his disciples thereafter, that the manner in which God offers and administers the reign of selfless love is calculated to eradicate fear and hence to diminish the anxieties spawned by self-defense and self-interest:

> *Do not be afraid*, little flock, for it is the Father's good pleasure to *give* you the kingdom.
>
> (Luke 12:32)

Unbelievers preoccupy themselves with self-interests, but since your heavenly Father knows everything that you need, let his kingship and righteousness preoccupy you, and everything that you really need will be provided.

(Matthew 6:32–3)

These admonitions of Jesus seem to mean that because God gives the kingdom and because that kingship is the rule of righteous selfless love, those who receive it have neither a reason to fear punishment nor a need to hope for reward in consequence of what they do in fulfilling their responsibility to the kingdom. Early on the Christian tradition concluded that the reality as well as the reign of God is love, and from its very beginning, Christian moral reflection grasped the insight, publicized most recently by Lawrence Kohlberg,[19] that fear is the crudest possible dynamic for the development of moral character and behavior. Ever since, it has been a fundamental, if often neglected, Christian teaching that

Love leaves no place for fear. Indeed, perfect love [i.e., God] exterminates all fear. Since fear has to do with getting punished, love is not yet perfected in the person who is afraid.

(1 John 4:18)

It strains the conscience to classify this canonical Christian passage with the famous sermon preached by the eighteenth-century Christian, Jonathan Edwards, on the topic of "Sinners in the Hands of an Angry God." Love does not fulfill its aims by generating fear, according to one honored current in mainstream Christianity. These Christians maintain also that love is not yet perfected in the person who behaves with a view to reward. Love seeks, they say, no reward; it seeks merely to effect its regard for the well-being of others and is thankful when permitted to do this.

Understandably, Christians are reluctant generally to claim that the rule of selfless love has become the governing option of their lives to the

---

19 See Lawrence Kohlberg, *The Philosophy of Moral Development* (San Francisco: Harper & Row, 1981).

extent that they have no fear and no eye to self-advantage. Nevertheless, as Christians they must acknowledge that striving for this ideal is their ultimate moral responsibility as participants in the reign of God's love. Fidelity to this moral obligation cost Jesus even more than giving up being himself in order to be the selfless Christ. It cost him his mortal life. Facing the prospect of an imminent death to be inflicted as punishment for crimes he never committed, Jesus, according to New Testament accounts, deliberated the choice between his desire to live and his desire to love so selflessly that even his death could be an act of love. He prayed, "Father, if you are willing, remove this cup [this death which will terminate my mortal life and your reign in it] from me. Nevertheless not my will but yours be done" (Luke 22:42). In the Christian context, the will of God intends that each person exercise his or her independence in *spontaneous regard for the welfare of others*. There is no abdication of the ethical, no acquiescence in the inevitable, no surrender of personal moral responsibility in the decision that Jesus expresses in the prayer, "Nevertheless not my will but yours be done." Christians understand this to mean that Jesus, whose fundamental motivational option was to do the Father's will, decided freely here to accept the divine Will as his own even if that required Jesus' death for the sake of others.

The decision of Jesus to give up his life, literally, so that his death, like his life and teaching, would manifest *selfless regard for others* constitutes for Christians the triumph of true morality in personal decision: Desire, duty, decision, and deed were perfectly unified *in selfless regard for the welfare of others*. Christ's free decision exemplifies for Christians the highest moral achievement possible for humans in this world. It defines decisively for them the moral demand made by God's reign whether in heaven, on earth, or in the individual human spirit. Consistent with his decision to make his own death an act of God's kind of love, Jesus, praying for his executioners even as they were crucifying him, said, "Father, forgive them. They do not know what they are doing" (Luke 23:34). This love, which moved Jesus to accept his own death and in dying to befriend those who sought themselves to be his enemies, is the moral demand that Christians seek to make irresistibly attractive to themselves and others in the face of the common human need for personal and social order in the world of human relationships. As Christianity's primary symbol of desirability, the kingdom of God identified as the rule of God's selfless love is the highest possible good. Faith, which is eager longing for the rule of this love, is the governing option of a Christian's moral behavior and serves to *minimize selfish motivation for good behavior*. In all these respects, then, the kingdom of God is the symbol that *defines all Christian ethical precepts and integrates them into its own comprehensive meaning and purpose for human life*. In the wider arena of world theology, as a notable instance of moral symbolism of desirability, the Christian symbol of the kingdom of God is an example of *defining desirable human conduct with reference to the ultimate desirability of the central spiritual reality of humankind.*

Mythological Symbolism of Desirability

Christians mythologically symbolize the supreme desirability of God's presence in Christ by depicting (1) each stage of Jesus' life under *an image of the ideal* that God wants for all human beings at the corresponding stage of their lives and (2) Jesus' whole life as *the ideal* for all who want to live eternally with God in heaven. This imagery is intended to express and evoke the conviction that throughout the historicized cosmos of Christian mythology the regnant will of God is nothing other than the selfless love present and presented in Christ. This conviction seeks to render the entire cosmos, known and unknown, a hospitable environment for any phase of human life and for short or long residence. A Christian folk hymn proclaims this conviction in the line, "Anywhere is home since Christ our Lord is there."

The celebration of Christ's birth has become a nearly universal symbol of goodwill. Christmas evokes images and acts of generosity in Christians and others alike. All distinctions of religious labels tend to recede as voices of all ages from all the earth's peoples join in the enchanting chorus, "Unto us a child is born, unto us a son is given." The idea that ultimate reality, otherwise incomprehensible even to humanity's greatest minds, has come to humanity in the helpless body of a baby is such an *irresistibly evocative image of desirability* that one hesitates and feels a bit remorseful to deal with it as a mythological construction of reality that requires a theological interpretation if one is to understand its larger meanings.

For Christians, one of the enlarged meanings of Jesus' birth is that the birth of every baby is an event in the life and love of God and should be planned and brought about with the care and design demonstrated in God's planned parenthood of Jesus. Christians have institutionalized, but compromised, this meaning in their sacrament of infant baptism. Based on the conviction that God took the initiative to reach out and incorporate all humanity into Christ while all were still sinners and unrepentant, the church reaches out to babies to incorporate them by infant baptism into the church and thus to give them an option on eternal life even though they cannot yet either understand or exercise the option. However, by limiting its formal and public recognition of birth, and hence limiting its recognition of the option for eternal life, to those babies who have at least one consenting Christian parent or guardian, the church compromises the universal meaning of Christ's mythic birth. That birth, in the wider, overriding symbolism of the Christian myth, proclaims every baby's birth to be an act of God's love calling for response with selfless love.

Between a child's birth and confirmation, the church cultivates the child's sense of living in relation to Jesus as the best friend and example available in the world. To Jesus "the first fond prayers are said," and Christian children are taught by numerous devices that Jesus embodies all the virtues of a perfect child. They learn this, for example, by singing such ditties as, "When Jesus was a little boy and played beside the street, I know that when his mother called he came on flying feet." The ideal of obedience to parents extolled in that little song translates, as the child grows older, into Jesus' obedience to God. God, the child learns, is the heavenly Father not only of Jesus but also of the child's parents, the child itself, and all others – those whom one dislikes as well as those whom one likes.

The incentive for transferring one's reference from parents and acquaintances to God is the New Testament's image of the boy Jesus at the age of twelve. Jesus had made a pilgrimage with his family to the temple at Jerusalem. He remained in the temple unnoticed by his parents as they departed with other relatives on the several days' journey homeward. Becoming aware that Jesus was not with them, they returned to Jerusalem after three days to look for him. They found him in the temple engaged in theological discussion with the teachers. After telling him how anxiously they had searched for him, his mother asked him why he had not followed his parents obediently. He astonished them with his own expression of astonishment at their imperceptivity: "Why were you searching for me? Did you not know that it is my responsibility to be in my Father's house?" (Luke 2:49). This is the image under which all pubescent Christian boys and girls are expected to exercise their option, independent of their parents, to decide to live their life selflessly in final accountability to God. The ritual of confirmation in which the adolescent makes this public confession serves also to raise the consciousness of the confirmand's parents to the Christian reality that their child's ultimate responsibility right now is to God and not to them. Like Jesus' parents, they "lose" their status when they find their child affirming his or her ultimate responsibility to God.

The church challenges adults to find in the words and deeds of the mature Jesus the *ideal* for every option in their own experience. We need to make only a selective illustration of this. To young people considering career alternatives, the church relates an incident in Jesus' life. A young man once asked Jesus to tell him a way to live that would guarantee to gain God's favor and eternal life for the young man (Matthew 19:16–30).

Jesus tried to disabuse the young man of his selfish preoccupation with his own life and his mistaken notion of needing to command God's favor. Jesus offered him the alternative of becoming a fulfilled person by joining with Jesus and others in responding to the basic needs and vital interests of others. The church makes Jesus' standard of service to others the decisive factor in a young person's choice of a life career.

Although Jesus did not marry, he seems to have taught that God intends marriage for humans in most cases. He held that God creates humanity as male and female, that male and female are created each for the other, that God ordains that each couple live together in a lifelong monogamous relation, and that God cautions the marriage partners and everyone else not to do anything to weaken or undermine that relation because it is a step in actualizing God's reign in their life together (Matthew 19:3–12). Except for marriage, Jesus is depicted as having lived a complete adult human life without ever sinning: "He was tempted in every way that we are, yet *he never sinned*" (Hebrews 4:15). Christians assume that the fullness of Jesus' adult experience and the perfection of his behavior entitle his teaching to the largest possible hearing, and so they retell his stories to evoke from all and sundry the motivation and behavior he commends.

Jesus taught by telling parables, mythological stories that teach what God wants by describing an instance of it on some imagined occasion. Jesus' parables present "what happened" in such elemental communication as not to be descriptive of an event, but rather prescriptive of universally desirable motivation and behavior. For example, a lawyer once asked Jesus, "Who is my neighbor?" (Luke 10:29–37) meaning to inquire also, Who is not my neighbor? Jesus answered with a parable about a Samaritan's good deed. Because the Samaritans had a racially mixed ancestry – Gentile and Jewish – and were often quite hostile to Jews, Jesus' Jewish contemporaries tended to despise them as mongrels and religious apostates who were unlikely to show sympathy or do a favor for any Jew. In his mythic story, Jesus made his imaginary Samaritan the heroic exemplar of good neighborliness:

A man was going down from Jerusalem to Jericho, and he fell victim to robbers who stripped and beat him and went off leaving him half dead. A priest happened to be going down that road, but when he saw him he passed by on the other side. Likewise a Levite [the designated lay-associate of a priest] came that same way, saw the man and passed by on the other side. But a Samaritan who was traveling came along where the man was, and when he saw him he had compassion and went to him and dressed his wounds, pouring on oil and wine. Then he put him on his own beast and brought him to an inn, where he took care of him. The next day he took out two denarii and gave them to the innkeeper, saying, "Take care of him, and if you need to spend more, I will repay you on my way back."

Then Jesus asked the lawyer, "Which of these three, do you think, proved to be a neighbor to the man who fell among the robbers?" When the lawyer answered that it was "the one who showed mercy," Jesus admonished him, "Go and behave the same way."

Christians retell this parable on the assumption that it reflects the wisdom and personal character of the adult Jesus. They retell it for the same reason that Jesus told it in the first place: to *evoke spontaneous and generous regard for others* from those who hear it. By retelling it they intend to say to themselves and others, "Make this story come true. Become and be this good Samaritan yourself." Similarly, they use other parables of Jesus, and stories about Jesus' own life, to *depict and evoke* the disposition, attitudes, and behavior that Jesus exhibited in his adult life and commended to all who would commit their life to God's kingship during their mortal life.

From the foregoing discussion it should have become evident that Christians appeal to mythological images of Jesus' life and teaching in order to amend and edify human life in the present world. Christianity assigns a positive value to the physical world itself by attributing its origin and reality to the creative love of God and by involving natural processes in God's Son–Word becoming actually present in the flesh, bone, and blood of Jesus. The New Testament asserts that the physical world itself aspires for the salvation of humans, suffers for the sake of human salvation, and will receive its own liberation along with the redeemed children of God (Romans 8:19–23). Christian teaching does not offer heaven or the hereafter as a prize for those who renounce the natural and temporal world. The official teachings of mainstream Christianity make a careful distinction, for example, between good sensuality and bad sensuality. Sensuality itself is not bad. Humans make it bad, but they can make it good and to that extent can hallow the whole world. Christian holiness does not drive out nature's powers; it develops them and directs them to good uses. All religions recognize explicitly – and we argue all humans recognize at least tacitly – that there is more to human life than its tenure in the moral world. Christianity offers heaven and hell as the only two destinies of human choice. It depicts life in heaven and hell as qualitatively continuous with life lived in this present sensual world and therefore urges that humans keep an eye on heaven's standard and a mind to serving Christ in this world:

A charge to keep I have, a God to glorify,
A never-dying soul to save, and fit it for the sky.

To serve the present age, my calling to fulfill;
O may it all my powers engage to do my Master's will!

Arm me with jealous care, as in Thy sight to live,
And, oh, Thy servant, Lord, prepare a strict account to give!

Help me to watch and pray, and on Thyself rely,
Assured, if I my trust betray, I shall for ever die.[20]

Heaven and hell respectively symbolize for Christians the eternal full-ness of salvation begun now in relation to God in Christ and the eternal deprivation of those who freely reject the overtures that God makes to humans in their history. Christianity uses these symbols to enhance hu-manity's present sense of responsibility rather than to make an end in itself of either gaining heaven or avoiding hell. That is the symbolic function of the Christian church's prayer, "Let your Kingdom come, let your will be done, on earth as it is in heaven." The church intends that praying this prayer will enable persons to become morally prepared for a long life, for unexpected death, even for the end of human history.

It should be noted that vain predictions of the day and hour when the sovereign God will end this world's purpose – though conspicuous in some forms of Christianity – are utterly contrary to the spirit of Chris-tianity as a humble acceptance of God's will in history. "Of that day and hour no one knows, not even the angels in heaven, nor the Son, but only the Father. Your part is to keep mindful and stay alert, for you do not know when the appointed time will come" (Mark 13:32). The church admonishes Christians to anticipate life in the hereafter with confident joy but to refrain from imagining elaborate details of the hereafter, an indulgence that tends to obscure the value and diminish the delight of present fellowship with Christ in the church:

And since our fellowship below in Jesus is so sweet,
What height of rapture shall we know when round his throne we meet.[21]

Dearly beloved, we are God's children already. What we shall be like later has not been made known, but we do know that when it is made known we shall be like him, for we shall see him as he is. Everyone who holds this hope will keep pure, as Christ is pure.

(1 John 3:2–3)

Christianity's mythological symbolism *depicts the ultimately desirable in evocative, concrete images* of Jesus' earthly life and stories in order to bring the character of heaven to Christians on earth. Christianity uses its mythological symbolisms of Jesus' life and stories to evoke Christ-like

20   Charles Wesley's hymn entitled, "A Charge to Keep I Have."
21   From Charles Wesley's hymn, "All Praise to Our Redeeming Lord."

living in others. This symbolism proclaims the inestimable value of earthly life with God in Christ by previsioning heaven as the continuation and perfecting of that life while showing hell to be the inevitable eternal consequence of having effectively rejected God in Christ from one's earthly life.

Elusiveness

Christianity not only acclaims God's love as undeniable and asserts its worth to be supremely desirable; it presents as a marvel the fact that the gracious manner of this love, on which their salvation depends, *exceeds human understanding and defies human control.* Christianity employs the term "grace" to denote this uncalled for, undeserved, and incomprehensible extension of God's independent love. They identify the necessity of this grace as the *missing link* required for humanity's conciliation and communion with God. The doctrine of grace epitomizes Christianity's witness to *the elusiveness of the central spiritual referent of humankind.* Our discussion of this witness does not need to be long. Once the Christian rationale of grace is understood, the entire Christian religion can be seen as a symbolic expression of the simultaneous accessibility and elusiveness of the ultimately real.

Intellectual Symbolism of Elusiveness

Christianity *attempts to make the elusiveness of ultimate reality reasonable* by showing that God's grace is necessary for humanity's salvation. The uncompromising theocentricity of the entire Christian religion grows out of its theocentric concept of salvation. Christians believe that the scheme for human salvation is designed, developed, and administered by the wisdom, bounty, and sole causality of God's love. Paul, in the first century, was perhaps the earliest Christian thinker to interpret all human experience in terms of the program of salvation that Christ represents as the embodiment of grace in history. Having analyzed and described that program as one that God alone has arranged and that God has opened to the whole human race, Paul exclaimed in wonder, admiration, and gratitude:

How inexhaustible are the resources, the wisdom, and the knowledge of God! How inscrutable are his judgments, how undetectable his ways! Who knows the mind of the Lord? Who has been his counsellor? Who has ever made a gift to him that deserved a gift in return? He is the source, the saving guide and the goal of all reality. To him be the glory forever more.

(Romans 1:33–6)

With this elegant economy of words Paul asserts in praise the unmitigated independence and infinite resources of God's reality; the elusiveness of God's demeanor; the unsurpassability of God's mind, judgment, and generosity; and the utter dependence of all other realities – from their beginning to their end – on God. Paul considered all of that to be a reasonable inference from his comprehension of God's saving program. Across the centuries, Christian experience and reflection have reaffirmed Paul's conclusion that God's reality is best understood from its creative maneuvers to save sinners.

In its conceptual representation of this theocentric arrangement for salvation, Christianity explains the necessity of grace in the following way. Human beings universally could have perceived clearly that God wants love to rule the world. Instead they have all rebelled against having a definitive communion of love with God. As a race and as individuals they could and should have perceived that the proper present and ultimate meaning of their life is to participate with God in a communion that opens solicitously to any other human being and embraces everyone who responds. Instead, human beings universally have willfully exchanged their God-given birthright – their finite freedom and their capacity to love – for bondage to the sin of self-will. This is the domino-effect *fall* that every human individual repeats, and it is enormously more serious than a person's merely *falling short* of the mark of moral aspiration. In choosing to live *from* the self *for* the self, the radical reality of a person *falls away from* companionship with God. From this "original sin" or "fall" in each person's life originate all other sins, including personal moral defects and misdemeanors. One must understand this notion of every human person's original sin if one wants to understand Christianity's reasoning for the necessity of grace, because, according to Christianity, it is this sin that permanently estranges people from God.

"Original sin" designates a person's fundamental commitment to be a self and to cherish and choose what pleases this self. It is a commitment that forms so subtly, on the basis of a decision that develops so early and deceptively, that a person cannot remember having ever experienced it as an actual option. Christian theology will not exculpate us even though we cannot remember choosing our selfish orientation. It will not permit us to say, "We were born this way and could not have been otherwise." The condition of being a self is one that each person brings about. Because it is a condition of *being* selfish, the human person *is* selfish whether it remains immobile or engages in activity. When one does express one's self, the expression is self-assertion and self-service. When a person's being is selfish, that personal being is selfish in itself, in its actions, and in its relations. It shuts out God and other humans from its being, and is indifferent to them except to use them for its self. Such a person whose

being is selfish does not even want to be otherwise. The selfward orientation of human persons impairs their judgment, conscripts their will, and
confuses their emotions so that they are unable to discern and despise
their truly corrupted condition, or to initiate and effect a break away from
it or even to imagine the possibility and satisfaction of selfless motivation.

Since the selfish sinner is unwilling, and unable to become willing, to
participate in a fellowship or communion of love with God and other
human beings, why has God not abandoned humans completely? Christianity answers that since God is ultimate and humans are finally accountable to God, and since the reality of God is a love that wills to commune
with humans right now as well as forever afterward, God is not indifferent
to humanity's unwillingness to love and to be loved rather than to be a
self. Because the reality of God in Christ is the love that aims for communion, that love cares whether humans accept or reject it. It would cease to
be righteous selfless love if it relented in its will to create communion with
those who have rejected it. Because it does continue to care infinitely for
those who are unwilling to commune with it, God's love requires that
humanity's estrangement be overcome and that a radical atonement (at-
one-ment) be established between loving God and selfish humanity.

How can God's love and humanity's selfishness be brought together in
a communing fellowship? Christianity asserts that this is a question for
God to answer, because humanity is in no disposition to renounce and
sacrifice anything of its own. Therefore, the motivation, the will, and the
resources to atone holy (loving) God and unholy (selfish) humanity are all
on God's side. This situation, according to Christianity, constitutes the
crisis point at which *grace*, the inexplicable extension of God's love,
becomes necessary. It supplies *the missing link* between God's love and
humanity's selfishness that is necessary for the salvation of humankind
from the sinful, fallen condition.

At the same time, Christian teaching maintains that the mere presence
of God's love does not suffice to induce selfishness to yield itself to
communion with God's love. The power of God's love has to be conducted in such a manner that it creates communion with selfish people
while they are still being selfish. Christians are instructed to see God's
love demonstrated in precisely that creative manner in Jesus Christ, and
they refer to it as "the grace of God given in Jesus Christ." What they see
in Jesus Christ and call grace is God's making a sacrifice that humans
ought to have made but refused to make. Christianity announces that
right here in human history – where humans ought to have sacrificed their
selfishness to God – the love of God acted vicariously for humanity in
Jesus Christ and sacrificed selfless love to selfish humanity. This grace,
this vicarious action of God's love, has supplied the *missing link*, in Christianity's scheme of salvation, a link that has joined holy (loving) God and
sinful (selfish) humans in a radical at-one-ment:

In Christ God was reconciling the world to God's reality, no longer holding humanity's transgressions against them. . . . Christ was innocent of sin, but for our sake God made him one with our sinfulness so that in him we might be made one with God's goodness.

(2 Corinthians 5:19, 21)

Christ died for us godless people. . . . Christ died for us while we were still sinners and in that act God demonstrates God's own love for us. . . . We were enemies when God reconciled us through the death of his Son, but now that we are reconciled we shall be saved all the more by the life of his son.

(Romans 5:6, 8, 10)

In this vicarious atonement with selfish humanity, God's love is believed to have compromised neither its own righteousness nor the righteousness it requires of human beings. Indeed, for Christianity, vicarious suffering and death demonstrate that God's love is righteous: It remains loving consistently and extends itself to others at literally any cost to itself – exactly the opposite of what selfishness does. It demonstrates also that the righteousness which God wants from every human being is also vicarious love.

The love of Christ overwhelms us when we reflect that since one man has died for all humans, then every human being ought to be dead, but he died for all so that living humans should no longer live selfishly, but for him who died and was raised to life for them.

(2 Corinthians 5:14–15)

Christians perceive that by yielding to human selfishness the love of God took a risk that has been realized: that humans would scorn, injure, and try to exterminate it, that yielding thus would involve a great waste of love. There is, however, a far more decisive consideration for the dignity and integrity of God's love than this realized risk. By sacrificing itself, this love of God created a communion and a community within which selfish humans have an assured possibility of a regeneration that will enable them to become righteous lovers of others and of God. This provision for human regeneration through the communion of a loving God and selfish humanity, in the community of the church, is a realistic, not facile, treatment of sin. The grace that, according to Christianity, accomplishes this regeneration is an expensive, not cheap, grace. By its vicarious sacrifice in Jesus Christ the grace of God's love shows itself to be qualitatively *other* than human reality. Rather this *otherness* does not constitute an elusiveness of inaccessibility. The elusiveness of grace is the *inexplicability* of its *given presence* in Jesus Christ and his church. Christian intellectual symbolism tries to make sense of the givenness of grace to self-centered humanity, for whom "common sense" dictates that no one should give or get something for nothing.

Over the centuries Christian thinkers have proposed numerous and elaborate variations on this elemental New Testament notion of grace. Christian reflection has consistently judged each proposal according to its fidelity to the idea that grace is God's way of giving salvation to sinful humanity for nothing, and according to its capacity to explain why God deals with humans quite without regard to their utter lack of desert or merit. A careful reading of Philip Watson's essay, "Developments of the Doctrine of Grace,"[22] will show that the history of Christian thought has sustained, in one way or another, the point we have made here: that grace, *the solicitous manner and generous conduct* of God's love, is *necessary* in Christianity's soteriology in order to create and account for a conciliating and saving communion between holy (loving) God and sinful (selfish) humanity. Christianity's case for the necessity of grace – *which humans can neither evoke, control, nor even influence* – exemplifies intellectual symbolization that points to the very principle of God's own unmitigated independence and thus provides an example of recognition of *the elusiveness of a central spiritual referent of the whole human race*. Having set forth the Christian rationale for the necessity of God's grace for human salvation, we can describe Christianity's other three symbolisms of elusiveness in brief compass.

Spiritual Symbolism of Elusiveness

Christianity's spiritual symbolism of the elusiveness of the central spiritual reality of humankind centers on the necessity of faith for human salvation. As we have noted already, the basic Christian sense of faith means the desire to have all that God is giving in Jesus Christ. In other words, faith means a person's desire to receive God's grace. It is necessary for a person to have and freely pursue this desire before God's uncoercive love will begin to work its saving influence in the person's life. The necessity of faith from the human side corresponds exactly to the necessity of grace from God's side. In specifically Christian terms, grace begets faith to be its human partner. Faith itself is a gift of grace, a work that God accomplishes through Christian preaching. As a response to the proclaimed presence of God in Christ, and as the desire for Christ, Christian faith always points to the necessity of grace as the *missing link* in Christianity's way of salvation. Therefore, Christianity's spiritual expressions of God's elusiveness *encourage the discipline of sustained faith* because faith itself is dependent on the independence, which is the elusiveness, of grace.

22 Philip S. Watson, *The Concept of Grace* (Philadelphia: Muhlenberg Press, 1959).

When Christianity implores people to sustain a disciplined desire for grace, it intends to assert unequivocally that salvation is, from first to last, a work of God. Paul, Christianity's foremost exponent of grace and faith, advised all who would "be worthy of the gospel of Christ," saying, "Work out your own salvation in fear and trembling, because God, in good will toward you, works in you both to evoke the desire and to accomplish its fulfillment" (Philippians 2:13). This is not a contradiction for Paul or other Christians. It asserts that grace itself, in its independent manner of action, makes a person's independent faith a necessity for salvation. Yet faith is possible only as a response to the initiative made by grace. "Faith comes from hearing the message of Christ proclaimed," Paul explained in another writing (Romans 10:17). Christians understand this to mean that personal faith originates when a person hears an appealing account of Christ's saving love, is inspired to have confidence in Christ, and is moved to desire Christ. The desire for Christ is a free choice in response to the message one has heard.

This decision may begin as a rather crude desire, as Bernard of Clairvaux,[23] among many others, has pointed out. At first it may be the selfish desire to "save" oneself rather than the desire to love selflessly. It may begin as weak faith, mixed with fear, diffidence, and doubt, but faith can grow. Christians typically analogize the stages of a person's growth in faith to three phases of a person's physical development: infant, young adult, and parent (cf. 1 John 2:12–14). Faith grows as a person becomes better acquainted with Christ and comes to desire Christ, not for being useful to that person's self, but for Christ's manifestation of God's selfless love. As faith grows, fear, diffidence, and doubt decrease. The self diminishes and the person increasingly desires Christ for the sake of expressing selfless love.

Faith, then, is the Christian alternative to self and is the technical Christian term for the cultivation and expression of human selfless love. Christians anticipate that when a person's faith grows to full maturity, selfless love will have superseded the self entirely as the principle that motivates that person's life and orders all of its experience. Christians differ among themselves concerning the likelihood that anyone will accomplish the complete displacement of selfishness in this life. They all agree, however, that this is the goal that every human should seek during this life because the displacement of human selfishness is the meaning and ultimate goal of God's salvation. The *discipline* of *sustained growth in faith* develops in a believer "the holiness [selflessness] without which no persons shall see the Lord" (Hebrews 12:14). God's grace does not force a person to become selfless, just as it does not force a person to have faith. It does require the pursuit of selflessness from all who consent to become

23 *The Love of God*, VII and XV.

incorporated into God's eternal life of love. To become selfless, according to Christianity, is the intended and inevitable result of a person's sustained faith in response to God's sustained grace. "By grace you are saved through faith" (Ephesians 2:8) describes a process of spiritual growth in which a person's disciplined faith freely responds to and works with God's grace to displace selfish dispositions with dispositions of goodwill, and to transform self-interested morality into spontaneous regard for the welfare of others. Christians call this a process of *spiritual* growth because they think that the Holy Spirit – the Spirit of God which is also the Spirit of Christ and is sometimes called the Spirit of grace – is God's mysterious power of transformation. This elusive power works in the spirit of a consenting and cooperating person to increase and mature that person's "love, joy, peace, patience, kindness, goodness, faithfulness, gentleness and mastery of self" (Galatians 5:22–3). This concept of a person's moral regeneration "by grace though faith" illustrates again the inseparability of Christianity's spiritual and moral symbolism of elusiveness. *Despite its elusiveness*, God's grace *requires* for its own saving work *the sustained discipline of a person's faith*, and faith working with grace builds up a person's moral character. This discussion of faith as Christianity's quintessential *spiritual* symbol of elusiveness leads naturally and unavoidably to a discussion of the moral symbolism of elusiveness.

Moral Symbolism of Elusiveness

Because the grace of God's love given in Jesus Christ constitutes the *missing link* in the Christian way of salvation, Christianity necessarily acknowledges that *good behavior in itself is insufficient for personal perfection*. Instead, Christianity emphasizes repeatedly that grace working through faith is the source and means of growth in personal perfection and that good behavior is an effect rather than a cause of that growth. Christians identify their quintessential *moral* symbol of elusiveness as "the righteousness of God," by which they mean the spontaneous love that God demonstrates in Christ. When by faith humans experience and express this love, Christians call it the righteousness of faith in order to emphasize that God has accomplished it and that it is not to be reckoned as an achievement of a person's self-motivated behavior.

Similarly Christians distinguish between the perfection that is possible for a person in this life and the perfection that God will bestow on that person in heaven. In this life and in heaven alike, perfection refers to selfless love. We noted in the preceding section that a person's faith, responding freely to God's grace and working steadily with God's Holy Spirit, progressively transforms that person's fundamental option from self-regard to spontaneous regard for God and humanity. This process of spiritual and moral growth begins through the agency of faith while we humans are still self-willing, self-asserting, and self-seeking sinners. The measure and manner of love with which a selfish sinner begins is self-evidently neither that perfection of love which God alone exemplifies, nor the perfection of love that the conditions of heaven will confer, nor even the fulfillment of the person' possibilities for loving under the condition of mortal existence. The beginner's love can be genuine, however, and the beginner's loving can be purified. Most Christians agree with Thomas Aquinas, who maintained that there is a perfection of love that honors God's purpose for human existence under the conditions of this world, and another perfection of love that God bestowed on the same persons in their existence in heaven. The earthly perfection of love my be instanced, Aquinas said, in two ways:

First by the removal from humanity's affections of all that is contrary to love, such as mortal sin [the rejection of God's intention for and communication to human-ity]; and there can be no love apart from this perfection, and therefore it is necessary for salvation. Secondly, by the removal from human affections . . . of whatever hinders the mind's affections from tending wholly to God. Love is possible apart from this perfection, for instance in those who are beginners and in those who are proficient.[24]

The earthly perfection of love, honoring the conditions of human exis-tence in this world, does not require, for example, the banishment of bodily desires. Because, according to Christianity, humanity's sin does not consist in bodily desires, personal perfection does not consist in the denial of bodily desires.[25] The perfecting of love in a human person in this earthly life consists instead in the diminution of selfishness and the in-creasing supremacy of selfless love as the sovereign option in a person's desires, thoughts, words, and deeds. This occurs "by grace through faith" as the Christian, desiring to become selfless, appropriates the cleansing powers and edifying gifts of the Holy Spirit. Serious-minded Christians petition God to bring about this perfection by praying daily some such collect for purity as: "Cleanse the desires of our hearts and the thoughts of our minds by the inspiration of thy Holy Spirit, *that we may perfectly love thee and each other* and thus worthily magnify thy holy name, through Jesus Christ our Lord." This prayer expresses what Christians think God wants to do for them and will do for them in this life if they are but willing to receive it. In this life, they believe, to the extent that a person is willing to be capacitated, faith can equip and enable that one to

24 *Summa Theologiae*, II, ii, q.clxxxiv, a.2. In this passage Aquinas characterizes the three degrees of the spiritual life as beginner, proficient, and perfect.
25 Ibid., q.clxxxiii, a.2.

love God and humanity solely for the sake of selfless loving, with total disregard for benefits to oneself. Faith can do this because God wants to give this spiritual and moral condition to every human and will give it to whatever extent a person desires it.

The desire to feel, think, speak, and act in no other way than the way of godly selfless love is the Christian ideal of the righteousness of faith. It is a desire believed to be evoked, nurtured, and fulfilled by God's grace in the communion God initiates and sustains with sinners. No human person can claim credit for it. It precedes a person's behavior and both defines and motivates all behavior that is good. Therefore, *good behavior cannot suffice for personal perfection* because moral achievement itself is an effect, not a participating cause, of the process by which grace saves humans through their faith. This derivative, dependent status of Christian morality points to grace and faith as the *necessary means* of human salvation and hence, in the wider context of a world theology, to *the elusiveness of the central spiritual reality of humankind.*

Mythological Symbolism of Elusiveness

The Christian sacraments and sacramental theology *illustrate the self-determination of God's grace* and therefore constitute a *mythological* symbolization of *the elusiveness of God's ultimate power.* We recognize that some Christians will be offended by our characterization of baptism, Eucharist (Holy Communion), and other distinctively Christian rites as mythological. Our respect for that Christian sensibility constrains us to remind the reader that we intend no disparagement, indeed no value judgment at all, in the use of the term mythological. We use the term here as elsewhere to designate *concrete images* of the effective operation of *a nonmaterial, ultimate reality* in the material world. According to Christianity, the sacraments are the physical means by which God effectively transmits to humans those powers of selfless love that are necessary for Christian life and human salvation. Christian imagination, reflecting its sense of the universal significance and pandemic meaning of Christ's historical revelation, depicts the universe under the image of a historically developing organism that is engendered and ordered by God's omnicompetent selfless love. This Christian mythology, consistent with the gospel and Christian theology, never represents God in any show of coercive force or display of sheer power. Such images of power, calculated to evoke dread and compel compliance, contradict the solicitous irrepressibility of God's love. Any disjunction of divine power from love constitutes, for consistent Christian reflection, a blasphemy. Even the slightest insinuation that love and power are ever separated in the reality or action of God is a blatant idolatry. In a truly Christian mythology, images of God's

coextensive love and power predominate and seek to elicit unmanipu-
lated, noncoerced consent and cooperation. Like the mythologies of
other religions, these Christian images *appeal for consent and response*
from those powers of intuitive insight and volition that function at deeper
levels of the human person than either discursive reasoning or conscious
feeling.

Theoretically, any part of a cosmos engendered and ordered by God's
omnicompetent love could symbolize that love and could function as the
sacrament (the physical instrument or means) by which God effectively
communicates the powers of saving love to the deepest levels of a human
spirit. Christianity holds, however, that God has ordained a limited
number of specific realities to serve as means of grace. For our discussion
here, it does not matter that Protestants disagree with Roman Catholics
and members of the Eastern churches on the number of these sacraments.
It does matter that all of these Christians subscribe to a basic sacramental
theology and practice that *illustrate in concrete images* the utter independence, and thus the elusiveness, of God's operation of grace in a Christian's life.

The paradigm or primordial sacrament in Christianity is Jesus Christ.
The very Word or reality of God's righteous selfless love is so indistinguishably united in the Christian imagination with Christ himself that
Christians identify the grace of God and also the grace communicated by
other sacraments as "the grace of our Lord Jesus Christ." Since it inheres
in the grace of Christ to establish communion and to create and build
community, it is inevitable that wherever Christ is, there the church will
develop as his body of believers with whom he is indistinguishably united
in communion and fellowship. Anything else which is to be called a
sacrament must exhibit the principle of unifying embodiment demonstrated in the incarnation of God's Word in Christ and in Christ's union
with the church: the indistinguishable embodiment of spiritual reality in
material reality.

Hugh of St. Victor (d. 1142) argued for as many as thirty sacraments
while Protestants generally hold that only baptism by water and the
eucharistic meal of bread and wine fulfill the requirements of a sacrament.
The vast majority of Christians, however, comprehending all of those in
both the Eastern and Roman Catholic churches, observe seven sacraments
putatively instituted by Christ. Each of these sacraments, manifesting its
distinctive operation of God's grace, accomplishes its own distinctive
realization in the Christian's life. In the rite of *baptism*, the physical
reality of water, bearing and conveying the Holy Spirit of God and
Christ, is poured on the head of the individual while the priest utters the
Trinitarian formula, and the baptized person, now "Christened" in name
and character, is empowered to reduce selfishness. *Confirmation* – by the

God-given power transmitted through the laying on of the hands of the bishop or presiding pastor – endows the freely consenting confirmand with the permanent authority and responsibility to participate in the mission of Christ's church to the whole world. By ingesting the consecrated bread and wine of the church's rite of *Eucharist,* a Christian thankfully receives the spiritual nourishment of Christ's vicarious sacrificial life and death and is strengthened for the whole Christian life. Administering the sacrament of *penance,* the church confers upon a person the insight and strength to acknowledge the grievous character and consequence of a particular sin and to assume as one's own cross some punishment prescribed by the church so that the sinner can share with Christ the suffering for sins committed. The candidates for *ordination* to the life of priestly service in the church submit to the laying on of episcopal hands and hearing the authoritative episcopal words conferring upon each of them the apostolic office of priest. Thereby they receive the irrevocable power and responsibility to perpetuate and shepherd the church as the permanent, historical symbol of God's irrepressible and ultimately irresistible grace. In the sacrament of *matrimony* the mutually consenting man and woman state, in the hearing of an officiating priest, their consent and vow to lifelong monogamous fidelity. They communicate to each other the unifying grace that betokens the union of Christ and his church and the eschatological restoration of humanity's "original" image of God ("God created humanity in his own image. . . . He created it male and female"; Genesis 2:27). The church anoints the sick and dying with an oil in the rite of *unction.* It thereby transmits the grace that enables the recipient to accept human weakness and death as the occasion for Christ to demonstrate that "my grace is sufficient for you, for my power is made perfect in weakness" (2 Corinthians 12:9).

According to the teaching of the churches that practice these seven sacraments, each of the sacraments transmits the grace of God given through Jesus Christ and is *the means* by which a Christian's faith appropriates grace. Each sacrament depends exclusively upon God for its validity and efficacy, not on the subjective disposition of the recipient and not upon the moral and spiritual excellence of the officiating priest or bishop. This teaching, as well as Christianity's theological concept of sacrament, *illustrates in concrete images,* independent of intangible considerations of the worthiness of the participants, the utter self-determination of God's grace. Thereby, they express mythologically *the elusiveness of God's grace,* which in turn provides the preeminent Christian example of *the elusiveness of a central spiritual referent for all humankind.*

Discussion of the sacraments as *concrete images* of the grace God gives in Christ provides a fitting conclusion to our presentation of Christianity's symbolic expressions of the undeniability, desirability, and elusiveness of its ultimate referent. The grace of God given in Jesus Christ is, according to Christianity, the supreme fact, value, and paradox. The saving behavior of God's love is God's alone to give at God's own discretion, and yet it is not grace until it is given, for grace is the way God's love behaves in the act of being itself. Christians regard Jesus to be the epitome of God's loving action, the paradigm of the *way* God's love behaves in order to effect human salvation. Christians find in Jesus – in his own ineradicable participation in human history and in his resurrected and permanent presence in the life of the historical church – *the central spiritual referent for all humankind*, and they identify that referent as the immaterial reality of a limitless, uncoercive love, irrepressibly and irresistibly intent upon making human life eternally good and happy, beginning now. Finding all this in Jesus, Christians call him the Christ and make him the governing *spiritual symbol* of their faith, the governing *moral symbol* of their values, the governing *intellectual symbol* of their wisdom, and the governing *mythological symbol* of their imagination. As we said at the beginning of this chapter, wherever one finds a distinctively Christian symbolic expression, one will find Jesus Christ to be its defining and unique constituent, for he is Christianity's one, original, originating, irreducible, and permanent datum.

CHAPTER SEVEN

Islam and the Central Spiritual Reality of Humankind

Islam originated in the Arabian peninsula with the revelation of a book, the Qur'ān, to the Prophet Muḥammad. The numerous installments of this revelation, which together made up the Qur'ān, occurred between 610 and 632 c.e., the year the Prophet died. For Muslims, followers of the Prophet Muḥammad and thus adherents of Islam, the Qur'ān constitutes the final and only fully authoritative revelation to humankind of the will of Allāh, the one and only God of all creation.

In addition to founding a new religion, Muḥammad initiated, through these revelations and his own efforts and skill, a remarkable political force, indistinguishable from Islam the religion. Less than twenty years after the death of Muḥammad, Islam presided over an empire larger than Alexander's or Rome's at its zenith. The empire eventually broke up, but the religion continued to expand until by the end of the first millennium, Islam had converted an enormous swath of territory from North Africa to North India.

Despite the cultural and racial groups assimilated in this meteoric rise to major world significance, Islam has remained to the present day remarkably homogeneous. The one major schism that divides Islam occurred early in its history as a result of a political dispute over who was the legitimate caliph of the emerging Islamic empire. One segment of Islam felt that only a male descendant of the Prophet Muḥammad could legitimately succeed Muḥammad as leader of all Muslims. Though Muḥammad had several wives, only one of his children was able to provide him with grandchildren. Therefore, there was only one line through which hereditary successors of the Prophet were possible: descendants of Muḥammad's daughter Fatima and her husband, 'Ali, Muḥammad's cousin and one of his closest associates. Because of their single-minded support of 'Ali, this faction of Islam came to be known as the Shī'a or "partisans," that is, partisans of 'Ali.

Shī'a frustration that 'Ali had not been named caliph, combined with their religious zeal and their resentment of some of the third caliph's political appointments, eventually resulted in armed conflict, political intrigue, and finally the assassination of 'Ali by one of his own disgruntled supporters. The result of this complex series of events was that Mu'āwiya, 'Ali's archrival, became the caliph of Islam. This setback did not diminish the Shī'ite conviction that only a descendant of 'Ali could legitimately preside over Islam, and the movement went underground.

Eventually Shī'ite Islam became dominant in the heartland of the defunct Persian empire, and a force to be reckoned with throughout the Muslim world. However, Shī'ite Islam's early experience as an underground movement resulted in the formation of several subsects. The central point of disagreement among these subsects concerns the identities and number of legitimate leaders, or Imāms, descended from 'Ali. Though Shī'ite Muslims disagree upon the identity of the last Imām, they all agree that the line of male descendants of 'Ali came to an end, and that the last Imām did not actually die. Instead, the Shī'a believe that the last Imām went into a miraculous concealment or occultation and remains mysteriously present in the world. The Shī'a as a whole believe that eventually this mysteriously present last Imām, the Mahdi, will return in triumph and preside in the name of Islam over a golden age of worldwide justice and peace.

Today, Shī'ite Islam accounts for about 20 percent of all Muslims, the other 80 percent being the Sunni or "traditionalists." There have been attempts to instigate a pan-Islamic reconciliation between Sunni Islam and the various sects of Shī'ite Islam, but these attempts have been unsuccessful for the most part. By and large, the various segments of Islam maintain their respective claims to be the only valid form of the religion.

Moreover, each of the segments of Islam tends to regard Islam – as they interpret and practice it – as the only adequate path to salvation. Such exclusion of other religions and of other forms of one's own religion is not, of course, unique to the history of Islam. Sectarian divisiveness and an exclusionist attitude toward other religions are prominent in the religious history of humankind as a whole. Nonetheless, exclusivism is more prominent in present day Islam than in the modern forms of the other religions we have examined. It appears, moreover, that exclusivism is an inherent part of Islam's symbolic expression of the ultimately real.

As a symbolic expression, exclusivism need not be condemned as narrowmindedness or feared as intolerance. Given its long history and the variety of cultures it has absorbed, Islam has been a remarkably tolerant religion, and the religion as a whole cannot be accurately characterized as narrowminded. Over the centuries Islam has tolerated many forms of spirituality in its midst, and Muslim thinkers have given careful consideration to alien modes of religion. On the whole, though, Islam has proved decisive in its rejection of doctrinal innovations that cannot be squared comfortably with Qur'ānic revelation. Absence of doctrinal innovation is the ideal of most religions; in Islam it is largely a reality. Both Sunni Islam and most of the sects of Shī'ite Islam endorse a religion remarkably similar to that propagated by the Prophet Muhammad nearly fourteen hundred years ago.

Even though most religious people the world over think that they adhere to an unadulterated form of their religion, the "exclusivism" with which Islam protects its original doctrines and practices has often been regarded as a negative aspect of the religion. This perceived exclusion of other modes of religion and behavior is perhaps the most notable of the characteristics that make Islam unattractive to Westerners. Other such apparent characteristics of Islam are its literalistic understanding of salvation in heaven and damnation in hell and its insistence upon predeterminism. Happily, precisely these three difficult aspects of Islam – exclusivism, literalism, and predeterminism – provide effective points of entry for our examination of Islam's ultimate referent under the headings undeniability, desirability, and elusiveness.

Undeniability

Spiritual Symbolism of Undeniability

Like the other theistic religions examined earlier, Islam asserts the necessary existence of God. As in Judaism and Christianity, this assertion may be regarded as a symbolic expression of the human necessity of assent to the *reality* of God. As in the cases of Judaism and Christianity, the necessity of assent to the reality of God is expressed in Islam as the necessity of assent to the doctrines of the religion that mediates this assent for its adherents. At the present time, Islam is more insistent than any other major religion on exclusive and unreserved acceptance of its doctrines in an orthodox form. Our purpose here is not to condemn or condone exclusivism in Islam or in any other religion, but rather to attempt to understand religious exclusivism as spiritual symbolism of the undeniability of an ultimate reality. For this purpose, Islam is an ideal example, since an exclusivistic attitude, though not necessarily an intolerant attitude, is written into the Islamic doctrine of God from its origins. Such exclusivism, and even active religious intolerance, may be regarded as a symbolic *appeal for personal consent to the inevitability of living with reference to an ultimate spiritual reality.*

In Islam, and in religions that share its exclusivistic attitude, rejection of other religious alternatives may be seen as symbolizing the ultimacy and urgency of establishing such *inevitable reference*. The ultimacy of such reference is reflected in Islam's ultimate claim to exclusive validity as a world view. The urgency of establishing such reference is expressed symbolically as the dire consequences of not affirming Islam to the exclusion of all other world views, whether religious or secular. Islam's exclusion of other religious orientations is manifest in its uncompromising claim to be the only true or salvific religion. Its exclusion of competing secular orientations appears as the aspiration of Islamic law to exert universal jurisdiction.

Islam's claim to be the only true religion is evident in the Muslim confession of faith, the *Shahāda*. This twofold confession – "There is no god but Allāh; Muḥammad is the prophet of Allāh" – does not merely proclaim monotheism. It implicitly rejects all other religions, even other forms of monotheism, which conceive of God differently from the Qur'ān or "recitation" that Muḥammad received from Allāh. This Qur'ān is regarded as the complete and final revelation of God's will for humankind. It supersedes and completes all previous revelations and precludes any further revelations from God. Thus, Muḥammad is no mere prophet, as for example Moses or Jesus, or other biblical figures recognized as prophets in the Qur'ān. He is the "seal of prophecy," the conduit of God's final and complete revelation. In making this twofold confession of faith, the Muslim asserts essentially that there is no valid object of religion other than Allāh, and that there is no valid means of addressing this object other than Islam, the religion proclaimed through Muḥammad.

Ideally, the *shahāda* will be the first words a Muslim hears upon birth and the last words heard before death. It will be heard and repeated countless times between these endpoints of human existence, and will figure prominently in every public or private religious observance in a Muslim's life. In such circumstances, the *shahāda* takes on an aura of undeniability that makes it the standard by which all other truths may be judged. In this light, the *shahāda* itself may be regarded as symbolizing the undeniability of Allāh. It becomes for the Muslim a prerational appeal for consent to the *inevitability of living with reference to the ultimately real.*

We are more concerned, however, with the exclusivism implicit in the *shahāda*. All Islam may be viewed as an elaboration upon the *shahāda's* confident avowal of ultimate truth. If the *shahāda*, with all its implications, is indeed true, it is obviously of universally ultimate concern. If it is true, failure to affirm Allāh in the manner prescribed in the Qur'ān, the ultimate revelation of his will, is an ultimately significant mistake. Such failure would indeed constitute complete disorientation in life. It would render one's life a futile foraging after insignificant or illusory criteria of value and meaning. If, in short, Allāh as revealed in the Qur'ān is the one omniscient and omnipotent God from whom all creation comes and to whom all creation returns on judgment day, then a Muslim does no one a service by passively tolerating ignorance or denial of this fact. Islam's exclusion of all other religions is, then, actually a claim to *include* all people in the ultimate plan revealed in the Qur'ān.

To some extent, such exclusion of other religious alternatives is implicit in the truth claims of each of the religions examined herein. Each of these religions, however, contains doctrinal elements that mitigate the urgency of this implicit exclusivism. In Hinduism and Buddhism, the doctrine of karma and rebirth allows the possibility of accomplishing in another lifetime proper orientation toward the respective ultimate truths that these religions claim to enshrine. The doctrine of grace in Christianity and the limited universalism of Judaism similarly make possible the coexistence of tolerance and claims to enshrine ultimate truth. Each of these religions has developed its own characteristic expressions of the undeniability of its ultimate referent and of the ultimacy and urgency of response thereto. From the standpoint of world theology, the apparent intolerance toward other faiths and toward internal doctrinal variation may be viewed as Islam's characteristic expression of the ultimacy and urgency of *living with reference to the central spiritual reality of humankind.*

This interpretation of Islamic exclusivism as a symbolic expression of the undeniability of a central spiritual reality gains force when one considers the doctrinal basis of Islam's exclusion of other modes of affirming and responding to the ultimately real. According to Islam, the primary impropriety of non-Islamic modes of addressing the ultimate referent of human life is *shirk*, "associationism." The term *shirk* means in essence "idolatry" and includes religious adoration of anything or anyone save Allāh, as well as associating anything or anyone with Allāh in his power. Allāh is strictly beyond compare. The Qur'ān proclaims *shirk* to be the only sin Allāh will not forgive.

Lo! Allāh forgiveth not that a partner should be ascribed unto him. He forgiveth (all) save that to whom He will. Whoso ascribeth partners to Allāh, he hath indeed invented a tremendous sin.

(Q 4:48)[1]

Shirk includes not only worship of nature and idols, but also employing images of any sort in worship, no matter how sophisticated their use: "And those who choose protecting friends beside Him (say): We worship them only that they may bring us near unto Allāh" (Q 39:3). It

---

1 We follow Muhammad M. Pickthall, *The Meaning of the Glorious Qur'ān* (London: Allen and Unwin, 1930; reprint, New York: Mentor, n.d.) for translation of Qur'anic passages. Square brackets enclose our clarifications.

includes angels and even excessive veneration of human beings, whether as saints, heroes, leaders, or exemplars: "They have taken as lords beside Allāh their rabbis and their monks and the Messiah son of Mary" (Q 9:31). It includes conceptual associations such as the Christian trinity, and finally, it even includes excessive sensual indulgence: "Hast thou seen him who chooseth for his god his own lust?" (Q 25:43).

According to Islam, some of the beliefs and practices of all other religions fall under one or another of these categories of *shirk*. Internally, debates between sects of Islam typically focus upon attributing *shirk* to opposing doctrines and denying it in one's own. In this way, the doctrine of *shirk* is the basis of Islamic exclusivism, both external and internal. If such exclusivism is regarded as a symbolic expression of the undeniability of an ultimate spiritual referent, the doctrine of *shirk* may be regarded as a conceptual exercise in the definition of this referent as "that than which nothing greater can be conceived." We argued in Chapter One that the undeniability of a central spiritual reality of humankind results from the existential necessity of behaving in response to a nonmaterial, ultimately desirable reality, which is concisely described in Anselm's definition. The Muslim repudiation of *shirk* expresses the incomparable greatness of Allāh by inexorably pushing one's contemplation of Islam's ultimate referent toward the greatest conceivable reality. If one conceives of Allāh in any terms save absolute, self-sufficient, incomparable greatness, one risks *shirk*. Attempting to avoid *shirk* leads one perpetually beyond limited understandings of Allāh, which rely on associating the ultimately real with philosophical concepts and mythological imagery. In this function, the doctrine of *shirk* may be regarded as a general symbolic expression of the unsurpassable greatness and hence undeniability of the central spiritual reality of humankind.

More specifically, the doctrine of *shirk* is spiritual symbolism of the undeniability of an ultimate spiritual referent in that it urges *personal consent to the inevitability of living with reference to an ultimate reality.* On the one hand, of course, fear itself, fear of the dire consequences of *shirk*, might inspire a limited form of *personal consent*, but more important, the gravity of the consequences of *shirk* may be taken to symbolize the gravity of the issue at stake for humankind. According to Islam, the human being is Allāh's viceregent on earth (Q 2:30), and even the angels were commanded to do obeisance to Adam when he was created (Q 2:34). Humans degrade themselves when they set any other than Allāh above themselves, for humans stand above all else in the created universe.

He (Moses) said: Shall I seek for you a god other than Allāh when He hath favored you above (all) creatures?

(Q 7:140)

Understood in this way, the doctrine of *shirk* is almost an anticipation of Feuerbach's criticisms of the degrading and debilitating effects of worshiping a humanoid God. The issue at stake with *shirk* is human dignity, whether people will grant valid, clean assent to their inborn spiritual urge or assent to it perversely, thereby trivializing their lives.

A similitude of those who disbelieve in their Lord: Their works are as ashes which the wind bloweth hard upon a stormy day. They have no control of aught that they have earned. That is the extreme failure.

(Q 14:18)

Eternal damnation, the penalty for *shirk*, may be seen as spiritual symbolism of the immediate degradation attendant upon dissipating one's spiritual life and, as a consequence, one's entire human life in superstitious, vain pursuits, and vague hopes and fears. The eternality of damnation may be regarded as indicating the immediate ultimacy of the failure to orient one's life consistently and coherently with reference to an ultimate spiritual reality.

With recourse to the concept of *shirk*, Islam expresses the unsurpassable greatness and undeniability of the central spiritual reality of humankind in a unique and effective way. By declaring *shirk* the deadliest of all sins, it expresses in a uniquely effective way the urgency of anchoring one's inevitable spiritual orientation in its source, the affirmation of unlimited perfection, rather than dissipating it in a welter of vain superstitions. By insisting that Islam is the only religion that avoids *shirk*, and positing conversion or the direst of consequences, it emphasizes the urgency of these concerns. By declaring the inferiority of all other religions in the course of all this, Islam has done nothing that other major religions had not done before it.

Some outside observers claim that Islam is also intolerant of individual differences within its own boundaries. It seems to place overmuch emphasis upon conformity in the externals of religion, the observance of religious injunctions and prohibitions. It seems to neglect and even suppress the intellectual and contemplative aspects of religion. Many Muslims would deny this, but it is clear that Islam does emphasize law and obedience more than than contemplation and knowledge.

Resistance of individual and sectarian deviation in Islam is a direct result of this emphasis on law and obedience. This emphasis, in turn, results from Islam's insistence upon *living with reference to Allāh* to the exclusion of all other orientations. Because of this emphasis upon law and obedience, conformity assumes unique importance in Islam. Conformity is important, moreover, not only in religious matters but also in areas regarded as secular in many other religions. Islam claims to enshrine not only ultimate truth, but also Allāh's will regarding all aspects of religious, social, political, and economic conduct. This claim of Islamic law (*sharī'a*) to universal jurisdiction may be regarded as further expression of the *inevitability of living with reference to an ultimate reality.*

Islam does not recognize any distinction between church and state, between sacred and secular. All waking life is to be pervaded by Islam, hence the phenomena of Islamic law and the Islamic state. Actually, many Muslims have abandoned the concept of the Islamic state governed exclusively by Islamic law. The majority of Muslims now live in secular states with secular law codes. These changes have not diminished the vigor of Islam in such countries. Therefore we may conclude that control of the state and the law is not indispensable for Islam. It appears likely that, like the Caliphate, actual Islamic states, in the classical sense of administering Muslim law exclusively, will vanish without weakening Islam itself.

Still, Islam claims the right to control society and the state. Such a claim, even if largely unheeded, demands explanation, especially since Islam makes it clear that if it is given the opportunity, it is prepared to legislate every aspect of society. This regulatory tendency in Islam is not without parallel in other religions. The so-called moral majority in the United States is eager to exercise control over society as a whole. Buddhism has often exerted great influence over societies by influencing their rulers and, in Tibet, actually controlled the government directly for many centuries. The Hindu caste system, codified in the Dharma Shastra, has claimed for millennia to enshrine the laws that, in a righteous society, would govern every aspect of the individual's behavior. Although the regulatory tendency is marked in Islam, it is not unique to Islam, and in seeking to understand it, we approach a phenomenon of universal religious significance.

Whether legislative control of society by any religion is a good thing or a bad thing is not our concern. We maintain only that aspiration for such control is understandable in terms of spiritual symbolism of the undeniability of the central spiritual reality of humankind. The grievous consequences of *shirk* and disbelief may be regarded as an expression of the inevitability of recognizing the ultimately spiritual orientation of human life. Islam's emphasis upon legislative control of society may be seen as an expression of the ubiquitous significance of this orientation.

We have suggested that the essence of the spiritual orientation of human life is preference, recognition of a "better," which implies a best, perfection. We urge this not as a philosophical argument but rather as an existential necessity, an affirmation, perhaps preconscious, that comes into play with every preference, no matter how trivial, for which there is no immediate material motivation. In claiming the right to regulate all as-

pects of life, whether the claim itself is reasonable or not, Islam emphasizes that every human action is a religious action, ultimately comprehensible only when viewed in the context of an ultimate, nonmaterial source
of meaning and purpose. Religious life is not confined to the mosque on
Friday afternoons, but is lived on the job, in the marketplace, and at
home, while eating, toiling, trading, making love or war, raising a family,
socializing, or disputing. A Qur'ānic verse reminiscent of the Buddhist
Satipaṭṭhāna Sutta urges one to "remember Allāh, standing, sitting and
reclining" (Q 4:104).[2] Buddhism urges mindful meditation in a similar
comprehensive list of human activities; Islam urges obedience of Islamic
law as it impinges upon every imaginable human activity. Each, in its own
way, emphasizes the pervasive influence of an ultimate spiritual reality in
human affairs. Islam employs spiritual symbolism, in the form of religious
law, as *an appeal for personal consent,* in the form of enthusiastic obedience, *to the inevitability of living one's entire life with reference to Allāh.*

The term Islam, meaning "submission," is often said to denote a twofold submission to Allāh: belief and obedience. The apparent extremes of
belief and obedience demanded by Islam have been the essential subjects
of the preceding discussions of *shirk* and *sharī'a* (associationism and law)
as spiritual symbols of the undeniability of a central spiritual reality of
humankind. In exhausting the significance of the term "Islam" itself,
spiritual symbolism subsumes the other symbolisms of undeniability in
Islam. Morality in Islam is subsumed almost entirely under obedience to
the law, the assumption being that it is for Allāh, not humans, to determine what is to be done and what is to be avoided. Morality in Islam is
not entirely a mechanical process of unthinking obedience to laws, but
there is a notable scarcity of moral philosophy that attempts to discover
the motivational principles for distinguishing good from evil and to encourage correct motivation in addition to correct action. Instead, correct
motivation is seen more as a question of complete submission to the will
of Allāh. Thus the concept of *shirk* is extended, notably by al-Ghazālī, to
include morality motivated by hope for the admiration of people, a heavenly reward, or by the arrogance of self-esteem, rather than by exclusive
devotion to Allāh.

Moral Symbolism of Undeniability

Even though mainstream Islam deemphasizes moral philosophy as such –
in favor of emphasis upon unquestioning obedience to divinely given law
– our definition of moral symbolism as *seeking to disclose, by exposing
self-contradictory behavior, the inevitability of living with reference to an*

2   See M 1:56:7; D 2:292.

ultimate spiritual reality is graphically illustrated in the Qur'ān itself. The opening *sūra* petitions Allāh to "show us the straight path, the path of those whom Thou has favored; not (the path) of those who earn Thine anger nor of those who go astray" (Q 1:1–7). "Going astray" is a common Qur'ānic assessment of the fate of those who disbelieve or disobey Allāh (e.g., Q 16:93), disobedience being tantamount to performing evil. Similarly, the synonyms *ḍalal* and *bāṭil*, signifying vanity, fruitlessness, or misguidedness, in the sense of not getting anywhere, are common Qur'ānic assessments of evil deeds, especially disbelief (*kufr*) and *shirk*. The following passage graphically depicts the evildoer as wandering helplessly from one blind alley to another in an endless maze with no exit.

39. As for those who disbelieve, their deeds are as a mirage in a desert. The thirsty one supposeth it to be water till he cometh unto it and findeth it naught, and findeth, in the place thereof, Allāh, Who payeth him his due; and Allāh is swift at reckoning.

40. Or as darkness on a vast, abysmal sea. There covereth him a wave, above which is a wave, above which is a cloud. Layer upon layer of darkness. When he holdeth out his hand he scarce can see it. And he for whom Allāh hath not appointed light, for him there is no light.

(Q 24:39–40)

This passage is a graphic representation of our argument in Chapter One that nonmaterial motivations must be viewed as converging upon a highest good. In the verses quoted above, disbelief represents failure to recognize the inevitable moral orientation of any reasonable nonmaterial motivation. The symbolism of mirages, waves, darkness, and clouds corresponds to the futility of responding randomly to divergent criteria that cannot be integrated in an overriding concept of a greatest good. Allāh's swift reckoning reflects the immediate consequences of *self-contradictory behavior* based on insufficient contemplation of the inescapable realities of human existence: failure to live a fully conscious human life with legitimate meaning and purpose.

The evildoer, of course, does not recognize that Allāh's reckoning is swift. It is swift only from the divine perspective, not from the human. From the human perspective, evildoers may escape the self-contradictory consequences of their actions for an entire lifetime or even for generations. They may even prosper and be admired for the apparent fruits of their consistently selfish actions. Similarly, the good may not enjoy tangible rewards for their goodness for the duration of a lifetime and may be repressed for generations. From the divine perspective, however, a human lifetime or an entire dynasty represents equally paltry moments of time. Islam consistently urges humankind not to view their lives and deeds from a mundane perspective, according to whether they result in prosperity or deprivation. Instead, Islam urges that human deeds and lives be viewed from the ultimate perspective of their eternal consequences as damnation or salvation. Many readers may reject the concepts of eternal damnation and salvation, but few will fail to recognize that in their context these represent powerful symbolic expressions of *the inevitability of living with reference to an ultimate spiritual reality*. In Islam, this inevitability is represented eschatologically as divine judgment and eternal reward or punishment. In the context of world theology, we suggest that this Islamic expression may be viewed as a graphic symbolic representation of the consequences of being bound by the nature of the human condition to attempt to respond consistently to the nonmaterial motivations that continually impinge upon human life. The Qur'ān urges such consistency upon the faithful as follows:

It is not righteousness that ye turn your faces to the East and the West; but righteous is he who believeth in Allāh and the Last Day and the angels and the Scripture and the Prophets; and giveth his wealth, for love of Him, to kinsfolk and to orphans and the needy and the wayfarer and to those who ask, and to set slaves free; and observeth proper worship and payeth the poor-due. And those who keep their treaty when they make one, and the patient in tribulation and adversity and time of stress. Such are they who are sincere. Such are the God-fearing.

(Q 2:177)

Although it urges the attempt, Islam recognizes and reiterates that humans are incapable of assuming a divine or ultimate perspective on their lives and deeds. Humans are therefore inherently and continuously tempted toward self-serving behavior, regardless of its consequences for others.

Say (unto them): If ye possessed the treasures of the mercy of my Lord, ye would surely hold them back for fear of spending, for man is ever grudging.

(Q 17:100)

Given the inherent selfishness of human beings, it is also often the case that self-serving, other-destroying behavior is applauded by individual people and whole societies. It is equally true that good behavior may be condemned and punished, not only by errant individuals, but by society as a whole. It is a simple historical fact that human beings and societies have never been able effectively to agree upon what is good and what is evil. The Qur'ān repeatedly emphasizes the inability of human societies to determine what is good, even what is good for themselves, by recalling the judgment and destruction of entire societies by Allāh, for example the people of 'Ad and Thamūd (Q 11:50–68). The Qur'ān repeatedly exhorts believers to recall the dismal fates of societies that have existed previously (Q 3:137; 6:11; 7:84; 10:39; 12:109; 16:36; etc.). At the same time the Qur'ān urges that human society does not and cannot evolve justice and goodness from its own resources, even after the cumulative experiences of many peoples.

38. He saith: Enter into the Fire among nations of the jinn (demons) and human-kind who passed away before you. Every time a nation entereth, it curseth its sister (nation) till, when they all have been made to follow one another thither, the last of them saith unto the first of them: Our Lord! These led us astray, so give them double torment. . . .
39. And the first of them saith unto the last of them: Ye were no whit better than us, so taste the doom for what ye used to earn.

(Q 7:38–9)

Such reasoning undergirds Islam's insistence that the criteria of morality reside entirely with Allāh. This insistence accounts for Islam's deemphasis of moral philosophy and its emphasis instead upon divine law (sharī'a). From the standpoint of Islam, moral philosophy is at best an indeterminate groping toward the good, doomed ultimately to falter short of its goal. At worst it can become a positive inducement toward evil. Entire nations – on the basis of principles derived from cumulative human attempts to define and encode the desirable – devise laws and customs that cause great inequality and suffering and which lead their adherents far astray from legitimately spiritual lives.

46. Have they not travelled in the land, and have they hearts wherewith to feel and ears wherewith to hear? For indeed it is not the eyes that grow blind, but it is the hearts, which are within the bosoms, that grow blind.
47. And they will bid thee hasten on the Doom, and Allāh faileth not His promise, but lo! a Day with Allāh is as a thousand years of what you reckon.
48. And how many a township did I suffer long though it was sinful! Then I grasped it. Unto Me is the return.
49. Say: O mankind! I am only a plain warner to you.

(Q 22:46–9)

Many would not accept the alternative proposed by Islam, but few could fail to accept that human attempts to discover and implement the principles of a truly just society have invariably failed. Islam insists that the principles of morality and its implementation are available to human-kind only through divine revelation. Muslims recognize that many prophets before Muḥammad have revealed these principles within the societies in which they lived, but that in each case these societies have failed to live up to these principles.

If they had observed the Torah and the Gospel and that which was revealed unto them from their Lord, they would surely have been nourished from above them and from beneath their feet. Among them there are people who are moderate, but many of them are of evil conduct.

(Q 5:66)

Islam asserts that through Muḥammad, whom Muslims regard as the final complete revealer of the entirety of the divine will for humankind, Allāh finally and definitively revealed not only the basic principles, but also the precise rules and procedures for society that will guarantee the actualization of good and welfare for all.

These principles, rules, and procedures are enshrined in the *sharī'a* or divine law of Islam. This divine law, which according to Islam constitutes the only reliable foundation for human society, is based on two sources, the Qur'ān and the Ḥadīth, a body of literature that records carefully verified words and actions of Muhammad. From these two sources alone, Muslims have derived a code of law that they regard as both necessary and sufficient for the establishment and maintenance of a just and moral human society. This attitude is of course diametrically opposite to the Christian admonition to render unto Caesar the things that are Caesar's, which serves as the ideological basis of the Western doctrine of the separation of church and state. As a result many Westerners find great difficulty in sympathizing with the Islamic concept of divine law governing an Islamic state. As moral symbolism of the undeniability of Allāh, however, the Islamic concept of *sharī'a* is immediately comprehensible. In claiming that Islamic law is an entirely sufficient basis for the governance of human society, indeed that it is the only sufficient basis, Islam *seeks to disclose the inevitability of living with reference to an ultimate spiritual reality by exposing self-contradictory behavior.*

Living in a society governed by laws, however primitive, is a universal of the human experience. No human lives other than in the context of some sort of community in which one is accountable to laws. Although most Muslims now live in societies governed primarily by secular legal codes, Muslims generally assert that this is an undesirable state of affairs and that it would be preferable to live in a society governed entirely by the *sharī'a*. In such a society, one would be held immediately accountable, by civil authorities, for actions and omissions for which one will ultimately be held accountable by Allāh. In such a society, civil authority itself would serve as a concrete, ever-present symbol of the will of Allāh and the ultimate accountability of humankind to that will. The self-contradictory nature of violating the laws of one's society and risking punishment is immediately apparent. The self-contradictory nature of violating divine law is less apparent to fundamentally selfish and wayward humans, but

Islam asserts that the risk and the punishment for such behavior are inevitable and absolute. The sociologist Emile Durkheim noted prominently the similarity between God and society, in that both are seen as establishing and enforcing laws. Durkheim's conclusion with regard to religion was negative, asserting that God is a deification of society, an unconscious abstraction by humankind of the power and authority that society exerts upon its members. Islam also notes the similar roles God and society play in human life but reverses Durkheim's conclusion by regarding legitimate society as an embodiment and instrument of God's will. As there is only one God, so ideally there should be only one society encompassing all of humankind and governed by the will of Allāh as explicitly revealed in the *sharī'a*. Many might not wish to participate in such a society, but the ideal of a universal Islamic society is cogent and powerful as *moral symbolism of the undeniability of a central spiritual reality of humankind.*

Mythological Symbolism of Undeniability

We suggested in Chapter One that the mythological dimension of religion *expresses undeniability as irresistibility by employing images of power.* In Islam, such mythological symbolism is particularly evident, couched primarily in terms of creation and eschatology. The Qur'ān also contains much anecdotal mythology with characters and plots similar to those in Arabian, Jewish, and Christian myths. In each case, narrative mythological material in the Qur'ān is expressly didactic in character. In most cases it illustrates the unity and greatness of Allāh and often seeks to validate the prophethood of Muḥammad. The large preponderance of mythological symbolism in Islam thus serves exclusively to reinforce the *shahāda:* "There is no God but Allāh. Muḥammad is the prophet of Allāh." In Islam, mythology is not, as it is in some religions, a distinct dimension from which moral or theological doctrines are extrapolated. This single-minded focus of Islamic mythology upon Allāh makes it an ideal illustration of the concept of mythology as symbolism disclosing the undeniability of the central spiritual reality of humankind.

Creation of the universe and "ownership" of the day of judgment stand out in the Qur'ān as the most potent symbols of the unsurpassable greatness and undeniability of Allāh, as the following quotation states:

2. Allāh it is who raised up the heavens without visible supports, then mounted the Throne, and compelled the sun and the moon to be of service, each runneth unto an appointed term; He ordereth the course; He detaileth the revelations, that haply ye may be certain of the meeting of your Lord.
3. And He it is who spread out the earth and placed therein firm hills and

flowing streams, and of all fruits he placed therein two spouses (male and female). He covereth the night with the day. Lo! Herein verily are portents for people who take thought. . . .

12. He it is who showeth you the lightning, a fear and a hope, and raiseth the heavy clouds.
13. The thunder hymneth His praise and (so do) the angels for awe of Him. He launcheth the thunder-bolts and smiteth with them whom He will while they dispute (in doubt) concerning Allāh, and He is mighty in wrath.
14. Unto Him is the real prayer. Those unto whom they pray beside Allāh respond to them not at all, save as (is the response to) one who stretcheth forth his hands toward water (asking) that it may come unto his mouth, and it will never reach it. The prayer of disbelievers goeth (far) astray.
15. And unto Allāh falleth prostrate whosoever is in the heavens and the earth, willingly or unwillingly, as do their shadows in the morning and the evening hours.

(Q 13:2-3, 12-15)

Islam regards the physical universe as Muslim, in that it *submits*, by way of natural law, to the will of Allāh. Human beings, however, are capable of a willing submission in that they may welcome submission to Allāh. The choice in Islam is not between submission and nonsubmission, for one does what Allāh wills in any case, even in disbelief and disobedience. The choice is rather one of welcoming this inevitable submission or struggling vainly against it, as the preceding passage urges powerfully. The undeniability of Allāh and the futility of recalcitrance are further illustrated in terms of symbols of final judgment, again in images of power.

7. Surely that which ye are promised will befall.
8. So when the stars are put out,
9. And when the sky is riven asunder,
10. And when the mountains are blown away.
11. And when the messengers are brought unto their time appointed –
12. For what day is the time appointed?
13. For the Day of Decision.
14. And what will convey unto thee what the Day of Decision is! –
15. Woe unto the repudiators on that Day! . . .

25. Have We not made the earth a receptacle
26. Both for the living and the dead,
27. And placed therein high mountains and given you to drink sweet water therein?
28. Woe unto the repudiators on that day!
29. (It will be said unto them:) Depart unto that (doom) which ye used to deny;
30. Depart unto the shadow falling threefold.

31. (Which yet is) no relief nor shelter from the flame.
32. Lo! it throweth up sparks like castles,
33. (Or) as it might be camels of bright yellow hue.
34. Woe unto the repudiators on that day!
35. This is the day wherein they speak not,
36. Nor are they suffered to put forth excuses.
37. Woe unto the repudiators on that day!
38. This is the Day of Decision, We have brought you and the men of old together.
39. If now ye have any wit, outwit Me.

(Q 77:7–39)

The absolute power of Allāh over all that lies between the termini of creation and judgment is frequently illustrated with brief references to anecdotal myths such as the destruction by storm of the people of ʿĀd (Q 41:15–16), the destruction by earthquake of the people of Thamūd (Q 7:74), or the destruction of Noah's contemporaries by flood (Q 11:25–48). In each of these cases, the calamity is a punishment for rejecting prophets sent to the respective peoples, as Muḥammad was rejected in Mecca. Allāh is also pictured as intervening in history as a savior. He rescued Mecca from an Abyssinian invasion by sending a flock of miraculous birds, which pelted the invader with smallpox-producing pebbles (Q 105:1–5). In other instances, Allāh's power over man and nature is illustrated in subtler myths, such as the granting of a child to Abraham's wife in old age (Q 11:69–73), or the three-hundred-year sleep induced upon the "seven sleepers" (Q 18:10–27). In none of the anecdotal myths recounted in the Qur'ān do the events have any normative significance of their own. Instead, the anecdotes are used as direct illustrations of the undeniability and irresistibility of Allāh. The concluding verses of the parable of the seven sleepers are a good illustration of the Qur'ān's lack of concern with the narrative details of myths.

23. (Some) will say: They were three, their dog the fourth, and (some) say: Five, their dog the sixth, guessing at random; and (some) say: Seven, and their dog the eighth. Say (O Muhammad) : My Lord is best aware of their number. None knoweth them save a few. So contend not concerning them except with an outward contending, and ask not any of them to pronounce concerning them. . . .

26. And (it is said) they tarried in their cave three hundred years and add nine
27. Say: Allāh is best aware how long they tarried. His is the invisible of the heavens and the earth. How clear of sight is He and keen of hearing! They have no protecting friend beside Him, and He maketh none to share in His government.

(Q 18:23–7)

Mythological symbolism in Islam expresses undeniability as the *irre-sistibility* of Allāh in all matters, great and small. Allāh's will is omnipresent in all creation and decisive even in apparently trivial events. The undeniability of Allāh is expressed mythologically in Islam as true omnipotence as opposed to the omnicompetence ascribed to God in Judaism and Christianity. Whether or not any theistic God exists or has any of the powers ascribed to God in the theistic religions, one can recognize such ascriptions as mythological symbolism expressing the undeniability in human life of assent to an ultimate referent of meaning and purpose.

Intellectual Symbolism of Undeniability

As some of the foregoing might suggest, Islam as a whole has seldom shown great interest in philosophy. To be sure, Muslims were instrumental in preserving much of Greek and Roman philosophy, and Muslims number among the great philosophers of history. Islam itself, however, has remained largely defiant of the implications of philosophical thought for religious doctrine, preferring to remain firmly based on revelation alone. The Mu'tazila movement, which attempted to square Qur'ānic revelation with rational thought, enjoyed some influence for a limited time. But this movement was eclipsed entirely by the conservative thought of ibn-Ḥanbal, al-Ash'arī, and finally al-Ghazālī. Al-Ghazālī employed philosophical methods resembling Hume's skepticism to argue that philosophy, by its own criteria, is incapable of arriving at certain knowledge even of mundane things. One cannot even establish beyond doubt that apparent causes have any real relationship to their apparent effects. If even such mundane things elude philosophical reasoning, argued al-Ghazālī, rational thought clearly cannot claim to evaluate revelation. Rejecting philosophical critique and evaluation, Islam has been largely consistent in not adducing philosophical support for its doctrine, which it regards as founded wholly upon revelation.

See ye not how Allāh hath made serviceable unto you whatsoever is in the skies and whatsoever is in the earth and hath loaded you with His favours both without and within? Yet of mankind is he who disputeth concerning Allāh, without knowledge or guidance or a Scripture giving light.

(Q 31:20)

Following the spirit of this verse, Islamic theology (*kalām*) and jurisprudence (*fiqh*) strictly limit the role of human reason in formulating their respective canons. The sources and methods of valid knowledge are strictly limited to the following: First in authority is the Qur'ān. Second to the Qur'ān is the Ḥadīth literature, accounts of the sayings and doings of the Prophet Muḥammad. Third is *ijmā*ʿ, the consensus of the Muslim community, usually limited to the early community of immediate associates of the Prophet. Fourth is *qiyās* or "analogy"; if the previous three sources do not speak definitively upon a given point, a close analogy may be made with a point upon which they do speak clearly in order to derive a valid answer. Beyond this, human reason may not go. Sunni Islam allows to only four people in history the prerogative of *ijtihād* or "opinion" based on the first principles of Islamic law. These are the jurists abū Ḥanīfa, Mālik ibn Anas, al-Shāfiʿī, and ibn Ḥanbal – and the latter two themselves rejected *ijtihād* as a means of valid knowledge! In Shiʿite Islam, *ijtihād* remains the prerogative of an elite of specifically designated religious leaders. Although these exalted persons must undergo rigorous scholarly training, it is by virtue of their alleged divine guidance, more than their exceptional intellectual power, that they have the prerogative of *ijtihād*. To be sure, there have been rationalist movements in Islam, but these have made little impact on the mainstream of the religion, and have made few inroads upon the absolute authority of revelation.

Nonetheless, Qur'ānic revelation appeals to the human intellect with what may broadly be termed *intellectual symbolism*. Most such symbolism, as one might expect, is of the cosmological sort, appealing for reasoned assent to the reality and power of Allāh on the basis of evidence in nature.

53. We shall show them our portents on the horizons and within themselves until it will be manifest onto them that it is the Truth. Doth not thy Lord suffice, since he is witness over all things?
54. How! Are they still in doubt about the meeting with their Lord? Lo! Is not He surrounding all things?

(Q 41:53–4)

The appeal implicit in many such passages, referring to Allāh's creation and governance of the universe, is explicit in the following verses.

Who hath appointed the earth a resting-place for you, and the sky a canopy: and causeth water to pour down from the sky, thereby producing fruits as food for you? And do not set up rivals to Allāh when you know (better).

(Q 2:22)

Lo! In the creation of the heavens and the earth and (in) the difference of night and day are tokens (of His sovereignty) for men of understanding.

(Q 3:190)

Is not He (best) Who created the heavens and the earth, and sendeth down for you water from the sky wherewith We cause to spring forth joyous orchards, whose trees it never hath been yours to cause to grow? Is there any God beside Allāh? Nay, but they are folk who ascribe equals (unto Him)!

(Q 27:60)

61. And if thou wert to ask them: Who created the heavens and the earth, and constrained the sun and the moon (to their appointed work)? they would say: Allāh. How then are they turned away?

63. And if thou wert to ask: Who causeth water to come down from the sky, and therewith reviveth the earth after its death? they verily would say: Allāh. Say: Praise be to Allāh! But most of them have no sense.

(Q 29:61, 63)

Passages such as the preceding may be viewed as symbolic expressions, cast in terms of cosmology, urging that *Allāh is real, and is the reality upon which all other realities depend and from which they derive their ultimate meaning.* Here, as in the other theistic religions, the reality of God is expressed in terms of necessary existence, and the derivative and dependent nature of other realities is expressed in terms of their created-ness – their contingent existence.

Alongside evidence in nature, Muslims regard the literary excellence of the Qur'ān as intellectually persuasive evidence of the existence of Allāh. The Qur'ān is widely regarded, even by non-Muslim speakers of Arabic, as the inimitable standard of Arabic literature. Its recitation can rouse aesthetic rapture in the faithful, a phenomenon known as the "lawful magic" of the Qur'ān. Muslims argue that a work of such beauty and majesty could not conceivably be the product of a human mind, and therefore must be divine. The Qur'ān itself issues the following challenge to any who would deny its status as revealed truth.

And if ye are in doubt concerning that which We reveal unto Our slave (Muhammad), then produce a *sūrah* of the like thereof, and call your witnesses beside Allāh if ye are truthful.

(Q 2:23)

Related to the theological proof based on the literary excellence of the Qur'ān is the cardinal Islamic doctrine of the illiteracy of Muhammad.

And thou (O Muhammad) wast not a reader of any scripture before it, nor didst thou write it with thy right hand, for then might those have doubted, who follow falsehood.

(Q 29:48)

Many non-Muslim scholars have expressed doubt that Muhammad really was illiterate, but in Islam, Muhammad's illiteracy is a doctrine analogous to the Christian doctrine of the virginity of Mary. It is not merely a historical proposition that may be proved or disproved. It is a premise, founded on trusted tradition, upon which intellectual appeals for the authenticity of divine revelation may be based. For Christians, this revelation is Christ himself. For Muslims, it is the Qur'ān. Humans cannot be virgins and have children, nor can they normally be illiterate and produce great literary works. In both the Muslim and the Christian cases, the improbability of such happenings, combined with the obvious and surpassing excellence of their product – Christ on the one hand and the Qur'ān on the other – combine powerfully to *establish that God is real.*

In Islam, as in Christianity, revelation – the Qur'ān in one case and Christ in the other – does not exhaust God. There is more to God than Christ and more to Allāh than his will as revealed in the Qur'ān. In each religion, however, the revelation that constitutes its wellspring is accorded the unique status of being uncreated and coeternal with God. Each of these revelations – Christ's exemplary life and the Qur'ān itself – thus becomes for its respective followers the ultimate norm of authority against which all other proposed truths may be evaluated. Even God cannot alter that which is uncreated and coeternal with God. In comparison to revealed truth, other apparent truths are unreliable, in the sense that they are created along with the universe they attempt to comprehend. Like one's sensual inclinations, one's intellectual inclinations can mislead one if pursued independently of revealed truth. For Muslims, as for Judaists and Christians, other criteria of truth, including rational criteria, are judged on the basis of their agreement with revelation, not vice versa. In terms of the present paradigm, the undeniability of the ultimately real is symbolically expressed as the undeniability of the revelation that discloses it.

In this way too, in addition to cosmological symbolism, Islam depicts Allāh as *the reality upon which all other realities depend and from which they derive their ultimate meaning.* The ontological dependence of the universe upon Allāh is paralleled by the dependence of all intellectual truths upon revealed truth. In terms of the present paradigm, the primary Islamic symbol of this dependence is the doctrine of the eternal Qur'ān.

According to this doctrine, though the Qur'ān is an accurate record of the revelations that Muhammad received from Allāh, it did not originate in the two decades during which these revelations occurred. Instead, being eternal in the form of a "guarded tablet" in heaven (Q 85:22), it preexisted its revelation. To many non-Muslims, this is absurd, since many Qur'ānic passages appear to be derived from biblical material, and since many address directly historical situations at the time of their revelation. If, however, one is willing to grant that it is conceivable that eternal truth could at some point in time break in upon the realm of temporality, there is no inherent contradiction in the notion that this breakthrough should occur in terms that address the preordained moment of revelation. If there is eternal truth, temporal truths and situations subsist entirely in the shadow thereof. There is no reason to assume that historical situations – including previous revelations like the Judaic and Christian scriptures, which Islam acknowledges as provisionally valid – should not abet the final revelation of this complete, eternal truth. Given the premise of an eternal truth, one might at most wonder how one could be certain that the Qur'ān is not only valid, and is not only one among other revelations of God's will, but also that the Qur'ān is the complete and final revelation of eternal truth.

Such certainty is possible, according to Islam, because humans have been created with foreknowledge of eternal truth ingrained in the very core of their being. Qur'ānic revelation is but a reminder (*dhikr*) of this preexisting, though often preconscious, foreknowledge. When human beings are true to themselves, Qur'ānic revelation itself is said to produce within them a certainty that other evidence of the existence of Allāh, including even miracles, can only approximate distantly.

49. But it is clear revelations in the hearts of those who have been given knowledge, and none deny our revelations save wrongdoers.
50. And they say: Why are not portents sent down upon him from his Lord? Say: Portents are with Allāh only, and I am but a plain warner.
51. Is it not enough for them that We have sent down unto thee the Scripture which is read unto them? Lo! herein verily is mercy, and a reminder [*dhikr*] for folk who believe.

(Q 29:48–51)

The concept of "reminder" or *dhikr* is of central importance in Islam. The words and gestures of the daily prayers of mainstream Islam are known as *dhikr*, as are the rituals of the Sufis. This again is essentially intellectual symbolism of the undeniability of an ultimate spiritual reality. Knowledge of the existence and unity of Allāh is represented as a remembrance rather than as an inferential assent, which could be regarded as speculative and therefore uncertain. The notion that knowledge of Allāh is a remembrance rather than an inference intertwines with the doctrine of foreknowledge in the following passage, which expresses foreknowledge in terms of a covenant.

171. And when We shook the Mount above them as it were a covering, and they supposed that it was going to fall upon them (and We said): Hold fast that which We have given you, and remember that which is therein, that ye may ward off (evil).
172. And (remember) when thy Lord brought forth from the Children of Adam,

from their reins, their seed, and made them testify of themselves, (saying): Am I not your Lord? They said: Yea, verily. We testify. (That was) lest ye should say at the Day of Resurrection: Lo! of this we were unaware.

173. Or lest ye should say: (it is) only (that) our fathers ascribed partners to Allah of old and we were (their) seed after them. Wilt Thou destroy us on account of that which those who follow falsehood did?

(Q 171–3)

Thus the backsliding of one's ancestors, the *shirk* that is passed on traditionally from generation to generation, does not absolve one from the responsibility of acknowledging the existence and unity of Allāh. This knowledge, by means of a covenant with the "Children of Adam," has been ingrained by Allāh in the human race as a whole. The following passage, though somewhat obscure, expresses this notion without recourse to covenant symbolism.

1. By the sun and his brightness,
2. And the moon when she followeth him, . . .

7. And a soul and Him who perfected it
8. And inspired it (with conscience of) what is wrong for it and (what is) right for it.

(Q 91:1–8)

The themes of reminder (*dhikr*) and the certainty (*yaqīn*) of foreknowledge are both appropriated as major elements of the Sufi expression of the undeniability of Allāh. Among the Sufis, *dhikr*, remembrance of Allāh, came to be expanded in scope far beyond formal repetitions in the ritual context. As Annemarie Schimmel writes, "The *dhikr* should permeate the mystic's whole being."[3] The primary meaning of *dhikr* in Sufism is the spiritual exercise of remembering Allāh, whether silently or through verbal repetitions. It is thus akin, as Schimmel says, to the Jesus prayer or the *nembutsu* of Japanese Amida Buddhism. (The Jesus prayer states, "Lord Jesus Christ, Son of God, have mercy on me, a sinner." The *nembutsu* states, "Homage to Amida Buddha.") The term *dhikr* retains in Sufism its connection with the doctrine of foreknowledge, as the following passage from the Sufi al-Kalābādhī, recalling Q 7:172 (quoted previously), illustrates.

Abu Muhamman Ruwaym said: "The people heard their first *dhikr* when God addressed them, saying, 'Am I not your Lord?' This *dhikr* was secreted in their intellects. So, when they heard the (Sufi) *dhikr*, the secret things of their hearts

3   Annemarie Schimmel, *Mystical Dimensions of Islam* (Chapel Hill: University of North Carolina Press, 1975), p. 171.

appeared, and they were ravished, even as the secret things of their intellects appeared when God informed them of this, and they believed."[4]

Sha'rānī, a sixteenth-century Sufi, writes of a sevenfold *dhikr*, beginning with verbal remembrance through formulaic repetitions, and culminating with the *dhikr* of "the most secret of secret," which, says Schimmel, "is the vision of the Reality of Absolute Truth (*ḥaqq al-yaqīn*)."[5] Thus the practice of *dhikr* in Sufism, in its widest sense, encompasses the entire mystical path from preliminary practices to realization of the certainty (*yaqīn*) of absolute truth (*ḥaqq*). Sufism may thus be characterized as a progressive recollection of the divine certainty ingrained in all human beings. In terms of the present model, it is the progressive realization of the human necessity of assent to an ultimate spiritual reality.

As if to emphasize that such assent is integral to human nature, the great Sufi al-Ḥallāj illustrates the three grades of certainty (*yaqīn*) with the simile of a moth drawn by nature to a flame. When the moth sees the flame, it represents intellectual certainty (*'ilm al-yaqīn*). When it draws near and feels the heat of the flame, it is gnostic or experiential certainty (*'ayn al-yaqīn*), "the vision of certainty." When finally it is consumed in the flame, it represents the final grade, "the reality of certainty" (*ḥaqq al-yaqīn*) where in there is self-annihilation through mystical union with Allāh.[6] Mainstream Islam characteristically condemns as *shirk* the Sufi notion of self-annihilation through union with Allāh. Al Ghazālī did much to alleviate this apparent conflict by interpreting the Sufi notion of union with Allāh as referring to a unity of wills rather than a unity of essence. Apparently contrary statements by Sufis such as al-Ḥallāj – who was executed by an Islamic inquisition for declaring "I am the Truth" – were interpreted by al-Ghazālī as being induced by mystical "intoxication." From the perspective of world theology, both the mysticism of al-Ḥallāj and the intolerance of his executors may be recognized as understandable and legitimate expressions of the undeniability of the central spiritual reality of humankind. In the case of al-Ḥallāj and in others like it, that the symbolic terms of these expressions were emphasized over their intent, that variance was emphasized over complementarity, can only be regarded profitably as human tragedy on the grandest scale.

Desirability

In addition to the exclusivism and intolerance that may appear to characterize Islam, at least in the largely unsympathetic Western imagination,

4 A. J. Arberry, *The Doctrine of the Sufis* (Cambridge: Cambridge University Press, 1935), p. 183.
5 Schimmel, *Dimensions*, p. 174.
6 Ibid., p. 142, from Ḥallāj's *Kitāb at-ṭawāsīn*.

the apparent literalism of the religion presents a further obstacle for those outsiders who would appreciate Islam. Recognizing this, many modern Muslim theologians offer interpretations of Islam that deemphasize its inherent literalism. In so doing, they revive the similar efforts of the Mu'tazila theologians of the eighth and ninth centuries. Regardless of such efforts, literalistic concepts of Allāh, heaven, and hell remain dominant in Islam. This literalism serves as an ideal focus for our discussion of Islam's symbolic expression of the *desirability of the central spiritual reality of humankind.*

Mythological Symbolism of Desirability

From the standpoint of world theology, it is evident that Islamic literalism is a result of an emphasis in the Qur'ān upon *mythological symbolism* expressing the desirability of Islam's ultimate referent. Such symbolism is so readily apparent that a brief discussion will serve to identify it. Despite the significant Qur'ānic disclaimer "Nothing is like Him" (Q 42:11), the Qur'ān's expression of Allāh is straightforwardly anthropomorphic. He is clearly male; he sits on a throne; he hears, sees, and speaks. He may become pleased or angry, and he moves about in heaven. He is just and merciful, and has many other specific attributes that together are known as the "99 names of Allāh."

Similarly, the eschaton over which Allāh will preside is imagined as an actual day of judgment. People on earth will be going about their business and will be surprised to hear a dreadful trumpet call and see the earth and sky rent asunder. On that day, all human beings who have ever lived will be resurrected in bodily form and will stand in awe before their Maker and be judged. The damned will be thrown into an abyss of roaring fire for eternity, and the blessed will enter a garden paradise complete with trees, rivers, couches, and fountains.

From early times in Islam there have been metaphorical interpretations of the Qur'ānic descriptions of Allāh, the eschaton, and the afterlife. Islam as a whole, however, has shown a decisive tendency to adhere to Qur'ānic literalism in these regards. Recognized as mythological symbolism, such literalism need not be regarded as naive on the one hand nor as a literal truth claim on the other hand. Instead, one may simply recognize that Islam insists upon an *evocative depiction* of an end point and aftermath of human history that serves to emphasize that all realities of mundane life *derive their value* in relation to an ultimate spiritual reality. Islam's literalistic eschatology serves to illustrate this situation by depicting an end point and aftermath of human history in the vivid terms of material reality, lest there be any doubt that all that is truly desirable in this mundane life is desirable because it is conducive to being among the blessed in the next life, a life every bit as concrete as this life. All that is not conducive to this blessed state, and in particular all that is conducive to damnation, is undesirable, regardless of its possible attractiveness.

And on the day when those who disbelieve are exposed to the Fire (it will be said): Ye squandered your good things in the life of the world and sought comfort therein. Now this day ye are rewarded with the doom of ignominy because ye were disdainful in the land without a right, and because ye used to transgress.

(Q 46:20)

According to Islam, the truly desirable realities of human life are spiritual values that presently reside in what we call the nonmaterial realm. After the judgment day, this will change. Allāh will obliterate the present material realm and bring about a "new creation" in which one's non-material virtue or sin will be concrete attributes of one's resurrected body, and one's just deserts will be physically manifest in the delights of the Garden or the torments of the Fire.

19. And (make mention of) the day when the enemies of Allāh are gathered unto the Fire, they are driven on
20. Till, when they reach it, their ears and their eyes and their skins testify against them as to what they used to do.
21. And they say unto their skins: Why testify ye against us? They say: Allāh hath given us speech Who giveth speech to all things, and Who created you at the first, and unto Whom you are returned.

(Q 41:19–21)

30. There doth every soul experience that which it did aforetime, and they are returned unto Allāh, their rightful Lord, and that which they used to invent hath failed them.

(Q 10:30)

Unlike Judaism and Christianity, Islam's overall evaluation of the material world is negative. There is a general consensus in Islam that the present world will not be transformed in the eschaton. It will be obliterated and replaced with a new universal order in which realities now regarded as spiritual will be concrete. Compared with this new creation, the present material world is deficiently real, its riches trivial and even insidious.

36. The life of the world is but a sport and a pastime. And if ye believe and ward off (evil), He will give you your wages, and will not ask of you your worldly wealth. . . .
38. Lo! Ye are those who are called to spend in the way of Allāh, yet among you there are some who hoard. And as for him who hoardeth, he hoardeth only from his soul. And Allah is the Rich, and ye are the poor.

(Q 47:36–8)

Al-Ghazālī writes:

[The wise man] considers the world as insignificant and the hereafter as great and everlasting. He considers this world and the next to be diametrically opposed to each other like two hostile friends of a man or like to co-wives.[7]

Thus, mythological symbolism in Islam emphasizes the desirability of the ultimately real by attempting to devalue the material reality that is so immediately appealing to the thoughtless. The merits of this devaluation, or the similar devaluation in Hinduism and Buddhism, are not at issue here. Our purpose is to analyze the dynamic of Islam's mythological symbolism of desirability. The essence of this dynamic is to *depict* an eschaton in *evocative*, literalistic terms that leave little to the imagination, a vivid image of a new world order in relation to which the present world pales to insignificance. In order to accomplish this, Islam's mythological symbolism of desirability asserts that in this new creation spiritual values that now must be embraced on the basis of faith will be the concrete, physical realities of life.

Spiritual Symbolism of Desirability

Islam's mythological symbolism of desirability sets the stage for its spiritual symbolism of desirability, which according to our definition *emphasizes the personal benefits of response to an ultimate spiritual reality.* The promised delights of the Garden and torments of the Fire, of course, clearly serve to emphasize the personal benefits of response to Allāh. Islam's appeal to fear of punishment and desire for reward in the hereafter, however, do not exhaust its expression of the ultimately desirable. Despite Islam's rich and literal descriptions of the sensual delights of the Garden, this in itself is not regarded as ultimately desirable. Instead what is ultimately desirable is *being with* Allāh. This concept of *being with* Allāh is expressed in the Qur'ān primarily in terms of "meeting with" (*liqā*) and "acceptance" (*ridwān*) by Allāh.

72. Allāh promiseth to believers, men and women, Gardens underneath which rivers flow, wherein they will abide – blessed dwellings in Gardens of Eden. And – greater (far)! – acceptance from Allāh.

(Q 9:72)

Literally *being with* Allāh in the blessed state is most closely approached in the human state by *being with* Allāh in will. Submitting to, and thus being in accord with Allāh's will is the very essence of Islam, the

---

7 Al-Ghazzālī, *Ihyā' 'Ulûm al-Dîn,* chap. 1, trans. Al-haj Maulana Fazul-karim as *Imam Ghazzali's Ihya Ulum-id-din* (Lahore: Sind Sagar Academy, 1971), 1:74.

religion of submission. This union of wills is thus something of a foretaste of the joys of the Garden. Such a notion becomes explicit in the writings of al-Ghazālī.

Al-Ghazālī was trained as an orthodox Islamic theologian. He was nonetheless attracted to the mystical path of the Sufis, despite mainstream Islam's hostility toward Sufism. As we have mentioned, al-Ghazālī was able to diminish this hostility by interpreting the Sufi's ecstasy of union with Allāh as a union of wills. Not only does this interpretation render Sufism more acceptable to mainstream Islam, but also it increases the power of Islam's spiritual symbolism of desirability by *emphasizing the personal benefits of living with reference to an ultimate spiritual reality.*

In Sufism itself, the primary expression of the desirability of *being with* Allāh is symbolism of "the beloved." Much Sufi poetry represents the desire to *be with* Allāh as the unrelenting and consuming passion to *be with* a lover whom one single-mindedly adores. Some of this poetry is practically indistinguishable from poetry written in the heat of the infatu-ation, adoration, and desire that characterize human sexual love.

For Shī'a Islam, *being with* Allāh is additionally symbolized by the Mahdi, the miraculously concealed last Imām. Though concealed from human eyes, the Mahdi or "guided one" is thought to be mysteriously present among humankind. The mysterious presence in this world of a divinely guided savior is the basis of the Shī'a acceptance of living religious leaders, who participate in this divine guidance. Though the foremost religious leaders of Shī'ism are not thought to be descendants of the Prophet, the mysterious presence of the last hereditary Imām is regarded as a conduit of divine guidance for these most respected figures of Shī'ite Islam. It is these leaders, known as Mujtahid, who enjoy the privilege of *ijtihād* or "authoritative opinion" with regard to matters of theology and law.

Shī'ite adoration of the Mahdi and the divinized Imāms who preceded him appears to Sunni Muslims as constituting or bordering upon *shirk,* but the notion of a divinely guided "perfect man" is a common theme throughout Islam. The Prophet Muhammad is regarded by all Muslims as being an infallible model of perfect human conduct. This is why the Ḥadith literature forms such an authoritative part of Muslim sacred lore. In addition to their own Ḥadith literature about Muhammad's deeds and speech, the Shī'a maintain a Ḥadith literature about 'Alī and the Imāms descended from him. Possibly as a result of Shī'a influence, belief in the coming of an infallible savior at the end of time is common, though not obligatory, among Sunni Muslims as well as Shī'ites.

Though often condemned as *shirk* by the ultraorthodox, the veneration of saints' tombs is widespread throughout Islam, Sunni and Shī'a. The most holy of these tombs belong to Sufi masters who are widely regarded as having attained in their lifetimes the status of the "perfect man." Sufism justifies its doctrine of the perfect man by citing the famous Qur'ānic verse:

We verily created man and we know what his soul whispereth to him, and We are nearer to him than his jugular vein.

(Q 50:16)

It is widely accepted among Sufis that in the innermost soul of every person there is a point at which the human intersects the divine. One who finds this point at the center of one's being becomes the perfect man, a flawless mirror simultaneously reflecting this world and the other, exhibiting both human and divine perfection. The tombs of such saints are widely thought to radiate *baraka*, a spiritual power of blessing, and devout Muslims will undertake long pilgrimages to partake of the sanctifying aura of these tombs. It is as if by being physically near even to the mortal remains of one who has been near to Allāh one comes nearer to Allāh oneself.

Regardless of disagreements in Islam about the proper assessment of the human potential for perfection and nearness to Allāh, we regard the foregoing examples of perfection in human form as symbolic of the desirability of an ultimate spiritual reality. Like the theme of the union of divine and human wills, they express yet another dimension of *being with* Allāh. Both the Sufi attempt to realize perfect humanness and the popular veneration of saints and Imāms *emphasize the personal benefits of response to an ultimate spiritual reality.* It is through access to this ultimate spiritual reality that humans become saints by *being with* Allāh. For ordinary folk, *being with* such people, by venerating their tombs and memories, is an expression of the ultimate desirability of *being with* Allāh.

Of the five religions we have examined, Islam displays most prominently symbolism of orientational centeredness. Orientation toward a center is yet another expression of the ultimate desirability of *being with* Allāh. Muslims are urged to pause at five appointed times during every day to face Mecca and pray. If possible, they should go to a mosque and pray in congregation with other Muslims. Every mosque has a *miḥrāb* or niche in its back wall which indicates the *qibla* or direction of Mecca. Muslims who are unable to attend the five daily prayer sessions – at dawn, midday, midafternoon, twilight, and the onset of night – are expected to ascertain for themselves the direction of Mecca and pray alone, or with others who are unable to reach a mosque. For prayer outside a mosque, some ritually pure surface is necessary. Most commonly a prayer rug is used, but when traveling, an unrolled turban will suffice, as will any such cloth that has not come in contact with impurities like dirt, blood, and mucus. These five daily prayers involve formalized words and prostrations that, if performed in a congregation, are to be performed in unison.

Thus, at the five daily times of prayer, Muslims throughout the world are arrayed like human spokes in a giant wheel, all focused upon Mecca. Of course, the Muslim world is so extensive that the phenomenon of time zones prevents all Muslims praying in literal unison at these five specified times, but in spirit, the Muslim world affirms its unity of intent five times a day by interrupting the daily routine to face Mecca and pray to Allāh.

Islamic symbolism of spatial centeredness is also evident in the yearly *ḥajj* or pilgrimage to Mecca. At least once in a lifetime every Muslim is expected to make this pilgrimage unless truly extenuating circumstances prevent it. Thus, once a year, Muslims from the entire world physically converge upon Mecca in millions to worship Allāh. Within Mecca, the focus of this pilgrimage is the Ka'ba, a cube shaped structure in the center of the spacious courtyard of the great mosque of Mecca. The high point of the several days of ritual observances at the *ḥajj* is a sevenfold circumambulation of the Ka'ba, which every pilgrim must perform.

Given Islam's repugnance for *shirk*, and thus for any form of idolatry, it is clear that this spatial focusing of the *ḥajj* and of prayer in no way signify that Allāh is somehow spacially present in the Ka'ba. Some unsophisticated Muslims may believe this, but the whole tenor of Islamic doctrine intimates that the spatial focusing of Islam upon the Ka'ba is to be regarded as spiritual symbolism of desirability, which reiterates the theme of *being with* Allāh. The spatial centrality of the Ka'ba in Islam symbolizes the centrality of Allāh in each Muslim's life. Facing or physically approaching the Ka'ba symbolizes conscious and willing acceptance of the centrality in one's life of an ultimately desirable spiritual reality. Facing or approaching the Ka'ba in unison, as a worldwide congregation of believers, is a powerful expression of adoration and verification of a central spiritual reality of humankind. This spatial symbolism of centeredness univocally *emphasizes the personal benefits of response to an ultimate spiritual reality* by depicting graphically the desirability of *being with* Allāh, united in will – individually and as a community – with the ultimate referent of Islam.

In order fully to appreciate the magnitude of this spiritual symbolism, one might imagine viewing the Muslim world from the perspective of outer space. As the edge of morning advances westward those who constitute the Muslim world, about one-seventh of humankind, turn their faces toward a single center and bow down in adoration. Or try to imagine living in that world, being born and raised among Muslims. Five times a day, every day, the people around you stop what they are doing and turn in unison to face the same direction and pray. It is difficult to imagine more powerful verification and reinforcement of one's own spiritual urge to affirm an ultimately desirable reality, but try to imagine the *ḥajj*. One is in the company of millions of the faithful from all over the world, all intent upon the Ka'ba, the spatial center of Islam. Try to imagine the solemn procession as millions, tightly packed together in the desert heat slowly turn seven times around the axis of the Muslim world, chanting "Allāh is great! Praise Allāh!" at this, the high point of their spiritual lives. When one is among Muslims, even if one cannot speak the language, there can be little doubt that Islam affirms the ultimate desirability of a spiritual reality regarded as central for humankind.

Reiterating this spatial centeredness of Islam are the Sufi and Shī'a doctrines of a hierarchy of saints that converges upon a *quṭb* or "axis" – that saint regarded as most blessed. The identity of the *quṭb* and the hierarchy converging upon it may, of course, differ from sect to sect. The different sects of Shī'ism identify as the *quṭb* whichever Imām they consider to be the Mahdi. Sufi orders sometimes regard their founders as the *quṭb* but most often regard the identify of the *quṭb* as a secret known only to an initiated elite of Sufi masters. Again, it is nearness to Allāh, the quality of *being with* Allāh, that identifies the *quṭb* from which all saintliness radiates. The term usually translated as "saint" is *walī*, which literally means "friend" – that is, a friend of Allāh. The supreme saint, the *quṭb*, is thus the closest friend of Allāh, and all saintship derives from nearness to Allāh. Although strict Muslims often disparage the veneration of saints as dangerously close to *shirk*, this practice may yet be regarded as another form of Islam's spiritual symbolism expressing the desirability of *being with* Allāh. Like all of Islam's symbolism of centrality, it may also be seen as expressing the universal human necessity of focusing one's spiritual life upon an ultimately desirable reality. Islam's spiritual symbolism of centrality thus intimates that the central spiritual reality of humankind is the *ultimate valuational norm from which other realities derive their value.*

Intellectual Symbolism of Desirability

Clearly all of the foregoing symbolic expressions of desirability in Islam rely upon the ultimate desirability of Allāh. *Intellectual symbolism* in Islam identifies Allāh *as the ultimate valuational norm and seeks thereby to make other expressions of desirability reasonable.* It *identifies* Allāh as the ultimate valuational norm not by recourse to rational argumentation, but by repudiating the ability of human reason to discover or comprehend what is ultimately good or even what is good for oneself. This repudiation of human reason is epitomized by the triumph of Ash'arite theology over Mu'tazila rationalism. The substance of their debate was Qur'ānic literalism versus abstract rationalism. In classical terms, it centered around the "99 names of Allāh."

The Muʻtazila, under the influence of Greek rationalism absorbed from various cultures dominated by Islam, reasoned that Allāh could not be said in any meaningful sense to have attributes. The attribution of qualities to Allāh placed limitations upon infinite being, resulted in an anthropomorphic concept of God and thereby constituted *shirk*. According to the Muʻtazila, all of the divine attributes, including the "99 names of Allāh," had to be understood metaphorically. The Muʻtazila position dominated Islam for a time, primarily due to the patronage of two caliphs, but in the end, even political leverage could not overcome the fact that Muʻtazila doctrines directly contradicted Qur'ānic revelation. The Qur'ān emphatically asserts that Allāh has hands, a face; that Allāh hears, speaks; and that Allāh is just, merciful, and so on.

It was the great jurist and theologian ibn Ḥanbal who first effectively challenged the Muʻtazila on this point, though literalist opposition to their rationalistic stance had been considerable all along. Ibn Ḥanbal, like many others, suffered persecution as a result of his outspoken resistance to the Muʻtazila position. As a result of his refusal to bend before this persecution, ibn Ḥanbal came to be regarded as a bastion of true belief and protector of the faith from the insidious errors of rationalism.

It was al-Ashʻarī, the architect of Islamic orthodoxy, who finally put to rest the controversy between the Muʻtazila rationalists and their literalist opponents. Al-Ashʻarī, and subsequently his followers, resolved the dispute decisively in favor of Qur'ānic literalism. Appealing to the Qur'ānic assertion that Allāh revealed the Qur'ān in "clear Arabic," al-Ashʻarī opens his treatise the *Ibāna* with the following declaration.

We seek right guidance from God, in Him is our sufficiency, and there is no might and no power except in God and He is the one upon whom we call for assistance. Now then: When we are asked, "Do you say that God has a face?" we answer "That is what we say, in contradiction of the heretics, for it is written: *the face of your Lord endures, in glory and honor* (55:27)." When we are asked "Do you say that God has hands?" we answer "That is what we say, for it is written *His hand is above their hands* (48:10). . . . And it is written *His two hands are stretched forth* (5:64); and it says in Ḥadīth *both His hands are right hands*. Literally so, and not otherwise."[8]

Having affirmed the anthropomorphic God as expressed literally in the Qur'ān, al-Ashʻarī deflects the charge of *shirk* and cuts the rationalistic ground from under his Muʻtazila opponents of with one ingenious stroke.

---

8   Ignaz Goldziher, *Introduction to Islamic Theology and Law*, trans. Andras Hamori and Ruth Hamori (Princeton, N.J.: Princeton University Press, 1981), p. 105.

He insists that we are to accept all of the attributes ascribed to Allāh in the Qur'ān "without how" (*bilā kayfa*) – without knowing how it could be that limitless, eternal, unitary, absolute being has specific attributes.

Similarly, and more importantly from the standpoint of the Islamic expression of the desirability of Allāh, al-Ash'arī insisted that there will be a literal resurrection of the dead, and that those admitted to the literal Garden will literally see Allāh. Again, all of this is to be accepted *bilā kayfa*, without knowing how. The resurrected body will be physical, will have literal hands and feet, and will literally see and hear, but all of its faculties will be qualitatively enhanced so as to be capable of enjoying the blessings of the Garden. The Garden too will be a physically existing place with literal fountains, trees, and fruits, but these blessings will be so infinitely enhanced as to be unimaginable to humans in their present state. Greatest of all of these blessing will be the *ru'yat* Allāh, the vision of God. Numerous passages in the Qur'ān state that the blessed will meet Allāh, and both Qur'ān and Hadith mention specific activities they will undertake in the presence of Allāh. The following verse is widely regarded as guaranteeing to believers that they will actually see Allāh in a physical form, albeit a form mere humans cannot even imagine.

22. That day will faces be resplendent,
23. Looking toward their Lord.

(Q 75:22–3)

Although al-Ash'arī's own intellectual heirs retreated somewhat from the strict literalism he espoused, this doctrine – the doctrine of a physical resurrection in a literal Garden where Allāh is present and can be seen – has remained overwhelmingly predominant in Islam. As the foregoing discussion shows, this doctrine cannot be dismissed as mere credulity, for it has been hammered out and tempered in a highly sophisticated forum of debate. We regard this doctrine as intellectual symbolism that *identifies the ultimate referent* of Islam as the Allāh described in the Qur'ān and none other. By shunning philosophical abstraction, it emphasizes that Allāh is indeed *the ultimate valuational norm* of human life, not an imaginary contrivance of intellectuals. The Qur'ān depicts Allāh as the omnipotent, all-merciful creator and ultimate judge of each human being. Conceived as such, Allāh is clearly and immediately recognizable as the ultimate referent from which all other realities *derive their value*. Islam's insistence that logical necessity not override or obscure the human necessity of assent to such an ultimate referent is the intellectual key that *makes reasonable other expressions of the desirability of Allāh*.

The Ash'arite position adopted by mainstream Islam is perfectly reasonable if one only grants the possibility of an unconditionally omnipotent God. There is nothing to stop such a God from creating a universal order to whatever specifications that God should will. The nature and possibilities of such a being will certainly not be determined by the dictates of human reason.

Recognizing the conflict between human reason and Qur'ānic revelation, the Ash'arites developed a full-scale critique of the principles of human reason. They emphasized the fallibility of the senses and rejected the possibility of reliable knowledge based upon observation of nature. They altogether reject causality, the basis of the concept of necessity in both nature and logic. According to the Ash'arites, a blow to the head precedes but does not cause pain. Allāh causes both the blow and the pain. Similarly, to borrow a common syllogism of Western logic, even if Socrates is a man, he is not necessarily mortal unless Allāh wills it. For the Ash'arites, there is no such thing as natural law. What appear to be unalterable laws of nature are only "habits of nature." Allāh has established these habits and can suspend them at any time, thus creating a miracle. One need not accept any of this to recognize it as an attempt to *make reasonable* Islam's various *other symbolic expressions of the ultimate desirability of Allāh*. Islam's intellectual symbolism succeeds in this attempt by forcing one to consider the implications of omnipotence. In doing so it discloses an intellectual aspect of the ultimate desirability of the central spiritual reality of humankind, the aspect of infinite possibility.

Moral Symbolism of Desirability

In the light of the foregoing intellectual symbolism, the relative paucity of Islamic *moral symbolism* of desirability is not surprising. Islam requires of its adherents a very strict morality. Some of the clear requirements for entering the Garden are truthfulness, honesty, generosity, humility, and resolve. There is, however, little of what could accurately be called normative moral thought in Islam. This again is explained by Islam's general mistrust of the human intellect. Just as, in the face of Allāh's supreme will and unlimited power, human reason cannot determine what is true, so in the face of Allāh's unlimited perfection, human reason cannot determine what is good.

Instead, Allāh ordains what is good for humankind. The requirements of morality have been proclaimed in the Qur'ān and clarified by the exemplary life of the Prophet Muḥammad. Given this guidance, what is morally good is thought to be simple and obvious, albeit demanding. The Qur'ānic verse thought to encapsulate this simple yet austere morality is the following, recited at the end of the Friday sermon in Sunni mosques.

Lo! Allah enjoineth justice and kindness, and giving to kinsfolk, and forbiddeth lewdness and abomination and wickedness. He exorteth you in order that ye may take heed.

(Q 16:90)

It is neither necessary nor appropriate for humans to wrestle with their consciences over the subtleties of moral principles. It is in fact an arrogance. Instead, we are merely to obey humbly the will of Allāh, remembering that in relation to the infinite perfection of Allāh, the morality he requires of human beings is slight indeed. The following verse reminds the faithful that Allāh is merciful in not requiring more of believers.

42. But (as for) those who believe and do good works – We tax not any soul beyond its scope – such are the rightful owners of the Garden. They abide therein.
43. And We remove whatever rancour may be in their hearts. Rivers flow beneath them. And they say: The praise to Allāh, Who hath guided us to this. We could not truly have been led aright if Allāh had not guided us. Verily the messengers of our Lord did bring the Truth. And it is cried unto them: This is the Garden. Ye inherit it for what ye used to do.

(Q 7:42–3)

By insisting the good that human beings are capable of doing is slight, and that even this nominal morality depends upon Allāh's guidance, Islamic moral symbolism *integrates its ethical precepts into its larger, overall expression of the meaning and purpose of human life.* Thereby it serves to *minimize selfish motivation for good behavior.*

Although Muslims are enjoined to fear the Fire and hope for entry into the Garden, they are frequently reminded that salvation will result not from their own efforts, but from the beneficence and guidance of Allāh. Thus, though morality in Islam may be instigated by fear of punishment and expectation of reward, *true morality is not ultimately based on fear of punishment or expectation of reward.* One cannot *expect* as a *reward* something one admits that one can in nowise deserve.

If Allāh took mankind to task by that which they deserve, He would not leave a living creature on the surface of the earth; but he reprieveth them unto an appointed term, and when their term cometh – then verily (they will know that) Allāh is ever Seer of His slaves.

(Q 35:45)

True morality in Islam is ultimately grounded in a *free decision to submit to the will of Allāh.* In the end, one's attainment of the Garden and avoidance of the Fire will result from Allāh's omnipotent will, not from one's own good deeds. Allāh, being unconditionally omnipotent, is not under the compulsion of any necessity to reward good behavior, or for that matter to punish evil. After al-Ash'arī, the orthodox position has been that the "eternity" of damnation will last as long as Allāh wills. In Islam, utter dependence upon the will of Allāh for the reward or punishment of one's actions *transforms self-interested morality into spontaneous regard for the welfare of others.* As noted previously, the arrogance of self-interested morality is regarded as a form of *shirk.* The Qur'ān warns against such arrogance as follows.

He is best aware of you (from the time) when He created you from the earth, and when ye were hidden in the bellies of your mothers. Therefore ascribe not purity unto yourselves. He is best aware of him who wardeth off (evil).

(Q 53:32)

The full significance of the material considered briefly in this section on moral symbolism will become more evident in the following examination of Islam's expression of the elusiveness of the central spiritual reality of humankind.

Elusiveness

Perhaps the most widespread stereotype of Islam is the notion of the Muslim as fatalist. In the popular imagination of the Western world, the Muslim is imagined as being resigned to his *"kismet,"* the words "if Allāh wills" constantly upon his lips. This widespread sterotype, like most stereotypes, is not entirely inaccurate. Like the other theistic religions we have examined, Islam has struggled over the centuries with the apparent incompatibility of human free will and divine omnipotence. Unlike them, Islam has been decisive in its affirmation of divine omnipotence, to the extent that predeterminism has been and remains a prominent feature of Islam. Predeterminism in Islam, then, may be viewed as an aspect of the expression of Allāh's absolute greatness, which in the present scheme is regarded as an intimation of the undeniability of the central spiritual reality of humankind. For the purpose of illustrating the Islamic expression of this reality, however, we have chosen to regard predeterminism in Islam as an expression of the elusiveness of the ultimately real.

Intellectual Symbolism of Elusiveness

The debate in Islam surrounding free will and determinism has focused mainly upon the question of predetermined salvation. Can one influence one's eschatological fate through one's own effort, or is salvation or damnation decreed in advance by Allāh? In Islam the question came down to a decision between effective affirmation of Allāh's justice or of his omnipotence, and it was in these terms that the philosophical debate over free will was pursued over several centuries. Characteristically, Islam eventually decided firmly in favor of Allāh's omnipotence. In doing so, it created one of the most existentially gripping expressions of the elusiveness of the ultimately real encountered among the world religions. The broad outlines of this debate provide an excellent sample of intellectual symbolism expressing the elusiveness of the central spiritual reality of humankind. A presentation of the doctrine of predeterminism in Islam also sets the stage for consideration of Islam's moral and spiritual symbolisms of elusiveness.

Qadarism, belief in free human will, was a pejorative term in Islam from early times. It is doubtful that anyone ever called himself a Qadarite, and the term fell into disuse after the ninth century. Derived from the triconsonantal root q-d-r, signifying "to measure out" and thus "to decree," the term is applied in the Qur'ān to Allāh's decreeing of events. Attributed to a human being, *qadar* implies *shirk*, arrogating to oneself the prerogative of Allāh. The term became such anathema that advocates of free will actually attempted to apply it to their opponents, as the following passage from al-Ash'arī, an opponent of the Qadarites, illustrates.

The Qadarites consider that *we* deserve the name of Qadar, because we say that God has determined (*qaddara*) evil and unbelief, and whoever affirms (*yuthbit*) the Qadar is a Qadarite, not those who do not affirm it. The reply to them is: The Qadarite is he who affirms that the Qadar is his own and not his Lord's, and that he himself determines his acts and not his Creator.[9]

Qadarism was most notably championed by the Mu'tazila movement, which maintained a position of limited free will in order to render reasonable the claim that Allāh is just. They reasoned that if some are to be eternally punished for their actions, these actions must be their own, not preordained by Allāh. Otherwise, Allāh could not be considered just. Such an argument appears harmless enough, even pious, but like other aspects of the pious rationalism of the Mu'tazila, it is directly contradicted in the Qur'ān and was thus unable to gain a firm foothold in Islam.

The Qur'ān repeatedly assigns to Allāh complete control over all as-

9 W. Montgomery Watt, *The Formative Period of Islamic Thought* (Edinburgh: University of Edinburgh Press, 1973), p. 117. From al-Ash'arī, *Kitāb al-ibāna 'an usul ad-diyāna* 73, trans. W. C. Klein as *The Elucidation of Islam's Foundation*, (New Haven, Conn.: American Oriental Society 1940), p. 113.

pects of his creation. There is, moreover, no attempt in the Qur'ān to dissociate evil from Allāh.

Naught of disaster befalleth in the earth or in yourselves but it is in a Book before we bring it into being – Lo! that is easy for Allāh.

(Q 57:22)

Not only natural evil, but also moral evil, usually in the form of disbelief, is said to originate with Allāh. Very often Allāh's creation of moral evil, which may result in a person's eternal damnation, is expressed in terms of "leading astray."

Had Allāh willed He could have made you (all) one nation, but He sendeth whom He will astray and guideth whom He will, and ye will indeed be asked of what ye used to do.

(Q 16:93)

As the preceding passage suggests and the following passage makes explicit, Allāh determines not only what will befall one; but also how one will respond to it. Misfortune form Allāh, then, cannot be regarded as a test or as a tempering of character, since Allāh also predetermines whether one succumbs to or triumphs over such misfortune.

6. As for the disbelievers, whether thou warn them or thou warn them not it is all one for them; they believe not.
7. Allāh hath sealed their hearing and their hearts, and on their eyes there is a covering. Theirs will be an awful doom.

(Q 2:6–7)

The second major Mu'tazila doctrine under which free will found expression was the principle that Allāh "commands good and forbids evil." On this basis, the Mu'tazila argued that Allāh could not possibly predetermine evil actions, as this would entail the creation of evil by Allāh, contrary to his own command to do good. Although such doctrines deviate from Qur'ānic revelation on the basis of human reason, the Mu'tazila was not the rationalistic school of thought it is often portrayed to have been. In general, its followers attempted to harmonize revelation with reason, but were not willing to reject revelation on the grounds of reason.

Thus characteristic Mu'tazila expressions of free will are actually rather conservative and limited affirmations in the form of Qur'ānic exegesis. For example, the Mu'tazila held that Allāh knew, but did not determine a person's actions in advance. Citing such passages as "He misleadeth thereby only miscreants" (Q 2:26), they argued that Allāh misled the damned only after they had first sinned of their own wills. Alternatively, in the form of a sort of moral version of triage, they suggested that because Allāh knew in advance where his guidance would bear fruit, he simply did not expend guidance upon hopeless cases. Moreover, since Allāh commands only good, the Mu'tazila held that Allāh does not "lead astray" sinners as several Qur'ānic verses seem to say. Instead, they argued, the Qur'ān should be understood as saying that Allāh "counts astray" those who sin by their own volition. Some even suggested that the "seal" Allāh puts upon the hearts of the damned is to be interpreted as an identifying mark, whereby the damned may be recognized on judgment day.[10]

Although the Mu'tazila position is pious, conciliatory, and by no means opposed to revelation, such arguments did not gain an enduring place in Islam. Like Qadarism before it, the Mu'tazila became anathema in Islam. The liberal role the Mu'tazila played in Islam was subsequently filled to a limited extent by the Māturīdite school of theology. Māturīdite theology is still regarded as orthodox, but compared with Ash'arite theology it has enjoyed little influence in mainstream Islam.

At any rate, Māturīdite theology does not actually affirm free will. It is content with the apparently self-contradictory position that one has a "choice" (ikhtiār) in his actions, but that Allāh creates all actions. Good actions, according to the Māturīdite school, Allāh creates by his "good pleasure" (riḍā); he does not create evil actions by his "good pleasure".[11] Note that the Māturīdites do not go so far as to say that Allāh does not create evil actions or that humans have any truly free will. Many modern Muslims believe in free will, but in most cases this is a result of modern, predominantly Western influences. Mainstream Islam remains predeterministic in outlook.

The doctrine of predeterminism attains its most authoritative statement in the overwhelmingly influential Ash'arite school of thought, the quintessential Muslim theology. Al-Ash'arī flatly denied free will. He held that though people must accept moral responsibility for their actions, the will to act is created by Allāh along with the action. Both the will to act and the action itself are only "acquired" by the human agent. In other words, free will is only an idea, created by Allāh, in the human mind. The Ash'arites, championed by the great al-Ghazālī, defended predeterminism with recourse to a quantum theory of time borrowed from their Mu'tazila opponents. According to the Ash'arite construal of this theory, time, in order to progress at all, must progress from moment to moment in discontinuous, indivisible leaps. Otherwise, the time between any two moments could be divided into an infinite number of infinitely small periods.

10 Watt, *Islamic Thought*, pp. 233–4.
11 *Shorter Encyclopaedia of Islam*, ed. H. A. R. Gibb and J. H. Kramers (Leiden: E. J. Brill, 1974), p. 406.

These periods, being infinitely small and infinite in number, would never accumulate, and one moment would never succeed another. They reasoned further that if time passes in discontinuous moments, one moment could not be the cause of another. Thus the Ash'arites concluded that the will to act in one moment could not be the cause of an action in a subsequent moment. Instead, Allāh creates ex nihilo each new moment, which, in the case of humans, contains both the will to act and the action itself.

The foregoing Ash'arite treatment of the doctrine of predeterminism is essentially an example of intellectual symbolism of the elusiveness of the ultimately real. The Islamic doctrine of predetermination expresses the elusiveness of Allāh as radical inaccessibility to human striving alone. Despite all of one's strivings, one will not attain salvation unless Allāh has preordained it. All is written, and what is written will occur. So says revelation. Islamic theology employs such intellectual symbolism to attempt to *make the elusiveness of Allāh reasonable*. That is to say, Islamic theology attempts to justify intellectually the *missing link* in Islam's scheme of salvation. This same *missing link*, expressed as predeterminism, forms the basis of both *moral* and *spiritual symbolism* of elusiveness in Islam.

Moral Symbolism of Elusiveness

Given this *missing link*, expressed as predeterminism, it is abundantly clear in Islam that *though morality is defined with reference to the ultimately real, good behavior is regarded as insufficient for personal perfection*. We have noted that in Islam morality as such is overshadowed by an emphasis upon obedience to the *sharī'a* or law. Islam probably specifies proper behavior in greater detail than any other major religion. Still, even with this comprehensive code of law governing every aspect of human behavior, obedience does not guarantee salvation. The following ḥadīth – a saying attributed to Muhammad – makes this clear.

(The Prophet said:) By God, one of you will work the work of the people of the Fire until there is between him and it less than an arm's length, and the book [of destiny] will overtake him and he will work the work of the people of the Garden and enter it; and another man will work the work of the people of the Garden until between him and it there is less than an arm's length, and then the book will overtake him, and he will work the work of the people of the Fire and enter it.[12]

12   Watt, *Islamic Thought*, p. 105, from the second part of al-Bukhārī, *Sahīh*, under Qadar, eds. L. Krehl and T. W. Juynboll (Leiden: E. J. Brill, 1862–1908).

Many such ḥadīths and Qur'ānic passages stand behind the following creedal formulation from Book 2 of al-Ghazālī's *Resuscitation of the Sciences of Religion* (*Iḥyā' 'Ulūm al-Dīn*).

He wills all that exists, and determines events. Thus all things . . . good or bad . . . acts of obedience or disobedience, they all occur solely according to his decision and determination, his wisdom and will. What he wills, takes place, and what he does not will, does not take place.[13]

Al-Ghazālī justifies this apparent arbitrariness of Allāh on the grounds that since Allāh's power and authority are absolute, there are no grounds upon which to evaluate or criticize his actions. Allāh's supremacy is so great, and human merit of reward so miniscule by comparison, that it is presumptuous to imagine that one's good deeds deserve any reward whatsoever.

It is proof of his generosity, and not a necessity, that he showers mercy and good things upon his servants, a pure gift on his part, for he could have punished his servants with every possible affliction, suffering and illness. And if he had done so, it would have been just of him, not bad and unjust.[14]

In recognition of this total control of events and thoughts by Allāh, Ash'arite theology urges that its followers add to the confession "I am a believer," the proviso, "if Allāh wills."

In addition to its prominence in orthodox, mainstream Islam, the notion of the inability of the human being to guarantee his or her own salvation through even the most obedient actions also plays a part in the renowned Sufi tendency occasionally to flaunt disobedience of the *sharī'a*. Such disobedience is often misconstrued as rejection of the *sharī'a* in favor of "free thinking," as rejection of the restrictions of organized religion in favor of spontaneous, creative, individualistic spirituality. It is tempting to construe Sufi disobedience as antinomian or even tantric, but in Sufi circles, notably among the Malāmatiyya or "blameworthy" Sufis, disobedience of conventional religious restrictions is practiced as an immunization against arrogant piety.[15] Overtly pious behavior inspires ad-

---

13   al-Ghazzālī, *Ihya' 'Ulum al-Din*, sec. 82; from *Philosophers Speak of God*, ed. Charles Hartshorne and William L. Reese (Chicago: University of Chicago Press, 1963), p. 107, which follows the German translation by Hans Bauer, *Die Dogmatik al-Ghazzali's Nach dem II Buch seines Hauptwerkes* (Halle: Buchdrückerei des Waisenhauses, 1912), pp. 10–11.

14   Ibid., al-Ghazzālī, sec. 82. Hartshorne and Reese, *Philosophers Speak of God*, p. 107. Bauer, *Die Dogmatik*, p. 13.

15   Schimmel, *Dimensions*, pp. 86–7.

miration in others which may lead one to the sin of pride and the illusion of self-sufficiency. More insidious, the sense of personal well-being that piety can produce may turn out to be, in Sufi terms, one of Allāh's ruses (*makr*). Even the highest states of mystical ecstasy may be divine ruses, concealing the pitfall of pridefully imagining that one's salvation is assured.[16]

Orthodox Muslim criticisms, as well as non-Muslim treatments of Sufism, generally overemphasize Sufi blasphemy and disobedience of the *sharī'a*. In reality, the vast majority of Sufis practice strict obedience of all the prescriptions and restrictions of Islamic law. Infrequent disobedience of the law expresses the *missing link* in Islam's scheme of salvation rather than indicating a rebellious spirit.

To be sure, the Sufi path, with its various sets of progressive stages (*maqām*) appears to be a sort of ladder or staircase to heaven. The Sufi aspirant, however, is constantly warned not to imagine that by following the path he may reach salvation through his own efforts. Many masters advise that before the initial path-stage of repentance (*tauba*) can be completed, the adept must "repent of repentance." It is arrogant to think that one's repentance will play a decisive role in one's eschatological destiny. Another early station on the path, renunciation (*zuhd*), is not completed until one renounces renunciation, and ceases to desire even salvation. These stages are preliminary to the crucial stages of *tawakkul*, "trust in Allāh," which involves abandoning any thought of self-reliance in the realm of spiritual progress.[17]

Since the Qur'ān often expresses predeterminism in terms of a fixed length of life (*ajal*) and provision of sustenance (*rizq*), these have become classical terms in which Islam has expressed its doctrine of predeterminism. Similarly, Sufism cautions the aspirant to be ever mindful that all sustenance, material and spiritual, comes from Allāh, not through one's own efforts. This concept leads to what may be considered the focal point of Sufi life, *faqr* or "poverty." The West, in fact, first heard of Sufis under the descriptive terms "fakir" (an alternative transliteration of the Arabic *faqīr*) and "dervish" (from the Persian *darvish*), both of which mean "poor person."

The poverty of the ideal Sufi, in addition to being a spiritual discipline, is an expression of absolute trust that Allāh will provide sufficient sustenance. Material poverty, however, is really only a symbol of spiritual poverty, the humble realization that all spiritual sustenance is also a gift from Allāh rather than the result of one's striving. At an advanced station on the path, the Sufi develops gratitude (*riḍā*) for the spiritual sustenance of Allāh in three stages: gratitude for the gift, gratitude for withholding

16 Ibid., p. 128.   17 Ibid., p. 110.

the gift, and finally gratitude for the gratitude.[18] Even the Sufi's thankful dependence upon Allāh cannot be regarded as his own accomplishment or realization.

Spiritual Symbolism of Elusiveness

This discussion of the *missing link* in the Sufi path to salvation has moved somewhat beyond the realm of moral symbolism of elusiveness into the related area of spiritual symbolism. The primary point, however, is to illustrate the prevalence throughout Islam of predeterminism as an expression of the *missing link* in the Islamic path to salvation. In mainstream Islam, where emphasis is upon obeying the law, the concept that one's obedience and even one's belief are predetermined by Allāh precludes any thought that one may guarantee spiritual salvation through one's own efforts alone. Sufism, far from being the self-sufficient departure from conservative Islam that it is often imagined to be, emphasizes this dependence upon Allāh throughout its path to salvation. Moreover, Sufism, like mainstream Islam, expresses this dependence in terms of predeterminism. Outsiders are likely to feel that Islam goes overboard in expressing the elusiveness of Allāh in such uncompromising terms. Be that as it may, in Islam, as in each of the religions we have examined, the elusiveness of the religion's ultimate referent is regarded as an essential corollary of the unsurpassable greatness and the undeniability of the ultimately real. Again, in Islam the conviction emerges that something unsurpassably great must of necessity be elusive of human effort. Like each of the other major religions, Islam employs an internally coherent and evocative symbolic complex that expresses, in its own unique way, the intertwined undeniability and elusiveness of the central spiritual reality of humankind.

Islam's insistence upon strict and uniform observance of religious law among the faithful seems on the surface to be incompatible with predeterminism. One may wonder at the extreme effort in Islam to enforce orthodox belief and practice if both are in reality predetermined by Allāh. This situation appears problematic, though, only to outsiders. For believers, the predetermination of one's belief and practice, including their results, and the necessity nonetheless for sincere exertion, all intersect in the realm of a lived paradox that is best understood as spiritual symbolism of elusiveness. Spiritual symbolism, we have suggested, *encourages sustained discipline despite the elusiveness of the ultimately real*. In each of the religions examined there is tension between the desirability of its ultimate referent and the elusiveness of this referent. In Islam, the dynam-

18   Ibid., pp. 125–6.

ic of this tension is particularly clear. Not to strive for Allāh's acceptance is tantamount to denying his reality and desirability; and yet to strive with any confidence of success is a denial of his greatness.

For the Muslim in daily association with this paradox, the confusion it causes in outsiders may itself appear confusing. Most of the major religions have attempted doctrinally to smooth over the rough edge where the utter transcendence of ultimate reality verges upon the necessity of human effort in response to an ultimate referent. Islam illustrates how little is accomplished, in terms of a living faith, by such doctrinal exercises. Logical consistency is the addiction of intellectuals, but not apparently a requisite of the lived human response to an ultimate spiritual reality. Islam shows, perhaps more clearly than any other major religion, that the human being can be quite comfortable with an undiluted form of the conflict that stands at the very core of human existence: the conflict between the existential necessity of affirming an ultimate criterion of desirability, and the logical necessity of declaring that such a criterion is unattainable by human effort alone. Thus, the Muslim is enjoined to "seek the next world as if you were to die tomorrow" and yet to be ever mindful that one does not thereby ensure or even advance one's own salvation. In Islamic terms, submission to Allāh must be unconditional. It must not take the form of a bargain, or even of supplication.

Such abject submission appears to demean human dignity only to outsiders to Islam who, not viewing the situation from the perspective of participation, adhere to the literal terms of the expression of submission. Just as English spoken with German sentence structure becomes gibberish, so does the spiritual symbolism of Islam become unintelligible unless one attempts more than merely to slot its terms into one's own world view. For this reason, we have suggested that each of the major religions makes recourse to spiritual symbolism to address the universal human predicament of reconciling the necessity for purposeful action with the absence of any readily apparent purpose beyond the mercurial demands of biology. Our human status does not allow us to be satisfied with the mere fulfillment of biological urges, and yet we do not find in the material world any purpose beyond these urges. The paradox that spiritual symbolism addresses, in Islam and the other religions we have examined, is a given of the human situation. It is not created by the religions in question. Nor is it solved merely by being recognized and abstracted in intellectual terms such as "spiritual symbolism." It does not go away when it is ignored by secularism, nor is its poignancy lessened when it is lived in the symbolic terms of Islam or any other religion. Instead, when practiced with the urgency they demand, each of the world religions provides a symbolic framework whereby the human imagination may reach beyond the foragings of the senses and intellect.

Mythological Symbolism of Elusiveness

Mythological symbolism illustrating the elusiveness of Allāh is relatively sparse in Islam. We noted previously that Islam's mythological symbolism in general is predominantly didactic, specifically intended to illustrate the unity and greatness of Allāh or the prophethood of Muḥammad. Shī'ite veneration of the mysteriously concealed Mahdi may be construed as a mythological expression of the elusiveness of Allāh, as may the Sufi notion of the *quṭb*, but these examples illustrate primarily the desirability of Islam's ultimate referent. In addition to Islam's straightforwardly didactic narrative material, there are stories with less immediately apparent meanings, stories that can be construed as mythological expressions of elusiveness. The following Qur'ānic story, the well-known story of al-Khiḍr, with a few changes in names and idiom, could just as easily come from a text of Zen Buddhism, where such expressions of elusiveness abound.

66. Then found they [Moses and his servant] one of Our slaves, unto whom We had given mercy from Us, and had taught him knowledge from Our presence.
67. Moses said unto him: May I follow thee, to the end that thou mayst teach me right conduct of that which thou has been taught?
68. He said: Lo! thou canst not bear with me.
69. How canst thou bear with that whereof thou canst not compass any knowledge?
70. He said: Allāh willing thou shalt find me patient and I shall not in aught gainsay thee.
71. He said: Well, if thou go with me, ask me not concerning aught till I myself make mention of it unto thee.
72. So they twain set out till, when they were in the ship, he made a hole therein. (Moses) said: Hast thou made a hole therein to drown the folk thereof? Thou verily hast done a dreadful thing.
73. He said: Did I not tell thee that thou couldst not bear with me?
74. (Moses) said: Be not wroth with me that I forgot, and be not hard upon me for my fault.
75. So they twain journeyed on till, when they met a lad, he slew him. (Moses) said: What! Hast thou slain an innocent soul who hath slain no man? Verily thou hast done a horrid thing.
76. He said: Did I not tell thee that thou couldst not bear with me?
77. (Moses) said: If I ask thee after this concerning aught, keep not company with me. Thou hast received an excuse from me.
78. So they twain journeyed on till, when they came unto the folk of a certain township, they asked its folk for food, but they refused to make them guests. And they found therein a wall upon the point of falling into ruin, and he repaired it. (Moses) said: If thou hadst wished, thou couldst have taken payment for it.

79. He said: This is the parting between thee and me! I will announce unto thee the interpretation of that thou couldst not bear with patience.
80. As for the ship, it belonged to poor people working on the river, and I wished to mar it, for there was a king behind them who is taking every ship by force.
81. And as for the lad, his parents were believers and We feared lest he should oppress them by rebellion and disbelief.
82. And We intended that their Lord should change him for them for one better in purity and nearer to mercy.
83. And as for the wall, it belonged to two orphan boys in the city, and there was beneath it a treasure belonging to them, and their father had been righteous, and thy Lord intended that they should come to their full strength and should bring forth their treasure as a mercy from their Lord; and I did it not upon my own command. Such is the interpretation of that wherewith thou couldst not bear.

(Q 18:66–83)

Such allegorical stories, though uncommon in mainstream Islam, are common in Sufism.

A primary reason for the scarcity in mainstream Islam of mythological symbolism *illustrating the elusiveness of Allāh* is the strict Qur'ānic prohibition of graphic depiction of animals or human beings in any form. The reason behind this prohibition is Islam's ubiquitous abhorrence of *shirk*, associating Allāh with any other being or thing. The spirit of this prohibition seems to inform even the narrative, mythological dimension of Islam, which hesitates even verbally to depict human beings in the type of superhuman struggle that might serve to *illustrate the elusiveness of Allāh*. Again, the Shī'a veneration of Imāms is a notable exception to this general tendency, as is the more widespread cult of saints. The primary function of both the veneration of Imāms and the cult of saints, however, is to make the ultimately desirable more accessible, not to express its elusiveness.

As one might expect, eschatological expressions of elusiveness play a more prominent role than narrative material in mainstream Islam. On the day of judgment, one will be confronted with a book in which one's good and evil deeds are exhaustively recorded; one's sins and merits will be weighed up in a balance, and tradition has it that one will have to walk across a bridge over hell that is as narrow as a sword's edge. Each of these trials is a mythological expression of the elusiveness of salvation, but like narrative mythological expressions they are not of the essence of Islam.

Islam's essential symbolism of the elusiveness of Allāh is conspicuous by its absence. The Qur'ānic prohibition of images of any kind results in an austere majesty in Islamic architecture. This architectural austerity is Islam's primary *illustration of the elusiveness of the ultimately real*. A person of any faith, or of none, can scarcely enter even a relatively insignificant mosque without sensing on the one hand Islam's dignity and unity of intent, and on the other hand Islam's recognition of the utter transcendence of that upon which it focuses. The walls and ceiling of a mosque may be adorned with geometric and floral designs, and there may be some calligraphy of Qur'ānic passages adorning the walls, but other than this the mosque will be empty. It is a place to pray. This prayer is focused upon a niche or *miḥrāb* in the back wall of the mosque that is oriented toward Mecca. Though this *miḥrāb* may be adorned, it will not be lavishly adorned, and is often intentionally plain. The *miḥrāb* is empty, except possibly for a lamp. This architectural feature derives from one of the most haunting Qur'ānic passages.

35. Allāh is the light of the heavens and the earth. The similitude of His light is as a niche wherein is a lamp. The lamp is in a glass. The glass is as it were a shining star. (This lamp is) kindled from a blessed tree, an olive neither of the East nor of the West, whose oil would almost glow forth (of itself) though no fire touched it. Light upon light. Allāh guideth unto His light whom He will. And Allāh speaketh to mankind in allegories, for Allāh is Knower of all things.

36. (The lamp is found) in houses which Allāh hast allowed to be exalted and that His name shall be remembered therein. Therein do offer praise to Him at morn and evening.

(Q 24:35–6)

Paradoxically, the empty *miḥrāb* is Islam's most potent mythological symbol of the elusiveness of Allāh. The *miḥrāb* is the focus of Islamic ritual, and yet it contains nothing. It *illustrates the elusiveness of the ultimately real* by providing nothing upon which the senses or the intellect might lay hold, and yet serving as a focus of intense devotion. When all is said and done, the entire intellectual, spiritual, and moral edifice of Islam rests upon the emptiness of the *miḥrāb*. This superabundant emptiness, though not overtly mythological, evocatively *illustrates the elusiveness of the central spritual reality of humankind*. As it is written in the four-lined *sūra* entitled "The Unity," which many regard as the essence of the Qur'ān:

1. Say: He is Allāh, the One
2. Allāh, the eternally Besought of all!
3. He begetteth not nor was begotten.
4. And there is none comparable to Him.

(Q 112:1–4)

Conclusion

We do not imagine that the foregoing attempt at "world theology" exhausts or even addresses the issue comprehensively or definitively. We hope at least to have called attention to the need and the possibility of integrating all of the religious expressions of humankind in a systematic manner. In the long run, our conclusions regarding characteristics of an ultimate reality commonly recognized by at least five of the world's major religions may be modified, expanded upon, or rejected outright in the course of critical discussion and expansion of our findings. In any case, we will be pleased to have encouraged serious, systematic contemplation and discussion of the vast and diverse amount of data that confronts and challenges any who would responsibly assert the validity of religion in general or of any single religion in the modern world. We are eager to draw attention to the fact that the present work builds upon and would be impossible without the cumulative efforts of numerous scholars from a wide variety of disciplines. Their combined input is both our debt and our strength. The disciplines involved include history, linguistics, anthropology, sociology, theology, philosophy, and others. Under the rubric of "religious studies" researchers representing an array of specializations have contributed over the past century or so to a vast fund of factual information regarding the religions of humankind. Regardless of the weaknesses in our own "world theology," we are confident that it is not merely the product of our intuition and imagination. We consider that it is instead a necessary undertaking in response to the existing corpus of factual information – now readily available – concerning the religions of the world.

The time is now well past when one could with any credibility assert the validity of one's own religion without reference to the truth claims of other religions and without recognition of the secular and antireligious traditions that now constitute appealing, well thought out, and long-standing alternatives to religion. Similarly, secular and antireligious traditions have reached a stage of maturity at which they must seriously and open-mindedly consider the cumulative force of the religious expressions of all humankind. Dogmatic, sectarian polemic – whether religious or secular in origin – is well and truly anachronistic at this, the dawn of the second millennium of the common era.

On the other hand, we certainly do not intend to encourage the sacrifice of particularity on the altar of universality. We urge instead that each of the particular traditions we have examined is valid on its own terms. This internal rationality and coherence, however, may often be obscure to outsiders to the particular tradition in question. For this reason we have attempted to construct a concrescent paradigm in the light of which at least five of the world's religions can be sympathetically comprehended universally. Ideally Esperanto – a proposed universal language – should facilitate communication among speakers of diverse, particular languages. No responsible proponent of Esperanto ever intended that it would displace the existing languages of the world. The briefest of reflection reveals that any universally comprehensible language would of necessity lack the color and nuance that renders each of the world's languages uniquely and enduringly expressive of the ideas, ideals, and emotions of those who speak it well. Similarly, we do not imagine that the world would be a better place without the existing variety of particular modes of religious expression that have developed in the long course of human experience on earth.

In this spirit, we fondly and eagerly hope that others will attempt to apply our paradigm to the many religious traditions that we have omitted from the present work. We are very much aware of the omission from the present study of several major religious traditions, for example, Bahaí, Daoism, Shinto, and Sikhism. We are even more anxiously aware of the omission of the so-called primitive or tribal religions as a whole. Many of these traditions, though nonliterate, are ancient and venerable repositories of cumulative reflection and experience. Any world theology worthy of the name should have the capacity to incorporate at least some of the nonliterate religious traditions. Furthermore, though we have made significant reference to secular world views, we have not attempted to incorporate any of them directly into our paradigm. Such incorporation may be possible in some cases. For example, the Marxist ideal of a truly just and egalitarian society is clearly a *nonmaterial, ultimate reality,* in that such a society does not exist and has not existed anywhere at any time. Even so, the Marxist ideal corresponds to our definition of "a reality," and for Marxists it is clearly *the reality in relation to which other realities derive their value and meaning.* As such it is *ultimately desirable* and, though *elusive,* is regarded as *undeniable* in the sense of being the *inevita-*

ble outcome of the *irresistible* revolutionary dialectic of class conflict and struggle.

Such extensions of the scope of our admittedly preliminary world theology we believe to be possible and desirable. We recognize that extension of the scope of our paradigm may require expansion or modification of the paradigm itself. We have certainly not intended to suggest that *undeniability, desirability,* and *elusiveness* are the only identifiable characteristics of *the central spiritual reality of humankind.* Nor do we imagine that *intellectual, spiritual, moral,* and *mythological* exhaust the categories of symbolic expression of this reality. We have, for example, treated the visual symbolism of painting, sculpture, and architecture only briefly and in passing. For most people, visual symbols are symbols par excellence. Our extension of the notion of symbolic expression beyond the vivid images of visual art and literature does not intend in any way to diminish the significance of artistic symbolism in the expression of human ideas and ideals. We can readily imagine, for example, treatments of architectural symbolism of *undeniability, desirability,* and *elusiveness.* At the same time – in line with our suggestion that some secular ideologies could be meaningfully and informatively treated in the context of world theology – we intuit dimly the possibility of the phrase *political symbolism* identifying a coherent complex of expressions of the *undeniable, desirable,* and *elusive* reality that, we have argued, impinges upon virtually all human lives and behavior. Regardless of our own assessment, at least one *undeniable* component of all of the world's religions is the human component. All religions, without exception, are human expressions. We urge that all human expressions are in essence symbolic. No expression entirely captures the reality to which it refers. Instead, all expressions *point to* a reality larger than the terms of the expressions themselves. Religious expressions are no exception, but neither are other modes of expression that may immediately appear to be nonreligious.

Another unexplored potential of the central paradigm of the present work is its usefulness in distinguishing with considerable precision between "religion" on the one hand and "superstition" and "pseudoreligion" on the other. "Superstitious" and "pseudoreligious" world views typically refer to a *nonmaterial reality* of some sort, and often consider it *ultimate* and *undeniable.* In many cases, however, this reality is regarded as fearsome rather than *desirable* and is dealt with through avoidance and propitiation rather than the life-ordering attempt to approach and actualize that characterizes response to the *ultimately desirable.* More precisely and more universally, superstition and the pseudoreligious may be identified by their failure to acknowledge the *elusiveness* that characterizes the *central spiritual reality of humankind.* The superstitious practice of magic, for example, guarantees results, provided the magical performance is adequate, regardless of how exalted the nonmaterial reality approached is conceived to be. More pertinently, one often encounters pseudoreligious television evangelists prepared to guarantee to the credulous that following instructions will result in salvation, or even in immediate earthly reward. We do not suggest that superstition and pseudoreligion should be ignored in the academic study of religion. At the same time, all academic study should produce a means of identifying and delimiting its subject matter and thereby identifying that which is tangential to its central concern. The present study implies for religious studies extension of existing subject matter by the inclusion of some apparently secular world views. At the same time, it suggests limitation of of the central concern of the academic discipline to those human endeavors that attempt to express the *undeniability, desirability,* and *elusiveness* of a central spiritual reality of humankind.

This brings us to our final point. The present work spans the discrete and distinct academic disciplines of theology on the one hand and religious studies on the other. We hope that this spanning does not blur the vital distinction between the two. In essence, our book, as a "world theology" attempts to construct a valid *theological theory* on the basis of factual information amassed by scholars of *religious studies.* Our theological statement, in turn, properly becomes additional data for religious studies to assimilate and evaluate. This situation illustrates the basic distinction between theology and academic religious studies. Theology – whether with reference to God or not – is *normative* of human belief and behavior. Religious studies is *analytical* of the beliefs and practices thus normed, and of the normative theologies themselves.

Because of its preliminary, exploratory nature, this study attempts to do both theology and religious studies. In this germinal stage of the endeavor to construct a world theology, the authors felt that this was unavoidable. There simply were not any existing theological categories – including the concept of God itself – that could be applied across the board to all religions. Such categories had to be informed by and derived from the empirical data of religious studies. At the same time, we clearly feel that our own interpretation and structuring of these data have implications for the interpretation and structuring of data in religious studies, as well as for the theoretical definition of the subject matter of the discipline itself.

We hope that in the future, the practice of world theology will proliferate to the extent that it will constitute a well-defined category of the data that academic religious studies routinely analyze. For the time being, however, we regard it as being of the utmost importance that this book be subjected to especially rigorous critical reflection by academics in the field of religious studies. On the other hand – from the standpoints of theologically normed world views – we are aware that some readers may find our representation and construal of their faiths to be inaccurate and in need of correction.

In either case, we eagerly await the feedback of our readers, whether published or offered privately through our publisher. It is important that errors of theological fact or interpretation be rectified. It is equally important, and even more important for the future practice of world theology, that the present work be adequately contextualized within the academic field of religious studies. The book now having passed beyond our hands, we leave it to our readers and colleagues to evaluate the extent to which it constitutes *data for* critical analysis by religious studies, and to what extent it constitutes a theoretical and methodological *contribution to* the analysis of data in religious studies.

9 780521 337472